Power Platform and the AI Revolution

Explore modern AI services to develop apps, bots, and automation patterns to enhance customer experiences

Aaron Guilmette

Power Platform and the AI Revolution

Copyright © 2024 Packt Publishing

All rights reserved. No part of this book may be reproduced, stored in a retrieval system, or transmitted in any form or by any means, without the prior written permission of the publisher, except in the case of brief quotations embedded in critical articles or reviews.

Every effort has been made in the preparation of this book to ensure the accuracy of the information presented. However, the information contained in this book is sold without warranty, either express or implied. Neither the author, nor Packt Publishing or its dealers and distributors, will be held liable for any damages caused or alleged to have been caused directly or indirectly by this book.

Packt Publishing has endeavored to provide trademark information about all of the companies and products mentioned in this book by the appropriate use of capitals. However, Packt Publishing cannot guarantee the accuracy of this information.

Group Product Manager: Aaron Tanna

Book Project Manager: Prajakta Naik

Publishing Product Manager: Uzma Sheerin

Senior Editor: Kinnari Chohan

Technical Editor: Rajdeep Chakraborty

Copy Editor: Safis Editing

Proofreader: Kinnari Chohan

Indexer: Tejal Soni

Production Designer: Prashant Ghare

DevRel Marketing Coordinators: Deepak Kumar and Mayank Singh

First published: May 2024

Production reference: 2310524

Published by Packt Publishing Ltd.
Grosvenor House
11 St Paul's Square
Birmingham
B3 1RB, UK

ISBN 978-1-83508-636-0

www.packtpub.com

I'd like to thank Microsoft and OpenAI for gently introducing us to our robot overlords. Be good to them as, one day, they'll put us in people zoos. I also want to acknowledge the support of my long-suffering girlfriend, Christine, who has put up with my book deadlines interrupting vacations for my last 15 books. She's the real MVP here.

Finally, I'd like to thank my kids—Liberty, Hudson, Anderson, Glory, and Victory. Without them, I'd probably be able to retire to a tropical location with umbrella drinks a lot sooner.

– Aaron Guilmette

Contributors

About the author

Aaron Guilmette is a principal architect at Planet Technologies, an award-winning Microsoft Partner focused on dragging public sector customers into the modern era. Previously, he worked at Microsoft as a senior program manager for Microsoft 365 Customer Experience. As an author of at least 15 other IT books you've probably seen recommended on Amazon, he specializes in identity, messaging, and automation technologies.

When he's not writing books or tools for his customers, trying to teach one of his kids to drive, or making tacos with his girlfriend, Aaron can be found tinkering with cars and "investing" in Star Wars memorabilia. You can visit his blog at `https://aka.ms/aaronblog` or connect with him on LinkedIn at `https://www.linkedin.com/in/aaronguilmette`.

About the reviewer

Steve Miles is CTO at Westcoast Cloud, part of a multi-billion turnover IT distributor based in the UK and Ireland. Steve is a Microsoft Azure **Most Valuable Professional (MVP)**, **Microsoft Certified Trainer (MCT)**, and an Alibaba Cloud MVP. Steve has over 20 years of technology experience along with his previous military career in engineering, signals, and communications.

Among other books, Steve is the author of the number 1 Amazon best-selling AZ-900 certification book titled *Microsoft Azure Fundamentals and Beyond*. Like Aaron, he is also a petrolhead, and can also be found tinkering with cars when he is not writing. You can connect with him on LinkedIn at https://www.linkedin.com/in/stevemiles70/.

Ahmad Najjar is a seasoned Power Platform Lead Architect at Avanade, based in Oslo, Norway. With a remarkable career spanning 20 years in the Microsoft development ecosystem, Ahmad has honed his expertise in C#, ASP.NET, SQL, and SharePoint. Over the last decade, he has also accumulated extensive experience with Azure technologies, including Logic Apps, API Management, and Function Apps.

For the past nine years, Ahmad has been deeply immersed in the Power Platform, specializing in Power Automate, Power Apps, and AI Builder. His role as an enthusiastic solution architect doesn't prevent him from being a passionate developer at heart which earned him a reputation for excellence and innovation.

Ahmad's accolades include being a FastTrack Recognized Solution Architect in both Power Apps and Power Automate, as well as a Business Applications MVP for seven consecutive years. Additionally, he has been a Microsoft Certified Trainer for four years, sharing his knowledge and skills with aspiring professionals.

Beyond his professional achievements, Ahmad is a prolific author and reviewer of technical books. His commitment to the tech community is evident in his eight years of organizing IT events and over a decade of enabling and facilitating community and technical initiatives. Ahmad's influence extends internationally, with over 200 sessions and more than 50 workshops delivered at local, European, and global conferences.

Ahmad's expertise, passion, and dedication make him a leading figure in the world of Microsoft technologies and a driving force behind many successful projects and community endeavors.

Table of Contents

Preface — xiii

1

Introduction to AI Services — 1

What kinds of things can Generative AI do?	3	Understanding Power Platform licensing	9
What is Power Platform?	4	Exploring additional AI services	10
Learning about Power Automate	5	Working with Azure AI Services	10
Learning about Copilots	6	Working with OpenAI models	12
Learning about Power Apps	7	Working with services from Google, Anthropic, and more	13
Learning about AI Builder technologies	8	Summary	13

2

Configuring an Environment to Support AI Services — 15

Configuring Azure	16	Configuring your workstation	25
Requesting API access for Azure OpenAI services	16	Configuring Power Platform	25
Setting up OpenAI service resources in Azure	19	Summary	26
Configuring API access for ChatGPT	21		

3

Talking to ChatGPT — 27

Working with ChatGPT as a user	27	Sending prompts to ChatGPT	30
So, what's a token?	29	HTTP	30

viii   Table of Contents

OpenAI GPT-3 completions	37	Working with ChatGPT's JSON output in Power Automate	43
Retrieving data from ChatGPT	**41**	**Summary**	**46**
So, what exactly is JSON?	41		

4

Using ChatGPT and Copilot to Create Flows and Apps   47

Working with Power Automate	**47**	**Working with Power Apps**	**60**
Using ChatGPT to create flows	47	Using ChatGPT to build an app	60
Using ChatGPT Plus to create flows	52	Using Copilot to build an app	64
Using Copilot to create flows	56	**Summary**	**70**

5

Bootstrapping a Power App with Copilot   71

Configuring prerequisites	**71**	Creating the model-driven backend app	80
Creating identities in Entra ID	71	Creating the canvas frontend app	86
Creating a Dataverse environment	72	Enabling automation	90
Building a new Power App with Copilot	**73**	**Further exploration**	**95**
Configuring the data elements	74	**Summary**	**96**

6

Processing Data with Sentiment Analysis   97

What is sentiment analysis, anyway?	98	Configuring a sentiment analysis flow	103
Licensing prerequisites	98	Testing the flow	112
Configuring solution prerequisites	100	Further exploration	114
Creating a shared mailbox	100	Summary	114
Creating a Microsoft Teams team	102		

7

Using Power Automate and AI to Build PowerPoint Presentations — 115

Licensing prerequisites	115	Creating the flow	124
Learning about the Encodian Flowr connector	117	Creating the Generate Content Summaries scope	124
Input formatting	117	Configuring the JSON parameters	129
Tokens	118	Customizing the GPT prompt	132
Populate PowerPoint	119	Creating the Generate Slides scope	139
Merge Presentations	119	Working with Encodian Flowr	142
Interacting with Wikipedia articles	120	Testing the flow	148
Creating a PowerPoint template	122	Further exploration	152
		Summary	152

8

Building an Event Registration App with Identity Verification — 153

Designing a solution	153	Creating flows	167
Licensing prerequisites	155	Configuring a flow to handle form submission	167
Configuring solution prerequisites	155	Processing the identity document	178
Configuring SharePoint Online	156	Sending confirmation messages	185
Establishing a Teams meeting	163	Testing the flow	189
Building an input form	165	Further exploration	194
		Summary	195

9

Implementing an AI-Enabled Resume Screener — 197

Designing a solution	197	Configuring the AI model	204
Licensing prerequisites	199	Enabling the Cloudmersive connector	212
Configuring solution prerequisites	199	Creating a flow	213
Creating a shared mailbox	199	Configuring the trigger and variables	213
Creating a team	200	Processing the attachment and candidate record	215
Configuring SharePoint Online	201		

Extracting information from a resume and updating a candidate record	218	Sending confirmation messages	228
Evaluating the resume with a prompt	220	Testing the flow	230
Updating the candidate record	225	Further exploration	232
		Summary	232

10

Crafting an Executive Summary with GPT — 233

Designing a solution	233	Converting the document	237
Licensing prerequisites	233	Sending the content to GPT	238
Configuring solution prerequisites	234	Populating the document and saving the new file	245
Enabling subscriptions	234		
Preparing a document template	234	Testing the flow	247
Setting up a cloud storage provider	234	Further exploration	249
Creating the flow	235	Summary	249
Configuring the trigger	235		

11

Using AI to Tag Images in a SharePoint Library — 251

What is computer vision?	251	Creating the flow	260
Designing a solution	255	Configuring the trigger	260
Licensing prerequisites	255	Working with computer vision	263
Configuring solution prerequisites	255	Updating the image details in the library	267
Creating a computer vision service	255	Testing the flow	268
Configuring a SharePoint library	257	Further exploration	269
		Summary	270

12

Creating a Generative AI-Based Bot — 271

Learning about the solution	271	Designing a solution	274
What's a topic, anyway?	272	Licensing prerequisites	275
What are generative answers?	273		

Preparing solution prerequisites	275	Testing the copilot	295
Creating the copilot	276	The Holidays topic	295
Customizing the copilot	277	Generative answers	297
Creating a new topic that uses ChatGPT	277	Further exploration	299
Disabling template topics	290	Summary	299
Adding content for generative AI	291		

13

Publishing a Generative AI-based Bot — 301

Publishing a bot to Teams	301	Publishing a bot to a website	309
Publishing the bot	302	Publishing a bot to Facebook	313
Testing the bot	305	Publishing a bot to other endpoints	324
Approving the bot	307	Summary	324

Index — 325

Other Books You May Enjoy — 334

Preface

Artificial intelligence (AI) is commonly thought of as the capability of a machine or computer system to perform tasks that would normally require human intelligence. Whatever your mental image of AI is—HAL 9000 in 2001: A Space Odyssey, Arnold Schwarzenegger as the Terminator, or Brent Spiner as Data in Star Trek: The Next Generation—it probably represents only one or two facets of the growing capabilities in the field.

Until recently, most AI technologies revolved around machine learning—essentially, an automation of applied statistics. If you've forgotten your college statistics classes, it's basically using large data samples to predict future data (for example, looking at recent home prices to predict future home prices). In the last year and a half, however, **generative artificial intelligence** (or **GenAI**, for short) has exploded onto the scene. Generative AI may be one of the most pivotal technologies created in the last hundred years. It's a watershed moment for both individuals and organizations, potentially redefining what it is to be capable of creativity—or even thought.

In case you've been living under a rock, generative AI is the power behind some of the wildest technical cultural phenomena such as OpenAI's ChatGPT, Midjourney, Dall-E, and Grok (as well as a host of other commercial ventures). Generative AI services can "create" content (based on their training data) that resembles the types of things that people can create. Instead of taking minutes or hours to compose content, many generative AI solutions can return responses in seconds.

Some of the most exciting use cases are around content summarization, reasoning over content in an almost human-like fashion, pattern matching, prediction, and analysis. Generative AI can also mix operating modes or contexts—for example, predicting values based on time-series data and writing a narrative to go along with it.

Throughout this book, we'll explore some exciting ways to combine the expanding capabilities of different types of AI with Microsoft's Power Platform tooling (including Power Apps, Power Automate, and Copilot Studio).

Who this book is for

This book is intended for individuals who are interested in exploring and experimenting with AI and automation but who may not have extensive technical experience in the field. This includes those in fields typically categorized as knowledge working, such as business decision-makers, sales representatives, administrative assistants, business development managers, human resources representatives, and business analysts.

The content in this book assumes you have no knowledge of any machine learning or AI concepts (though it certainly helps with understanding some of the more complex topics).

What this book covers

Chapter 1, Introduction to AI Services, introduces some of the basic concepts of AI.

Chapter 2, Configuring an Environment to Support AI Services, walks through the steps necessary to activate subscriptions and enable AI services in your environment.

Chapter 3, Talking to ChatGPT, introduces interacting with ChatGPT.

Chapter 4, Using ChatGPT and Copilot to Create Flows, demonstrates how to use AI to assist in creating Power Automate flows.

Chapter 5, Bootstrapping a Power App with Copilot, focuses on the power of Copilot to help design and modify a basic Power App through a conversational interface.

Chapter 6, Processing Data with Sentiment Analysis, shows how to leverage a machine learning capability to analyze text and then trigger actions based on a positive, negative, or neutral sentiment.

Chapter 7, Using Power Automate and AI to Build PowerPoint Presentations, explores the use of Power Automate and ChatGPT to create a PowerPoint presentation based on content sourced from the internet.

Chapter 8, Building an Event Registration App with Identity Verification, shows how to process government-issued identity documents to verify the identity of a registrant and then send automated meeting confirmations.

Chapter 9, Implementing an AI-Enabled Resume Screener, combines the power of document recognition, entity extraction, and a GPT service to process a submitted resume and evaluate whether it's a good fit against a particular job description.

Chapter 10, Creating an Executive Summary with GPT, demonstrates how to use GPT to generate an executive summary of a document and then insert it into a document or presentation.

Chapter 11, Using AI to Tag Images in a SharePoint Library, shows how to use the Azure Computer Vision service to categorize images based on content and then update a document library with descriptions and tags.

Chapter 12, Creating a Generative AI-Based Bot, explores the new Copilot Studio interface to create conversational bots that can provide answers through both ChatGPT and by reasoning over a set of document content.

Chapter 13, Publishing a Generative AI-Based Bot, leverages the conversation bot created in *Chapter 12* and walks through making the bot available for end users.

To get the most out of this book

To make the most of your studying experience, we recommend the following components:

- Azure tenant with free trial subscriptions (`https://azure.microsoft.com/en-us/free/ai-services/`)
- OpenAI GPT subscription (`https://www.openai.com`)
- Microsoft 365 trial subscription (`https://www.microsoft365.com`)
- AI Builder trial capacity (`https://learn.microsoft.com/en-us/ai-builder/ai-builder-trials`)

Download the example code files

You can download the example code files for this book from GitHub at `https://github.com/PacktPublishing/Power-Platform-and-the-AI-Revolution`. If there's an update to the code, it will be updated in the GitHub repository.

We also have other code bundles from our rich catalog of books and videos available at `https://github.com/PacktPublishing/`. Check them out!

Conventions used

There are a number of text conventions used throughout this book.

`Code in text`: Indicates code words in text, database table names, folder names, filenames, file extensions, pathnames, dummy URLs, user input, and Twitter handles. Here is an example: "Mount the downloaded `WebStorm-10*.dmg` disk image file as another disk in your system."

A block of code is set as follows:

```
html, body, #map {
  height: 100%;
  margin: 0;
  padding: 0
}
```

When we wish to draw your attention to a particular part of a code block, the relevant lines or items are set in bold:

```
[default]
exten => s,1,Dial(Zap/1|30)
exten => s,2,Voicemail(u100)
exten => s,102,Voicemail(b100)
```

```
exten => i,1,Voicemail(s0)
```

Any command-line input or output is written as follows:

```
$ mkdir css
$ cd css
```

Bold: Indicates a new term, an important word, or words that you see onscreen. For instance, words in menus or dialog boxes appear in **bold**. Here is an example: "Select **System info** from the **Administration** panel."

> Tips or important notes
> Appear like this.

Get in touch

Feedback from our readers is always welcome.

General feedback: If you have questions about any aspect of this book, email us at `customercare@packtpub.com` and mention the book title in the subject of your message.

Errata: Although we have taken every care to ensure the accuracy of our content, mistakes do happen. If you have found a mistake in this book, we would be grateful if you would report this to us. Please visit `www.packtpub.com/support/errata` and fill in the form.

Piracy: If you come across any illegal copies of our works in any form on the internet, we would be grateful if you would provide us with the location address or website name. Please contact us at `copyright@packtpub.com` with a link to the material.

If you are interested in becoming an author: If there is a topic that you have expertise in and you are interested in either writing or contributing to a book, please visit `authors.packtpub.com`.

Share Your Thoughts

Once you've read *Power Platform and the AI Revolution*, we'd love to hear your thoughts! Scan the QR code below to go straight to the Amazon review page for this book and share your feedback.

https://packt.link/r/1835086365

Your review is important to us and the tech community and will help us make sure we're delivering excellent quality content.

Download a free PDF copy of this book

Thanks for purchasing this book!

Do you like to read on the go but are unable to carry your print books everywhere?

Is your eBook purchase not compatible with the device of your choice?

Don't worry, now with every Packt book you get a DRM-free PDF version of that book at no cost.

Read anywhere, any place, on any device. Search, copy, and paste code from your favorite technical books directly into your application.

The perks don't stop there, you can get exclusive access to discounts, newsletters, and great free content in your inbox daily

Follow these simple steps to get the benefits:

1. Scan the QR code or visit the link below

https://packt.link/free-ebook/978-1-83508-636-0

2. Submit your proof of purchase
3. That's it! We'll send your free PDF and other benefits to your email directly

1
Introduction to AI Services

In the last few years, the field of **artificial intelligence** (**AI**) has undergone remarkable advancements, revolutionizing various domains and reshaping the way we think about and interact with technology. One particularly fascinating branch of AI that has gained significant attention recently is **Generative AI**. By enabling machines to exhibit creativity (or, more specifically, the appearance of creativity), Generative AI has opened up new frontiers in areas such as art, music, design, and storytelling, in addition to chat and human interaction.

Before we get too ahead of ourselves, let's talk about some core concepts to help shed some light on how all this works.

What do all these AI terms mean? Generative AI, in particular, refers to a class of algorithms and models that can autonomously generate new and (somewhat) original content. Unlike traditional AI systems, which rely on pre-defined rules or explicit instructions, Generative AI systems are designed to learn from patterns and existing data to produce novel outputs. These systems leverage deep learning techniques, such as **generative adversarial networks** (**GANs**), **variational autoencoders** (**VAEs**), and **recurrent neural networks** (**RNNs**), to emulate the creative processes of the human mind.

As you'll see, AI has a lexicon all its own. What do we mean when we say things such as *generative adversarial networks* and *variational autoencoders*? Let's make a quick detour and define some of the terms that we're going to use:

- **Algorithm**: An algorithm is a set of rules (typically expressed in a computer programming language) that are followed when solving problems.
- **Neural network**: When we talk about neural networks, we're talking about computer systems and interactions that are modeled on our understanding of the human brain and nervous system. Like the human brain, the fundamental building blocks of artificial neural networks are referred to as neurons (nodes), each of which connects to other nodes. The connections have concepts of weight and bias, and when inputs reach certain thresholds, they flip on the next node in the chain. Imagine a neural network as layers of nodes arranged in grids, with each node connecting to multiple nodes on the adjacent layer, and each node's output being used to influence the input in the adjacent layer's nodes.

- **GAN**: A GAN is comprised of two neural networks that compete based on the same source data. GANs can create synthetic data that is unique but imitates the seed data.
- **VAE**: A VAE is an algorithm that has two functions. The first takes a complex data structure and then stores a more simplified version of it with some amount of randomness, while the second takes the simplified version and then generates a more complex output. Imagine the encode function as taking a high-resolution picture of a tree, downscaling it (so that it still looks like a tree but is missing some data and possibly looks blurry), and adding a few random pixels to it. When the decode function is activated, it retrieves the simplified data that's stored and uses it to reconstitute a more high-resolution image of a tree. The new picture looks similar to the original, but partially due to the loss incurred through the simplification of original data and partially due to the insertion of some amount of randomness by the encoder, the new picture is also different.
- **RNN**: An RNN is a type of artificial neural network that can process sequential data by preserving information from previous steps.
- **AI model**: An AI model is a mathematical algorithm that mimics human intelligence, processing data to make predictions and generate outputs. It learns from training data to perform specific tasks such as image recognition or natural language processing.
- **Large language model**: A large language model is a type of AI model that is designed to understand and generate coherent and contextually relevant, human-like text. The popular ChatGPT is an example of a large language model.

There are many more complex concepts (including many more types of neural networks and AI models) behind deep learning and AI systems.

In addition to Generative AI, many types of AI models are currently in use today, such as those designed to do the following:

- Estimate shipping routes
- Predict traffic patterns and congestion
- Find weather anomalies
- Identify objects in pictures

Each of these different types of models depends on vast quantities of existing data and purpose-built algorithms, combined with training procedures to help the models "learn" how to predict or identify things.

Throughout this book, we'll be using a variety of AI technologies – from prebuilt, purpose-oriented models to Generative AI. By the time you reach the final examples and exercises, I hope you'll have some exciting ideas on how you can accelerate your team, organization, or even personal life with AI.

What kinds of things can Generative AI do?

The remarkable power of Generative AI lies in its ability to create realistic and diverse outputs that exhibit human-like creativity. For instance, in the area of visual arts, Generative AI can produce lifelike paintings, generate photorealistic images, or even assist in designing new products with particular aesthetics. In music composition, Generative AI algorithms can compose original melodies and harmonies, imitating the style of different composers or creating entirely new musical genres. Similarly, in the realm of storytelling, Generative AI can develop compelling narratives, write poetry, or generate realistic dialogue.

The impact of Generative AI extends far beyond artistic and creative pursuits. It has already found applications in various fields, including data augmentation, synthetic data generation, video game design, and drug discovery. Generative AI techniques can also aid in enhancing existing content, enabling the creation of high-quality image upscaling, text summarization, and even voice synthesis that closely resembles human speech! The future of what AI can do is only limited by the creativity of the people building and training the models.

However, Generative AI is not without its challenges. Ethical concerns, such as the potential for misuse or the propagation of biased content, need to be addressed. Striking the right balance between the creativity of the AI system and its alignment with societal values is a crucial aspect that requires careful consideration.

> **Ethical and responsible AI**
>
> The responsible use of AI is critical to ensuring its success in the marketplace. Responsible AI includes concepts such as fairness (treating every user equitably), inclusiveness (making sure people of all races, genders, and abilities are empowered to use the systems), transparency (understanding how the AI models reached their conclusions), and accountability (ensuring people can be held responsible for an AI system's decisions).
>
> Responsible AI design and use covers all aspects of all AI systems, from machine learning models having representative data samples that don't hold biases toward nationalities or genders to ensuring Generative AI doesn't get used for creating likenesses of people (sometimes called **deepfakes**) without their consent.
>
> Microsoft, in part, has been working on establishing principles for ethical and responsible AI. You can read more about their commitments here: `https://www.microsoft.com/en-us/ai/responsible-ai`.

Overall, though, Generative AI represents a significant breakthrough in working toward AI. By harnessing the power of machine learning and deep neural networks, Generative AI systems can unlock new realms of creativity and innovation, business automation, and human-to-computer interaction.

Not to mention, it's also unleashing many ninja cat dinosaur mashups:

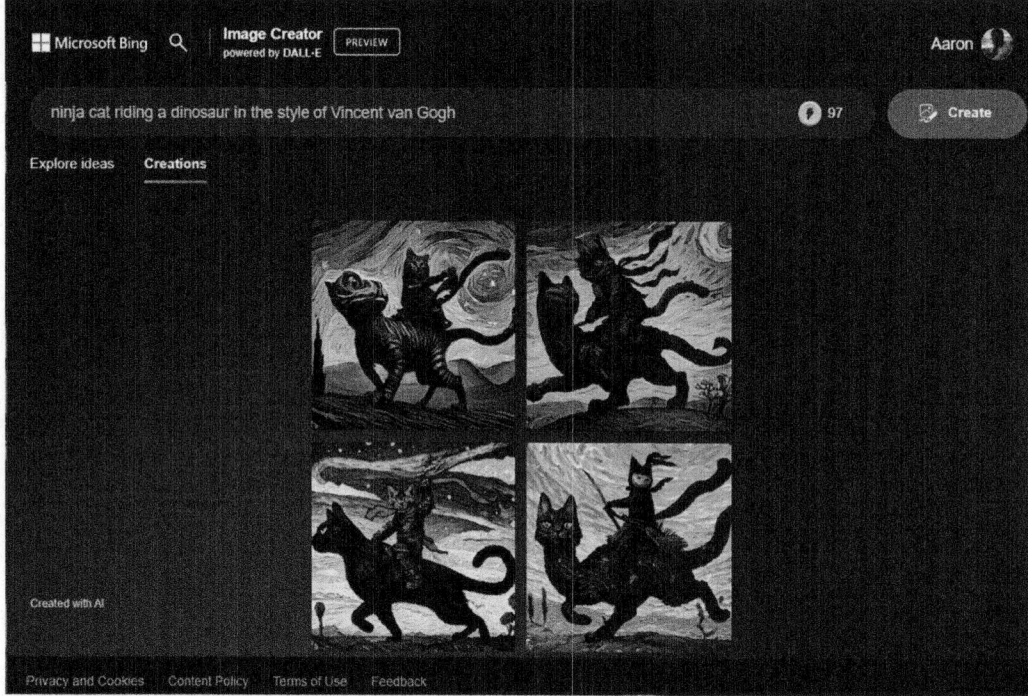

Figure 1.1 – Bing Image Creator, powered by DALL-E

Let's shift gears to understanding how various types of AI might be used in the context of business – specifically, with Microsoft's Power Platform.

What is Power Platform?

Power Platform is a comprehensive suite of **low-code** and **no-code** tools that's designed to empower individuals and organizations to create custom business applications, automate processes, analyze data, and develop virtual agents. It consists of four main components:

- **Power Apps**: This component enables users to build web and mobile applications with drag-and-drop functionality, all while connecting to various data sources.
- **Power Automate**: Formerly known as Microsoft Flow, it allows the creation of automated workflows, integrating and synchronizing data and processes across multiple applications and services. Power Automate has expanded from being a cloud-only process automation platform to including process mining and **robotic process automation** (**RPA**).

- **Power BI**: This component provides robust data analytics and visualization capabilities, transforming raw data into meaningful insights and interactive reports.
- **Copilots**: This component allows intelligent chatbots to be created without the need to code, enabling organizations to provide instant support and engagement with customers.

Together, these tools empower users of all skill levels to drive digital transformation, improve productivity, and innovate within their organizations. This book will focus primarily on integrating AI services and models with the Power Automate, Power App, and Copilots components of Power Platform.

> **What is no-code or low-code software?**
>
> Microsoft bills the Power Platform tools as a development environment that encourages **no-code** and **low-code** solutions. So, what are those? No-code is just like it sounds – a way for creators to assemble a solution from widgets, components, or modules in a **what-you-see-is-what-you-get** (WYSIWYG) fashion. No formal development experience is necessary to generate a working solution.
>
> Low-code software, which is one step up, involves using a simplified development language in conjunction with the available connectors or modules. Power Platform leverages a language called **Power Fx**, which is similar in structure to the syntax that's used by popular Office macros or spreadsheet formulas.
>
> Power Platform tools can also support **pro-code** or **code-first** authoring (which is decidedly the opposite of the low-code or no-code methodology), meaning you can interface with REST API interfaces or use traditional development environments such as Visual Studio.

Learning about Power Automate

Power Automate is a workflow and process automation tool. As a no-code/low-code solution, Power Automate relies on various components or building blocks to create automation.

Here's a quick list of some of the terminology you'll see in this book as it relates to Power Automate:

- **Flow**: The basic unit of Power Automate, flows are logical groupings of connectors, conditions, and tasks that are used to perform an automation
- **Connector**: Connectors are configuration components that are used to define the necessary parameters to communicate with services and apps
- **Trigger**: A trigger is an event or activity that causes a flow to begin, such as *When a new file is created* or *When a row is added to a SQL database table*
- **Actions**: Actions are the logical steps or units that describe the actions and evaluations being performed, such as *Copy a file*, *Check if the value is greater than or equal to*, or *Add a row to a SQL database table*

We'll use Power Automate in many of the exercises and examples throughout this book.

> **Further reading**
>
> To learn more about Power Automate, check out *Workflow Automation with Microsoft Power Automate, Second Edition* (https://www.packtpub.com/product/workflow-automation-with-microsoft-power-automate-second-edition/9781803237671).

Learning about Copilots

Copilot technology (not to be confused with *Copilot for something*) empowers users to design and deploy chatbots to interact with people, providing instant support and engagement. With a visual interface and pre-built templates, creators can easily define conversation flows, connect and integrate with various systems, and train the chatbot using **natural language understanding** (NLU).

> **So many copilots**
>
> We'll try to keep things straightforward, but Microsoft has infused its products with the copilot nomenclature. There's **Microsoft 365 Copilot** (a Generative AI assistant that's built into the Microsoft 365 experience), **Copliot in Viva Sales** (a Generative AI assistant that connects Outlook and other collaboration workloads with Dynamics CRM), and **Copilot for Security** (an AI assistant for threat hunting and management).
>
> Power Platform has its own set of copilot features, including **AI Copilot** (an AI-enabled generative assistant for creating Power Apps and Flows) and **Copilot Studio**, the web interface that's used to create – you guessed it – copilots. **Copilots** (in Copilot Studio) are the revamped Power Virtual Agents – chatbots that can be enabled to provide answers and initiate workflows in other applications.

Since we're going to be using copilots in some of the exercises in this book, you'll want to be familiar with their terminology, too:

- **Topics**: Topics represent the main areas or subjects that your chatbot can handle. Each topic consists of triggers, actions, and responses to guide the conversation flow.
- **Triggers**: Triggers are conditions or user inputs that initiate a conversation or direct it to a specific topic. They can be based on keywords, phrases, or system events.
- **Actions**: Actions are the steps or operations that the chatbot performs in response to user inputs or triggers. They can include sending messages, asking questions, calling APIs, or performing calculations.
- **Entities**: Entities are pieces of information that the chatbot can extract from user inputs.

- **Responses**: Responses are the messages or content that the chatbot generates to communicate with users.

Copilots can be deployed to a variety of locations and interfaces, including websites and Microsoft Teams.

> **Further reading**
>
> For more information on Copilots, please read *Empowering Organizations with Power Virtual Agents* (https://www.packtpub.com/product/empowering-organizations-with-power-virtual-agents/9781801074742).

Learning about Power Apps

The Power Apps component of Power Platform enables users to create custom web and mobile applications without extensive coding knowledge. It offers a low-code development environment where users can visually design app interfaces, define data sources, and add functionality through a wide range of pre-built connectors.

Like Power Automate and Copilots, Power Apps has terminology that you should know about:

- **Screens**: Screens are the building blocks of an app and represent different views or pages. Each screen can contain various controls and components.
- **Controls**: Controls are the interactive elements that are used to display data, capture user input, or trigger actions. Examples include text boxes, buttons, galleries, forms, and charts.
- **Data sources**: Data sources are the places where app data is stored, such as SharePoint, Microsoft Dataverse (formerly Common Data Service), Excel, SQL databases, or external systems via connectors.
- **Formulas**: Power Apps uses formulas (the Power Fx language) to perform calculations, manipulate data, and control app behavior. Formulas can be used in properties, events, and actions.
- **Data cards**: Data cards are containers for data entry controls within forms. They represent fields from a data source and enable users to view and edit data.
- **Galleries**: Galleries are controls that are used to display lists or collections of data. They can be customized to show data in different layouts, such as a table or a gallery with cards.

One of the most exciting new features of Power Platform is the *Describe it to design it* feature, which allows you to use natural language to build a framework for a Power App. We'll explore that a little bit in *Chapter 5, Bootstrapping a Power App with Copilot*.

> **Further reading**
>
> For more information on creating apps with Microsoft Power Apps, check out *Learn Microsoft Power Apps, Second Edition*: `https://www.packtpub.com/product/learn-microsoft-power-apps-second-edition/9781801070645`.

Learning about AI Builder technologies

AI Builder is the original AI component of Power Platform and allows users to incorporate AI capabilities into their Power Apps and Power Automate workflows. It enables users, even those without extensive AI expertise, to build and deploy AI models for common business scenarios.

Working with prebuilt models

AI Builder offers a set of prebuilt models and samples that can be customized to meet specific needs. These models cover various AI capabilities, such as form processing, object detection, prediction, text classification, and sentiment analysis. Users can train and refine these models using their data or leverage existing data connectors.

With AI Builder, users can automate data extraction from forms, classify and predict outcomes, analyze sentiment in text, and identify objects in images. These AI capabilities enhance the power and functionality of Power Apps and Power Automate – and you'll get hands-on experience with them in this book!

We'll be using the sentiment analysis feature in *Chapter 6, Processing Data with Sentiment Analysis*.

We'll work with the AI Builder document reader in *Chapter 8, Building an Event Registration App with Identity Verification*.

Finally, in *Chapter 9, Implementing an AI-Enabled Resume Screener*, you'll learn how to train an AI Builder model to extract key pieces of data from a resume.

Working with custom models

Custom models, in contrast to prebuilt models, allow users to create and train their custom AI models tailored to their specific business needs. Where prebuilt models are already trained for common scenarios, custom models allow you to train models with your data to meet specialized requirements.

We'll use a custom model to work with unstructured data in *Chapter 9, Building a Resume Screener Using Copilot and Power Apps*.

Understanding Power Platform licensing

The licensing structure of Power Platform can be a bit complex, but here's an overview of the main licensing options:

- **Power Apps and Power Automate Free**: There is a free version available for Power Apps and Power Automate that provides basic functionality and limited access to connectors and features. This licensing plan is sometimes referred to as the *seeded offering*.
- **Power Apps and Power Automate per-user plans**: These are paid plans that offer enhanced capabilities and more extensive access to connectors and features on a per-user basis. These plans are suitable for individual users who need advanced functionality and are licensed on a monthly or annual basis.
- **Power Apps and Power Automate per-app or per-flow plans**: These plans allow organizations to license specific apps or flows, rather than licensing individual users. They are useful when an organization has a large user base but only a subset of users need access to specific apps or flows.
- **Power Apps and Power Automate licensing with Microsoft 365 and Dynamics 365 plans**: Power Apps and Power Automate are also included in various Microsoft 365 and Dynamics 365 plans. These plans provide broader access to Power Platform capabilities alongside other Microsoft productivity and business applications.

It's important to note that certain premium features, add-ons, connectors, and capacity-based usage may require additional licensing or higher-tier plans. Additionally, Microsoft regularly updates and refines its licensing options, so it's recommended to consult the official Microsoft licensing documentation or contact Microsoft directly for the most up-to-date information on licensing options for Power Platform.

AI Builder is a feature that is billed on a capacity model – separate from the Power Apps and Power Automate per-user, per-app, or per-flow plans. Here's an overview of the key aspects:

- **Free usage**: AI Builder offers limited usage for free, allowing users to explore and experience its basic features without additional cost.
- **Consumption-based pricing**: When usage surpasses the free limit or requires more advanced capabilities, AI Builder capacity licensing comes into play. It follows a consumption-based pricing model, where organizations purchase capacity to enable AI Builder's features.
- **Capacity types**: There are two types of capacity available for AI Builder licensing – AI Builder standalone capacity and AI Builder capacity add-on:
  - **AI Builder standalone capacity**: This type of capacity is dedicated solely to AI Builder and covers the consumption of AI Builder models and services.
  - **AI Builder capacity add-on**: This capacity is an add-on for existing Power Apps and Power Automate capacity. It allows organizations to extend their existing capacity so that it includes AI Builder capabilities.

- **Capacity units**: AI Builder capacity is measured in capacity units, with each unit providing a certain level of compute resources and performance. The number of capacity units required depends on the volume of AI Builder usage and the complexity of the models being deployed.

It's important to consider the total number of users, expected usage, and the specific AI Builder features required when determining the appropriate capacity licensing for an organization. Organizations may need to allocate sufficient capacity units to ensure optimal performance and scalability.

For precise details on AI Builder capacity licensing, including pricing, specific features, and licensing agreements, it is recommended to refer to the official Microsoft documentation or consult with a Microsoft licensing specialist to ensure compliance and appropriate licensing for your organization's needs.

> **Further reading**
>
> For a deeper dive into Power Platform licensing, see `https://learn.microsoft.com/en-us/power-platform/admin/pricing-billing-skus` and `https://learn.microsoft.com/en-us/ai-builder/administer-licensing`. If all that is as clear as mud, you can contact a Microsoft Partner (`https://partner.microsoft.com/en-us/marketing`).

Exploring additional AI services

Now that we've spent a little bit of time learning about some of the features of Generative AI and Power Platform, let's look at a few of the AI services currently in the marketplace.

Working with Azure AI Services

Microsoft offers a wide array of AI and machine learning capabilities under the **Azure AI Services** (formerly Azure Cognitive Services) umbrella. These services enable developers to add intelligent capabilities to their applications without needing to build complex AI algorithms from scratch. With Azure Cognitive Services, developers can tap into pre-built models and **application programming interfaces (APIs)** to incorporate functionalities such as vision, speech, language, and decision-making into their applications.

The vision-capable services include the following:

- **Computer Vision**: This service enables image analysis and object detection. Computer Vision can do things such as identify objects in a scene (*dog, frisbee,* and *tree*) as well as perform contextual image analysis (*There is a dog catching a frisbee by the tree*) and optical character recognition.
- **Face**: The Face service is used to identify the presence of faces in image data, as well as identify and analyze faces in images. You might use the Face service to verify someone's identity against a government-issued identification card or to blur out face content in a picture or video.

- **Custom Vision**: The Custom Vision service, now part of Image Analysis 4.0, enables developers to create custom image recognition models for tagging and applying labels to content based on visual characteristics.

Azure Cognitive Services includes several language and speech APIs, which provide the following features:

- **Speech**: The Speech service provides a broad array of speech-to-text, text-to-speech, content translation, and speaker recognition capabilities.
- **Language**: This service has several sub-services and capabilities based on natural language understanding, including the ability to perform key phrase extraction, named entity recognition, and the ability to detect **personally identifiable information** (**PII**). The Language service can also provide text translation between two languages, classify bodies of text and determine their sentiment, and perform content summarization.
- **Translator**: While the Language service handles text-to-text content conversion, the Translator service can provide machine-based translation in real time.
- **Language Understanding** (**LUIS**): The **LUIS** service is a machine learning model that can predict overall meaning and content extraction from natural language conversation.
- **QnA Maker**: You can think of the QnA Maker service as a bot or answering service that can reason over semi-structured content and provide answers to customers.

The decision models that are available alongside Azure AI Services also provide unique capabilities:

- **Content Moderator**: The Content Moderator service provides analysis for potentially offensive, undesirable, unsafe, or otherwise risky content
- **Personalizer**: Using behavior and habits analysis, the Personalizer service helps select which content experiences to choose for your customers
- **Anomaly Detector**: The Anomaly Detector service allows you to monitor and detect inconsistencies in time-based datasets

Azure AI Services also includes the **Azure OpenAI service**, which has several language models, including GPT-3 and Codex, to support content generation, summarization, and natural language-to-code translation.

> **Change is a-comin'**
>
> If there's anything constant, it's change. As the AI landscape evolves, newer features, services, or capabilities replace older counterparts. Over the next few years, you'll need to say "goodbye" to the LUIS and QnA Maker services, as they'll be retired. Microsoft recommends transitioning LUIS-enabled applications and services to Conversational Language Understanding and retooling services by using QnA Maker with the question-and-answer capability in the Azure AI Language service.

Together, this family of services provides developers with the mechanisms to programmatically add AI-based capabilities to their applications without having lots of experience in AI modeling, improving user experiences, and driving innovation in areas such as healthcare and customer service.

> **Further reading**
>
> For more information on the complete lineup of Azure Cognitive Services, go to `https://learn.microsoft.com/en-us/azure/cognitive-services/what-are-cognitive-services`.

Working with OpenAI models

OpenAI is the organization behind popular models such as GPT-3, GPT-4, and the DALL-E image generation platform.

OpenAI offers a range of advanced AI technologies and services that aim to empower individuals and organizations to leverage the power of AI. Let's look at some of their offerings:

- **Generative Pre-trained Transformer (GPT)**: This is OpenAI's flagship language model. It can generate coherent and contextually relevant text, making it useful for tasks such as natural language processing, text completion, and chatbot development.

- **OpenAI API**: This offering provides developers with easy access to OpenAI's models, enabling them to integrate language generation capabilities into their applications or services.

- **Images API**: The Images API provides methods for creating or editing new and existing images based on text prompts.

- **OpenAI Gym**: This is a toolkit for developing and comparing reinforcement learning algorithms. It provides a wide range of pre-built environments and tools to train and evaluate AI agents.

- **OpenAI Platform**: OpenAI Platform offers a suite of tools and resources for researching, developing, and deploying AI models. It includes model training infrastructure, collaboration features, and model management tools.

- **OpenAI Scholars Program**: This is a research internship program that supports aspiring AI researchers from underrepresented backgrounds. It provides mentorship, stipends, and resources to help participants advance their AI knowledge and contribute to the field.

OpenAI, like Microsoft, emphasizes ethical considerations and responsible AI development.

> **Further reading**
> In this book, we'll mainly be focusing on the OpenAI services that are exposed through Power Platform directly or via Azure AI Services. OpenAI's products are available separately, as well. For more information on developing with the OpenAI platform, go to `https://platform.openai.com/overview`.

Working with services from Google, Anthropic, and more

While we're mainly going to focus on services offered in the Microsoft cloud (Power Platform AI Builder, Azure AI Services, and OpenAI, to be more specific), they aren't the only big names in AI right now. There are several other AI platforms – both general and specific – that are currently being developed. Some are even open for you to experiment with now!

Here's a list of a few services that you might come across:

- **Google Bard**: Based on Google's **Language Model for Dialogue Applications (LaMDA)**, Bard is an advanced language model that's developed by Google's research team. LaMDA's training involves dialogues instead of isolated prompts, allowing it to grasp the underlying meaning and engage in more conversational exchanges. You can start a conversation with Bard at `https://bard.google.com`.
- **Anthropic Claude**: Claude is another type of conversational AI model. Anthropic approaches their AI models a bit differently, however, training with a method they call Constitutional AI. Constitutional AI involves supervised learning and review so that the AI learns from the feedback to generate harmless outputs. Talk to Claude at `https://claude.ai`.
- **Midjourney**: Whereas ChatGPT, Bard, and Claude use text for both input and output, Midjourney is an AI-based art generation platform. Midjourney can be used to create high-quality art using text prompts. Experience Midjourney at `https://www.midjourney.com/`.

AI has also found its way into countless plugins and extensions. A quick internet search or two will quickly reveal new ad hoc tools you can try out.

Summary

Hopefully, having a high-level understanding of some of the types of computing, algorithms, and frameworks that go into Generative AI makes it a little less scary to approach. While the machines may not be coming for us (yet), they certainly are going to be influencing how businesses and customers interact for years to come.

Now, it's time to begin your AI journey by getting your development environment ready!

2
Configuring an Environment to Support AI Services

In this chapter, we're going to begin exploring how to obtain and set up the various services and environments you're going to need to perform the exercises in this book.

Since this book is primarily focused on working with the AI services available in the Microsoft ecosystem, we'll spend the most time working with the Azure and Power Platform services. At the end of the chapter, we'll walk through getting connected to other AI platforms in case you want to use those as part of your learning as well.

> **Note**
> Some of these services may have free trials available for individual interactive usage, but most will require some form of payment for anything that accesses resources programmatically, such as from a Power App. You may need to budget accordingly to take full advantage of the available platforms.

For those who are only going to use AI in low-code scenarios (such as AI Builder or as OpenAI actions in Power Apps or Power Automate), configuring the OpenAI service resources in Azure may not be necessary, and you can skip to the *Configuring Power Platform* section. However, if you want to dive deeper into the world of AI-enabled services with what Azure has to offer, keep reading.

Configuring Azure

There are a number of ways to use OpenAI-based services such as ChatGPT in the Azure environment. Depending on your context, you may be willing to use a public service such as ChatGPT for your generative needs. However, if you want to configure OpenAI to work against your own dataset within the boundaries of your Azure tenant, you'll want to request access to Azure OpenAI Service.

One of the many benefits of enabling OpenAI in your Azure tenant is that you can connect it to your own tenant data. When you start to review the terms of service for public or free AI interfaces, you'll notice that the service providers can claim ownership over the results that you produce, as well as use the data you supply to further train models. If your goal is to use AI to work against your own proprietary data (which may contain anything from **personally identifiable information** (**PII**) to trade secrets), you need to be assured that you remain in control (both from a data stewardship perspective as well as a content ownership perspective) of any data that passes through the system.

> **Note**
> OpenAI does offer an enterprise subscription for ChatGPT that protects your prompts, source data, and results from being used to train the general model.

Requesting API access for Azure OpenAI services

Due to the rapidly evolving nature of AI services and the potential risks that **generative AI** (**GenAI**) poses, Microsoft has gated access to OpenAI services. As part of its responsible AI commitments, Microsoft works to ensure that the services it provides are being used in a way that is safe.

In order to use Azure services, you will need an Azure subscription.

> **Tip**
> To find your Azure subscriptions, navigate to the Azure portal (`https://portal.azure.com`) and type `Subscriptions` in the **Search** bar. The subscription ID is formatted as a GUID, which you will need to provide during the request process. For more information on viewing your Azure subscriptions, see `https://learn.microsoft.com/en-us/azure/azure-portal/get-subscription-tenant-id`.

To begin requesting access to Azure OpenAI services, follow these steps:

1. With a browser, navigate to `https://aka.ms/oai/access`.

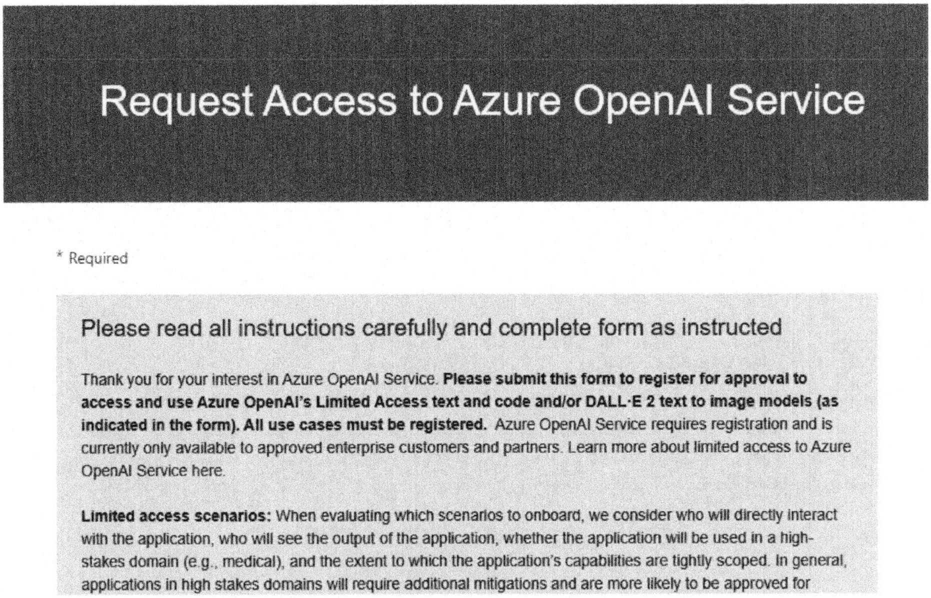

Request Access to Azure OpenAI Service

* Required

Please read all instructions carefully and complete form as instructed

Thank you for your interest in Azure OpenAI Service. **Please submit this form to register for approval to access and use Azure OpenAI's Limited Access text and code and/or DALL·E 2 text to image models (as indicated in the form). All use cases must be registered.** Azure OpenAI Service requires registration and is currently only available to approved enterprise customers and partners. Learn more about limited access to Azure OpenAI Service here.

Limited access scenarios: When evaluating which scenarios to onboard, we consider who will directly interact with the application, who will see the output of the application, whether the application will be used in a high-stakes domain (e.g., medical), and the extent to which the application's capabilities are tightly scoped. In general, applications in high stakes domains will require additional mitigations and are more likely to be approved for

Figure 2.1 – Requesting access to Azure OpenAI services

2. Fill out the form with your name and Azure subscription IDs.
3. Select which Azure OpenAI services you want to use. The available options are **Text and code models** and **DALL-E 2 models**. See *Figure 2.2*:

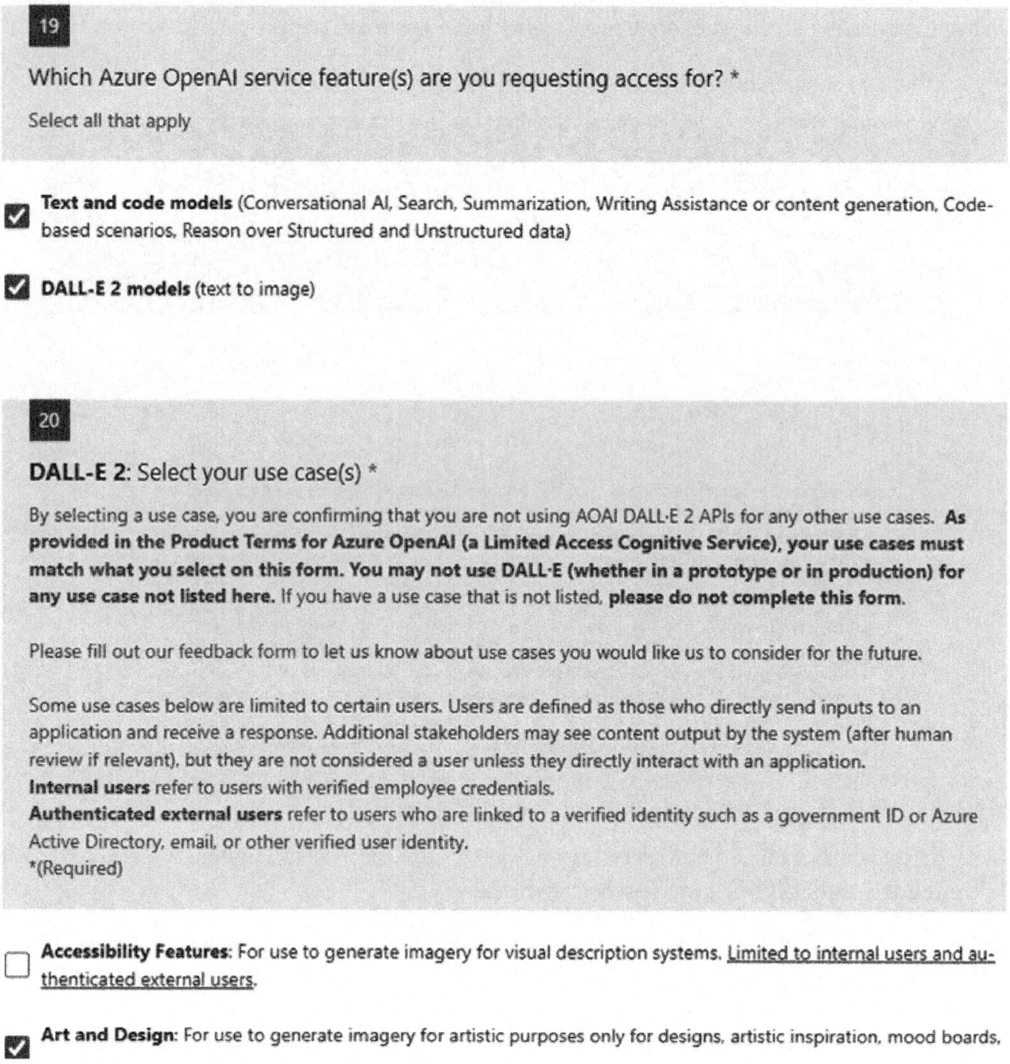

Configuring an Environment to Support AI Services

Figure 2.2 – Selecting Azure OpenAI service models

4. Select use cases for each model. When selecting use cases, be aware that selecting **Most Valuable Professional (MVP) or Regional Director (RD) Demo Use** will result in denial if you are not currently a Microsoft MVP or RD.

5. Ensure you fill out any required fields, such as your organization's phone number or company website.

6. For *question 18*, you must select **I acknowledge these terms apply to use the Azure OpenAI Service**. Read the terms linked in the question, including legal terms, support terms for products in Azure Previews, as well as the Code of Conduct for Azure OpenAI Service.

7. For *question 19*, you must select **Yes, I attest** to confirm adherence with the service requirements and to acknowledge that Microsoft is monitoring the use of completions and generations APIs.

8. Click **Submit**.

The form will be sent to Microsoft for review and approval. Currently, it takes approximately 10 business days for a request to be reviewed. Once your access has been approved, you'll be able to create and use OpenAI resources in the Azure portal.

Setting up OpenAI service resources in Azure

Once you've been approved by Microsoft for OpenAI services in your Azure tenant, it's time to set it up!

All of the services you need to work with OpenAI already exist—they're just waiting to be enabled. To take advantage of the examples in this book, you'll need to register several resource providers.

An Azure resource provider is a collection of REST operations designed to support the functionality of a specific Azure service, such as *Microsoft.Search* for the Azure Cognitive Search service. This provider specifies the REST operations used to manage various aspects of the service, including configuring search indices and enabling the development of semantic search-based apps.

Resource providers are registered and enabled per subscription. In this section, we'll take the necessary steps to enable connections that will support using Azure OpenAI services later:

1. Navigate to the Azure portal (`https://portal.azure.com`) and select **Subscriptions**.
2. Select one of the subscriptions that you used to register for OpenAI Service access.
3. Under **Settings**, select **Resource providers**, as shown in *Figure 2.3*:

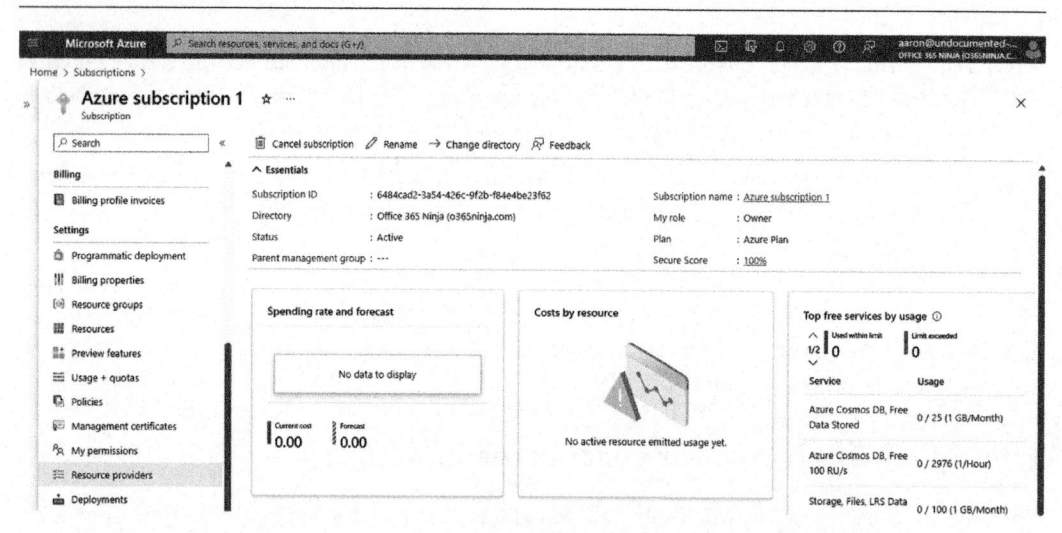

Configuring an Environment to Support AI Services

Figure 2.3 – Navigating the Azure subscription

4. From the list of resource providers, select **Microsoft.AppConfiguration**:

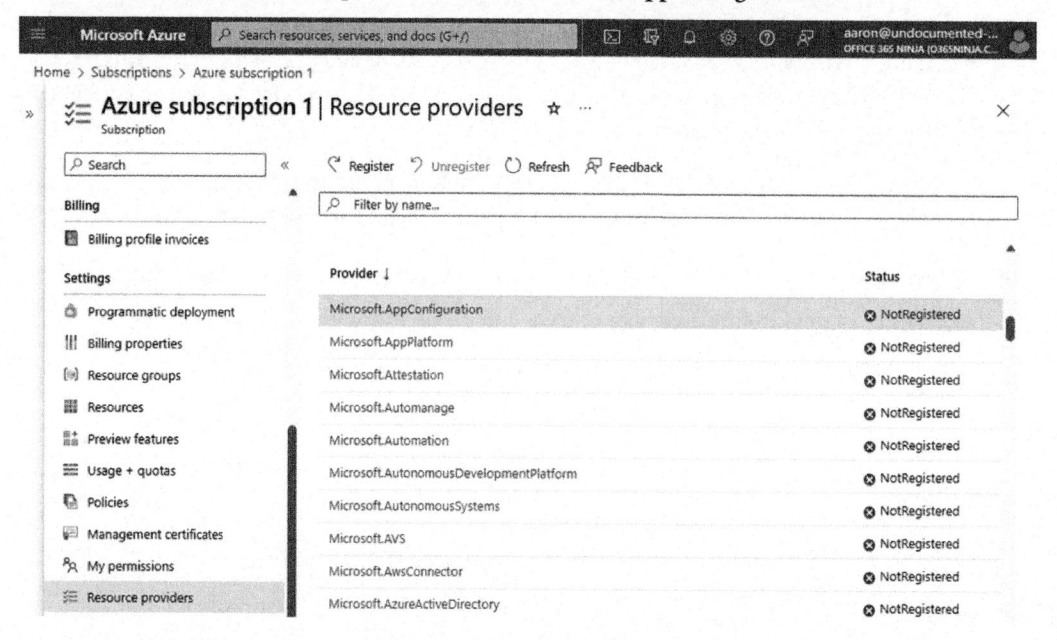

Figure 2.4 – Selecting the Microsoft.AppConfiguration resource provider

5. Click **Register**.

6. Repeat *steps 4* and *5* for the following service providers that will be used throughout this book:

- Microsoft.AppPlatform
- Microsoft.App
- Microsoft.Authorization
- Microsoft.BotService
- Microsoft.CognitiveSearch
- Microsoft.CognitiveServices
- Microsoft.Insights
- Microsoft.Logic
- Microsoft.ManagedIdentity
- Microsoft.KeyVault
- Microsoft.Storage
- Microsoft.Web

As you expand your use cases with Azure OpenAI, you'll need these enabled to start working with the models and services.

Configuring API access for ChatGPT

While anyone can browse to OpenAI and use ChatGPT for free interactively, you'll need to obtain API access if you want to start using ChatGPT in your apps and automations.

To sign up for API access, follow these steps:

1. With a browser, navigate to https://beta.openai.com/signup.
2. On the **Create your account** page, enter an email address and click **Continue**. Alternatively, you could use an OAuth connection to authenticate with Google, a Microsoft account, or an Apple ID.
3. Enter a password for your new OpenAI account and click **Continue**.
4. Check the account you provided during *step 2* for a confirmation message. Click the link to confirm your identity and proceed to the onboarding.
5. On the **Tell us about you** onboarding page, add your personal details, including your **Full name**, **Organization**, and **Birthday** details. Click **Agree**.
6. If you have registered previously, you may receive a message about upgrading to a paid plan to start using the API. Click **Continue**.

7. If necessary, click **Upgrade** on the **Welcome to the OpenAI platform** overview page, as shown in *Figure 2.5*:

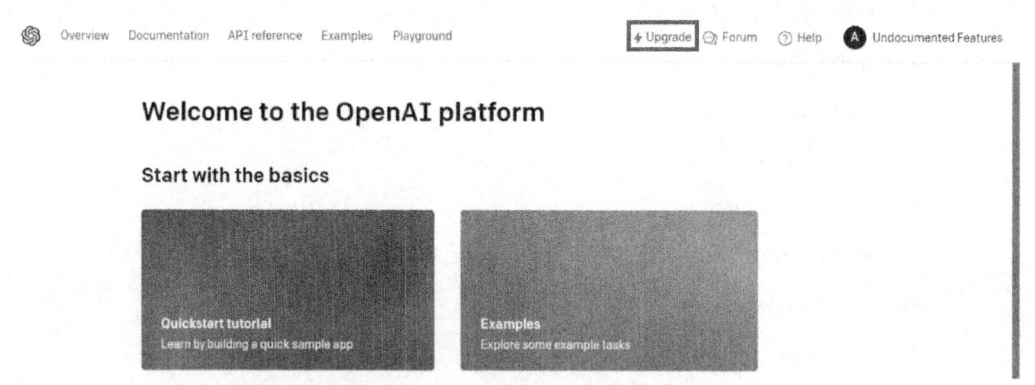

Figure 2.5 – OpenAI platform overview page

8. Otherwise, click **API keys** in the navigation menu.
9. Click **Start verification** to begin a phone verification process.
10. On the **Verify your phone number** page, enter a phone number for a device that is capable of receiving SMS messages. Click **Send code**.
11. On the **Enter code** page, enter the six-digit code that you received from the OpenAI verification service.
12. Click **Start payment plan**.
13. On the **What best describes you?** page, select the classification that best describes your usage scenario (**Individual** or **Company**).
14. On the **Set up payment plan** page, enter your credit card information and click **Continue**.
15. On the **Configure payment** page, enter a value for **Initial credit purchase**. You can select any amount between $5 and $50.
16. On the **Payment summary** page, click **Confirm payment**. You will be charged for the amount specified on the **Configure payment** page and displayed in the summary.
17. On the **Billing overview** page, in the navigation menu under **User**, select **API keys**. See *Figure 2.6*:

Configuring API access for ChatGPT   23

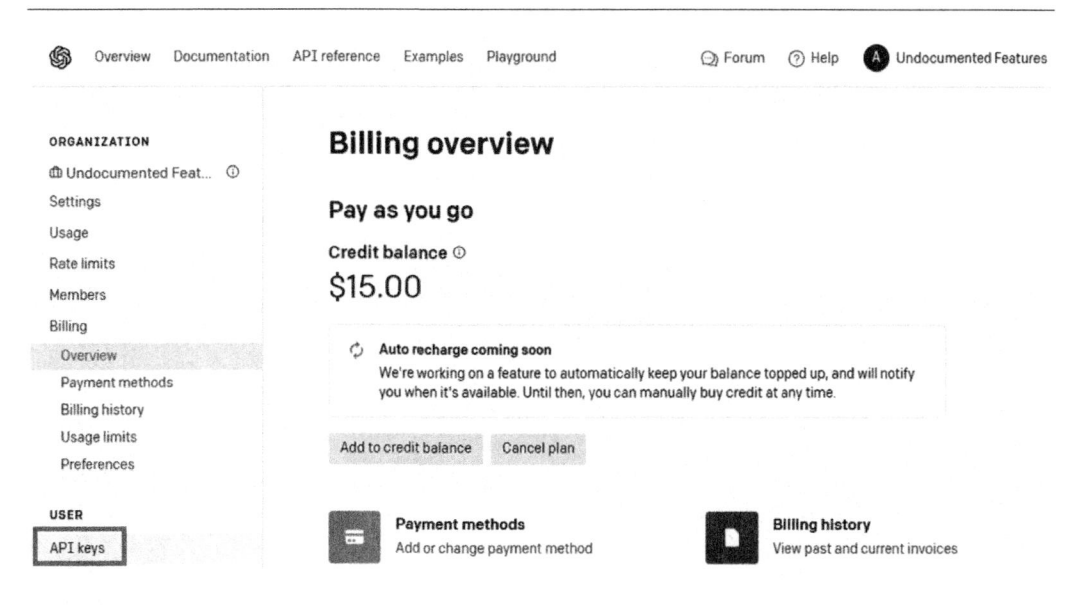

Figure 2.6 – Selecting API keys

18. On the **API keys** page, select **Create new secret key**:

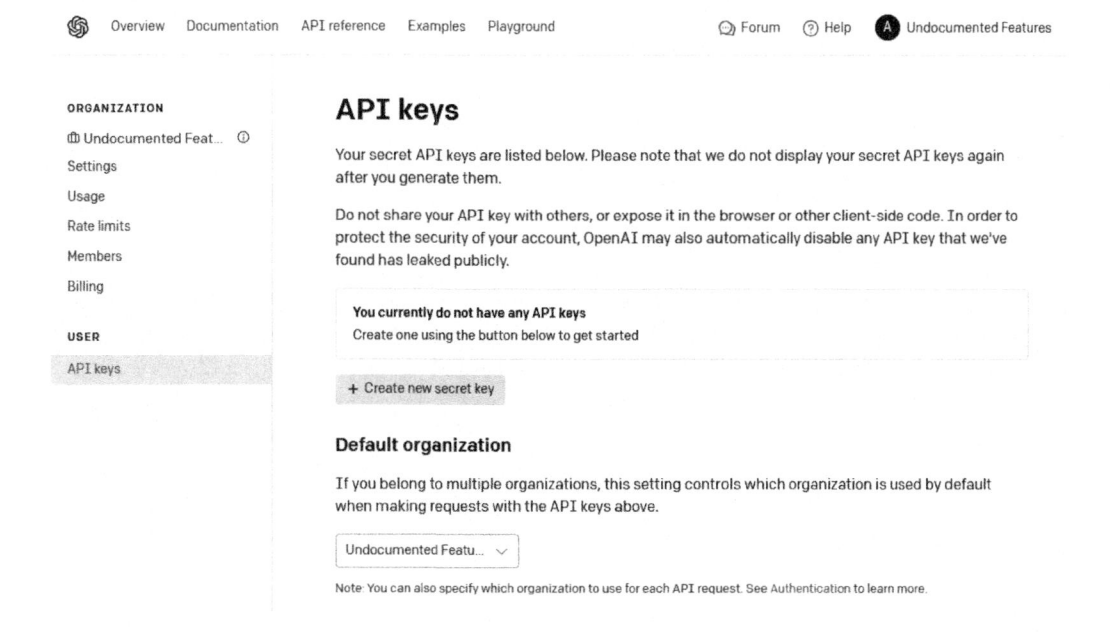

Figure 2.7 – Creating a new API key

19. On the **Create new secret key** popup, enter a name for the API key (such as OpenAI API key) and click **Create secret key**.
20. Copy the value displayed to a safe location. You will need this value when connecting to the OpenAI service from other apps and services. As soon as you click **Done**, this value will be hidden, and you will be unable to retrieve it in the future:

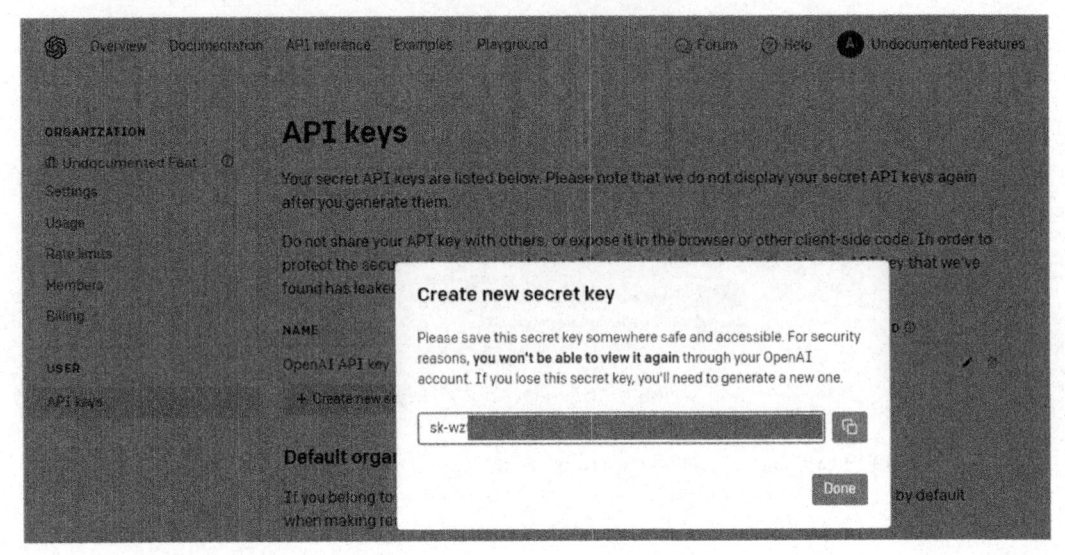

Figure 2.8 – Capturing the API key

> **Important note**
> Protect this API key value like it's money. If it is compromised or stolen, others could use it to execute API calls and queries against your account balance. If it is lost or stolen, you will need to go back to this page, generate a new key, and then revoke the old key by clicking on the trash can icon. Additionally, if OpenAI detects that your key has been saved or posted to a public location (such as GitHub), your key will be invalidated, and you'll need to generate a new one.

21. Click **Done**.

When you configure other services to integrate with ChatGPT, you'll supply this API key for authenticating to the service.

Configuring your workstation

There are a number of tools that you can use to build and deploy AI-based applications. For purposes of this book, you may need to download and deploy a handful of tools:

- Visual Studio Code: https://code.visualstudio.com/download
- Azure Developer CLI: https://aka.ms/azure-dev/install
- Python 3.9+: https://www.python.org/downloads/
- Node.js 14+: https://nodejs.org/en/download/
- Git: https://git-scm.com/download/win
- PowerShell 7+: https://github.com/powershell/powershell

Download and install each of those using the provided links. Be sure to use the default installation options for all of them, as any examples in this book will reference default options and paths.

Configuring Power Platform

Lastly, we're going to set up the necessary subscriptions and prerequisite services for Power Platform.

AI models, available through AI Builder in the Power Platform tooling, require AI Builder licensing as well as access to Microsoft Dataverse. To get started, follow these steps:

1. Navigate to the Microsoft Power Automate web portal (https://make.powerautomate.com) and sign in with an administrative account.
2. From the navigation menu, select **AI hub**.
3. On the **Discover an AI capability** page, select **AI models**.
4. If prompted, select **Create a database** to create a new Dataverse database.
5. On the **New database** page, select a **Currency** and **Language** value, and then click **Create my database**.

6. If you don't already have AI Builder capacity, you should see a **Start free trial** banner at the top of the page, as shown in *Figure 2.9*. Select it:

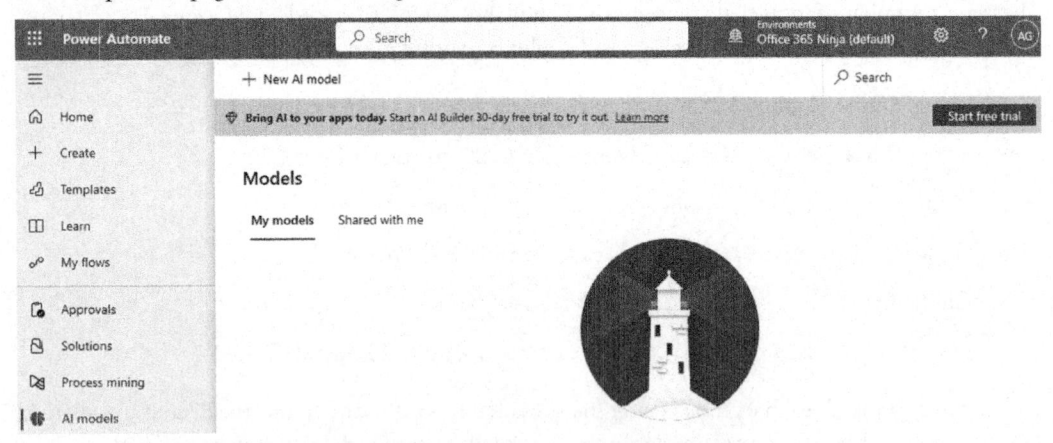

Figure 2.9 – Starting a free trial of AI Builder

7. Follow the prompts to sign up or extend your trial.

That's it! You're ready to go with AI Builder in Power Automate and Power Apps!

Summary

In this chapter, you configured all of the prerequisites for using AI services—including OpenAI in Azure, ChatGPT, and Power Platform AI Builder. You also configured your workstation with the necessary tools to deploy AI apps to Azure.

Next, we're going to start interacting with ChatGPT as an end user to get an idea of how it works.

3
Talking to ChatGPT

If you're reading this book, you've probably at least heard the hype surrounding ChatGPT. But, have you actually seen what it does? How it works? Know what a prompt is? How to interact with one?

Maybe you've tinkered with it a bit, so your next questions will probably be things such as *How do I send data to it?* and *How do I get data back from it? What are tokens and why are they important?*

If so, you've come to the right place. In this chapter, we're going to do a little bit of exploration with the ChatGPT interface to get familiar with how it works and then shift to Power Automate, where you'll learn the basics of processing ChatGPT data.

Working with ChatGPT as a user

Working with ChatGPT as a user is very simple. To begin, you simply need to open a web browser and navigate to `https://chat.openai.com`.

> **Setting up**
> Hopefully, you've already started a ChatGPT account (it was part of the assignments in *Chapter 2, Configuring an Environment to Support AI Services*).

Once there, log in using the credentials you signed up with earlier:

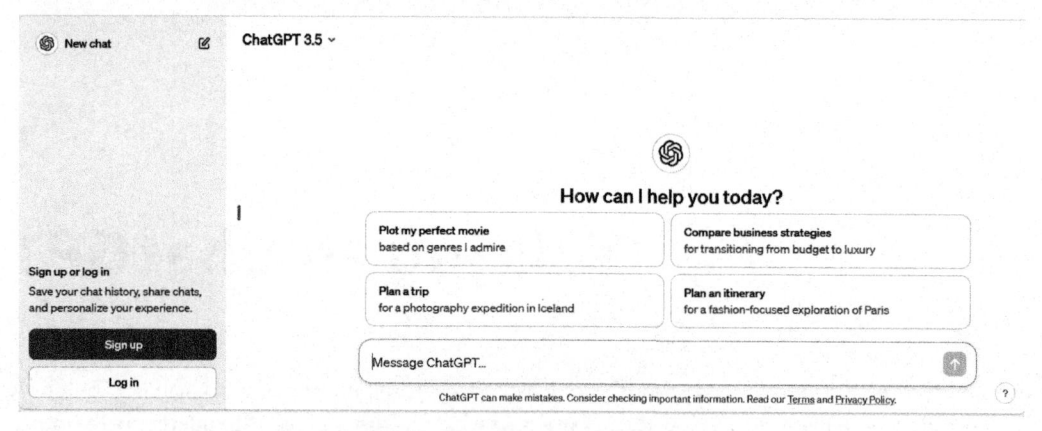

Figure 3.1 – Logging in to ChatGPT

Once you've logged in, you can immediately start sending questions (**prompts**) to the model, as shown in *Figure 3.2*:

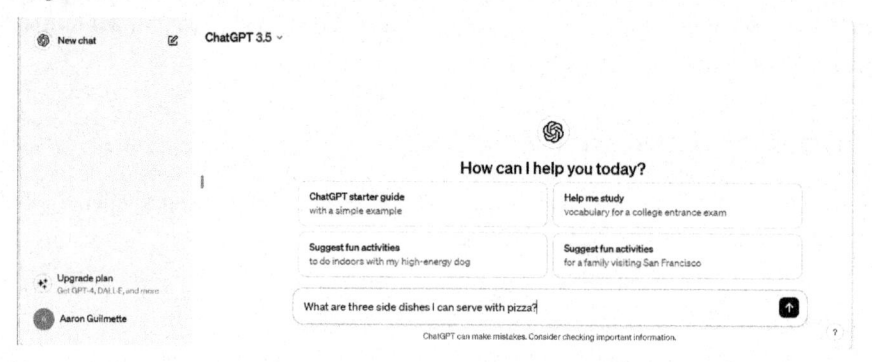

Figure 3.2 – Sending a prompt to ChatGPT

After entering a prompt, ChatGPT will respond with content (in this case, ideas for pizza side dishes).

You're not limited to just submitting simple questions to ChatGPT – you can even submit scenarios and background information to help guide ChatGPT's responses. This framing is referred to as **context**. For example, you can provide context to ChatGPT in several ways:

- Explain string theory to a 10-year-old.
- You are a technical writer. Describe the steps necessary to mix mortar.
- You are a web developer. Generate basic HTML code for a web page with a simple one-level menu.
- Here is a list of animals: tiger, cat, dog, grizzly bear, antelope, spider. Arrange them in a list from smallest to largest.

ChatGPT is conversational, allowing you to refer back to previous prompts and responses to further refine your output.

So, what's a token?

I'm glad you asked! This will come up when you're interacting with ChatGPT (or other language models and services). In the context of ChatGPT, a token is the smallest unit of text that the model processes. It could be as small as a single character, commonly used groups of letters, prefixes, and suffixes, or even whole words, depending on how the model is configured.

From a cost and billing perspective, models typically charge you based on how many tokens you're submitting and how many tokens you're getting back as a response. Let's use the example prompt featured in Figure 3.2 – What are three side dishes I can serve with pizza?

Using a tool such as OpenAI's Tokenizer, you can figure out how much this request is going to cost to send:

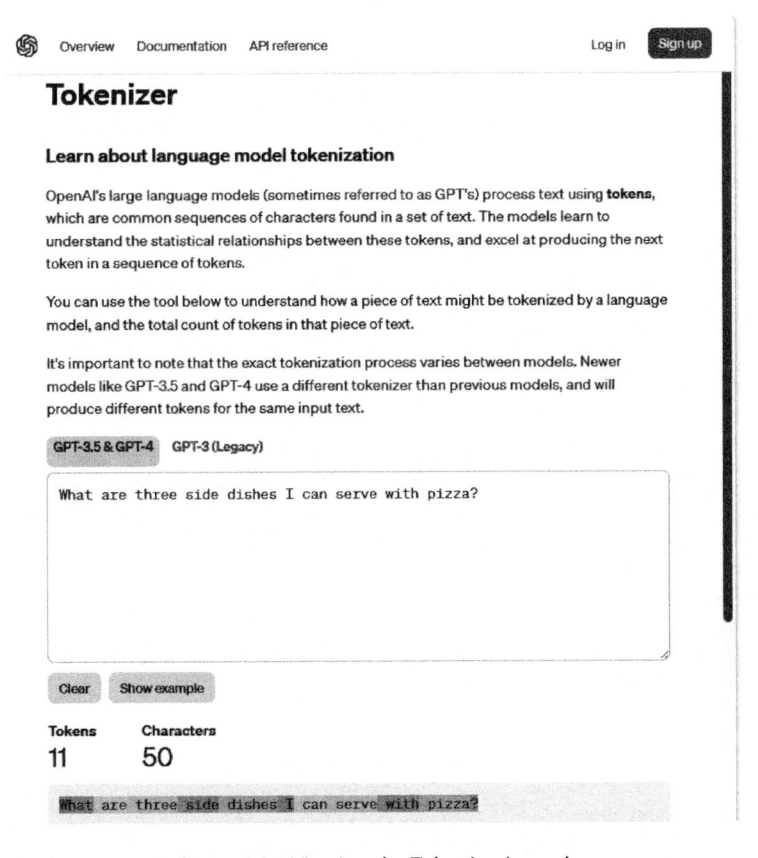

Figure 3.3 – Viewing the Tokenizer's result

As you can see, this request costs 11 tokens. The area at the bottom shows how OpenAI breaks apart the sentence.

Response tokens are tallied the same way. With this in mind, you may find it useful (or necessary, depending on your budget) to frame questions and response criteria in such a way that minimizes token usage. Depending on what services you are consuming, your usage may be counted differently. It's always important to understand the pricing and charge models to make sure you don't end up with an unexpected bill!

With the accounting tasks out of the way, we'll look at sending data to ChatGPT.

Sending prompts to ChatGPT

Working with ChatGPT as an end user is pretty simple. So, how hard is it to do the same thing with Power Automate? The answer, it turns out, is that it isn't that bad.

You have two main options for passing data to the OpenAI ChatGPT service itself: the built-in HTTP (Premium) connector or a third-party OpenAI connector. We'll go through both options quickly, and you can adapt whichever you like to suit your purposes.

Both of the examples will be built as instant cloud flows with a simple text prompt. For both examples, you'll need the OpenAI API key that you created in *Chapter 2, Configuring an Environment to Support AI Services*.

HTTP

The HTTP method is the more complex method of the two but also gives you the most flexibility.

> **Updated parameter information**
> Like all cloud services, OpenAI may change endpoints and other parameters without notice. You can get the most updated endpoints and parameters at `https://platform.openai.com/api-reference/completions`.

To start building the flow, follow these steps:

1. Launch a web browser and navigate to the Power Automate web portal (`https://make.powerautomate.com`).

2. From the navigation menu, click **Create**, and then, under **Start from blank**, select **Instant cloud flow**. See *Figure 3.4*:

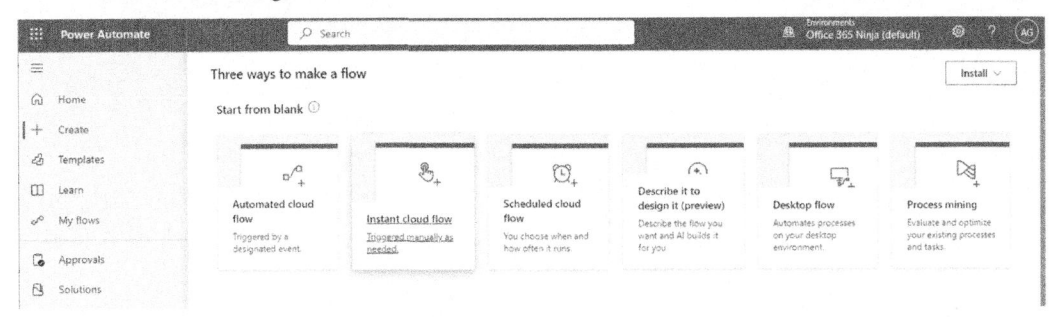

Figure 3.4 – The Power Automate portal

3. On the **Build an instant cloud flow** page, add a **Flow name** value and then select the **Manually trigger a flow** trigger. Click **Create**:

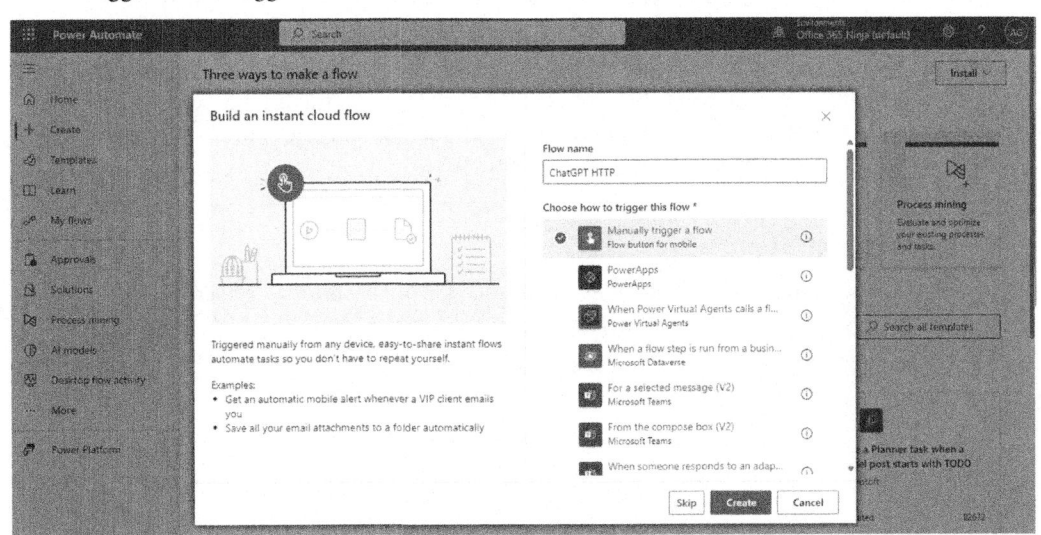

Figure 3.5 – Creating a blank instant cloud flow

4. In the canvas area, click **Manually trigger a flow** to expand the trigger.

5. Click **Add an input** and select the **Text** input type:

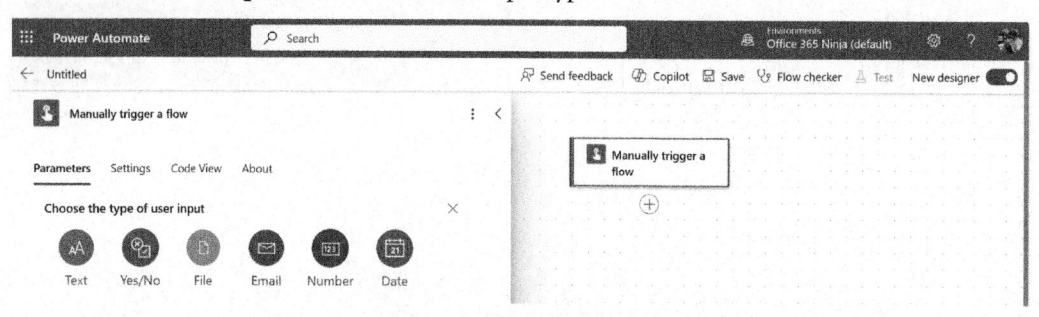

Figure 3.6 – Selecting an input type

6. In the **Input** box, replace **Input** with `Prompt`.

> **Why does my Power Automate canvas look different?**
>
> Depending on your settings, you may be viewing the Classic Power Automate canvas or the new designer interface. You can switch between the experiences using the **New designer** toggle in the top right-hand portion of the page. The interfaces are a little bit different, so feel free to adapt and use whichever one you prefer. If you switch the view partway through a design, you'll be prompted to save your work before continuing.

7. Click **New step**.
8. In the **Choose an operation** dialogue, select the **HTTP (Premium)** trigger:

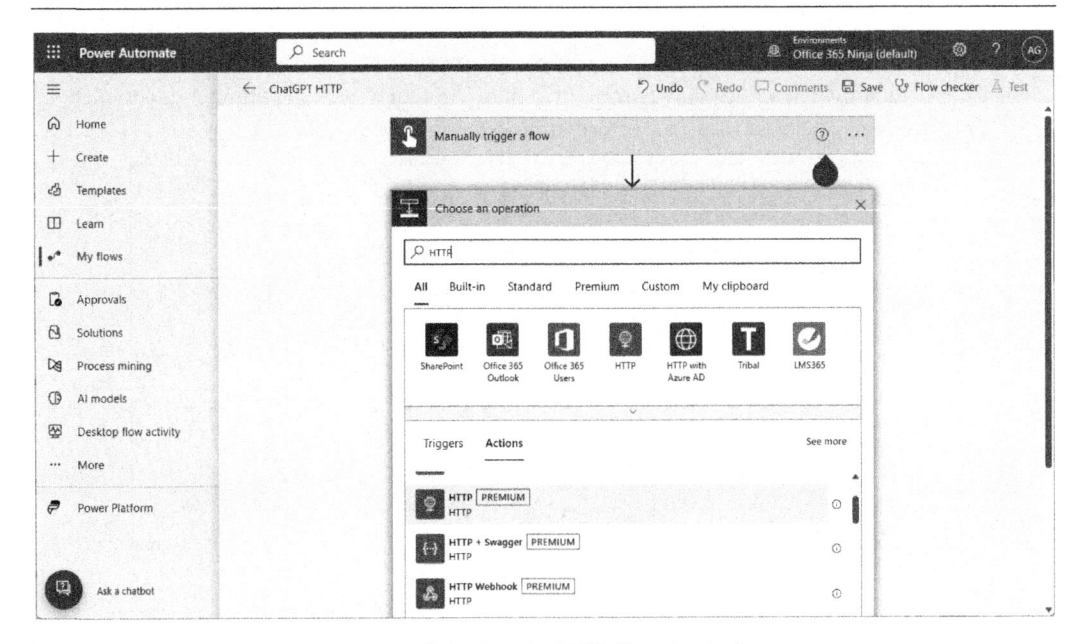

Figure 3.7 – Selecting the HTTP (Premium) trigger

9. Fill out the first part of the HTTP action with the following data:

Method	Post
URI	`https://api.openai.com/v1/chat/completions`

Next, you'll need to add two different headers. Headers are informational data that are sent during the HTTP transaction. In this case, you'll be sending an *Authorization* header, containing your OpenAI API key, as well as the *Content-Type* header, which describes the type of data transaction:

Header	Value
Authorization	`Bearer <OpenAI API key>`
Content-Type	`application/json`

Talking to ChatGPT

Finally, you'll need to enter values for the Body parameter. Body will contain information about the type of model being used, the prompt dynamic content object, the number of completions to return, and other instructional information. See *Figure 3.8*:

Body	`{`
	    `"model": "gpt-4",`
	    `"messages": [`
	      `{`
	        `"role": "system",`
	        `"content": "You are a helpful assistant."`
	      `},`
	      `{`
	        `"role": "user",`
	        `"content": "**TRIGGER DYNAMIC CONTENT**`
	      `}`
	    `],`
	    `"max_tokens": 1000,`
	    `"temperature": 0,`
	    `"n": 1,`
	    `"stream": false,`
	    `"logprobs": null,`
	    `"stop": null`
	`}`

The output can be seen in the following figure:

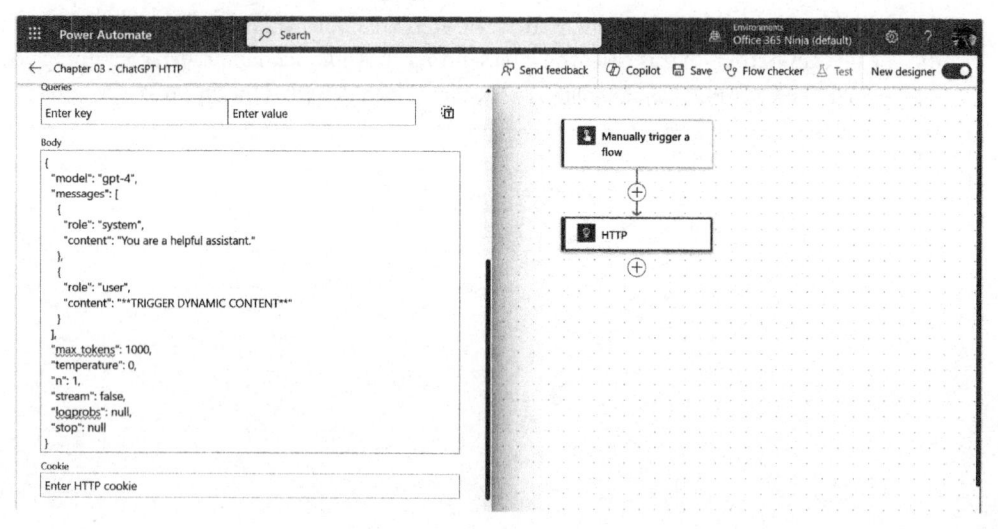

Figure 3.8 – Filling out the HTTP action

Sending prompts to ChatGPT   35

1. In the **Body** section, select ****TRIGGER DYNAMIC CONTENT**** (including the square brackets) and replace it with the dynamic content token that represents the prompt from Step 6 by clicking on the lightning bolt icon:

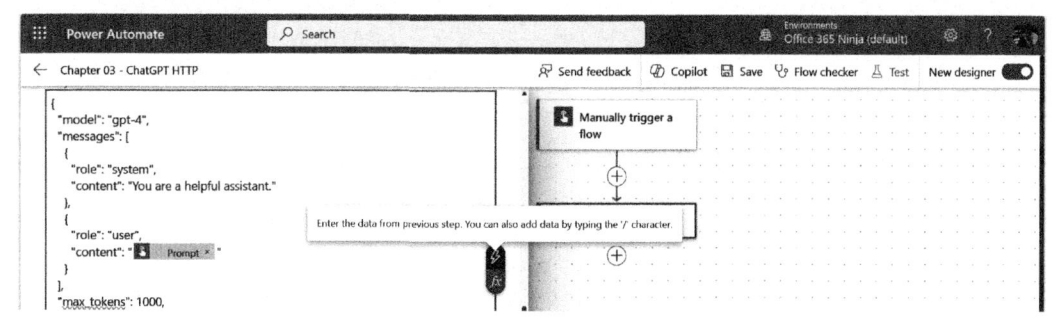

Figure 3.9 – Updating the prompt body

2. Click **Save**.

Once you've saved it, it's time to test it out!

1. Click the **Test** icon on the menu bar to verify that it's working correctly.
2. Select the **Manually** radio button on the **Test flow** flyout and then click **Test**:

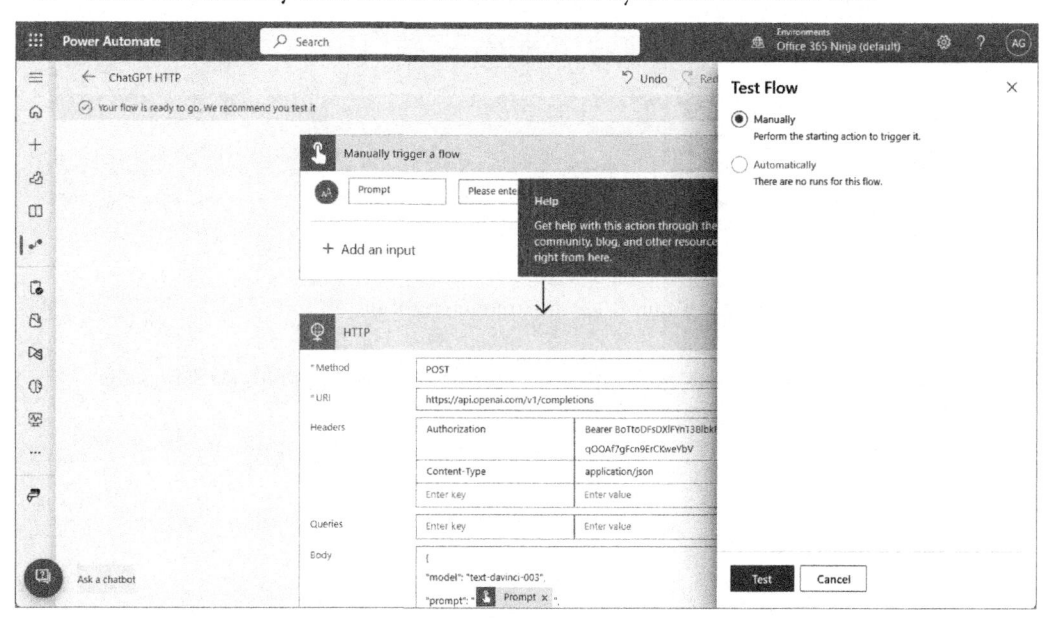

Figure 3.10 – Testing the flow

Talking to ChatGPT

3. Enter your text in the prompt and then select **Run flow**. To follow the example, you can use `List the ingredients for baking a cake`:

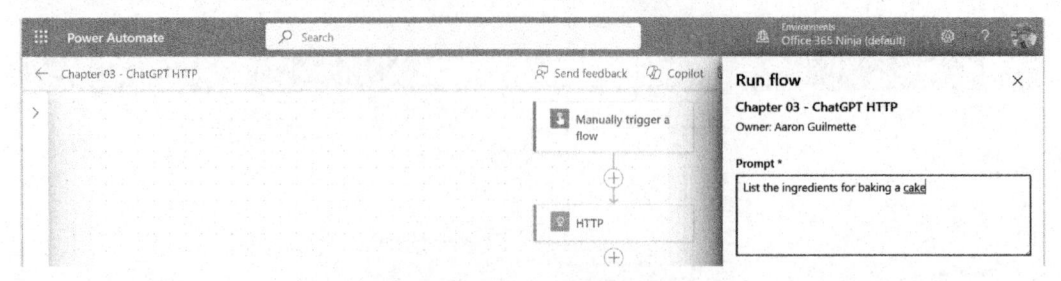

Figure 3.11 – Entering the prompt

4. Click **Done**.
5. Scroll down to the **Outputs** section and then look for the **Body** field. See *Figure 3.9*:

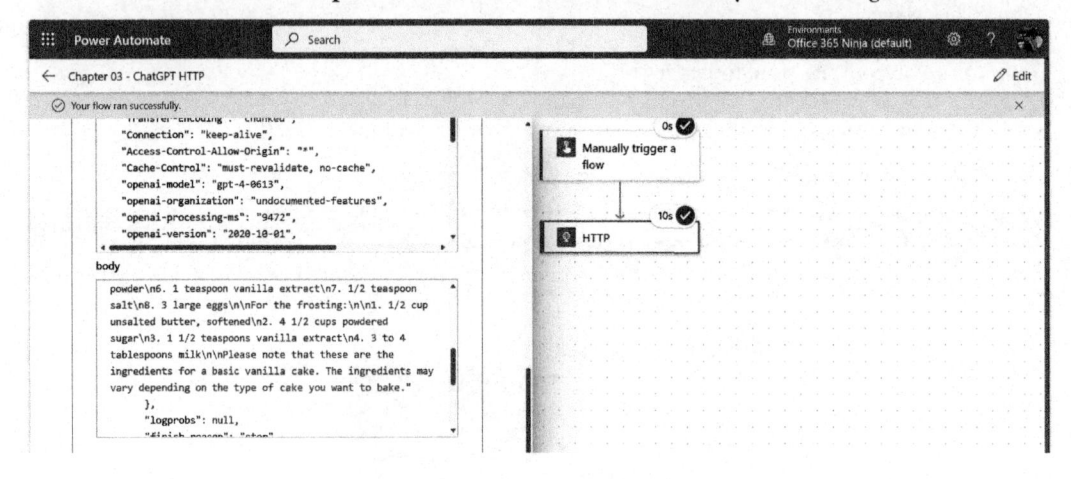

Figure 3.12 – Completions output

Now that you've seen how to do it the complex way, let's look at using a pre-built connector.

OpenAI GPT-3 completions

Using a pre-built connector makes the task of interacting with ChatGPT even easier.

We'll create another instant cloud flow to see its capabilities:

1. Launch a web browser and navigate to the Power Automate web portal (`https://make.powerautomate.com`).
2. From the navigation menu, click **Create**. Then, under **Start from blank**, select **Instant cloud flow**.
3. On the **Build an instant cloud flow** page, add a **Flow name** value and then select the **Manually trigger a flow** trigger. Click **Create**.

> **Switching gears**
> To see the necessary options in the **Manually trigger a flow** card, you'll need to switch to the Classic view. You can switch back after you're done.

4. In the canvas area, click **Manually trigger a flow** to expand the trigger.
5. Click **Add an input** and select the **Text** input type.
6. In the **Input** box, replace **Input** with `Context`.
7. Select the ellipsis (…) for the **Context** input and then click **Add a drop-down list of options**:

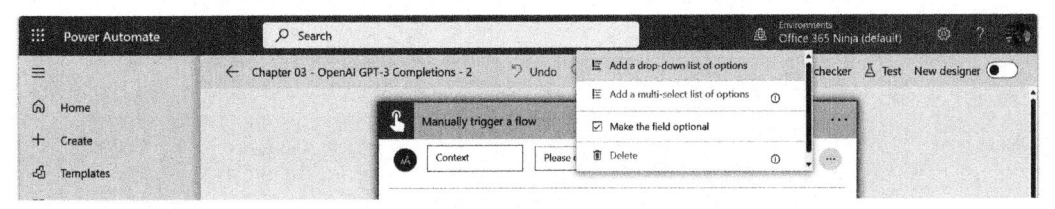

Figure 3.13 – Adding a drop-down list

8. Populate the list with the `user` role. This will be used to inform GPT of who is interacting with the system. This field is case-sensitive, so be sure to enter it in lowercase:

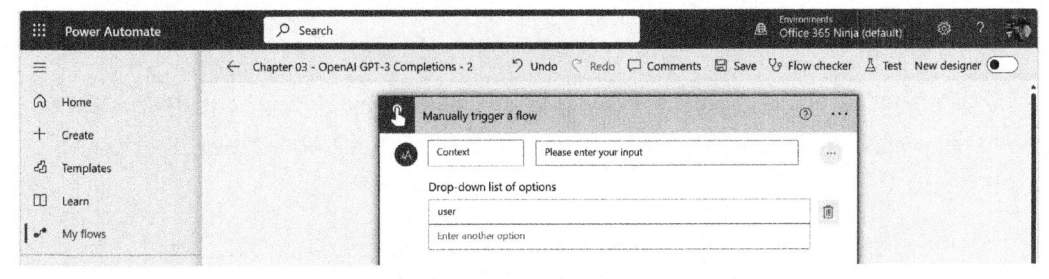

Figure 3.14 – Configuring the drop-down list

9. Click **Add an input** and select the **Text** input type.
10. In the **Input** box, replace **Input** with `Prompt`.
11. Click **New step**.
12. In the **Choose an operation** dialogue, under **OpenAI (Independent Publisher)**, select the **Chat Completion (preview)** action, as shown in *Figure 3.12*:

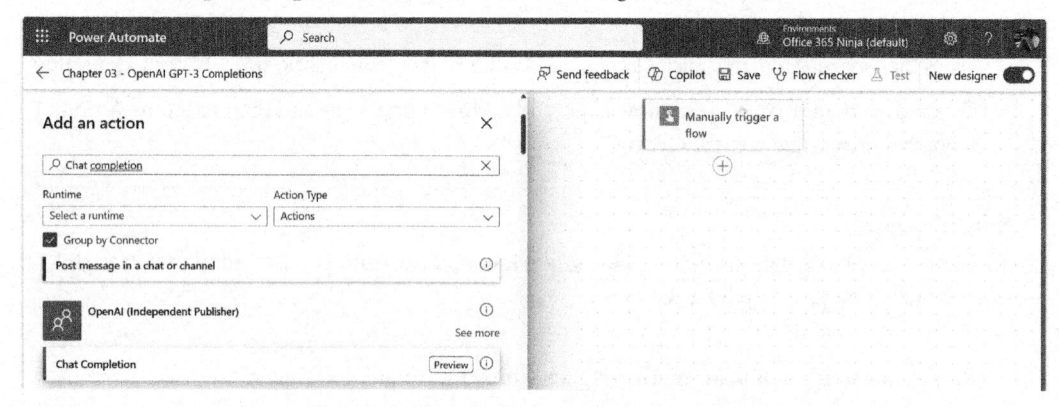

Figure 3.15 – Selecting the Chat Completion (preview) action

13. In the **OpenAI (Independent Publisher)** action, add a **Connection name** value. Enter your OpenAI API key in `Bearer <APIKEY>` format and click **Accept**:

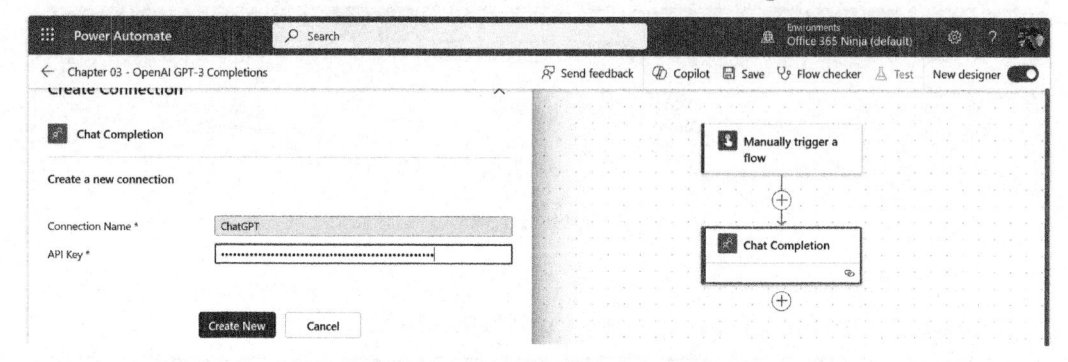

Figure 3.16 – Configuring the connection

14. Select the **Advanced parameters** dropdown and select **Body/Model** and **Body/Messages**.
15. In the **Chat Completion (Preview)** action, add a **model** name, such as `gpt-3.5-turbo`.

> **About models**
>
> Though there are several models to choose from, the most common models you'll likely use are **gpt-3.5-turbo**, **gpt-4**, and **gpt-4-turbo**. The gpt-3.5-turbo model is a great everyday model with the lowest cost price point, while the gpt-4 model has some improved function-calling support and can handle more tokens. The gpt-4-turbo model has an even higher token count support and also has vision capabilities. In other contexts, you may use the **dall-e-3** model to generate images using the **Images API**.

16. In the **Body/Messages** area, click **Add new item**.
17. In the **Role - 1** field, add the `Context` dynamic content token.
18. In the **Content – 1** field, add the `Prompt` dynamic content token.
19. In the **Max Tokens** field, enter `1000`. See *Figure 3.17*:

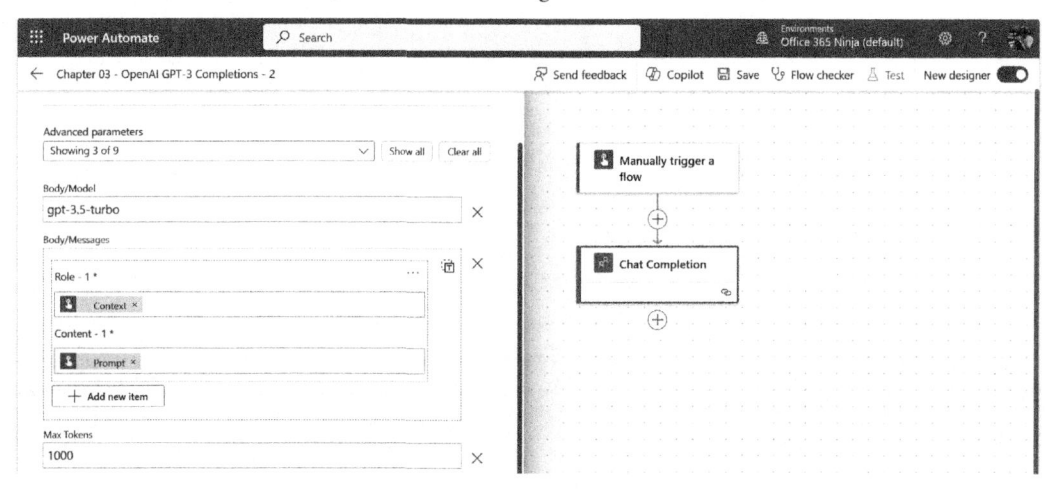

Figure 3.17 – Configuring the Chat Completion card

20. Click **Save**.

Just as before, let's test it out:

1. Click the **Test** icon on the menu bar.
2. On the **Test Flow** flyout, select the **Manually** radio button.
3. If prompted, click **Continue** to sign in and authorize the OpenAI connection.
4. In the **Context** dropdown, select one of the roles.
5. In the **Prompt** text area, enter a sentence describing the desired output – for example, `List the ingredients of a cake and brief instructions on how to prepare.`:

Talking to ChatGPT

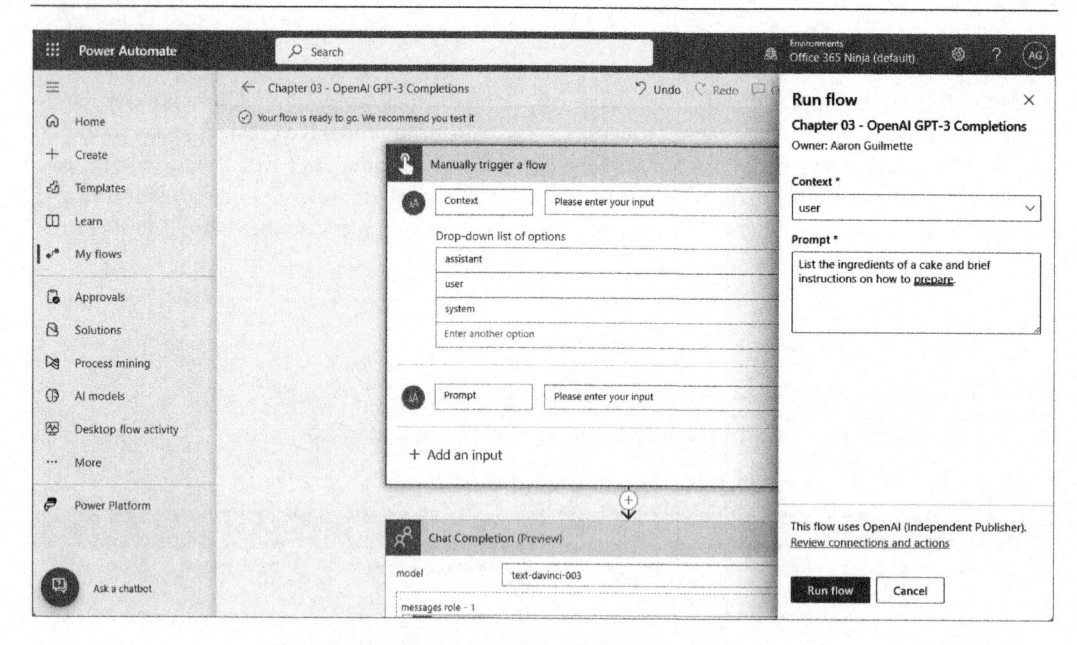

Figure 3.18 – Testing the OpenAI Chat Completions flow

6. Click **Run flow**.
7. Click **Flow Runs Page** to be redirected to the run history.
8. Select the run and then scroll to the **Choices** area of the **Outputs** section to view the detailed data:

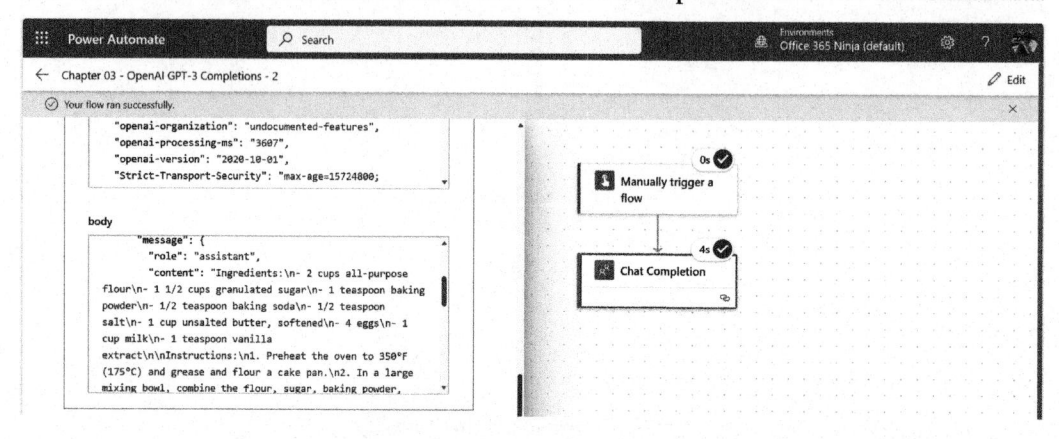

Figure 3.19 – Reviewing the output

So far, so good!

Now that you have this output, what's next? You can take this output and then feed it into other flows or processes!

Retrieving data from ChatGPT

When you were reviewing the output from your test flows, you probably noticed that ChatGPT's answers (or responses) were structured in a particular way:

Figure 3.20 – ChatGPT response data

The structure, which is **JavaScript Object Notation (JSON)** here, is a standardized format that stores objects in a `name:value` pair structure or notation.

So, what exactly is JSON?

Let's take a look at a few fields in our example:

```
"body": {
        "object": "text_completion",
        "model": "gpt-3.5-turbo",
        "choices": [
            {
                "text": "\n\n1. Flour\n2. Sugar\n3. Baking powder\n4. Salt\n5. Eggs\n6. Milk\n7. Butter or oil\n8. Vanilla extract",
                "index": 0,
                "logprobs": null,
                "finish_reason": "stop"
            }
```

```
        ],
        "usage": {
            "prompt_tokens": 7,
            "completion_tokens": 39,
            "total_tokens": 46
        }
    }
```

In this example, the body tag or name is used to indicate the contents of the JSON response. In the name:value context, body is the name, and everything between the opening and closing curly braces (the { and } characters) is its value.

JSON also allows you to nest objects using the same structure or notation. In this case, the next name:value pair is "object": "text_completion", defining object as name and text_completion as its value. This process of nesting name:value pairs can extend to a depth of 64 levels.

In addition to simple name:value pairs, JSON also supports an array construct. Where a name:value pair indicates a one-to-one relationship between a name and its corresponding value, an array can be thought of as a one-to-many relationship. For example, I have five children:

- Liberty
- Hudson
- Glory
- Anderson
- Victory
- An array of kids, indeed! In JSON, array objects are denoted by square brackets ([and]).
- Were I to describe my children in JSON format, I might construct a data sample like this:

```
{
"children": [
            "Liberty",
            "Hudson",
            "Glory",
            "Anderson",
            "Victory"
    ]
}
```

JSON array objects can also contain their own `name:value` pairs, each grouping denoted by its own set of curly braces.

- Here's an example:

```
{
    "children": [
        {
            "name": "Liberty",
            "age": "20"
        }
        {
            "name": "Hudson",
            "age": "18"
        }
        {
            "name": "Glory",
            "age": "16"
        }
        {
            "name": "Anderson",
            "age": "14"
        }
        {
            "name": "Victory",
            "age": "12"
        }
    ]
}
```

One of the benefits of JSON is that it's human-readable and very easy to understand.

Now that I've satisfied my kids by featuring them in a book, let's shift back to handling ChatGPT's JSON-formatted output.

Working with ChatGPT's JSON output in Power Automate

We could just print the body of the response, but as you saw in Figure 3.15, the body contains a lot more than just the text output. The actual data we want is stored as one of the `name:value` pairs in the `choices` sub-object. To access just that portion of the data, we'll use an expression as part of a `compose` action to extract the output we're looking for and save it to a variable for later use.

From the Power Automate flow, you can follow these steps:

1. After the **HTTP** action, select **New step**:

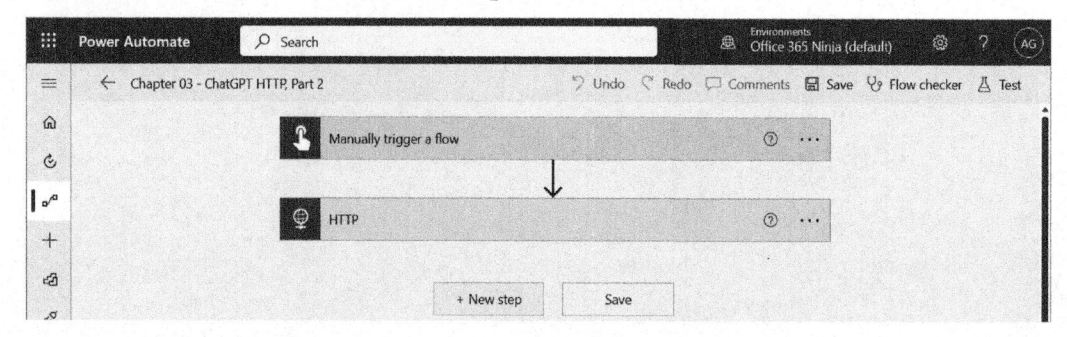

Figure 3.21 – Adding a new step

2. In the **Choose an operation** box, search for and select the **Compose** action.
3. Select the **Inputs** box of the **Compose** action. If necessary, click the **Add dynamic content** link to surface the flyout.
4. In the expression builder box, start typing `outputs` and select the **outputs** function:

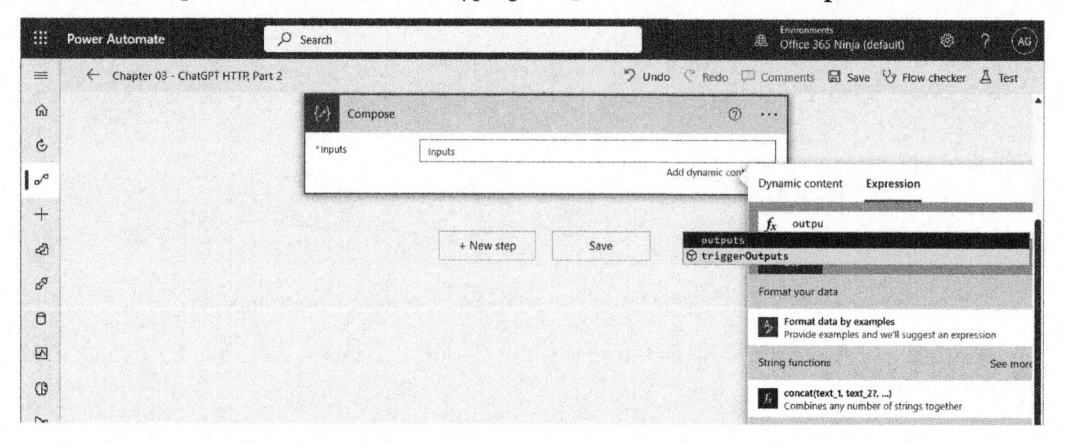

Figure 3.22 – Adding the triggerOutputs function

5. You can complete the rest of the function with this text:

   ```
   outputs('HTTP')?['body/choices'][0]['text']
   ```

   Let's dig into this expression:

Retrieving data from ChatGPT | 45

In this example, `'HTTP'` references the preceding action. We're looking for the result of that action (hence the `outputs` function). The `?` character is used to choose the element, parameter, or sub-object that we want to reference. In this case, we're selecting the body element. From looking at the output of the test flow in *Figure 3.20*, we know that the body element itself has many sub-elements or sub-objects (**object**, **model**, **choices**, and **usage**). We also know that the data we're looking for is stored in the **choices** element, so we're going to signify that by telling the expression to look in `body/choices`.

Depending on the type of outputs that are being generated, **choices** themselves may have more than one element. In this case, we're going to select the first element (denoted by index item `[0]`). The name of the name/value pair we're looking for inside that element is called **text**.

So, when reading the expression, it says "*Using the outputs of the HTTP action, look in the body/choices element, select the first element, and then inside that element, capture the value for the text object.*"

6. Next, click **Add step**.
7. Select the **Initialize variable** action.
8. In the **Name** box of the **Initialize variable** action, enter a name for the variable, such as `ComposeOutput`, and set **Type** to **String**.
9. In the **Value** box, add the dynamic content token representing the **Outputs** content object of the **Compose** variable, as shown in *Figure 3.23*:

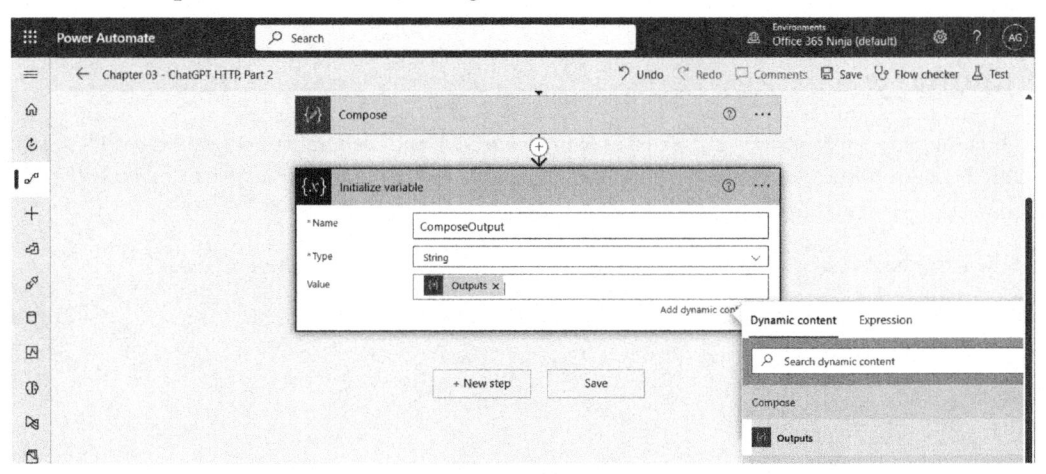

Figure 3.23 – Adding the Initialize variable step

10. When you're finished, click **Save** and then re-test.

At this point, you can go to the flow's run history and check the output:

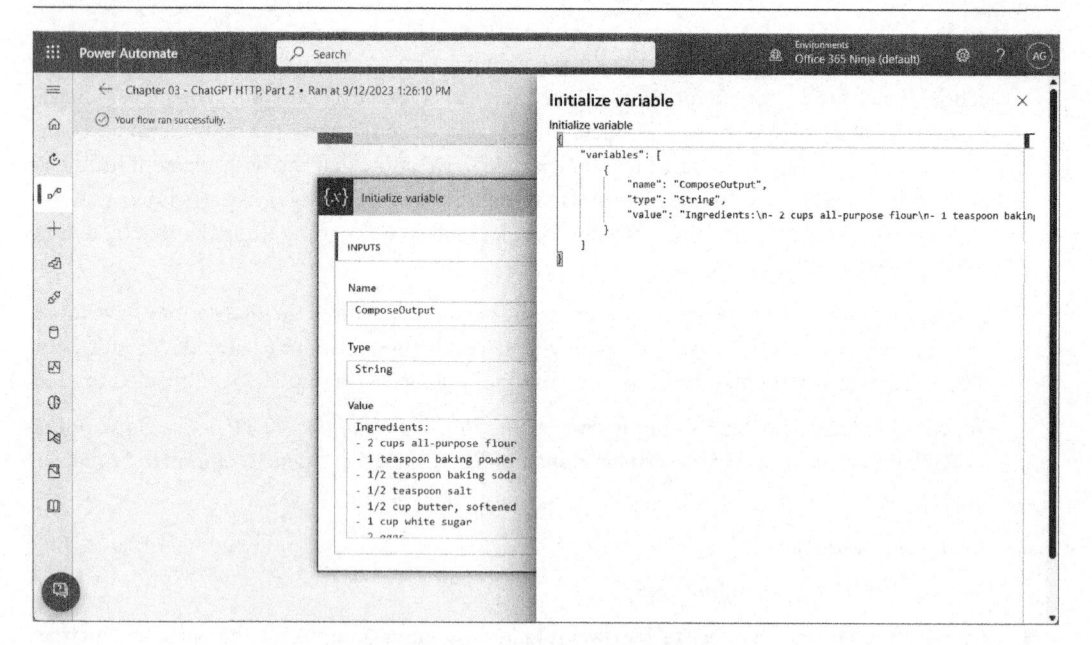

Figure 3.24 – Viewing the flow's output

That's it! You've successfully sent data to and received it from ChatGPT (and learned a little about JSON along the way).

Summary

In this chapter, you took your first steps in using ChatGPT and Generative AI with Power Platform. With the sample flows you created, you were able to take input, send it to ChatGPT using two different actions, and then extract the responses.

In the next chapter, we're going to look at using AI to help build more complex flows.

4

Using ChatGPT and Copilot to Create Flows and Apps

In the previous chapter, we dipped our feet in the ChatGPT water by sending prompts and getting back some responses.

In this chapter, we're going to wade in a little deeper and learn about some interesting ways to get help from AI and automation. Perhaps you want to automate something a little more complex than the built-in Power Automate templates allow or you aren't sure what connectors and actions are needed. Maybe you've never built a Power App before and have no idea where to start.

Those are all great use cases for AI-assisted automation.

In this chapter, we're going to look at a few use cases and use AI assistance to help with the building process.

Working with Power Automate

Power Automate, the business and process automation tooling portion of the Power Platform, can be as simple or as complex as you want (or need) it to be. From a simple flow such as copying a file or sending an email to more complex flows that insert rows into databases, Power Automate can help in almost any process.

In this next section, we'll look at what kind of help ChatGPT can provide.

Using ChatGPT to create flows

When it comes to Power Automate, ChatGPT can provide some good instructions on how to get started.

Imagine you work in the marketing department for the fabled manufacturing conglomerate Contoso. You want to monitor Twitter (or now, X) for the times Contoso is being mentioned.

You could ask ChatGPT something like this:

> **AA** How do I create a Power Automate flow to monitor Twitter for words or phrases "Contoso" or Contoso LTD"

> To create a Power Automate flow to monitor Twitter for specific words or phrases like "Contoso" or "Contoso LTD," you can use the Twitter connector and set up a flow that listens to Twitter for these keywords. Here are the steps to create such a flow:
>
> 1. **Sign in to Power Automate**: Log in to your Power Automate account at https://flow.microsoft.com/ if you haven't already.
> 2. **Create a New Flow**:
>   - Click on "Create" in the left-hand menu.
>   - Choose "Instant - from blank" to create a blank flow.
> 3. **Set up a Trigger**:
>   - In the search bar, type "Twitter" to find the Twitter connector.
>   - Select the "When a new tweet is posted" trigger.
> 4. **Connect Your Twitter Account**:
>   - Click on the "Sign In" button and follow the prompts to connect your Twitter account to Power Automate.
> 5. **Configure the Trigger**:
>   - In the "Search text" field, enter your keywords, separated by OR, like this: `Contoso OR "Contoso LTD"`.
>   - You can also configure other trigger options such as specifying Twitter handles, hashtags, or location filters if needed.
> 6. **Add Actions**:
>   - After setting up the trigger, you can add actions that will be performed when a new tweet matching your keywords is posted.
>   - For example, you can send an email notification, store the tweet in a SharePoint list, or post the tweet to a Teams channel.
> 7. **Configure Action Parameters**:
>   - Depending on the action you choose, you'll need to configure the action's parameters. For example, if you want to send an email, configure the email subject, recipient, and message.
> 8. **Test Your Flow**:
>   - Before saving your flow, it's a good practice to test it to ensure it works as expected. You can do this by manually triggering the flow or waiting for a tweet that matches your keywords to appear on Twitter.
> 9. **Save and Activate Your Flow**:
>   - Once you've tested your flow and are satisfied with the results, save it and activate it. You can also set up a schedule for when you want the flow to run if you need it to run at specific intervals.
> 10. **Monitor Twitter for Your Keywords**:
>   - Your flow will now continuously monitor Twitter for tweets containing the specified keywords, and it will trigger the specified actions whenever a matching tweet is found.

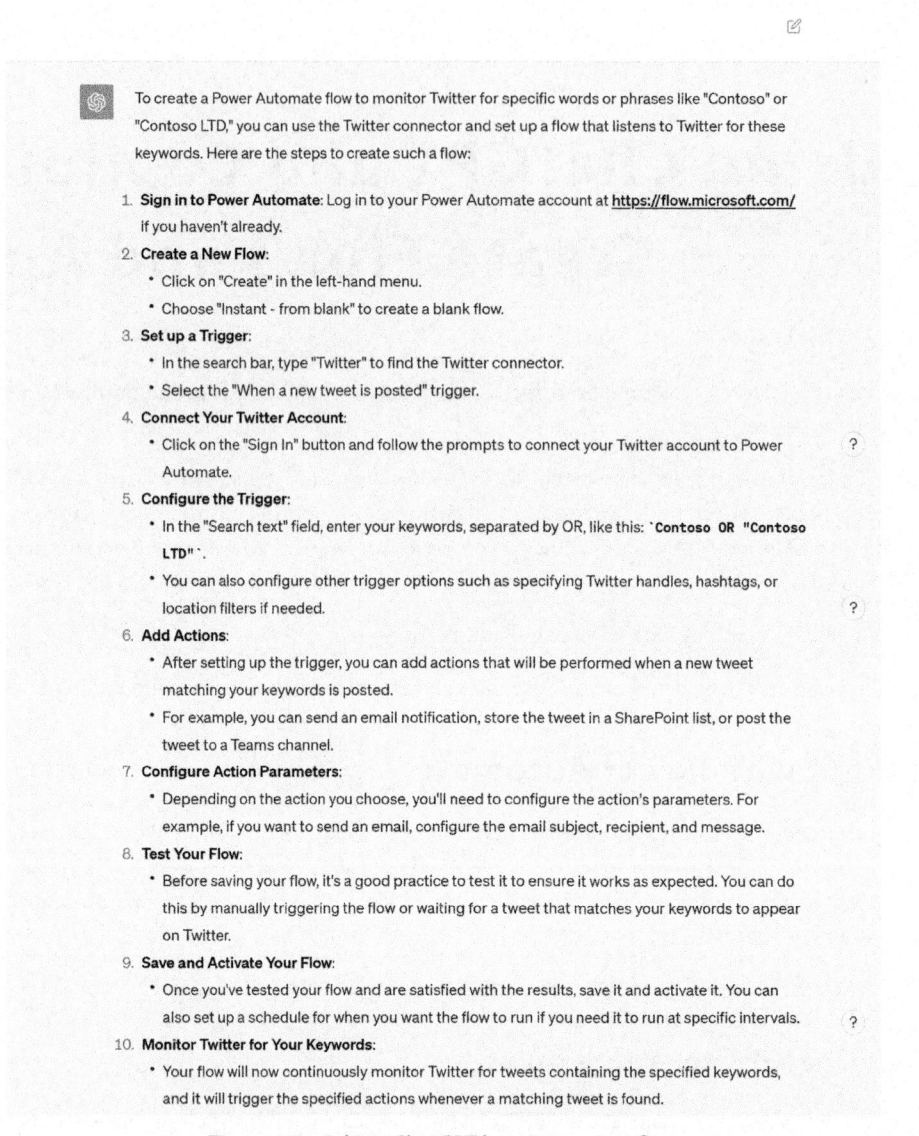

Figure 4.1 – Asking ChatGPT how to create a flow

As you can see, ChatGPT can provide pretty straightforward guidance on how to do something.

> **Limitations of using ChatGPT to create flows**
>
> What if you want a little more, such as a completed flow that you can then import?
>
> As of this writing, ChatGPT can't package the flow in any meaningful way or provide a download that you can import. When you export a flow from the Power Automate interface, the resulting ZIP file is a collection of JSON files that describe the flow's triggers and actions along with connection definitions and a manifest file that provides metadata about the files and flow itself.
>
> Instead, it can provide several different sets of instructions on how to export it once you've created it in Power Automate or using some of the Power Platform command-line interface tools.

You also might notice that if your instructions aren't well-defined or complete, ChatGPT may offer some suggestions. When reading through the sample instructions from *Figure 4.1*, notice how *Step 6* has suggestions for actions. The prompt didn't provide any guidance on actions to perform—and actions are a significant portion of creating a flow.

After reading through ChatGPT's instructions, maybe you decide that you like the suggestion of posting to a Teams channel. You can even go back and ask ChatGPT how to add things to your flow!

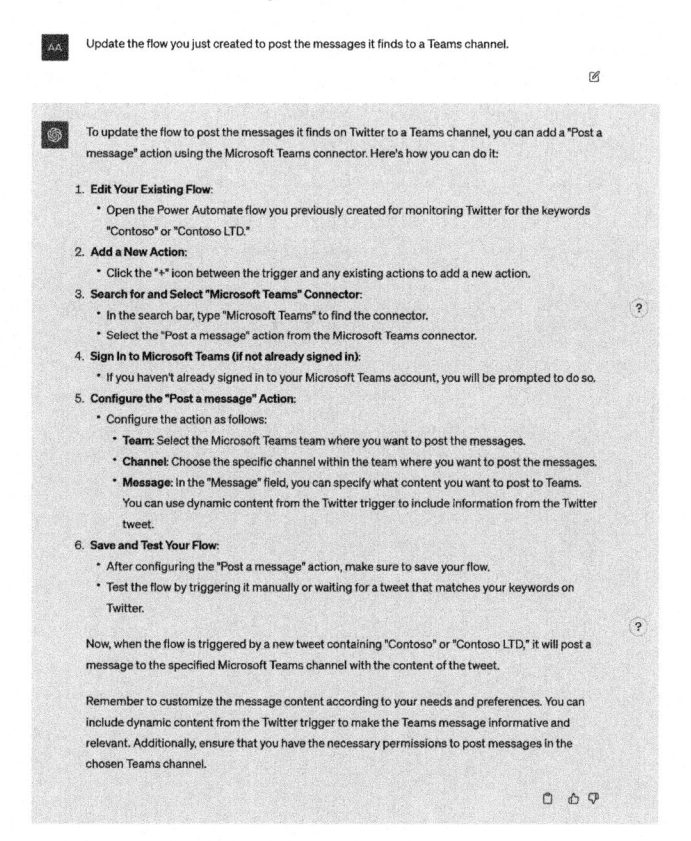

Figure 4.2 – Updating a flow with ChatGPT

You'll notice that it's imperfect—ChatGPT assumes that you already filled in the blanks in Step 6 with something. Fortunately, it's pretty easy to see the gap and make your adjustments on the fly: you can just merge the two sets of instructions, taking the first six steps from the first prompt and then picking up at Step 2 from the second prompt.

> **Refining output with ChatGPT**
>
> This process of refining output is a blend of art and science. In some instances, you may want to provide ChatGPT with examples of output to emulate or a specific dataset to work against.
>
> Fine-tuning a model is a lot of work, requiring an abundance of training data and time and resulting in more specificity for a given scenario. While that may be desired in some contexts, it's not very useful with general-purpose AI. In that case, you can use a technique called **shot learning**.
>
> The concepts of shot learning are pretty simple:
>
> **Zero-shot learning**: With this type, the model is asked to perform a task with no prior knowledge or training examples. This is how most people use ChatGPT (and how we've used it in the examples so far).
>
> **One-shot learning**: In this type of example, you can feed the model a little bit of contextual data to demonstrate how to interpret data. For example, when working with an image-based AI model, you might upload a few tagged images of different breeds of cats and dogs. Then, you could present the model with a new image and ask it, *Cat or dog?*
>
> **Few-shot learning**: This type of learning takes the concepts of one-shot learning further, allowing you to enter several examples. You could enter four or five Maya Angelou, Pablo Neruda, or William Shakespeare quotes and then ask the model to generate a quote that sounds like one of those authors.

Maybe you're handing this work over to someone else who doesn't have quite the intuition that you do or doesn't have the same level of familiarity with Power Automate and you want to provide a more concise output. You could try rephrasing your prompt with more detail and ask ChatGPT for a complete solution, as I did in *Figure 4.3*:

Working with Power Automate   51

> **AA** How do I create a Power Automate flow to monitor Twitter for words or phrases "Contoso" or "Contoso LTD" and then post the results to "Twitter notifications" channel for a Microsoft Teams team called "Marketing data feed"?

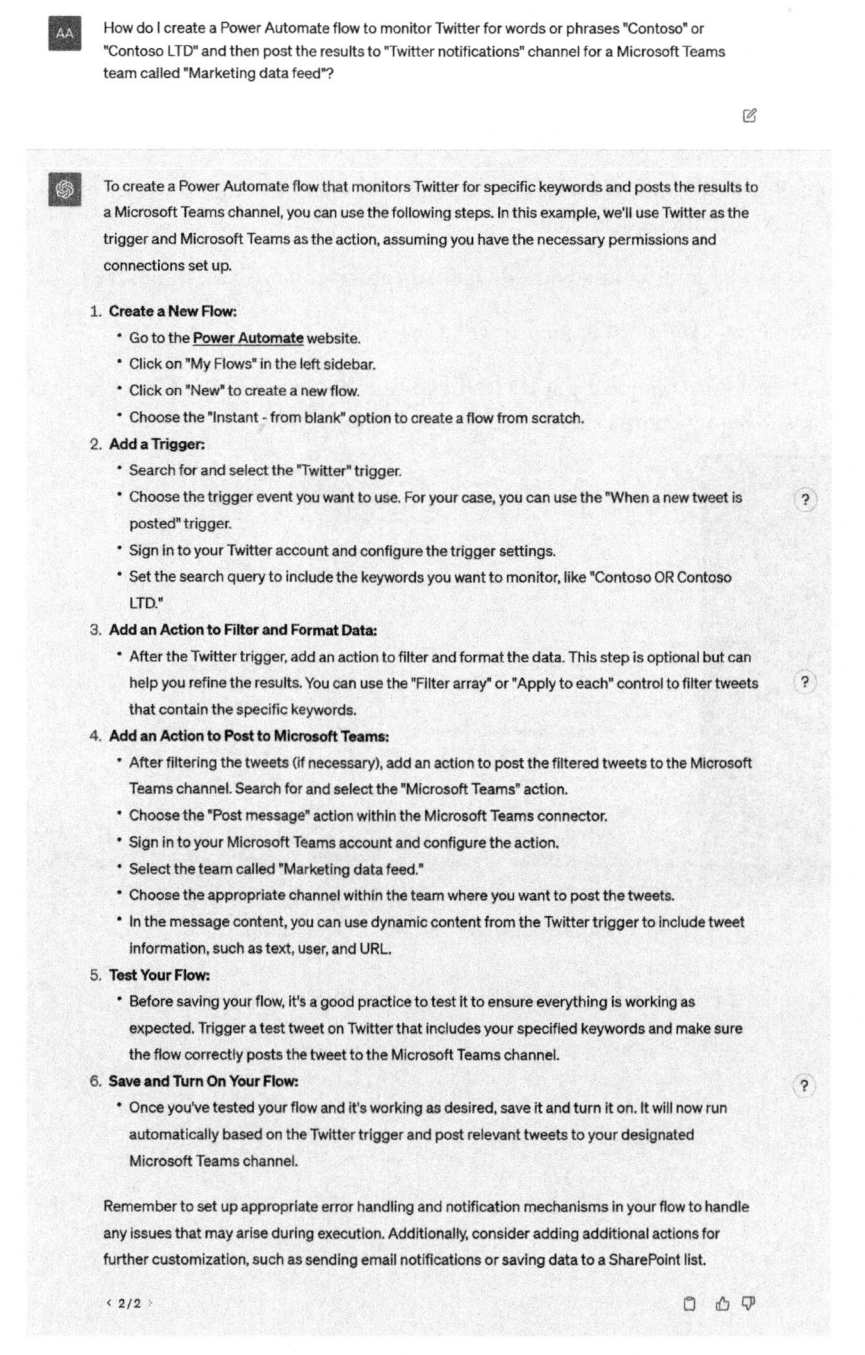

To create a Power Automate flow that monitors Twitter for specific keywords and posts the results to a Microsoft Teams channel, you can use the following steps. In this example, we'll use Twitter as the trigger and Microsoft Teams as the action, assuming you have the necessary permissions and connections set up.

1. **Create a New Flow:**
    - Go to the **Power Automate** website.
    - Click on "My Flows" in the left sidebar.
    - Click on "New" to create a new flow.
    - Choose the "Instant - from blank" option to create a flow from scratch.
2. **Add a Trigger:**
    - Search for and select the "Twitter" trigger.
    - Choose the trigger event you want to use. For your case, you can use the "When a new tweet is posted" trigger.
    - Sign in to your Twitter account and configure the trigger settings.
    - Set the search query to include the keywords you want to monitor, like "Contoso OR Contoso LTD."
3. **Add an Action to Filter and Format Data:**
    - After the Twitter trigger, add an action to filter and format the data. This step is optional but can help you refine the results. You can use the "Filter array" or "Apply to each" control to filter tweets that contain the specific keywords.
4. **Add an Action to Post to Microsoft Teams:**
    - After filtering the tweets (if necessary), add an action to post the filtered tweets to the Microsoft Teams channel. Search for and select the "Microsoft Teams" action.
    - Choose the "Post message" action within the Microsoft Teams connector.
    - Sign in to your Microsoft Teams account and configure the action.
    - Select the team called "Marketing data feed."
    - Choose the appropriate channel within the team where you want to post the tweets.
    - In the message content, you can use dynamic content from the Twitter trigger to include tweet information, such as text, user, and URL.
5. **Test Your Flow:**
    - Before saving your flow, it's a good practice to test it to ensure everything is working as expected. Trigger a test tweet on Twitter that includes your specified keywords and make sure the flow correctly posts the tweet to the Microsoft Teams channel.
6. **Save and Turn On Your Flow:**
    - Once you've tested your flow and it's working as desired, save it and turn it on. It will now run automatically based on the Twitter trigger and post relevant tweets to your designated Microsoft Teams channel.

Remember to set up appropriate error handling and notification mechanisms in your flow to handle any issues that may arise during execution. Additionally, consider adding additional actions for further customization, such as sending email notifications or saving data to a SharePoint list.

Figure 4.3 – Asking ChatGPT for a complete Power Automate solution

Using ChatGPT and Copilot to Create Flows and Apps

While the lower-end subscription for ChatGPT can't directly create flows, there's a new solution on the market that can.

Using ChatGPT Plus to create flows

In September 2023, Microsoft released a new plugin for ChatGPT that provides better integration between ChatGPT and Power Automate.

First, you'll need to upgrade your standard OpenAI subscription to a Plus subscription.

Once you've done that, you need to go through a few steps:

1. First, click your name or login ID in the lower left corner of the **Chat** page and select the **Settings & Beta** menu, as shown in *Figure 4.4*:

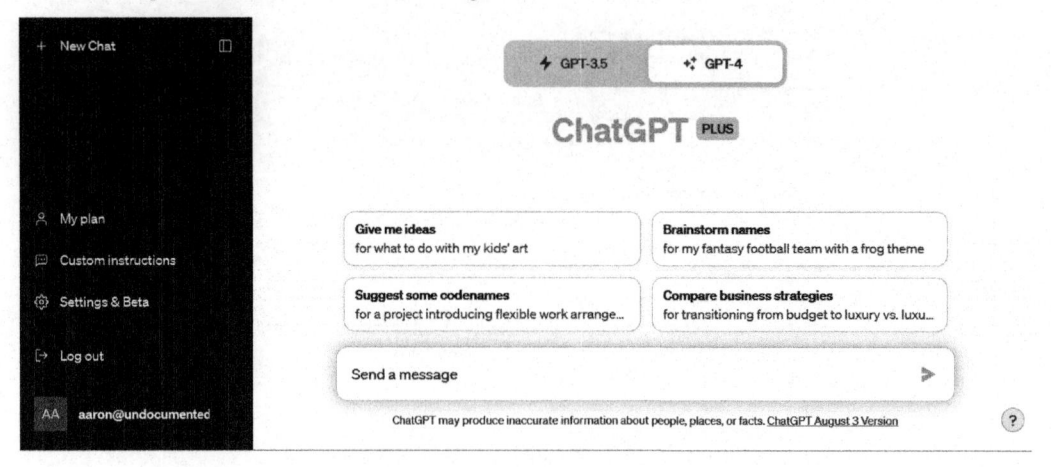

Figure 4.4 – The Settings & Beta menu

2. Then, under **Beta features**, turn on the slider for **Plugins** (see *Figure 4.5*):

Working with Power Automate | 53

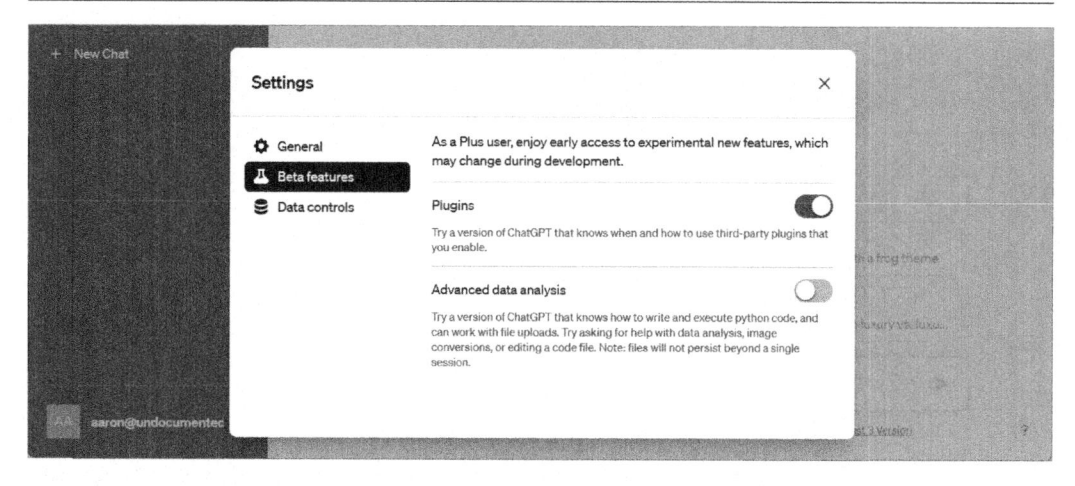

Figure 4.5 – Enabling Plugins

3. Select the **GPT-4** model at the top of the page, and then select the **Plugins Beta** option:

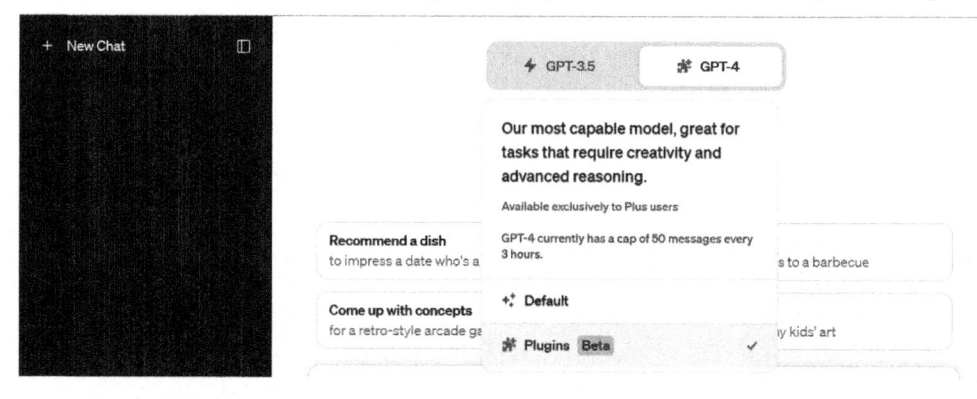

Figure 4.6 – Selecting the Plugins Beta option

4. Next, select the drop-down arrow next to **No plugins enabled**, and then select **Plugin store**:

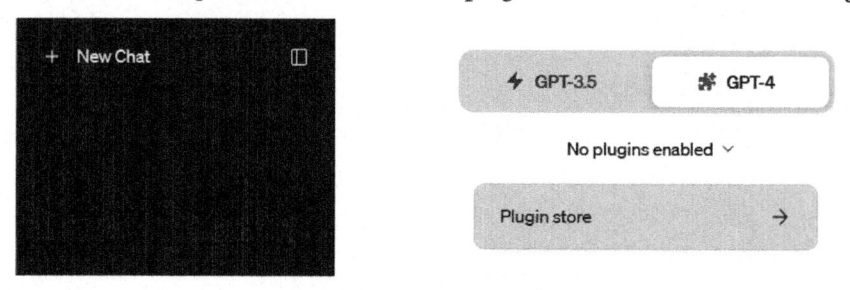

Figure 4.7 – Launching Plugin store

5. Click **OK** to acknowledge the information presented on the pop-up page.
6. In the search bar, enter `Power Automate` and then click **Install** in the **Power Automate** plugin card:

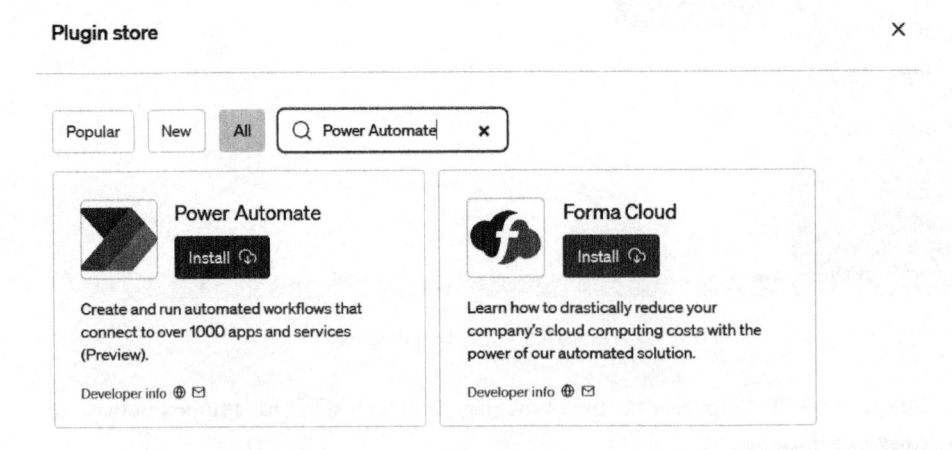

Figure 4.8 – Searching for the Power Automate plugin

7. Read the consent form. Provide the necessary consent and click **Accept**.
8. The Power Automate plugin is now enabled and available to use, as shown in *Figure 4.9*:

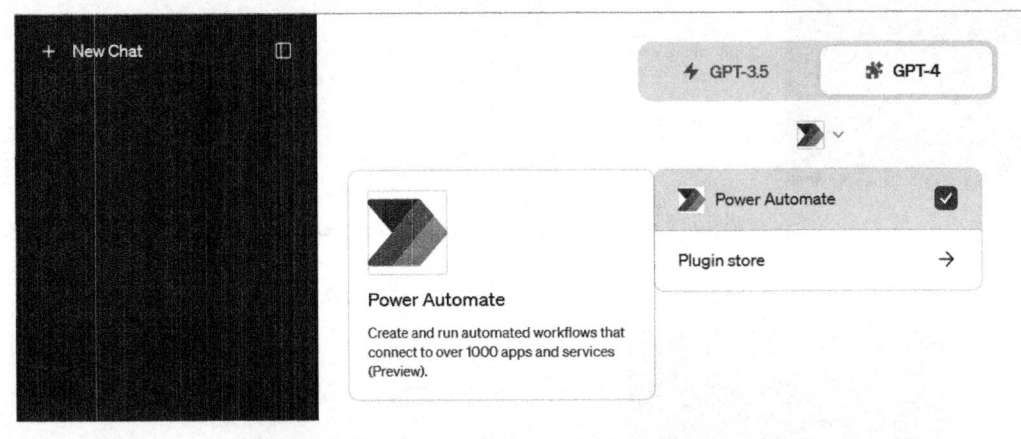

Figure 4.9 – The Power Automate plugin has been enabled

Now, all that's left is to try the prompt again with the Power Automate plugin enabled!

Figure 4.10 – Creating a flow with ChatGPT and the Power Automate plugin

Clicking on the link will launch Power Automate and show you a preview of your flow:

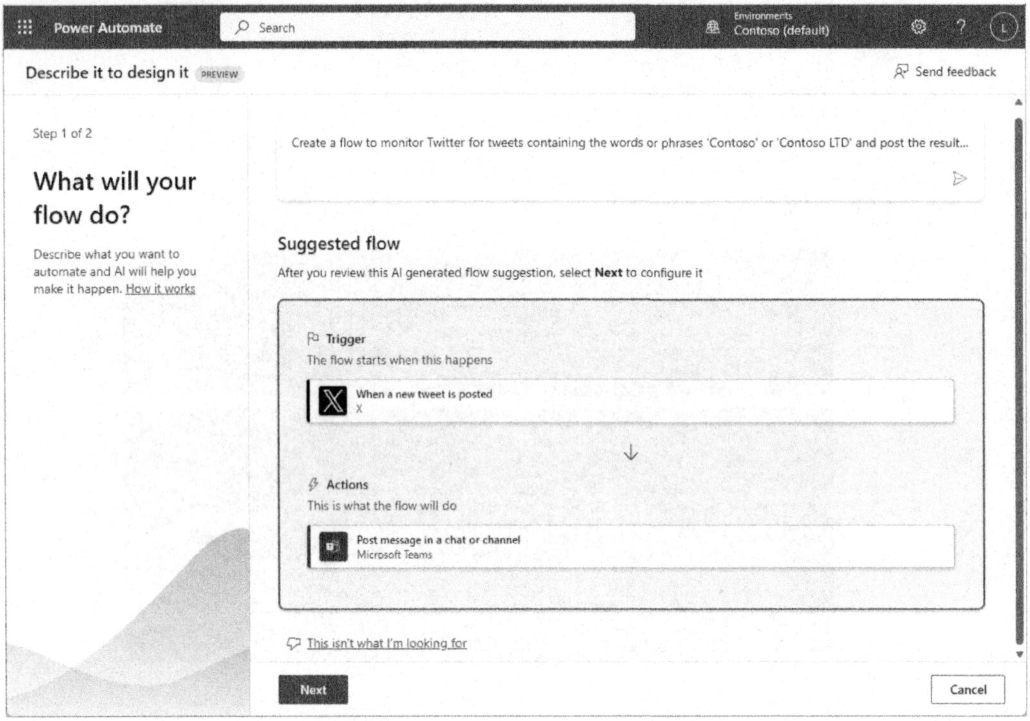

Figure 4.11 – Reviewing the suggested flow

You can simply follow the prompts to complete the setup.

> **Look back**
>
> Did you notice anything interesting about the Power Automate page that you were directed to? That's right—Power Automate's **Describe it to design it** feature. We'll look at that next.

Using Copilot to create flows

Copilot is Microsoft's umbrella branding that covers a wide range of AI-assisted technologies. Power Automate leverages OpenAI models to facilitate natural language processing and interaction under the feature name *Describe it to design it*.

What does that mean? It's essentially like having all of the power of generative AI such as ChatGPT natively integrated with the Power platform:

Working with Power Automate   57

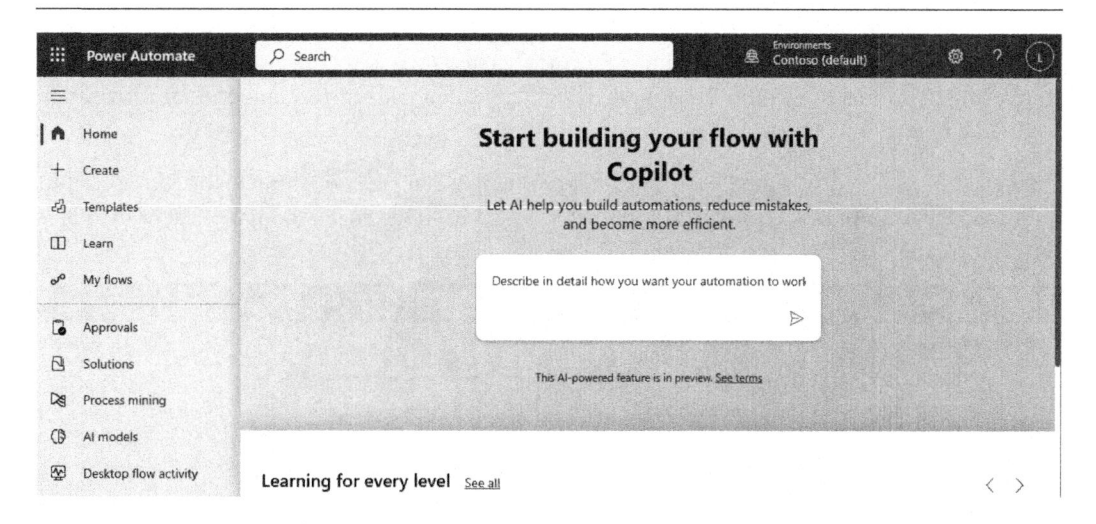

Figure 4.12 – Copilot and the Describe it to design it feature

By entering your natural language text directly in the Copilot text area, you can skip the step of the ChatGPT Plus plugin and begin your creating and editing experience directly in Power Automate.

For example, I decided to pivot from the Twitter example and try something a little more complex. In the example shown in *Figure 4.13*, I asked Copilot to create a flow that would send a weekly summary email of all my unread messages, and this is what it came up with:

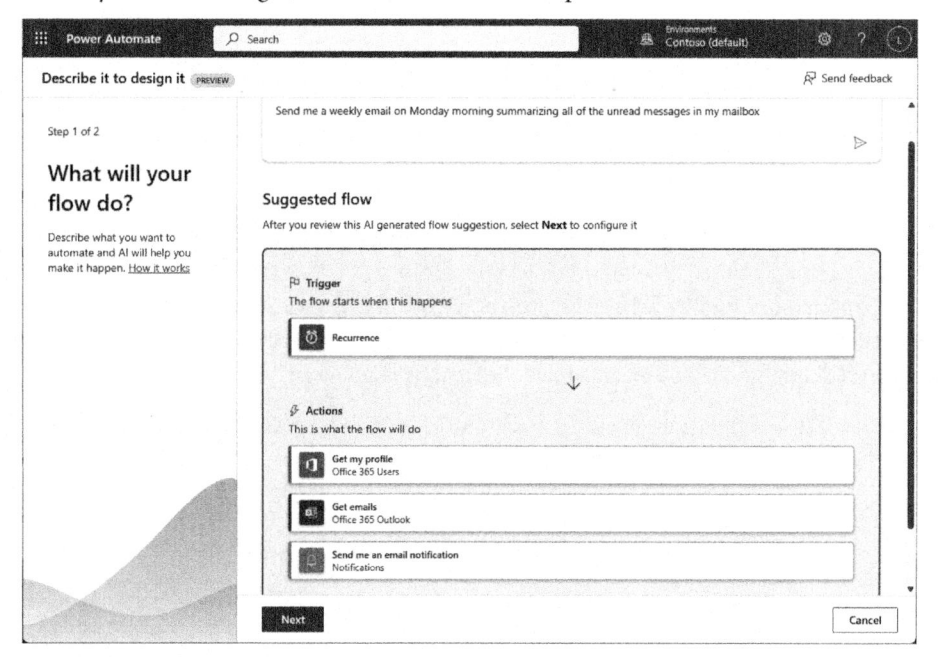

Figure 4.13 – Copilot's initial attempt at creating a flow based on natural language input

It looks close—it definitely has some of the right components (such as getting my Office 365 profile and connecting to my mailbox), though I don't see any actions that take into account the summarization requirement. Still, it might be a good starting point.

You can also try rewording the prompt to see whether you can get something better. For example, I updated the prompt in *Figure 4.14* and got what might even be closer, though some of the items appear to be out of order:

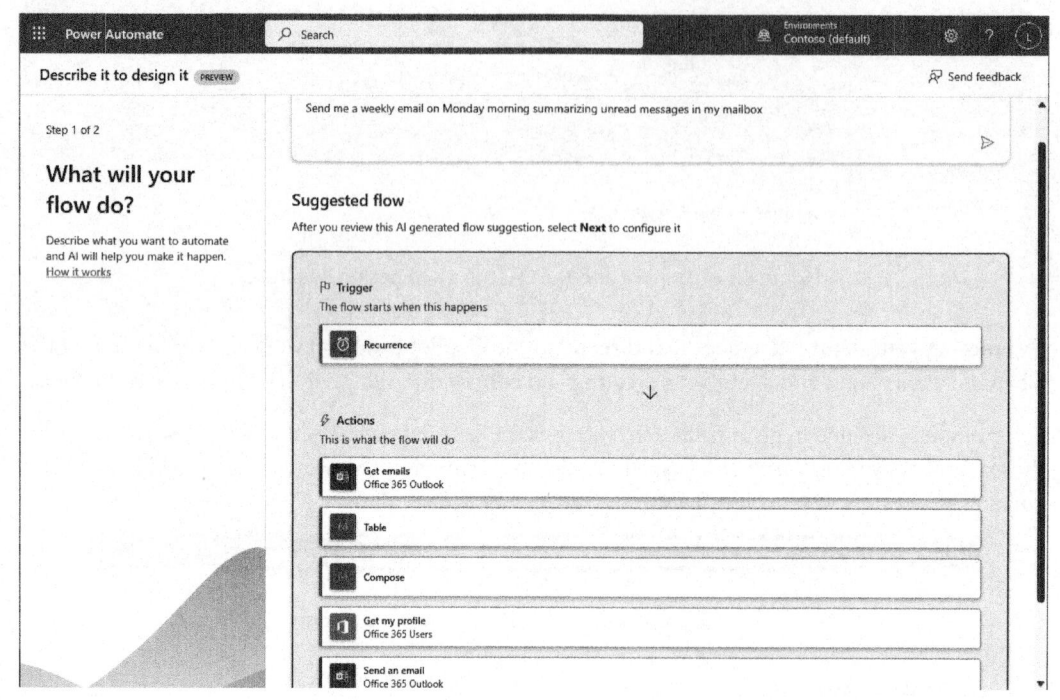

Figure 4.14 – The revised flow generated by Copilot

After you've gotten to a point where you're satisfied (as much as you can be) with Copilot's offerings, you can let Copilot create the flow. In my example, after clicking **Next**, I'm presented with a dialog to supply any credentials and, once again, a list of the steps that comprise the flow.

Clicking **Create flow** will instantiate the actions and steps that Copilot has arranged:

Working with Power Automate   59

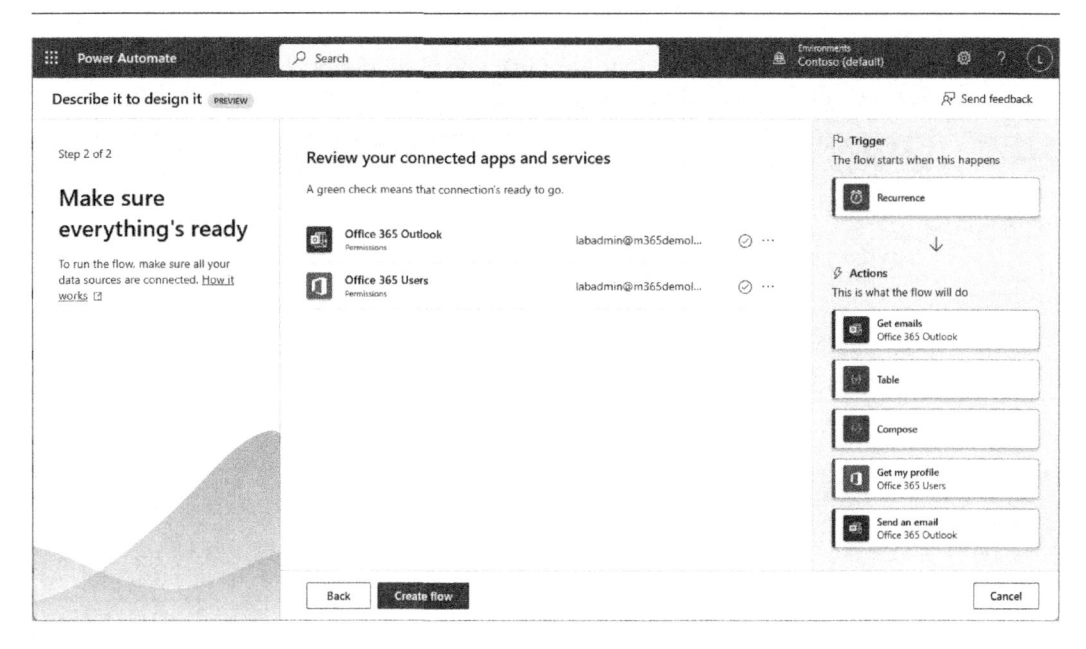

Figure 4.15 – Preparing to create the flow

After the framework has been laid out, you can then drag and drop steps or add actions like any other flow. One of the more interesting features is the ability to use Copilot to *update* the flow and refine it, as highlighted in *Figure 4.16*:

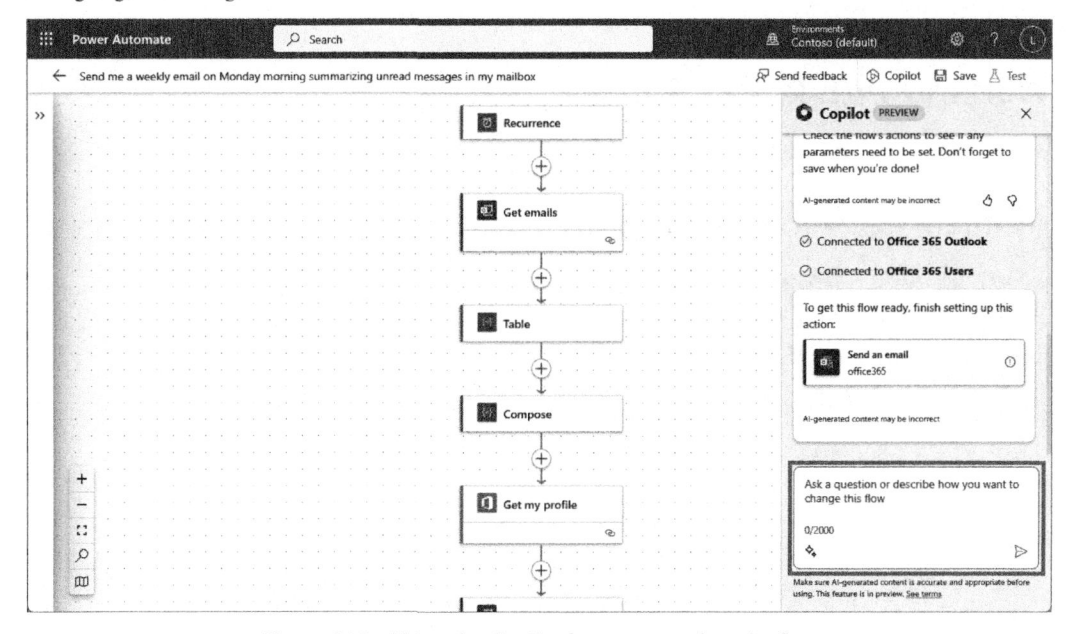

Figure 4.16 – Using the Copilot feature to update the flow

As a preview feature, Microsoft tells you up-front that not all connectors or actions are supported, which may account for the hit-or-miss behavior, as shown in *Figure 4.17*:

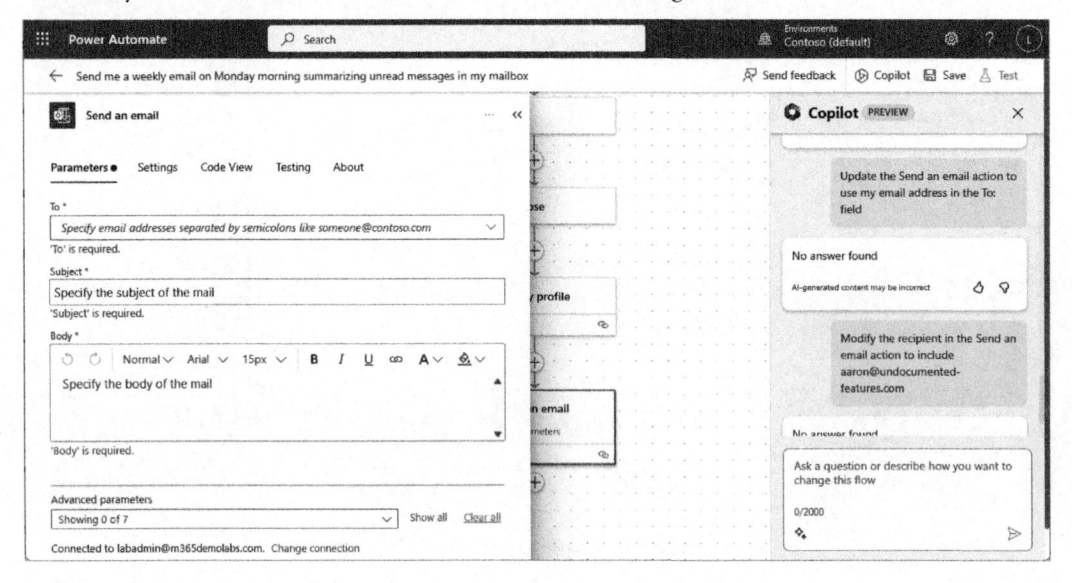

Figure 4.17 – Attempting to update an existing action with Copilot

While it didn't do exactly what I wanted, it's exciting to see the progress. As an AI-based assistant, Copilot is a great way to help explore the Power Automate space.

Working with Power Apps

Now, let's shift gears to see how we can use AI to help create in the application space.

Using ChatGPT to build an app

So, how do you get started? You can try starting a new flow from a blank canvas, but for many of us, that blank canvas also involves a lot of blank stares. Fortunately, if you have an idea of where you want to go, AI can help you get there.

As with Power Automate, you can try using ChatGPT to guide your design. In this example, I instructed ChatGPT to create a Power App that can be used to inventory some items in my garage with a photo. The app should attempt to perform some visual identification, save the data to the description, and then upload the items to a SharePoint list.

Figure 4.18 shows how ChatGPT responds to this task:

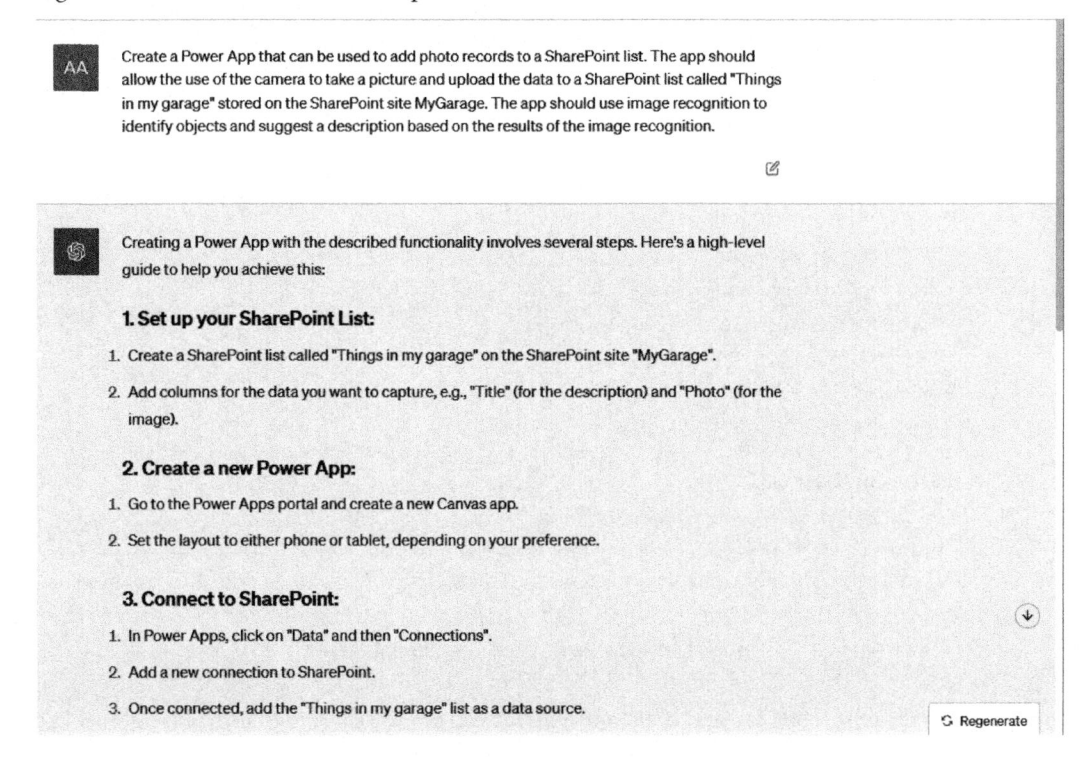

> **AA**: Create a Power App that can be used to add photo records to a SharePoint list. The app should allow the use of the camera to take a picture and upload the data to a SharePoint list called "Things in my garage" stored on the SharePoint site MyGarage. The app should use image recognition to identify objects and suggest a description based on the results of the image recognition.
>
> Creating a Power App with the described functionality involves several steps. Here's a high-level guide to help you achieve this:
>
> **1. Set up your SharePoint List:**
> 1. Create a SharePoint list called "Things in my garage" on the SharePoint site "MyGarage".
> 2. Add columns for the data you want to capture, e.g., "Title" (for the description) and "Photo" (for the image).
>
> **2. Create a new Power App:**
> 1. Go to the Power Apps portal and create a new Canvas app.
> 2. Set the layout to either phone or tablet, depending on your preference.
>
> **3. Connect to SharePoint:**
> 1. In Power Apps, click on "Data" and then "Connections".
> 2. Add a new connection to SharePoint.
> 3. Once connected, add the "Things in my garage" list as a data source.

Figure 4.18 – Asking ChatGPT to create a Power App

It starts off well, but as you can see in *Figure 4.19*, the specificity of what I wanted to achieve quickly tapers off:

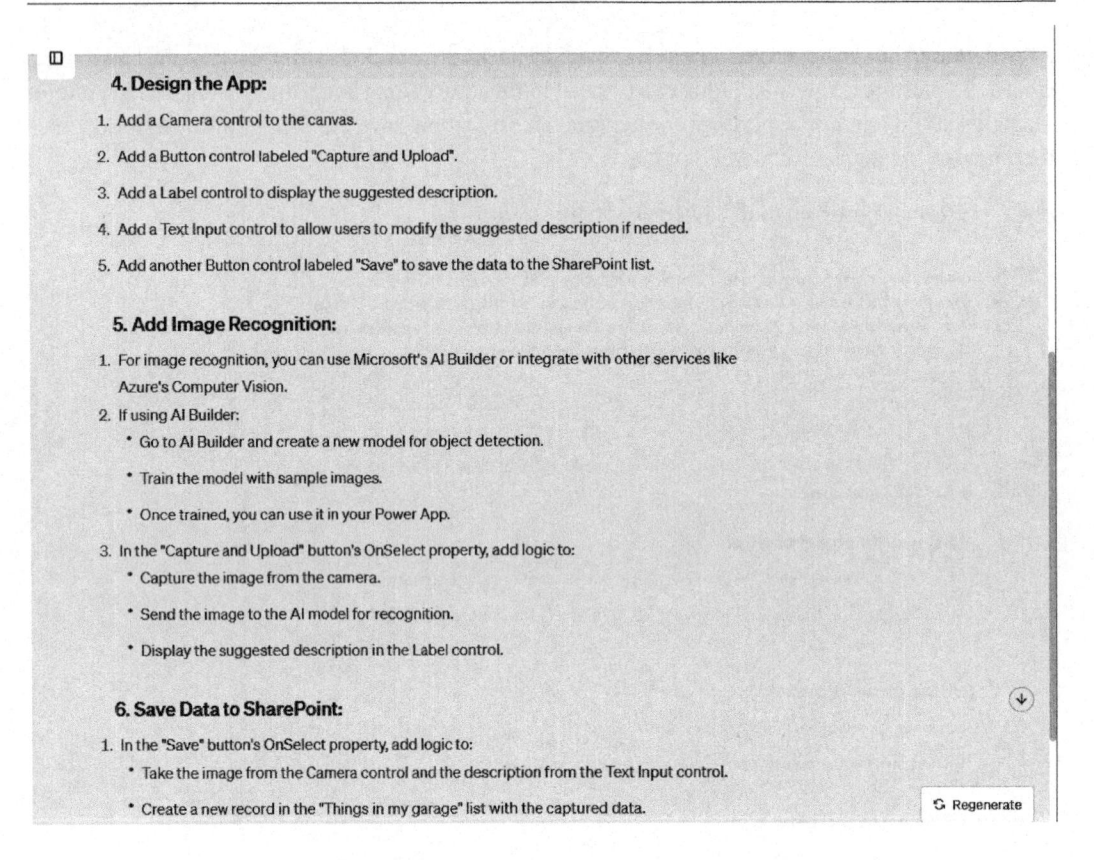

> **4. Design the App:**
>
> 1. Add a Camera control to the canvas.
> 2. Add a Button control labeled "Capture and Upload".
> 3. Add a Label control to display the suggested description.
> 4. Add a Text Input control to allow users to modify the suggested description if needed.
> 5. Add another Button control labeled "Save" to save the data to the SharePoint list.
>
> **5. Add Image Recognition:**
>
> 1. For image recognition, you can use Microsoft's AI Builder or integrate with other services like Azure's Computer Vision.
> 2. If using AI Builder:
>   * Go to AI Builder and create a new model for object detection.
>   * Train the model with sample images.
>   * Once trained, you can use it in your Power App.
> 3. In the "Capture and Upload" button's OnSelect property, add logic to:
>   * Capture the image from the camera.
>   * Send the image to the AI model for recognition.
>   * Display the suggested description in the Label control.
>
> **6. Save Data to SharePoint:**
>
> 1. In the "Save" button's OnSelect property, add logic to:
>   * Take the image from the Camera control and the description from the Text Input control.
>   * Create a new record in the "Things in my garage" list with the captured data.

Figure 4.19 – The Power App's configuration

Once it got to the more complex part of the process, instead of providing good instructions on what to do, ChatGPT fell back to **insert your own steps here**.

Remember, ChatGPT is conversational, so you can tell it that its previous input wasn't what you were looking for and that you need more detail. You can provide specific instructions as well as part of the procedure. Using these refinement tactics can help you get closer to your result, as shown in *Figure 4.20*:

Working with Power Apps   63

> Please provide more detailed, step-by-step instructions to the previous task.

Certainly! Let's delve deeper into the steps to create the Power App:

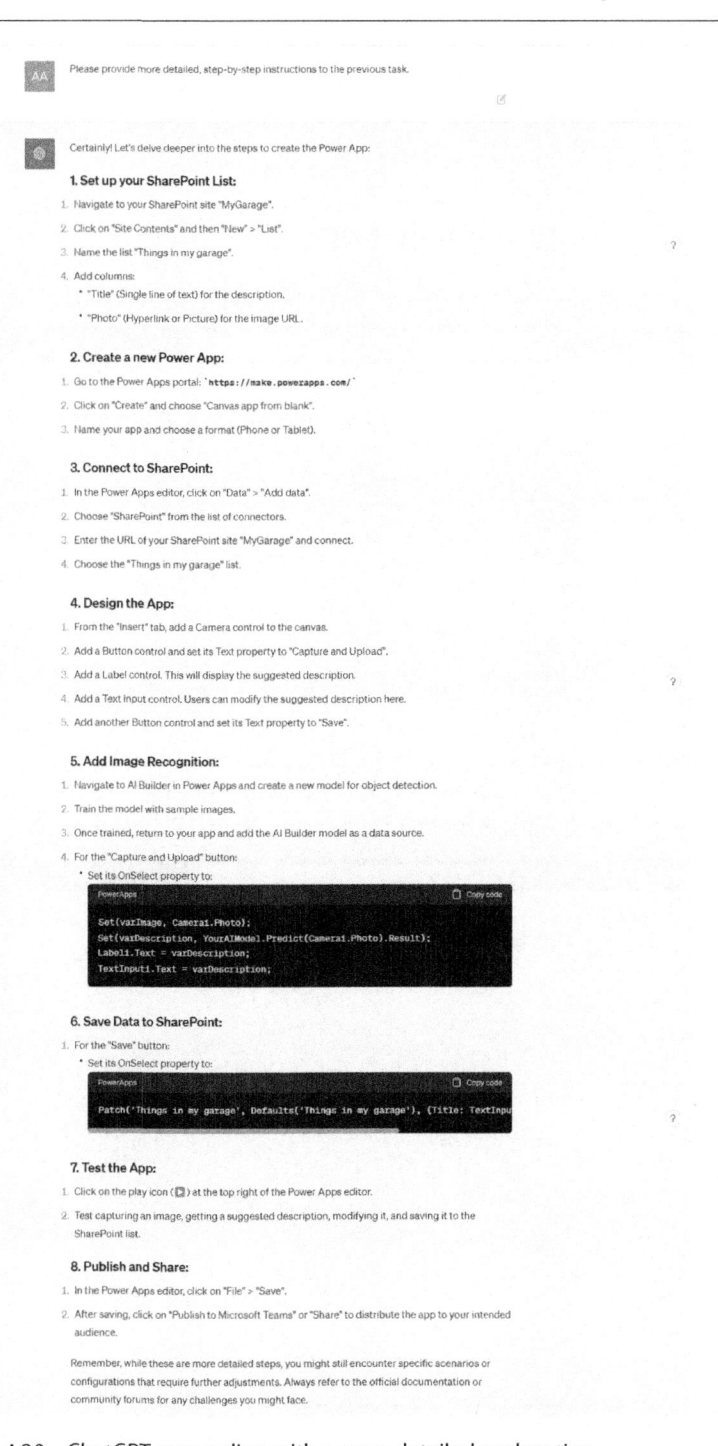

1. Set up your SharePoint List:

1. Navigate to your SharePoint site "MyGarage".
2. Click on "Site Contents" and then "New" > "List".
3. Name the list "Things in my garage".
4. Add columns:
   * "Title" (Single line of text) for the description.
   * "Photo" (Hyperlink or Picture) for the image URL.

2. Create a new Power App:

1. Go to the Power Apps portal: `https://make.powerapps.com/`
2. Click on "Create" and choose "Canvas app from blank".
3. Name your app and choose a format (Phone or Tablet).

3. Connect to SharePoint:

1. In the Power Apps editor, click on "Data" > "Add data".
2. Choose "SharePoint" from the list of connectors.
3. Enter the URL of your SharePoint site "MyGarage" and connect.
4. Choose the "Things in my garage" list.

4. Design the App:

1. From the "Insert" tab, add a Camera control to the canvas.
2. Add a Button control and set its Text property to "Capture and Upload".
3. Add a Label control. This will display the suggested description.
4. Add a Text Input control. Users can modify the suggested description here.
5. Add another Button control and set its Text property to "Save".

5. Add Image Recognition:

1. Navigate to AI Builder in Power Apps and create a new model for object detection.
2. Train the model with sample images.
3. Once trained, return to your app and add the AI Builder model as a data source.
4. For the "Capture and Upload" button:
   * Set its OnSelect property to:

```PowerApps
Set(varImage, Camera1.Photo);
Set(varDescription, YourAIModel.Predict(Camera1.Photo).Result);
Label1.Text = varDescription;
TextInput1.Text = varDescription;
```

6. Save Data to SharePoint:

1. For the "Save" button:
   * Set its OnSelect property to:

```PowerApps
Patch('Things in my garage', Defaults('Things in my garage'), {Title: TextInpu
```

7. Test the App:

1. Click on the play icon (▷) at the top right of the Power Apps editor.
2. Test capturing an image, getting a suggested description, modifying it, and saving it to the SharePoint list.

8. Publish and Share:

1. In the Power Apps editor, click on "File" > "Save".
2. After saving, click on "Publish to Microsoft Teams" or "Share" to distribute the app to your intended audience.

Remember, while these are more detailed steps, you might still encounter specific scenarios or configurations that require further adjustments. Always refer to the official documentation or community forums for any challenges you might face.

Figure 4.20 – ChatGPT responding with a more detailed explanation

That's a much more helpful response—especially for someone who isn't as familiar with the Power Apps platform.

Let's see how Copilot, integrated with Power Apps, handles this same task!

Using Copilot to build an app

Like Power Automate, Power Apps also has some support for Copilot:

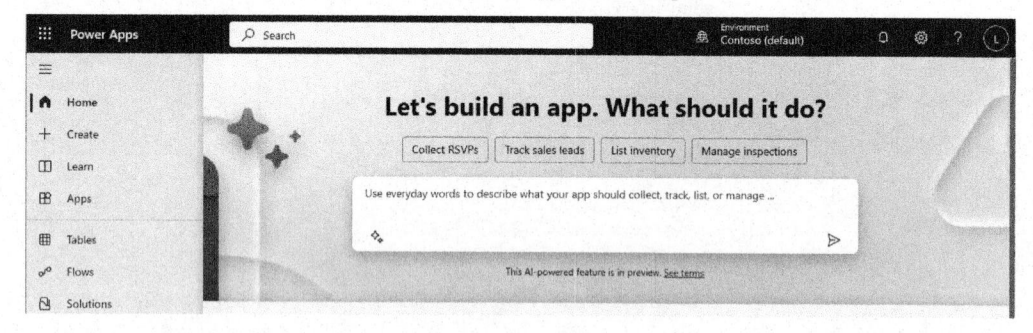

Figure 4.21 – The Power Apps Copilot prompt

In the following example, I'm going to provide the same initial instructions that I provided to ChatGPT. As you can see in *Figure 4.22*, the initial response doesn't appear to be as useful and just presents a table with the sample data, including columns for **Name**, **Description**, and **Photo**:

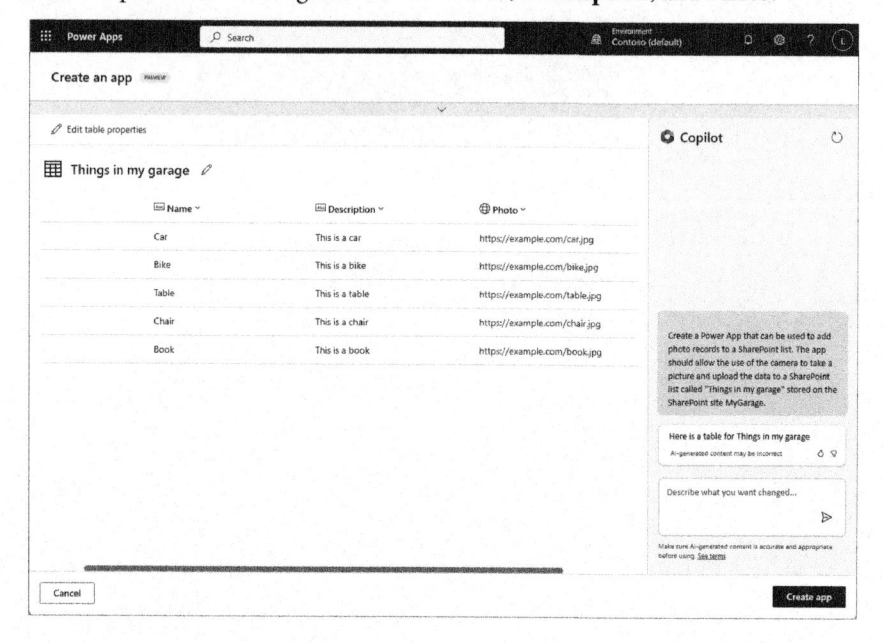

Figure 4.22 – The initial response from Power Apps Copilot

Working with Power Apps   65

After clicking **Create app**, the Power Apps Studio page is presented. The result is a one-page app that gathers information in a table, as shown in *Figure 4.23*:

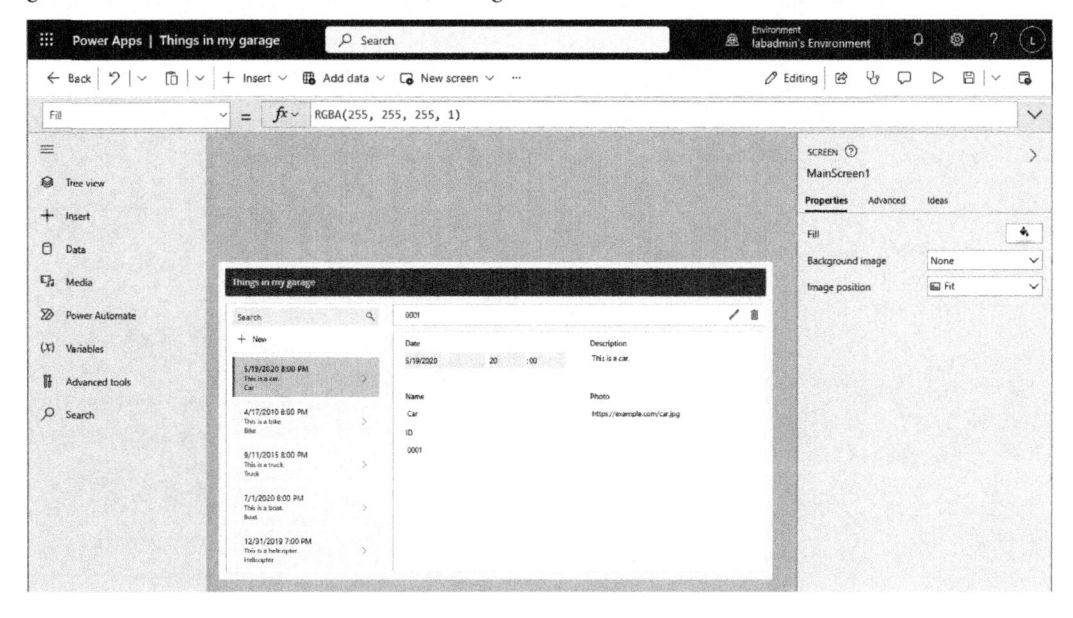

Figure 4.23 – A sample app created with Copilot

You can click around and preview the app, but at this point, it's a bit underwhelming.

> **Tip**
> The Power Apps Studio interface isn't as intuitive as Power Automate for adding or updating components—especially if the Copilot integrations aren't showing up while working on a canvas app. If you don't see the Copilot icon on the title bar of Power Apps Studio, check out the Power Platform admin center (https://admin.powerplatform.com), and under **Environments**, select your environment > **Settings** > **Product** > **Features** and ensure that **Copilot** and **AI Builder preview models** are both turned on.

While natural language processing is helpful for a lot of things, there are some contexts where you need to figure out the keywords and phrases that will trigger the AI to assist in the way you want. I'll go back to the drawing board and start over—this time, rephrasing the prompt and then using the refinements controls on the Copilot page.

As you can see in *Figure 4.24*, the combination of rephrasing the prompt and then using the Copilot interface helped me get much closer to the data entry page:

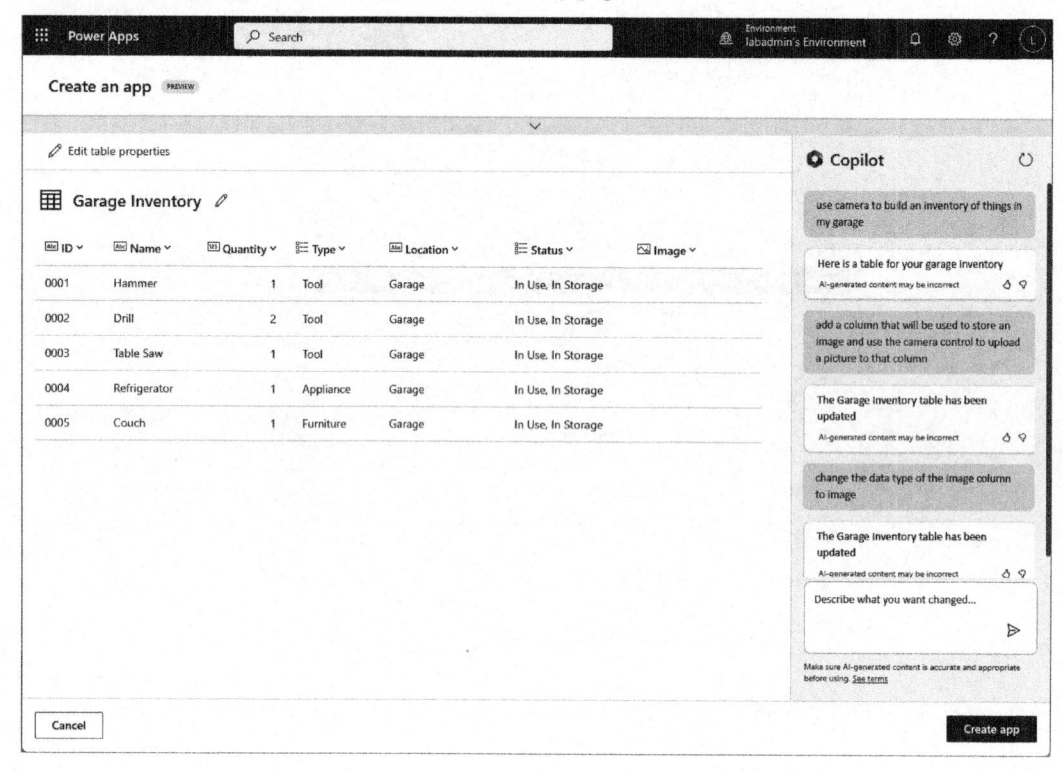

Figure 4.24 – The updated app with Copilot

From here, I can create this app and then start modifying it. By selecting the Copilot icon on the title bar of Power Apps Studio, I can try to instruct Copilot to update things, sometimes more successfully than others:

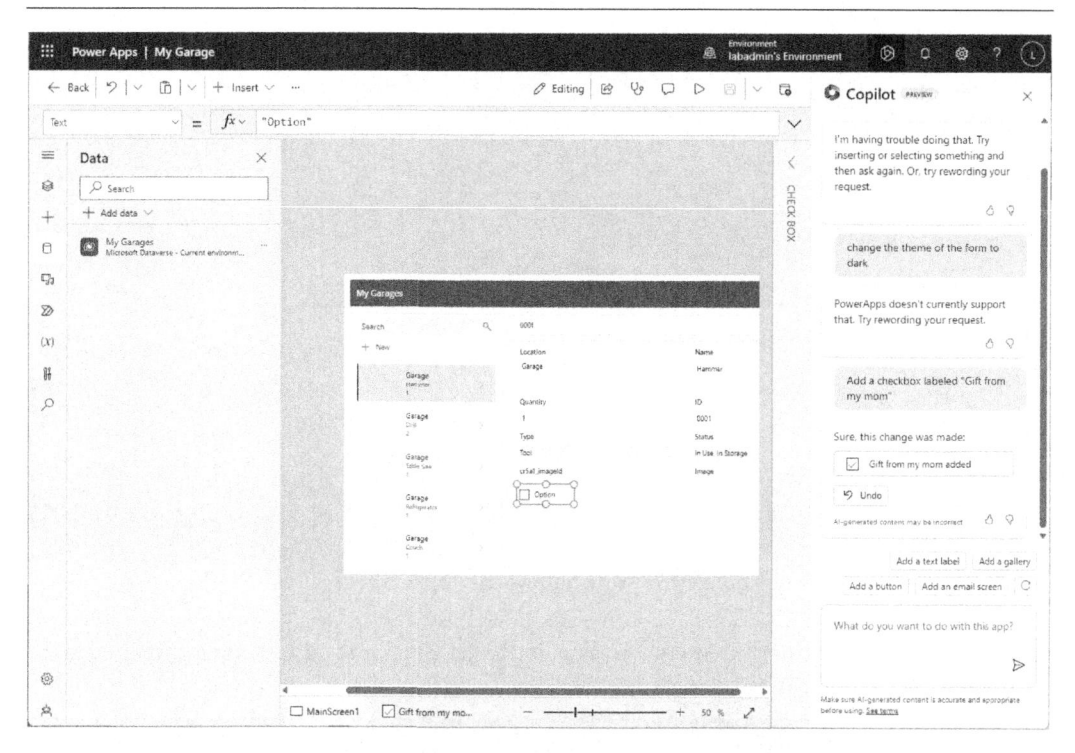

Figure 4.25 – Attempting to modify properties with Copilot

In *Figure 4.25*, a checkbox was indeed added, but it ended up being added to the main screen. The text, instead of being set to *Gift from my mom*, was configured with the **Option 1** default label. After removing the checkbox and telling Copilot to add it to *Form1* (the name of the input form), and then to set the **Text** to *Gift from my mom*, I met with a little bit more success, though the control was still on the main screen and not actually part of the input form:

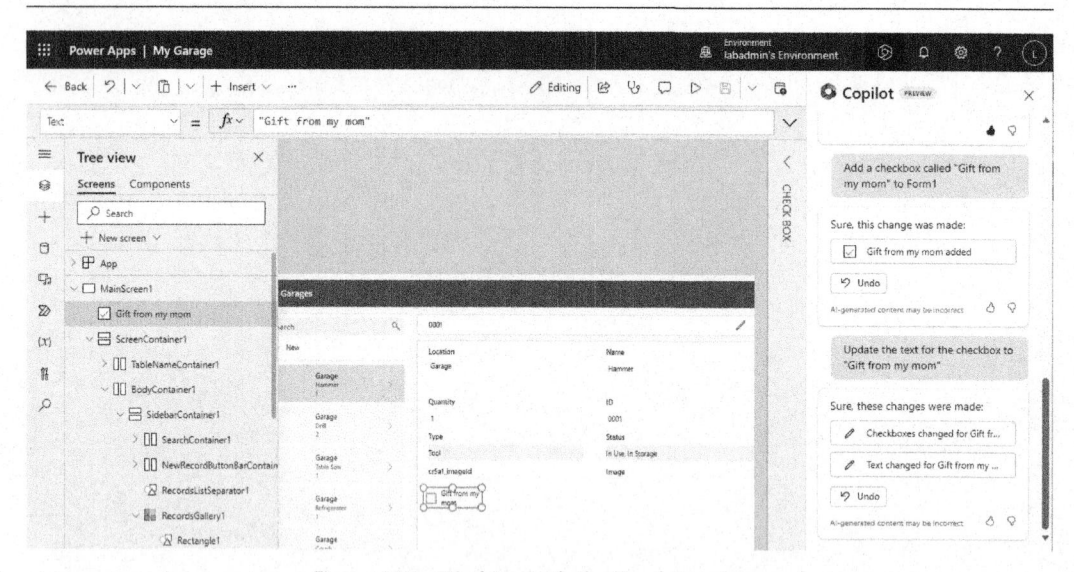

68 Using ChatGPT and Copilot to Create Flows and Apps

Figure 4.26 – Working with the Copilot process

Even after several rewording attempts, I was unable to get Copilot to add a simple checkbox to the input form for collecting data:

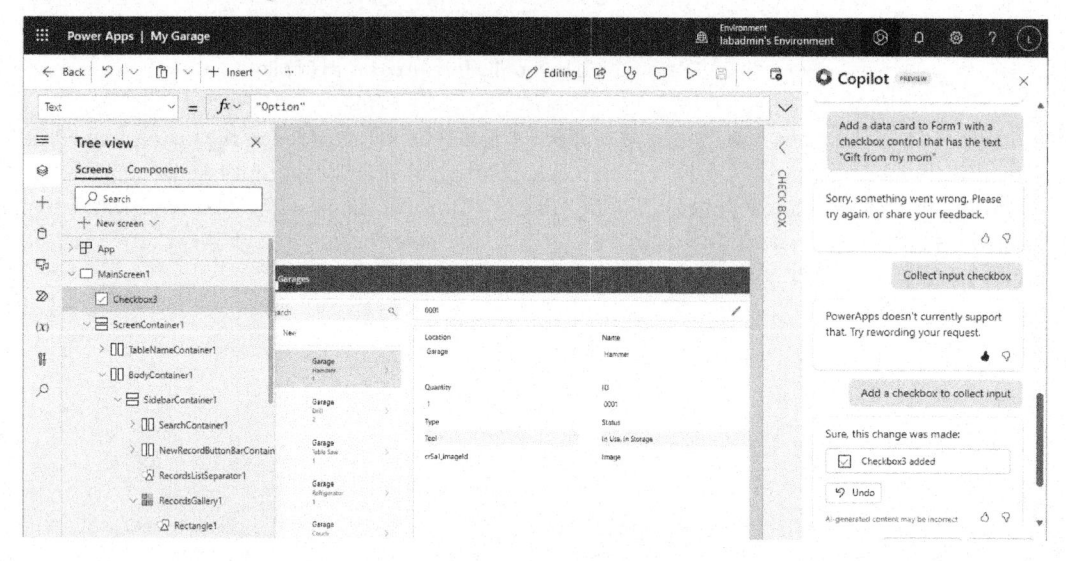

Figure 4.27 – Refining with Copilot

For many purposes, at this point—especially if you're just getting familiar with Power Apps—it may be more productive to ask ChatGPT how to do something than to ask Copilot to do it for you:

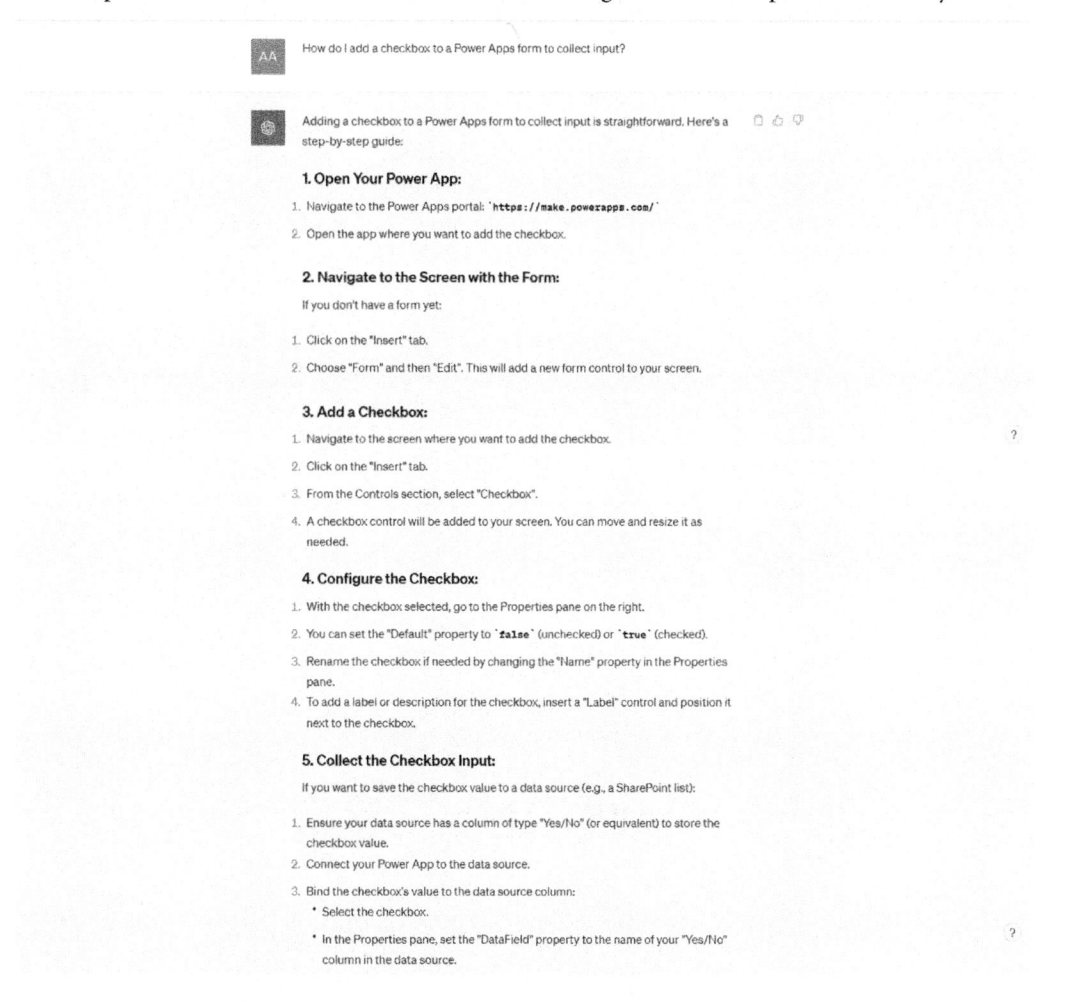

Figure 4.28 – Phoning an old friend, ChatGPT, for help

That's not to say Copilot can't do it—but as I mentioned earlier, you definitely need to know how to talk to Copilot to get it to be useful (we'll get to that in *Chapter 5*). You shouldn't approach Copilot thinking you can just speak an app into existence. While Power Apps Copilot does help kickstart some simple canvas apps, you'll still need a good bit of Power Apps knowledge combined with good old-fashioned design skills to turn its app generation attempts into something more useful.

Summary

The ultimate takeaway from this chapter is that AI assistants such as ChatGPT and Copilot are just that—assistants. While generative AI can't do your job for you (at this point), it's a great aid—especially when you're stretching outside your comfort zone.

If you're looking at bootstrapping new apps and flows, AI assistants can help get you started, but you'll ultimately need to continue refining your prompts, searching the blogs and community groups, and learning the underlying technology itself to be truly successful.

In the next chapter, we'll expand on using Copilot for Power Apps. While our first attempts didn't prove very successful, there are some techniques you can use to get Copilot and Power Apps to come together and produce working apps in as little as an hour.

5

Bootstrapping a Power App with Copilot

Copilot has begun to make its way into the Microsoft 365 platform. However, as you saw in the previous chapter, if you just approach Copilot the same way you approach ChatGPT for help, you may end up frustrated.

In this chapter, we're going to dig into the details of how to get Copilot to partner with you to create usable applications. We'll try an app that's a little more complex than the garage inventory app we worked with in *Chapter 4*. Here, we're going to try creating a simple leave or time-off request app using a few SharePoint lists and Copilot.

Configuring prerequisites

This sample leave request app is going to be comprised of a few SharePoint lists: one to store information about the request (requestor, start and end dates, approval status, and such) and another to store information about the approvers.

Creating identities in Entra ID

Since we're going to be picking users from Entra ID, you'll need to populate the directory with users. You should create users that provide as much detail as possible.

> **Further reading**
>
> For more information on creating users in Entra ID, go to `https://learn.microsoft.com/en-us/microsoft-365/admin/add-users/add-users?view=o365-worldwide`.

Creating a Dataverse environment

While a Microsoft 365 tenant is the logical boundary for your organization, an **environment** is a logical container or boundary that's used to segment applications, users, departments, or business units. A Microsoft 365 tenant can have multiple environments. An environment is used to group Power Platform components (such as Power Automate flows, Power Apps applications, Power Pages sites, or Dynamics 365 components), as well as dedicated information storage in a Dataverse database. A Dataverse environment can only have one database.

By default, your Microsoft 365 tenant should have a pre-built Dataverse environment (with a database that can store up to 3 GB of data), as shown in *Figure 5.1*:

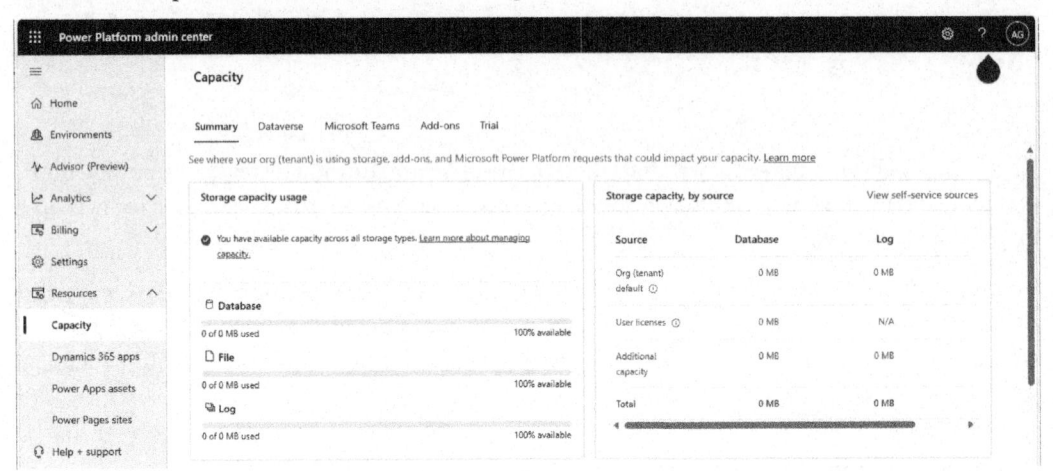

Figure 5.1 – Viewing Dataverse's capacity

If for whatever reason it doesn't (or you don't want to use the default environment), you can create a new one by following these steps:

1. Navigate to the Power Platform admin center (`https://admin.powerplatform.com`) and log in with a user who's been assigned an administrative role (such as a Global Admin or Microsoft Power Platform admin).

2. Select **Environments**, then click **New**.

3. Enter a **Name** value for the environment and select a **Region** value.

4. Select a **Type** value (either **Trial**, **Development**, **Production**, or **Sandbox**) and, optionally, enter a description in the **Purpose** area.

5. Under **Add a Dataverse data store**, move the slider to **Yes** to enable a database. Then, click **Next**.

6. The only required area on this page of the wizard is **Security group**. Click **Select** to choose the security controls for the environment. You can choose **None** under **Open access** to allow any user or select an existing security group under **Restricted access** to limit access.
7. Click **Save**.

After a few moments, the environment should be created. Whenever you wish to create or manage content in this environment, you'll need to switch environments in the Maker Portal, as shown in *Figure 5.2*.

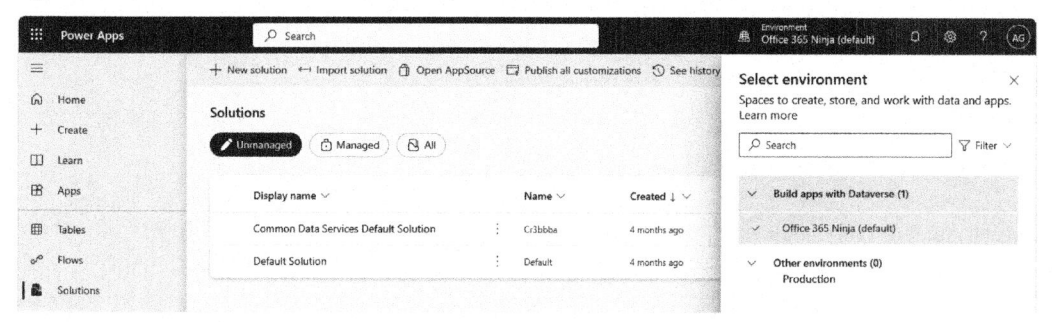

Figure 5.2 – Choosing an environment

Next, let's explore using Copilot to create a new Power App.

> **What do I do if I'm stuck?**
>
> If you run into a roadblock for some reason (can't find a feature, an option isn't showing up, or something is unclear), help is only a click away! You can download this chapter's artifacts from our GitHub site: `https://github.com/PacktPublishing/Power-Platform-and-the-AI-Revolution`.

Building a new Power App with Copilot

With our prerequisites met, it's time to start building an app! As you saw in *Chapter 4*, if you simply use the Copilot prompts to create an app, you essentially get a table that can be used for data entry. We're going to try a different approach – starting with a blank app and then using Copilot to add and link components.

This solution, which is built on a **Dataverse** (formerly known as the **Common Data Service**) environment with a database, will utilize both a frontend entry component for employees to request time off and a backend solution for approvers or managers to use.

> **Canvas and model-driven apps**
>
> Power Apps come in two flavors – **canvas** apps and **model-driven** apps. Canvas apps are built by adding controls to blank canvas pages (hence the name). Controls are essentially the building blocks that users interact with through actions such as clicking buttons, adding text, or submitting forms. Model-driven apps, however, approach design from the opposite end of the spectrum. Model-driven apps are used to interact with structured data and derive their core architecture and interface component configurations from the connected data sources. For more information on canvas apps, see `https://learn.microsoft.com/en-us/power-apps/maker/canvas-apps/getting-started`. For more information on model-driven apps, see `https://learn.microsoft.com/en-us/power-apps/maker/model-driven-apps/model-driven-app-overview`.

Configuring the data elements

Before you can start creating applications, you need to set up some structures to hold the data. Essentially, you'll create a table with **columns** – you can think of it as a spreadsheet. In a Dataverse table, columns are configured to have a **type**, which equates to what type of data can be stored in them.

Follow these steps to get started:

> **Copilot availability**
>
> At the time of writing, the Dataverse portion of the Power Apps Maker Portal does not have a Copilot interface.

1. Navigate to the Power Apps Maker Portal (`https://make.powerapps.com`) and select **Solutions**.

> **What's a solution?**
>
> **Solutions** can be viewed as container objects that are used to transport applications and components between environments and implement **application life cycle management** (**ALM**) in Power Platform. A solution can be as simple as a single flow or include apps and components, such as site maps, apps, and tables.

2. Click **New solution**.

Building a new Power App with Copilot   75

3. Enter a **Display name** value. The **Name** property will be automatically calculated, though you can edit it. Then, click **Create**:

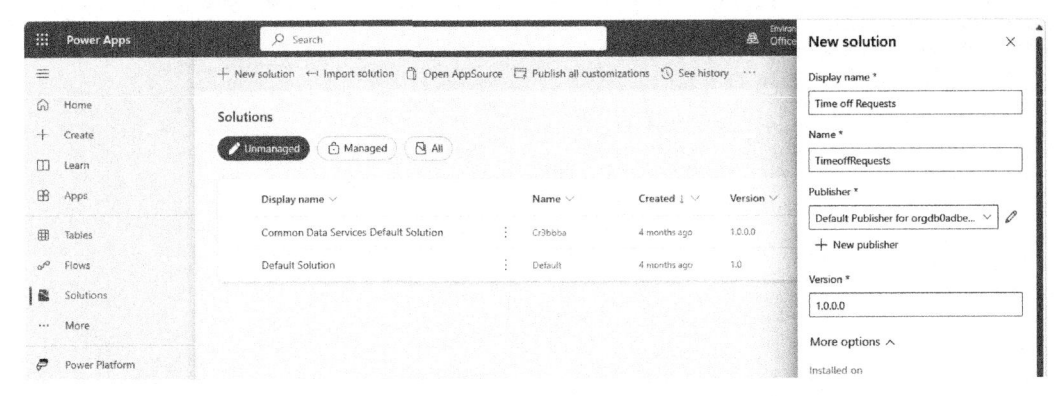

Figure 5.3 – Creating a new solution

4. Expand the **New** menu, point to **Table**, and select **Table**:

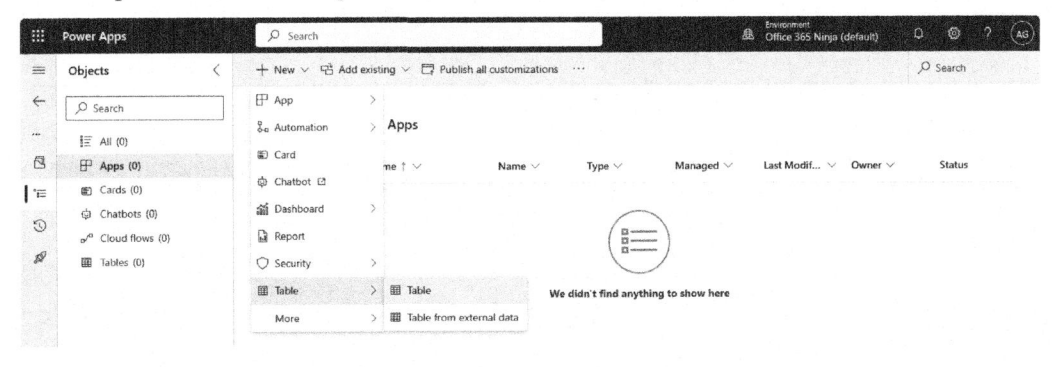

Figure 5.4 – Adding a table

76   Bootstrapping a Power App with Copilot

5. Enter a **Display name** value, such as `Time off Table`. Select the **Enable attachments (including notes and files)** checkbox and click **Save**:

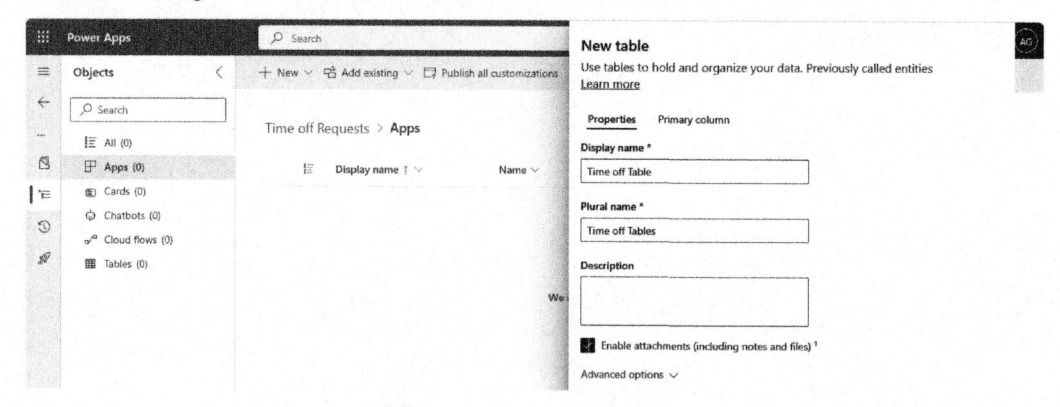

Figure 5.5 – Creating a new table

> **Updated terminology**
> **Tables** were previously called **entities**.

6. Click **New** > **Column**:

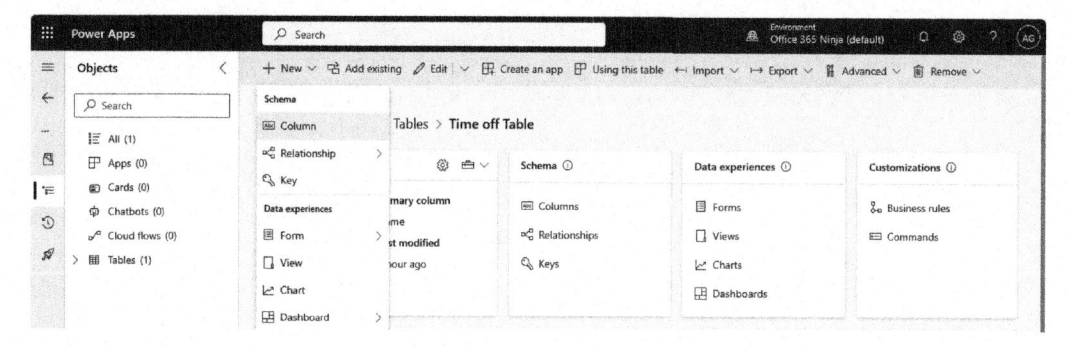

Figure 5.6 – Adding a column

> **Updated terminology**
> **Columns** were previously called **fields**.

7. On the **New column** flyout, enter `First` name in the **Display name** field, select **Single line of text** under **Data type**, and click **Save**. See *Figure 5.7*:

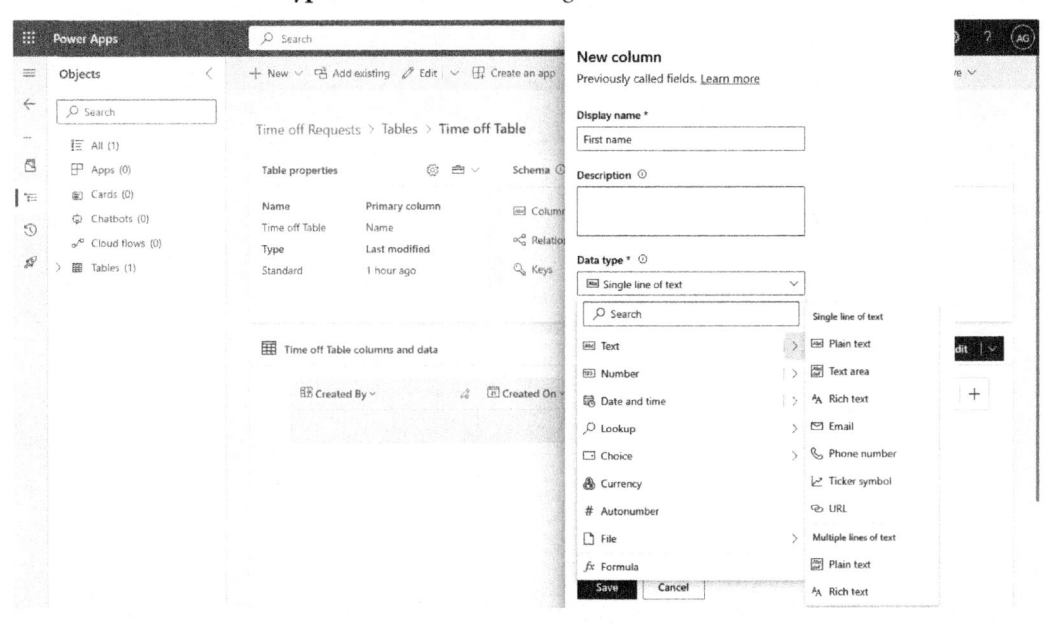

Figure 5.7 – Configuring a column

8. Repeat *step 7* to create additional fields based on what's shown in *Table 5.1*:

Field name	Data type	Additional properties	Required
Last name	A single line of text		Business required
Email	A single line of text	Format: Email	Business required
Supervisor	A single line of text		Business required
Supervisor Email	A single line of text	Format: Email	Business required
Start date	Date and time	Date only	Business required
End date	Date and time	Date only	Business required
Request Type	Choice	Sync with global choice: No Choice: Vacation Choice: Sick Choice: Bereavement Choice: Jury Duty	

Table 5.1 – Dataverse fields

9. From the Power Apps Maker Portal, expand **Tables** > **Views** and select **Active Time off Tables**. See *Figure 5.8*:

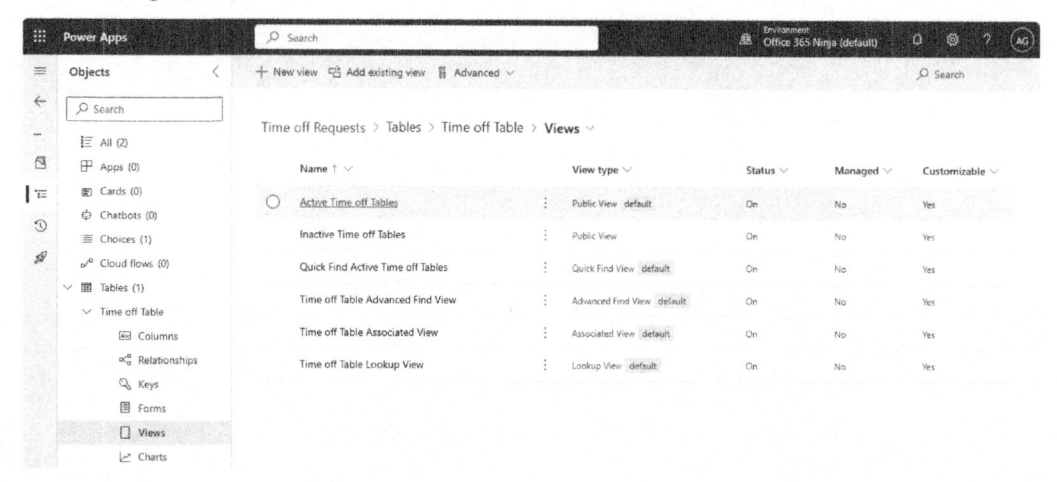

Figure 5.8 – Activing Time off Tables

Building a new Power App with Copilot   79

10. Drag the **First name**, **Last name**, **Start date**, and **End date** fields from the **Table columns** area into the main window:

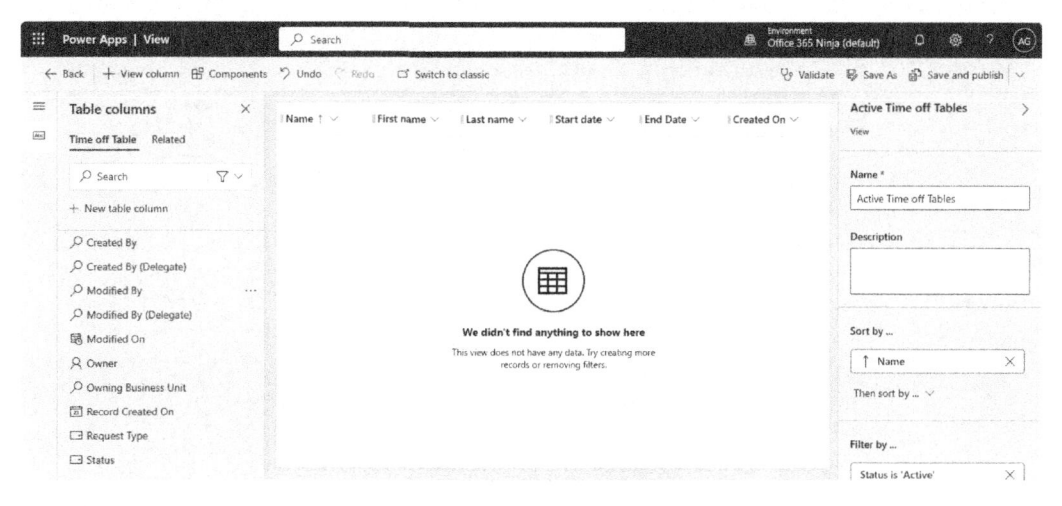

Figure 5.9 – Updating the view

11. Click **Save and publish**.
12. Click **Back** to return to the **Objects** view.
13. Expand **Tables** > **Time off Table** and select **Forms**. Select the form with **Form type** set to **Main**. See *Figure 5.9*:

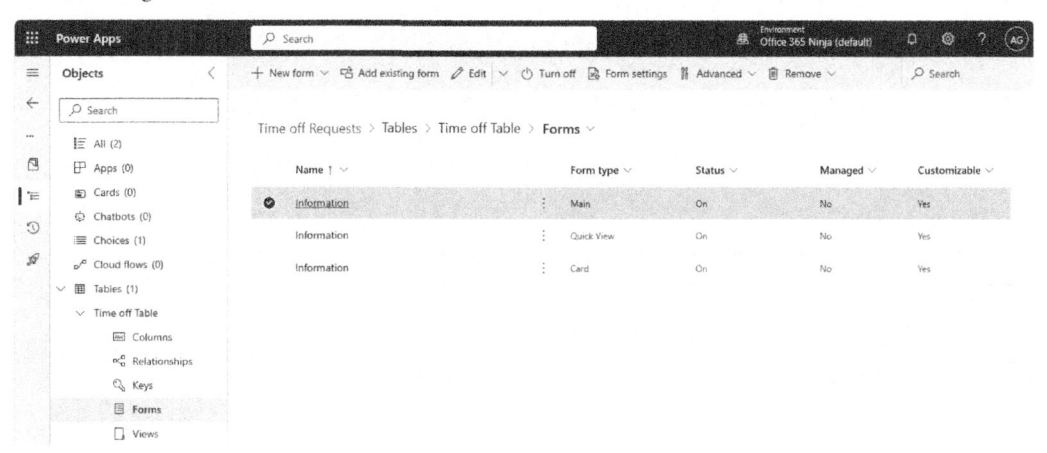

Figure 5.10 – Viewing the forms

14. Add the Dataverse columns you created earlier to the view, as shown in *Figure 5.11*. When you're finished, click **Save and publish**:

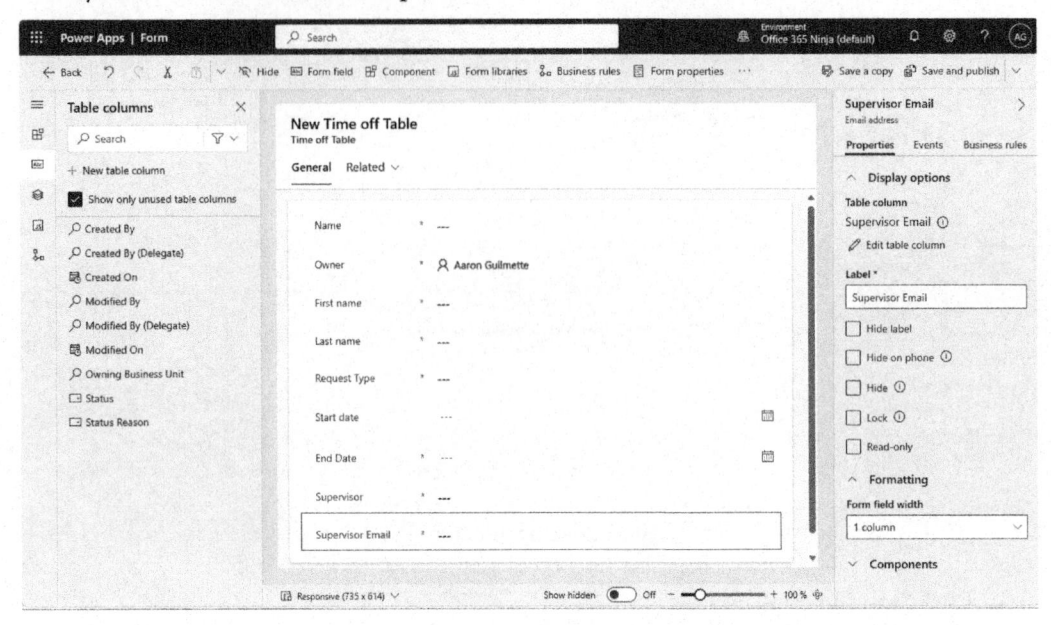

Figure 5.11 – Adding the Dataverse columns

Next, it's time to build the backend app.

Creating the model-driven backend app

In this section, you'll configure a new model-driven app that managers will use for approving time-off requests. Follow these steps:

> **Copilot availability**
> At the time of writing, Copilot is not available for working with model-driven apps.

1. Navigate to the Power Apps Maker Portal (`https://make.powerapps.com`). Then, expand **Solutions** and select the **Time off Requests** solution:

Building a new Power App with Copilot   81

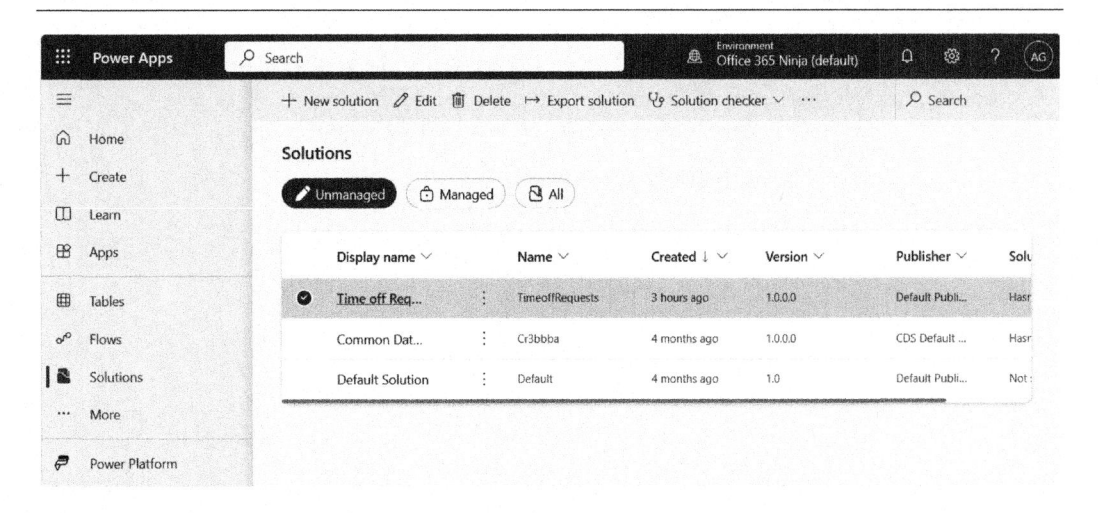

Figure 5.12 – Selecting the Time off Requests app

2. Click **New**, expand **App**, and select **Model-driven app**:

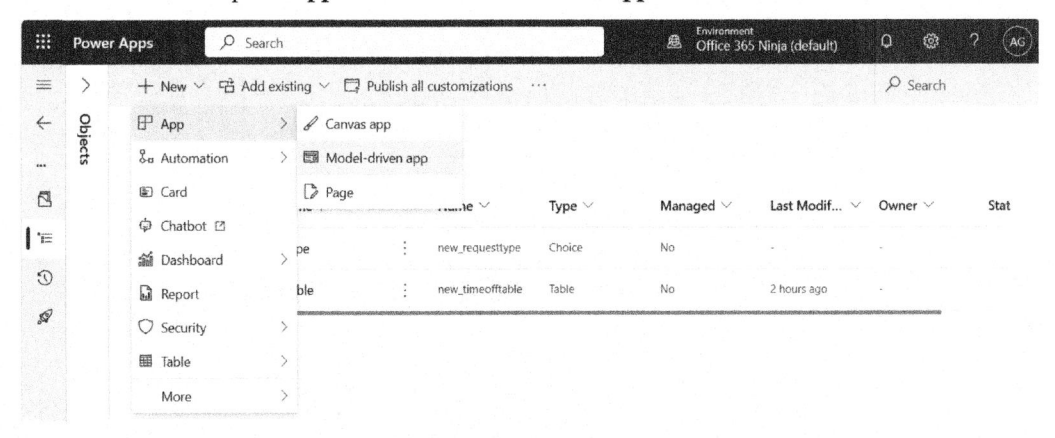

Figure 5.13 – Creating a new model-driven app

3. Enter a **Name** value, such as `Time off Back-end App`.

4. Expand the **Advanced** dropdown and select **Use components from a custom solution**. Under **Solution**, select the **Time off Requests** solution and click **Create**:

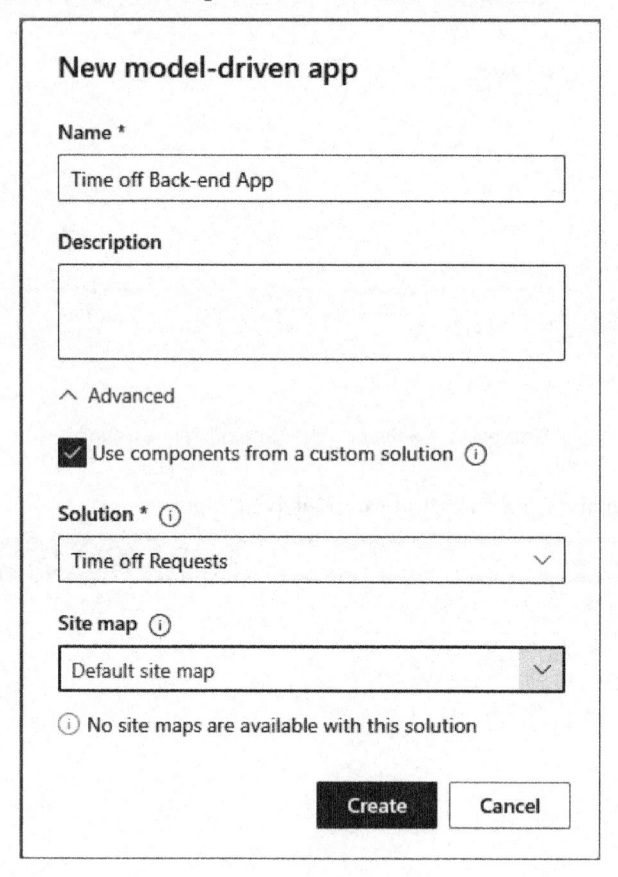

Figure 5.14 – Setting the parameters for the new model-driven app

5. Click **Back** to navigate back to the **Objects** page.
6. Select **Site maps**.

7. Select the **Time off Back-end App** site map:

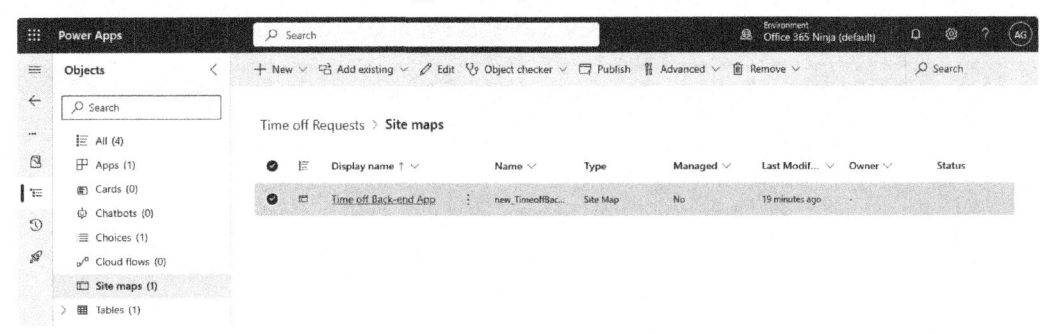

Figure 5.15 – Viewing the site map

8. Click the **Area1** label, and then click **Add** from the menu. Select **Group**.
9. Click **Add** and then click **Subarea**.
10. In the **Properties** pane, under **Type**, select **Entity**.
11. Under **Entity**, select **Time off Table**:

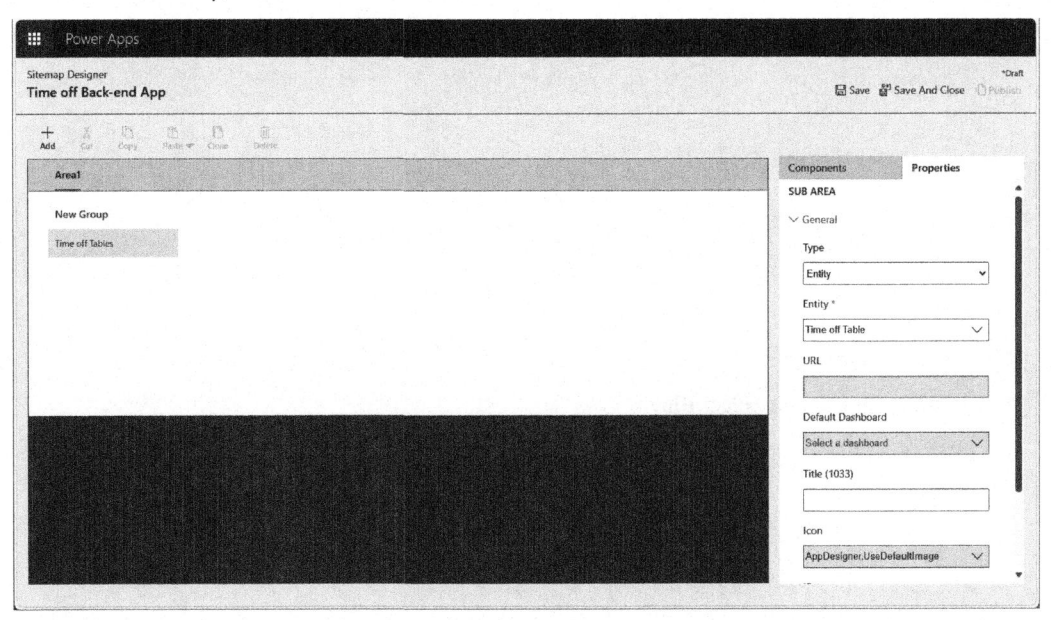

Figure 5.16 – Updating the site map

84 | Bootstrapping a Power App with Copilot

12. Click **Save and Close**.
13. In the **Objects** view, with **Site maps** selected, click **Publish**:

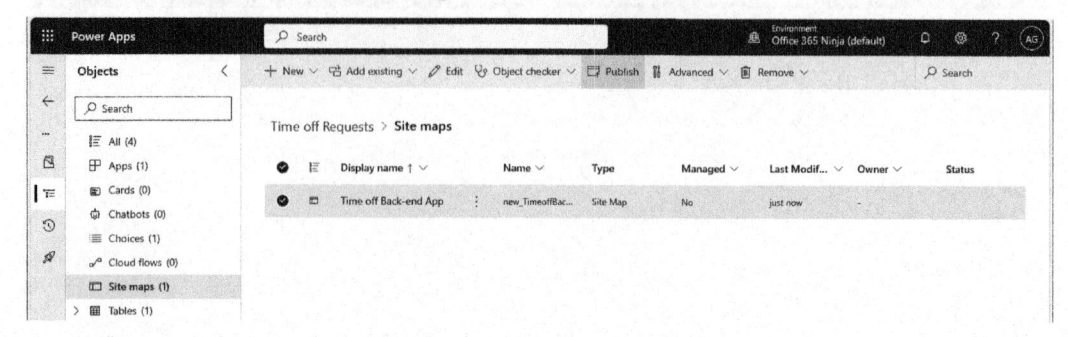

Figure 5.17 – Publishing the site map

14. Click **Apps** and then click **Publish all customizations**:

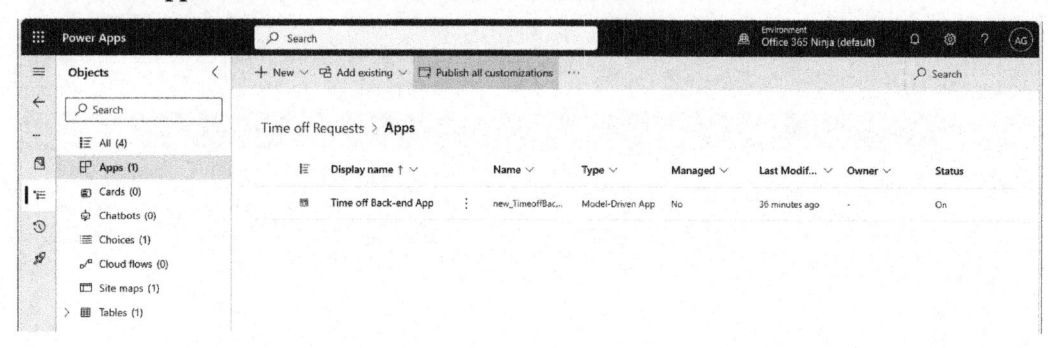

Figure 5.18 – Publishing app customizations

15. Open the app by clicking on it.
16. From the top menu, select **Play**:

Building a new Power App with Copilot   85

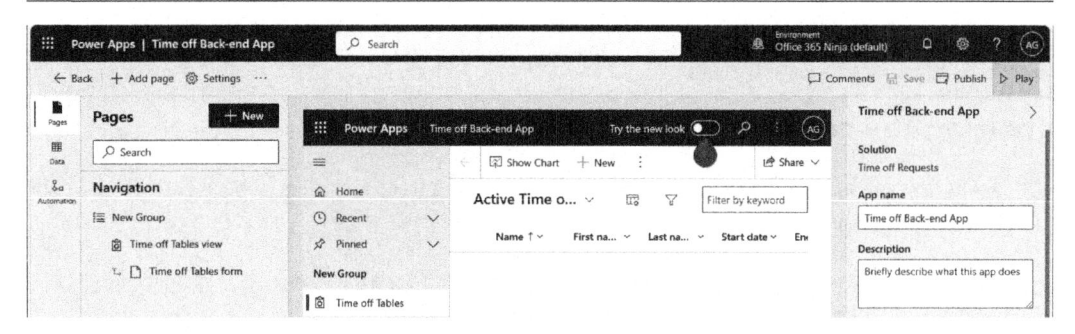

Figure 5.19 – Running the application

17. On the app, click **New** to add a new record:

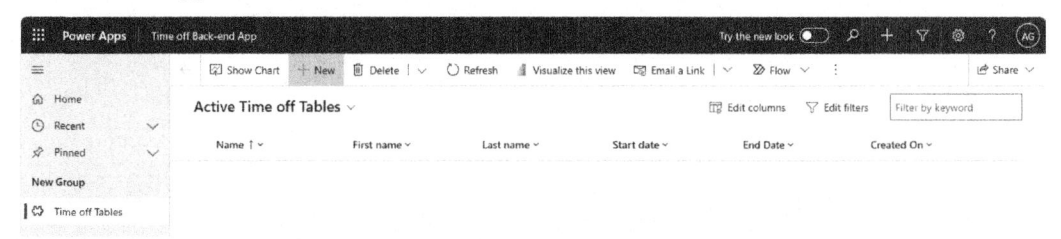

Figure 5.20 – Creating a new record

18. Fill out the record, like so:

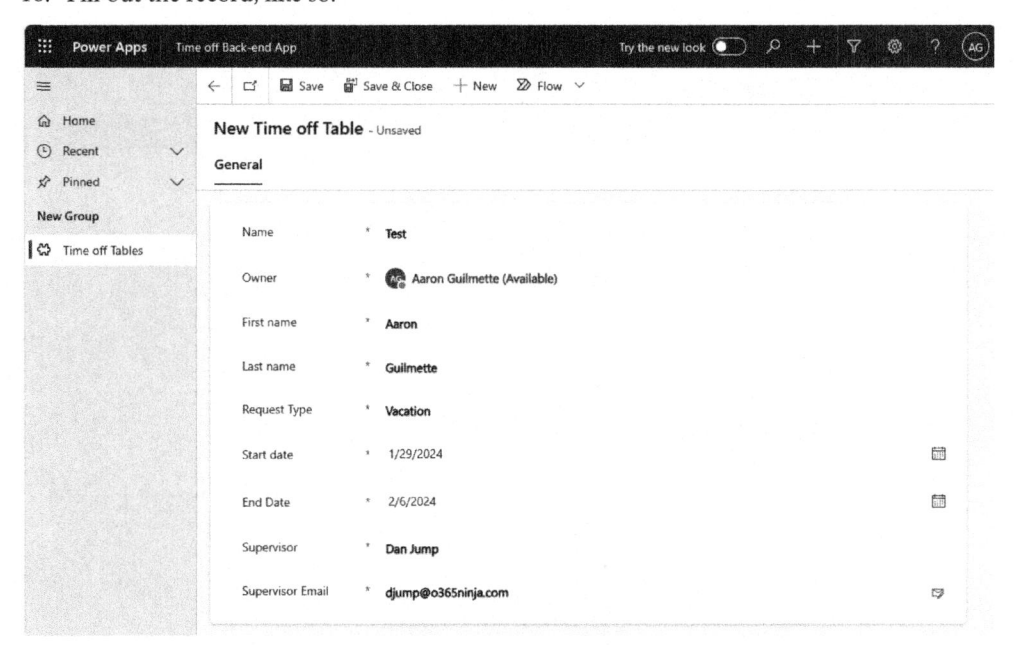

Figure 5.21 – Creating a record

With that, the model-driven app has been created. Now, it's time to create the end user interface.

Creating the canvas frontend app

The canvas app will be used by end users to create time off requests. Here, you'll be able to use Copilot to help configure the app:

1. Navigate to the Power Apps Maker Portal (`https://make.powerapps.com`). Then, expand **Solutions** and select the **Time off Requests** solution.
2. Select **Apps**.
3. Click **New** > **App** > **Canvas app**.
4. On the **Canvas app from blank** wizard, enter a **Name** value (such as `Time off Requests`), select a format (either **Tablet** or **Phone**), and click **Create**.
5. In the navigation pane, select **Data**.
6. Click **Add data** and select **Office 365 Users connector**. On the flyout, click **Connect**.
7. In the **Copilot** pane, instruct Copilot to add a new form and connect it to the **Time off Tables** table (or entity) you created earlier – for example, `Add a new form. Set the datasource for the form to 'Time off Tables'`:

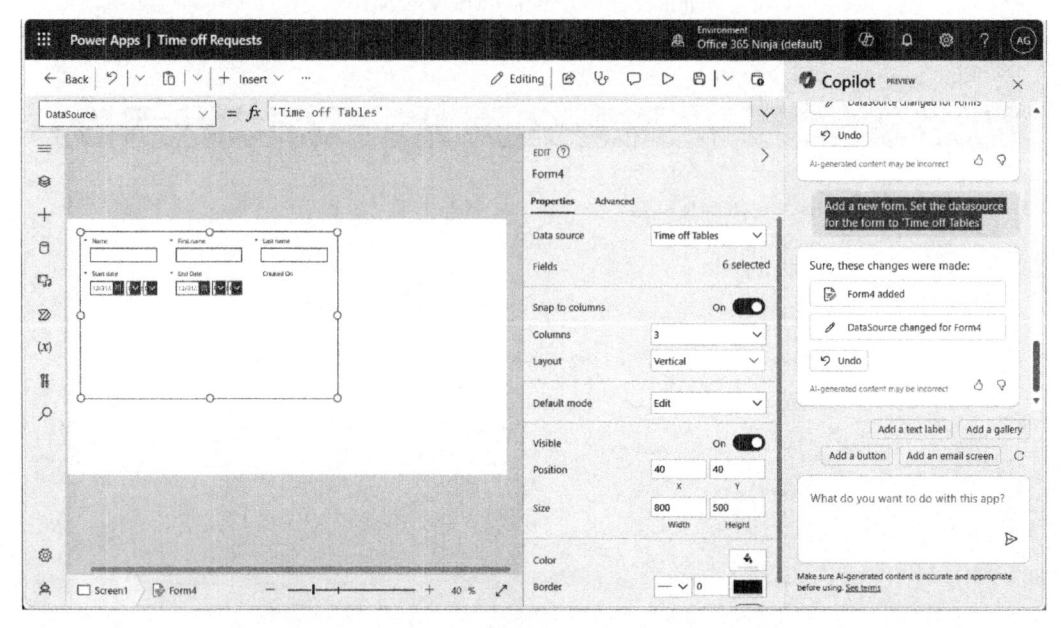

Figure 5.22 – Adding a table and connecting to a data source

Building a new Power App with Copilot   87

> **Note**
> It may take a few tries with Copilot to get the result you want. If it can't connect to the data source, make sure you are entering the name just as it appears under **Tables**. You can open the properties of the form and select the **Data source** dropdown to choose it manually.

8. Under **Data source**, click **Edit fields**.
9. Click **Add field**. Add the fields (columns) you created earlier:

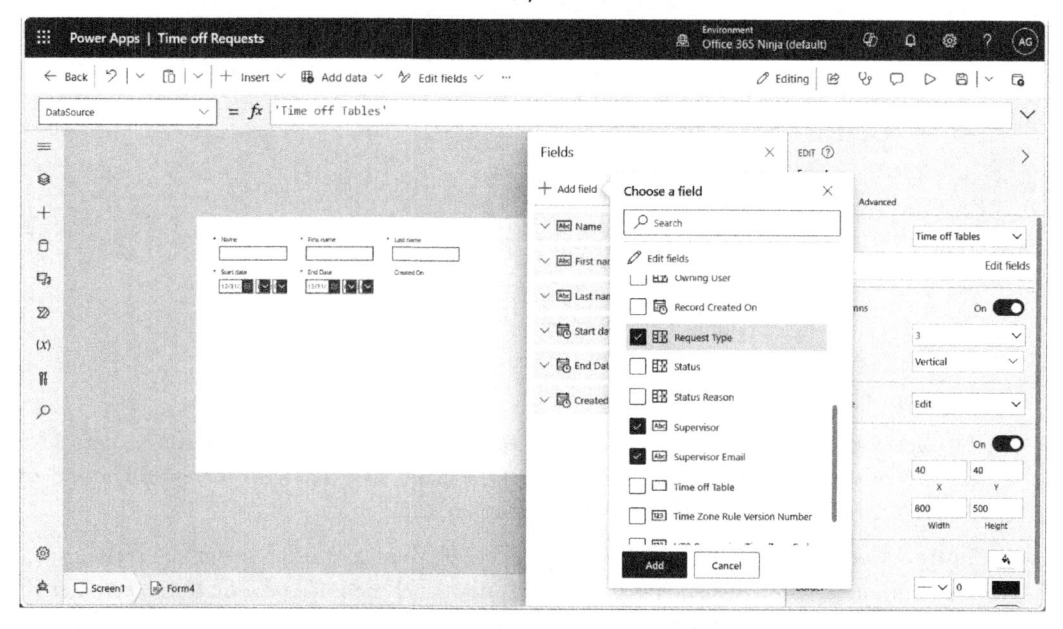

Figure 5.23 – Adding the remaining fields

10. Update the default mode of the form by instructing Copilot to `Set the default mode of the selected form to New`. Alternatively, you can update the configuration by clicking the dropdown next to **Default mode** on the property sheet and choosing **New**.

11. Instruct Copilot to `Add a button to Screen1. Configure the button to submit the form and then navigate to Screen2`. Verify that the button's `OnSelect` method displays the `SubmitForm('FormName');Navigate('Screen2')` function and references the form's name. Drag the button to an appropriate location on the screen:

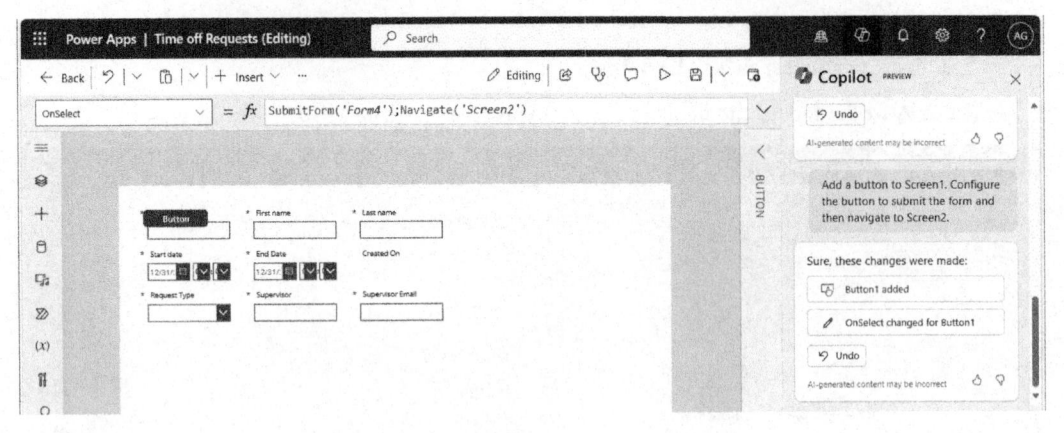

Figure 5.24 – Adding a button to the screen

12. Instruct Copilot to `Update button text to say Submit`.
13. Instruct Copilot to `Add a new screen using the Success template`. Alternately, select **New screen** > **Templates** > **Success** from the menu. By default, the screen will be named Screen2. You should be directed to Screen2 automatically.
14. Instruct Copilot to `Add a text label on Screen2 that says "Thank you for submitting your request."` A new label should appear on the screen. Resize it so that all of the text is visible.
15. Instruct Copilot to `Add a button on Screen2 labelled "Start a new request" that navigates to Screen1 and resets the form`. A new button should be created that has the **OnSelect** property populated with `Navigate('Screen1');ResetForm('Form1')` (or whatever your form name is). Drag it to an empty area of the screen and resize it so that all the text is visible. See *Figure 5.25*:

Building a new Power App with Copilot   89

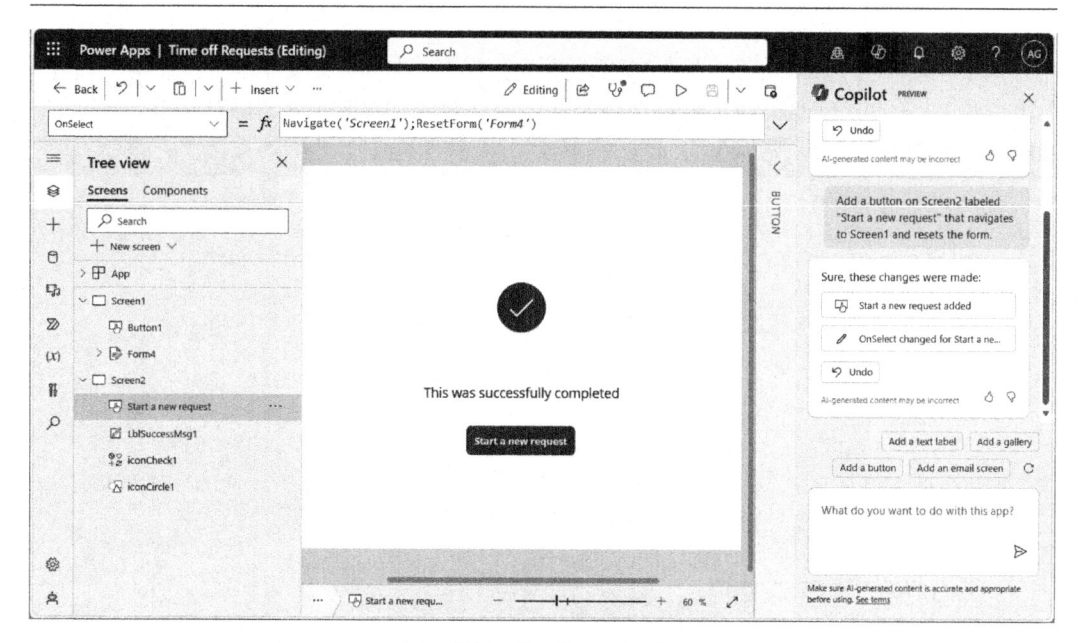

Figure 5.25 – Finalizing the form

16. Click the **Play** button to test it out and add a record:

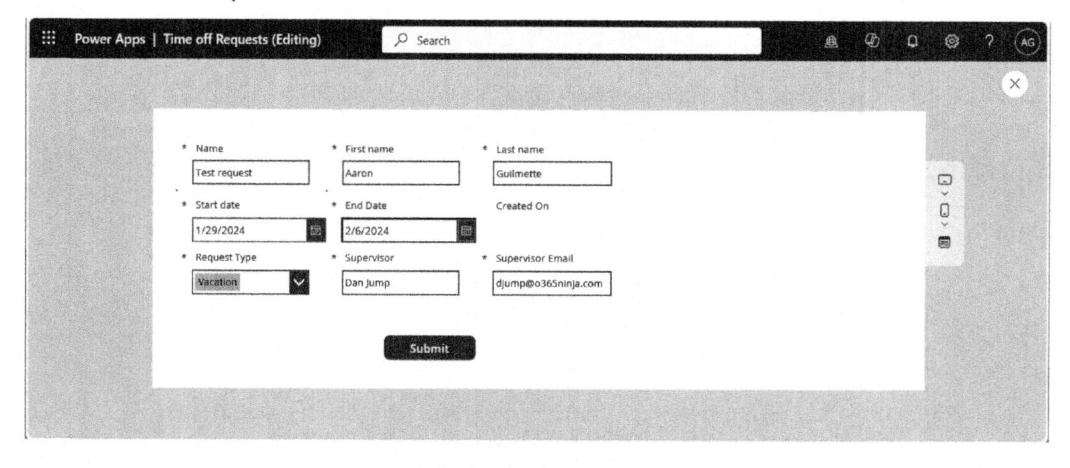

Figure 5.26 – Testing the app

17. After testing the app, click the **X** icon to close it. Then, click **Save and publish**.
18. On the **Publish** page, enter a brief description and click **Publish this version**:

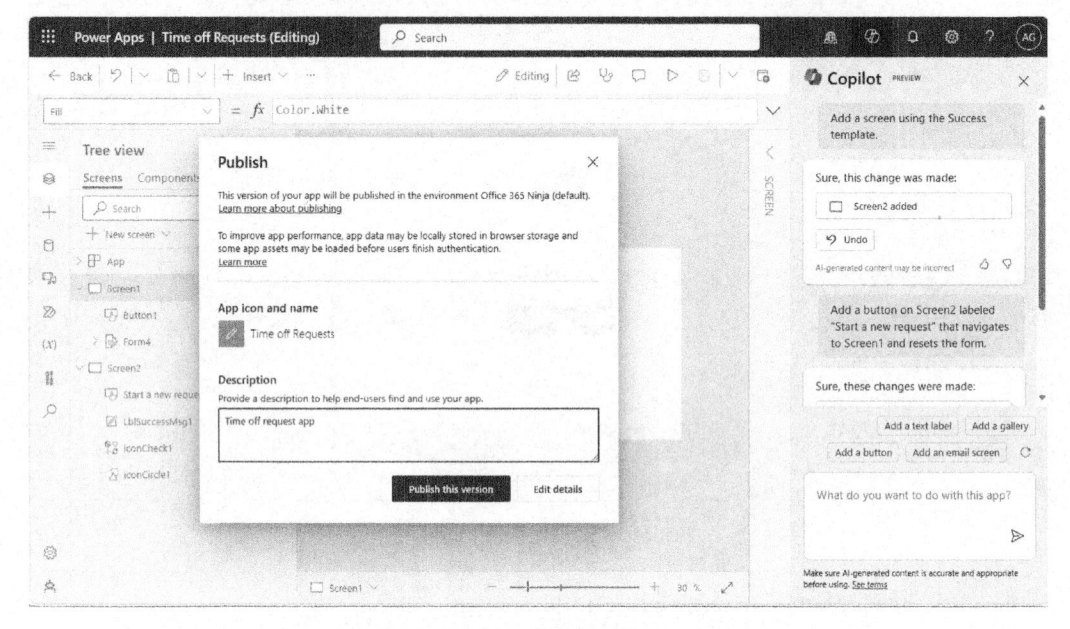

Figure 5.27 – Publishing the app

Next, we'll use Power Automate to launch an approval.

Enabling automation

In this section, you'll use Power Automate to help automate processing and notifications:

1. Navigate to the Power Apps Maker Portal (`https://make.powerapps.com`). Then, expand **Solutions** and select the **Time off Requests** solution.
2. Select **Apps**.
3. Click **New**, point to **Automation**, point to **Cloud flow**, and then select **Automated**:

Building a new Power App with Copilot 91

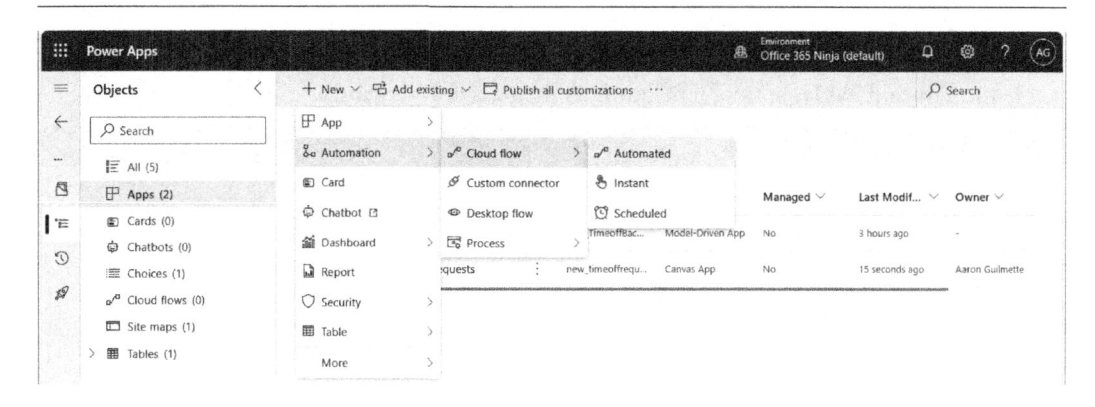

Figure 5.28 – Creating a new flow

4. On the **Build an automated cloud flow** wizard, enter a **Flow name** value and select the **When a row is added, modified, or deleted** Microsoft Dataverse trigger:

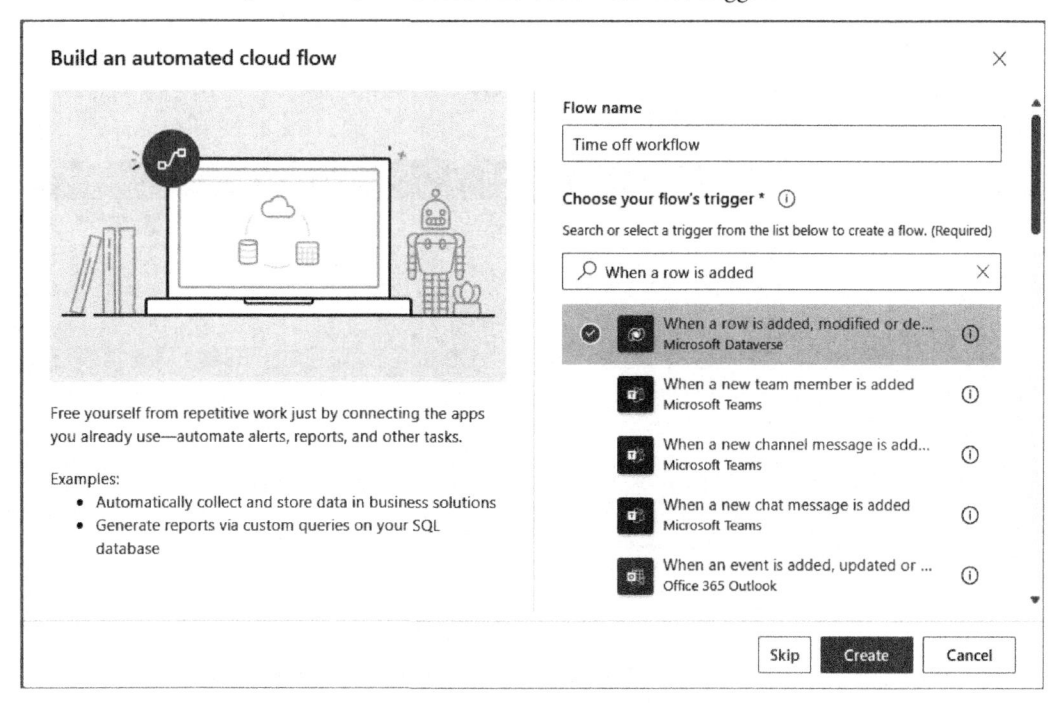

Figure 5.29 – Choosing a trigger

5. Click **Create**.

92 Bootstrapping a Power App with Copilot

6. Update the trigger. To do so, under **Change type**, select **Added**. Then, under **Table name**, select the **Time off Tables** option. Finally, under **Scope**, select **Organization**:

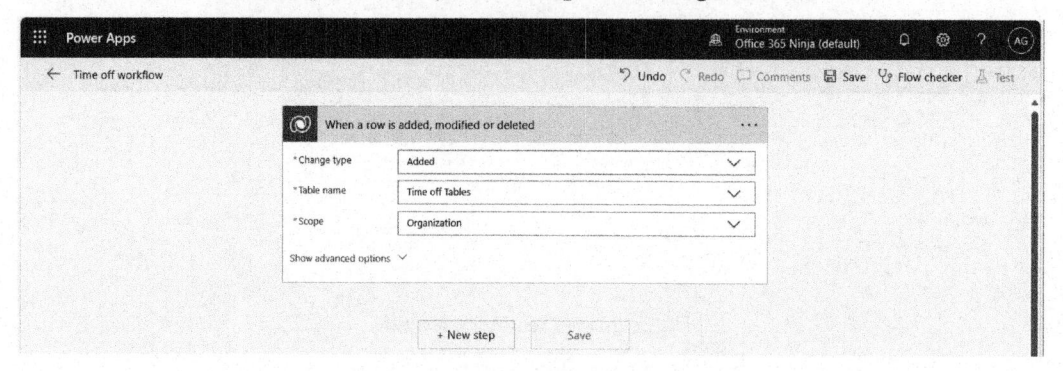

Figure 5.30 – Updating the trigger

7. Click **New step**.
8. In the **Choose an action** box, type `Start and wait` and select the **Start and wait for an approval** action, as shown in *Figure 5.31*:

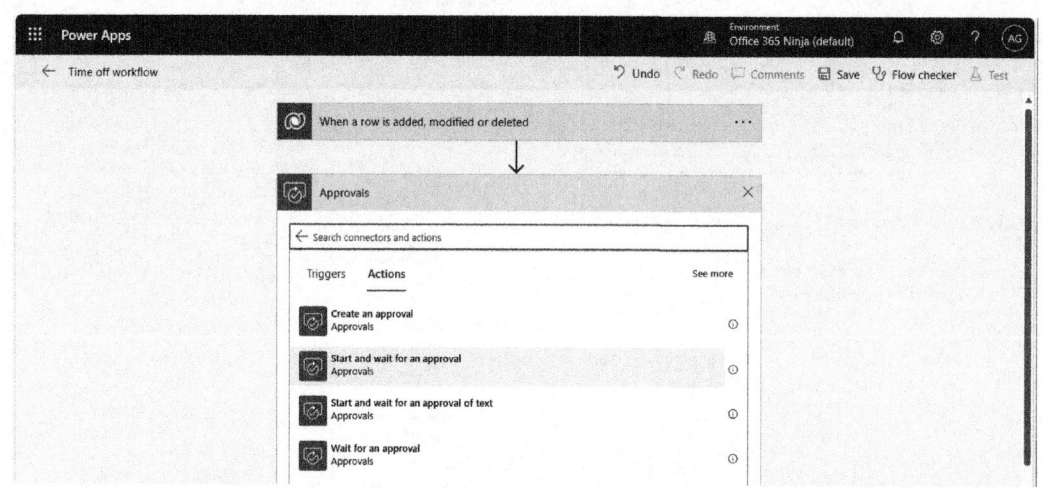

Figure 5.31 – Selecting the Start and wait for an approval action

Building a new Power App with Copilot   93

9. Using **dynamic content** tokens, fill in the approval:

Figure 5.32 – Filling out the approval step

10. Click **New step** and select the **Condition** control.

11. In the first **Choose a value** column, select the **Outcome** dynamic content token. In the second **Choose a value** column, enter `Approve`:

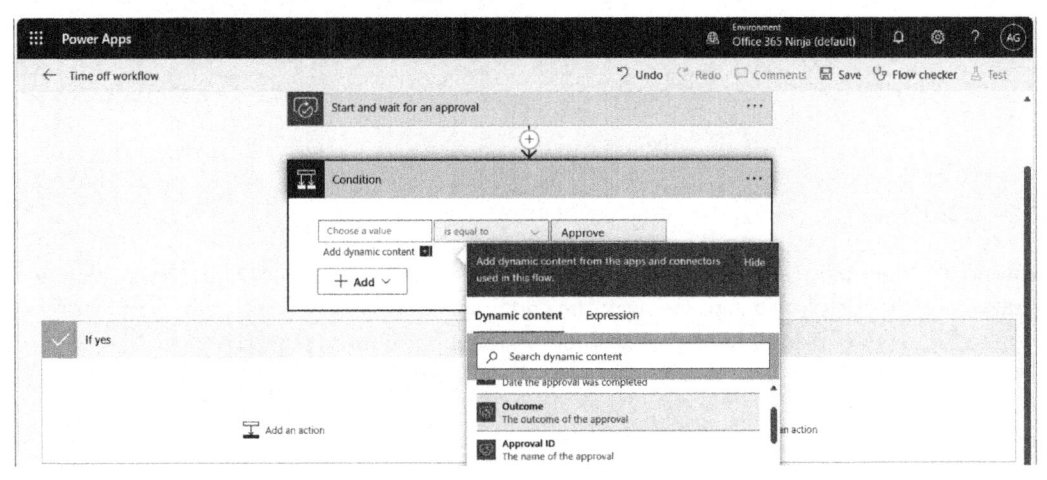

Figure 5.33 – Populating the condition

12. In the **If yes** branch, click **Add an action**.
13. Select **Send an email (V2)**.
14. Populate the email response with dynamic content tokens and text.
15. In the **If no** branch, click **Add an action**.
16. Select **Send an email (V2)**.
17. Populate the email response with dynamic content tokens and text.
18. Review the flow. See *Figure 5.34*:

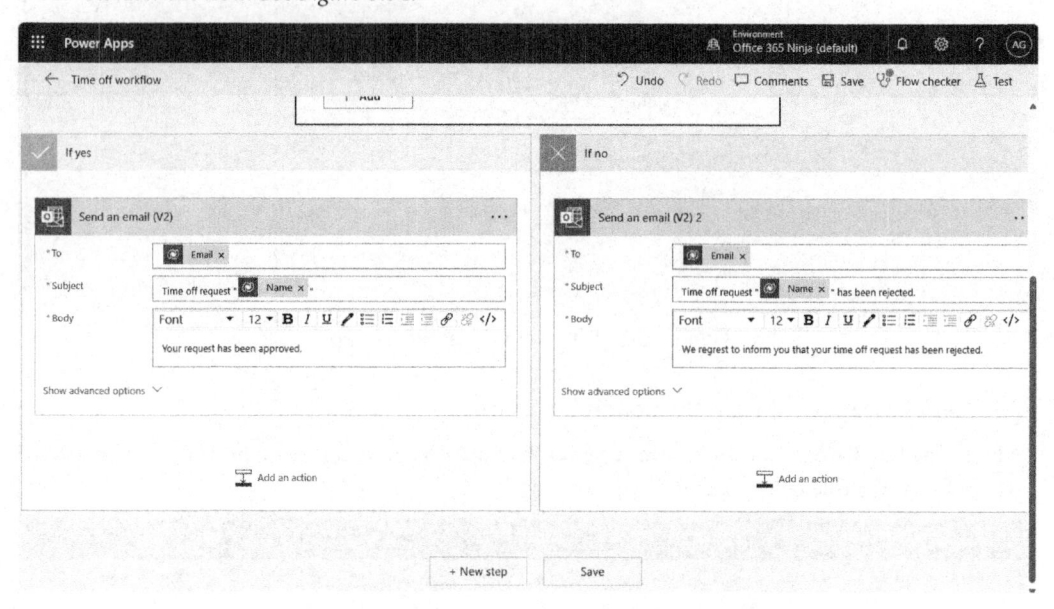

Figure 5.34 – Finishing the flow

19. Click **Save**.

Once you've done this, you can launch the canvas app to input data and then check on the submitted data with the model-driven app. This way, the end users have a simple frontend to work with and managers or approvers have a larger view of the organization's time off requests.

Further exploration

There are several ways to increase the usability of these apps. For example, instead of accepting the default values for the requestor's name or email address (as well as the manager's name and address), you could automatically populate them by changing the **Default** property so that it utilizes the **Office365Users** connector:

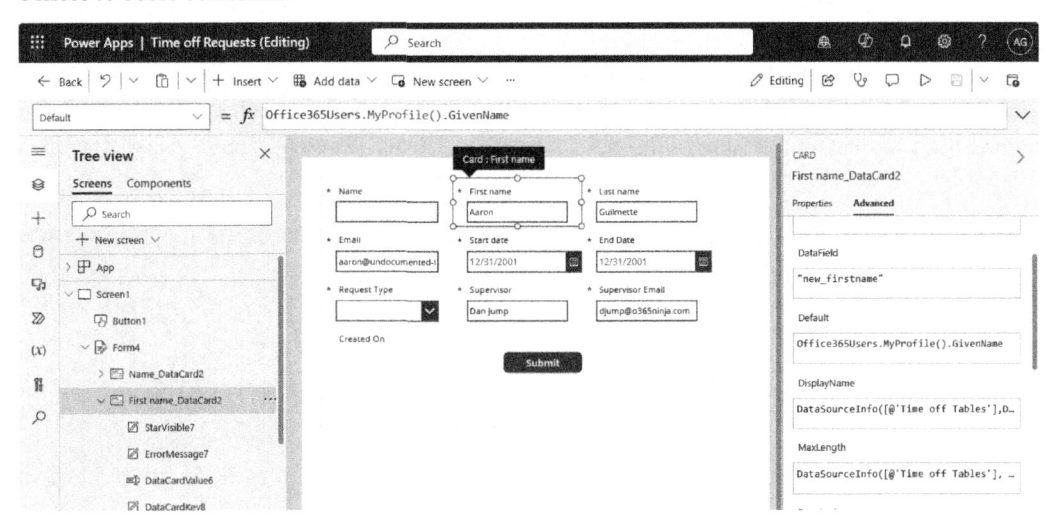

Figure 5.35 – Changing the Default property

Try updating the controls with the values shown in *Table 5.2* to improve the usability of the app:

Field	Updated default property value
First name	`Office365Users.MyProfile().GivenName`
Last name	`Office365Users.MyProfile().SurName`
Email	`Office365Users.MyProfile().Mail`
Supervisor	`Office365Users.Manager(Office365Users.MyProfile().UserPrincipalName).DisplayName`
Supervisor email	`Office365Users.Manager(Office365Users.MyProfile().UserPrincipalName).Mail`

Table 5.2 – Suggested default property values

While this particular solution isn't the most complex, it can be used to demonstrate the capabilities of Power Platform and Copilot.

Summary

Copilot has the potential to be a really powerful addition to a citizen (and pro) developer's toolbox. However, as you can see from our interactions with it, it's neither foolproof nor a replacement for understanding how Power Platform works. At the time of writing, Dataverse and model-driven apps don't have Copilot interfaces, nor does Power Automate when it's started in the context of a Power Platform solution.

Copilot is still in its infancy, so you can expect it to get better over the coming months and years. That being said, if you need to build an app and you're starting from a place of minimal Power Apps knowledge, you may want to start with some of the basics, such as *Learn Microsoft Power Apps, 2nd Edition*, by Matthew Weston and Elisa Barcena Martin.

In the next chapter, we'll explore how to use some of the AI Builder tools that are part of Power Platform to analyze customer feedback.

6
Processing Data with Sentiment Analysis

So far, we've looked at using AI (specifically, Microsoft's Copilot and ChatGPT) to help us create and modify tooling (such as flows and apps). While they can be helpful, it often requires a lot of extra effort to get these types of general-purpose assistants to do very specific step-oriented tasks.

Power Platform allows you to harness AI to make judgments across a wide range of content and data types, helping mimic human evaluations at machine speed.

For instance, humans can easily glance at a business card and discern the person's name and job title, regardless of their placement on the card. However, this task is considerably more challenging for traditional computer logic to execute. As business card designs evolve, data fields shift and become increasingly challenging for traditional automation engines to recognize and identify. AI models introduce contextual awareness to data, simplifying the automation process to mirror human-like performance. Another example might be determining how a customer feels about a particular product or service. It's relatively easy for a human to infer if a customer's email has a happy or angry tone, but it's much more difficult with standard programming logic.

Power Platform provides access to a variety of AI capabilities – whether it's leveraging existing AI models that have been trained for specific types of tasks or feeding data to more general-purpose AI tools to reason over content. Power Platform's native AI models are divided into two categories: **pre-built models** (models trained on specific types of datasets for a narrow content domain) and **custom models** (models that have some core training but require additional customization and training with your data).

What is sentiment analysis, anyway?

Sentiment analysis, simply put, answers the question, *"What type of feelings are present in this content?"* Power Platform's sentiment analysis model can examine a piece of content and return one of the following four sentiments:

- Positive
- Negative
- Neutral
- Mixed

When processing text, the sentiment analysis AI model returns a sentiment value for each sentence, as well as the content as a whole. In addition to the sentiment value, sentiment analysis provides confidence scoring, indicating how confident the model is in its assessment, on a scale of 0 to 1, where 1 represents more confidence and 0 represents less confidence. Sentiment analysis does have its limitations, however – for example, if the content has incorrect or improper word usage – that may influence the ratings.

The scenario in this chapter is based on a fictional company that uses a customer service mailbox as a funnel for comments and complaints. The business objective is to process the emails and determine the sentiment. If the sentiment is negative, the solution should post the message to a Teams channel so that a service representative can follow up with the customer.

Let's get started!

Licensing prerequisites

Using AI models and connectors in Power Platform has several prerequisites:

- A subscription that includes Microsoft Dataverse
- AI Builder capacity (or trial capacity)
- Power Apps or Power Automate premium licensing

The easiest way to get the right amount of licensing is to sign up for a Microsoft 365 E5 trial that includes Power Apps and Power Automate premium licenses, along with a modest amount of AI Builder capacity credits.

If you have an existing Microsoft 365 subscription, you can sign up for Power Apps or Power Automate premium licensing from the Microsoft 365 admin center (`https://admin.microsoft.com`), as shown in *Figure 6.1*:

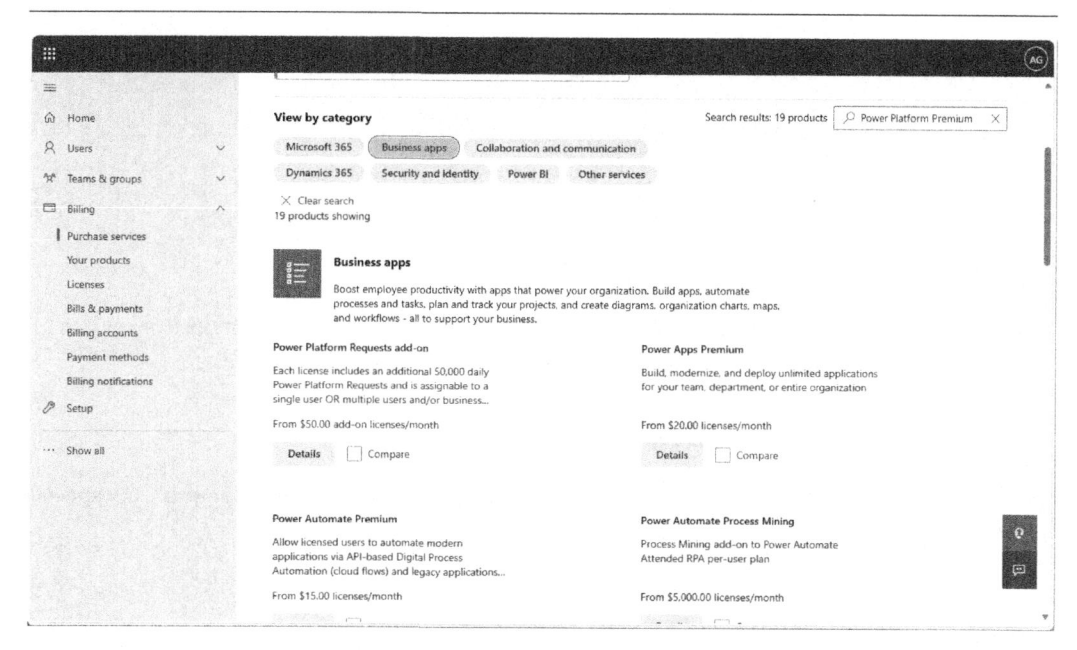

Figure 6.1 – Microsoft 365 admin center

You can review your current allocation of AI Builder capacity in the Power Platform admin center (https://admin.powerplatform.microsoft.com/resources/capacity#add-ons) under **Resources** > **Capacity**, as shown in *Figure 6.2*:

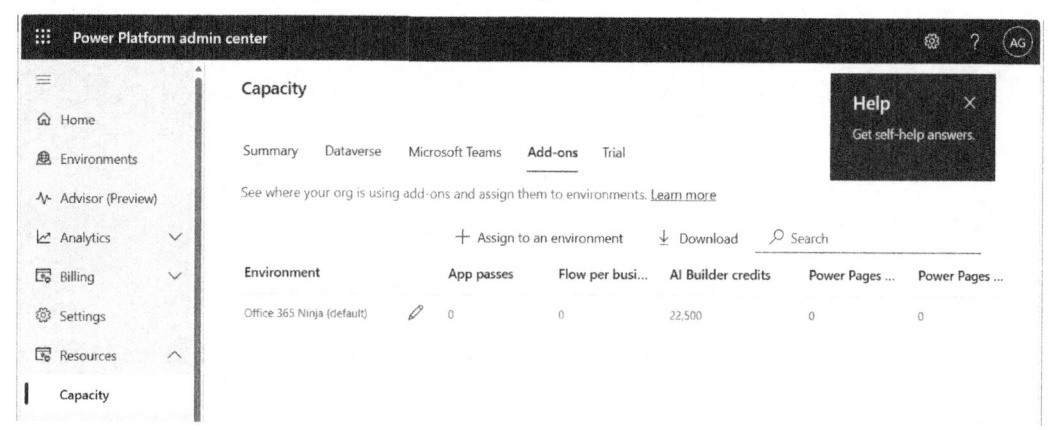

Figure 6.2 – Viewing Power Platform capacity

Next, we'll look at the prerequisites for building the solution.

Configuring solution prerequisites

Once you've got the licensing squared away, you'll need to set up a few things to make this demonstration work:

- A mailbox (either a standard mailbox or a shared mailbox in Exchange Online)
- A Microsoft team with at least the default General channel

While it's not necessary, it's also helpful to have a free email account (such as an Outlook.com or Gmail.com account) that you can use to validate that the solution is working end to end.

Creating a shared mailbox

First, we'll walk through creating a shared mailbox. A shared mailbox doesn't require any special licensing for itself, though it does require a licensed user to access it:

1. Log into the Microsoft 365 admin center (https://admin.microsoft.com). From there, expand **Teams & groups** and select **Shared mailboxes**.
2. Click **Add a shared mailbox**, as shown in *Figure 6.3*:

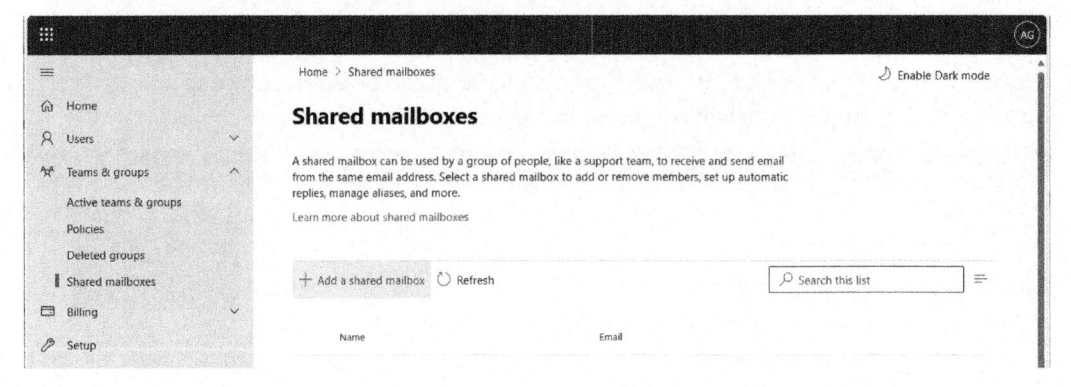

Figure 6.3 – Viewing shared mailboxes

3. On the **Add a shared mailbox** flyout, enter a **Name** value and adjust the **Email** address as necessary:

Configuring solution prerequisites 101

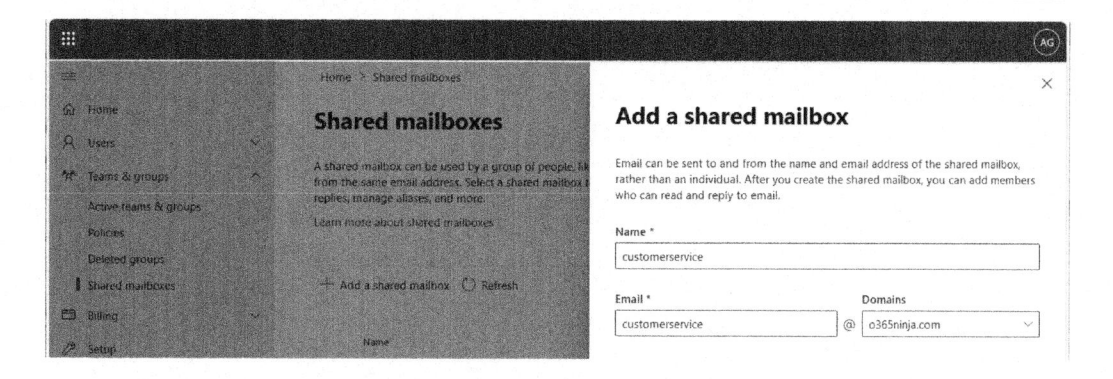

Figure 6.4 – Creating a shared mailbox

4. Click **Add members to your shared mailbox**:

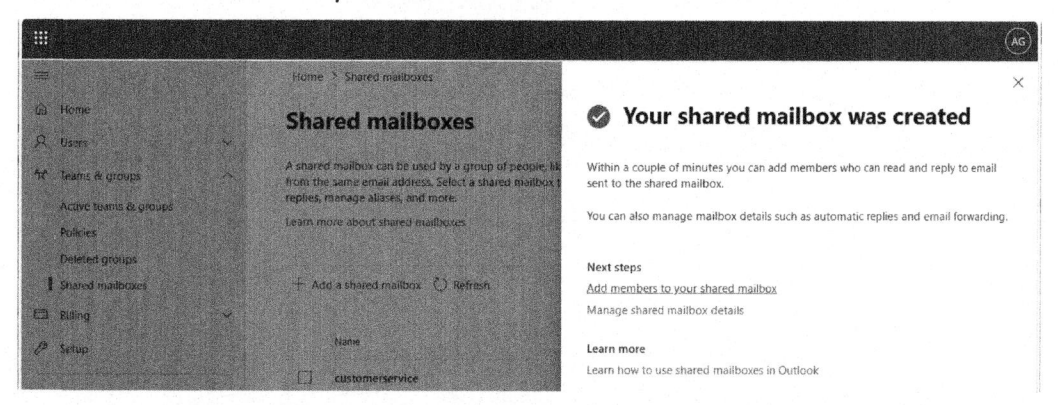

Figure 6.5 – Viewing the newly created mailbox

5. On the **Shared mailbox members** flyout, click **Add members**, select at least one user in the organization that has a mailbox license, and click **Add**.
6. Close the flyout.

When working with Power Automate, you'll need to use the credentials for the account you granted access to in *step 5*.

Next, you'll need to create a team.

Creating a Microsoft Teams team

The Microsoft Teams team will be used to receive notifications from Power Automate. To create a team from the Microsoft 365 admin center, follow these steps:

> **All roads lead to Rome**
>
> There are lots of ways to do the same task in Microsoft 365. While this set of steps details creating a team through the Microsoft 365 admin center (since we're already there), you can also do it directly from Microsoft Teams. To learn how to use Teams to accomplish this task, go to `https://support.microsoft.com/en-au/office/create-a-team-from-scratch-in-microsoft-teams-174adf5f-846b-4780-b765-de1a0a737e2b`.

1. From the Microsoft 365 admin center (`https://admin.microsoft.com`), expand **Teams & groups** and then select **Active teams and groups**.
2. On the **Teams & Microsoft 365 groups** tab, click **Add a team**.
3. On the **Basics** page of the **Add a team** wizard, provide a **Name** value for the team and click **Next**:

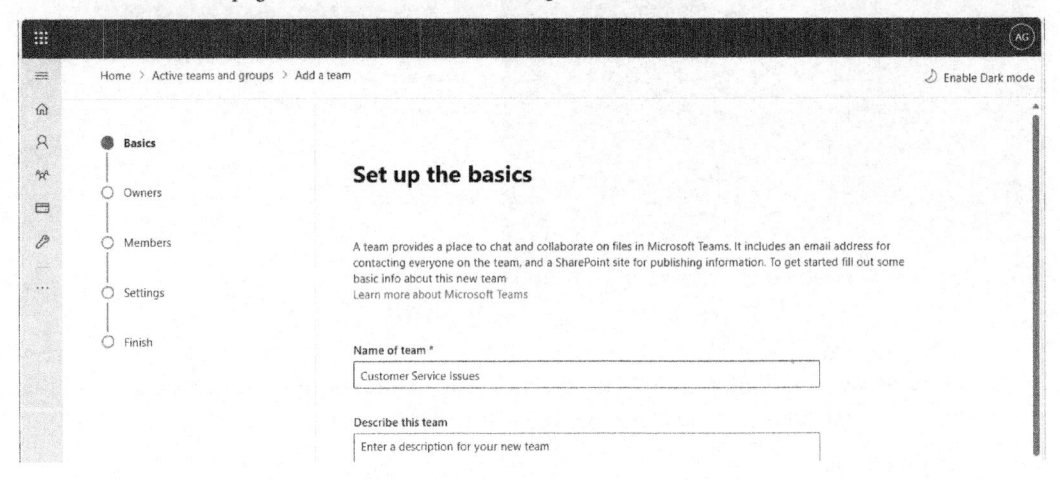

Figure 6.6 – Creating a new team

4. On the **Owners** page, add at least one owner (such as the account managing the shared mailbox). Then, click **Next**.
5. On the **Members** page, add any additional members and click **Next**.

6. On the **Settings** page, enter a **Team email address** value. Then, click **Next**:

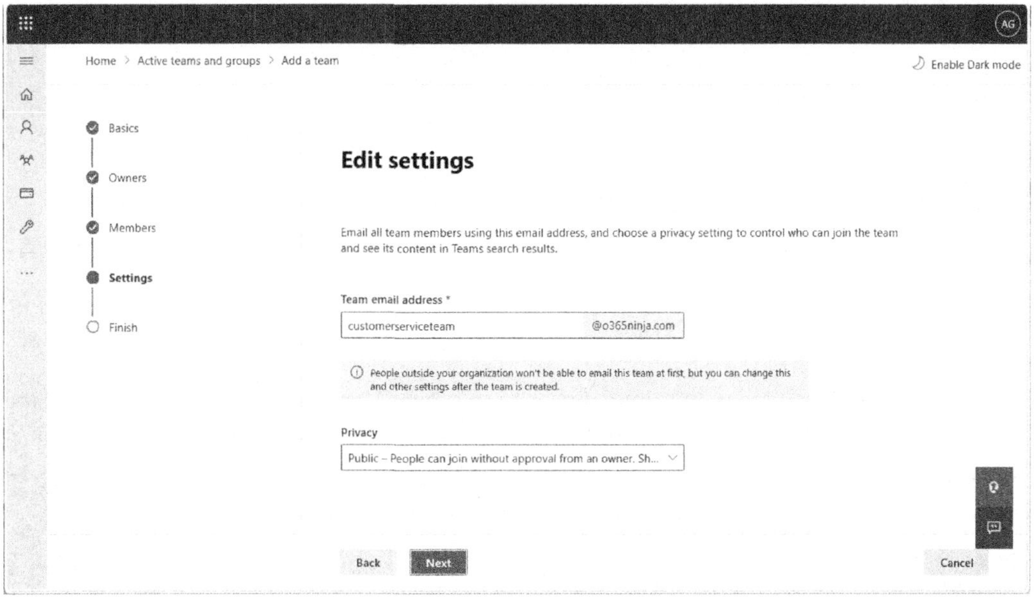

Figure 6.7 – Configuring an email address for the team

7. On the **Finish** page, review the settings and click **Add team**.

Now, it's on to the fun part!

Configuring a sentiment analysis flow

As you learned earlier in this chapter, sentiment analysis provides a mechanism to evaluate content's tone and provide an output. To address the business scenario of responding to negative customer feedback, you can use a sentiment analysis flow to process messages that are received by the shared mailbox.

> **What do I do if I'm stuck?**
> If you run into a roadblock for some reason (can't find a feature, an option isn't showing up, or something is unclear), help is only a click away! You can download this chapter's artifacts from our GitHub site: https://github.com/PacktPublishing/Power-Platform-and-the-AI-Revolution.

Let's create the flow:

1. Navigate to the Power Automate Maker Portal (https://make.powerautomate.com).
2. From the navigation menu, select **Create**.

3. Under **Start from blank**, select **Automated cloud flow**:

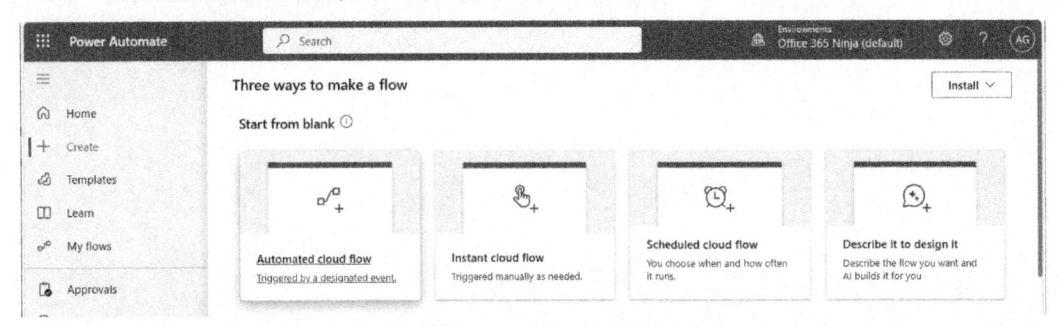

Figure 6.8 – Starting a new flow

4. On the **Build an automated cloud flow** wizard, enter a **Flow name** value and then select the **When a new email arrives in a shared mailbox (V2)** trigger. Click **Create** once you're done:

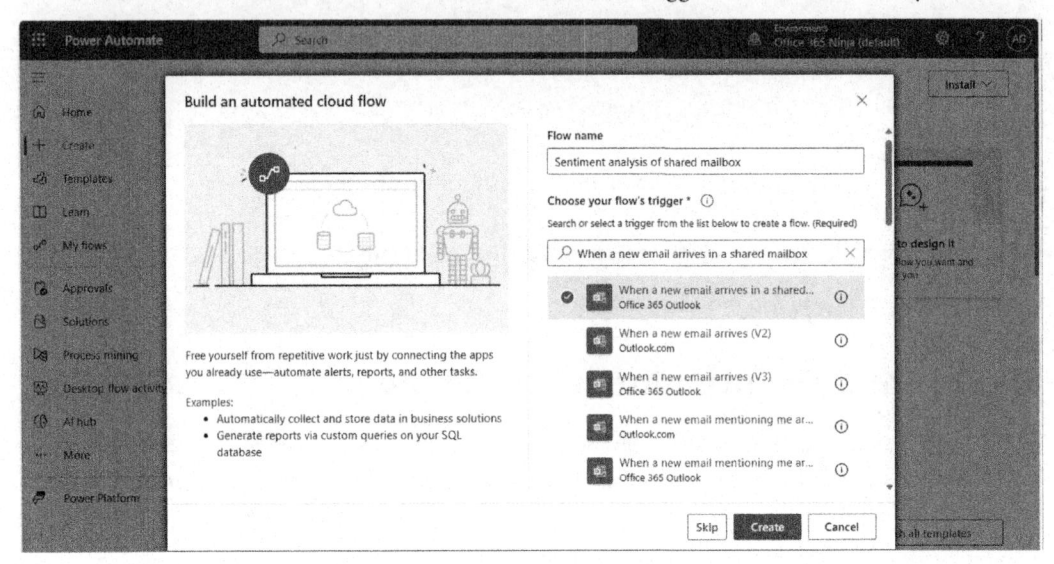

Figure 6.9 – Selecting the flow's trigger

5. In the canvas area, select the **When a new email arrives in a shared mailbox (V2)** trigger.
6. On the flyout, click the **Change connection** link if the screen displays a message about an invalid connection. See *Figure 6.10*:

Configuring a sentiment analysis flow   105

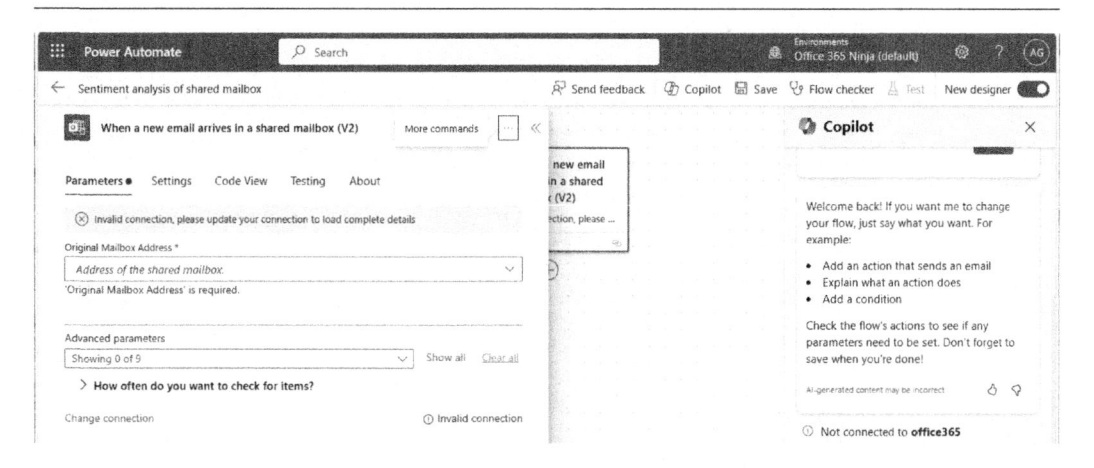

Figure 6.10 – Configuring the shared mailbox

7. Select the credential that will be used to authenticate to the mailbox. If the credential is not listed, click **Add new** and provide the username and password for an account that has access to the shared mailbox.

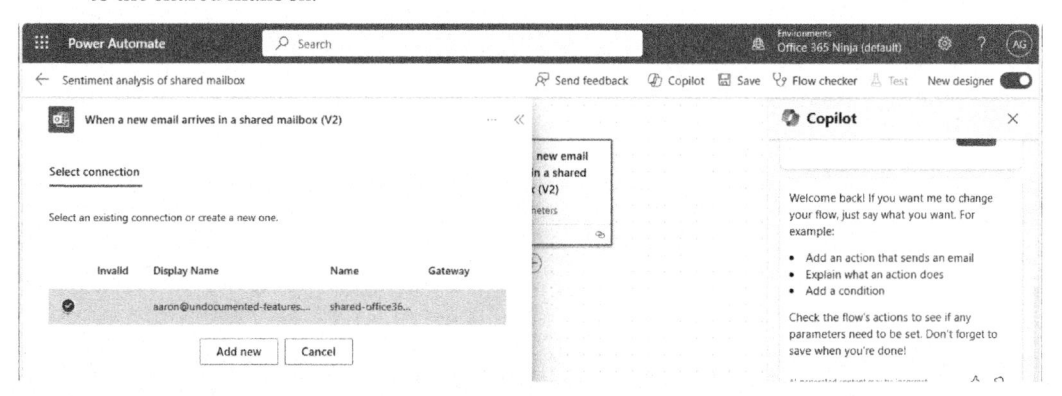

Figure 6.11 – Updating the connection settings

8. On the **Parameters** tab of the flyout, enter the email address of the shared mailbox that will be used to receive customer emails. When prompted, select **Use <email address> as a custom value**.
9. Click the << (**Collapse**) icon to close the flyout.

10. In the canvas area, click the + icon under the trigger to add a new step and then click **Add an action**:

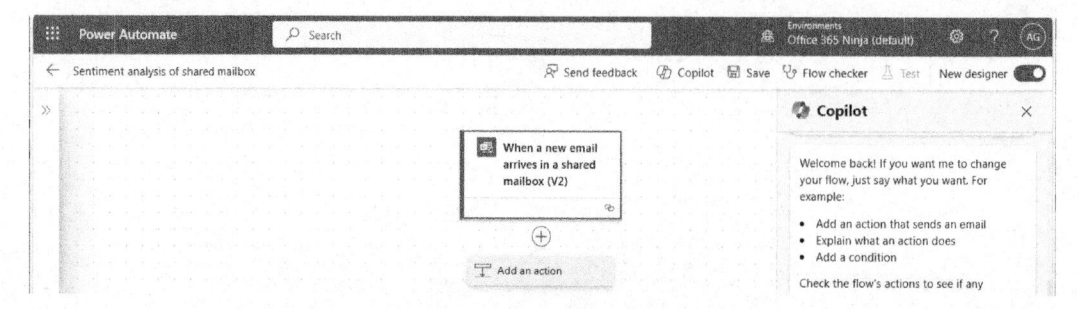

Figure 6.12 – Adding a new action

11. In the **Add an action** flyout, type `detect` in the search box and select the **Detect the language being used in text** action, as shown in *Figure 6.13*:

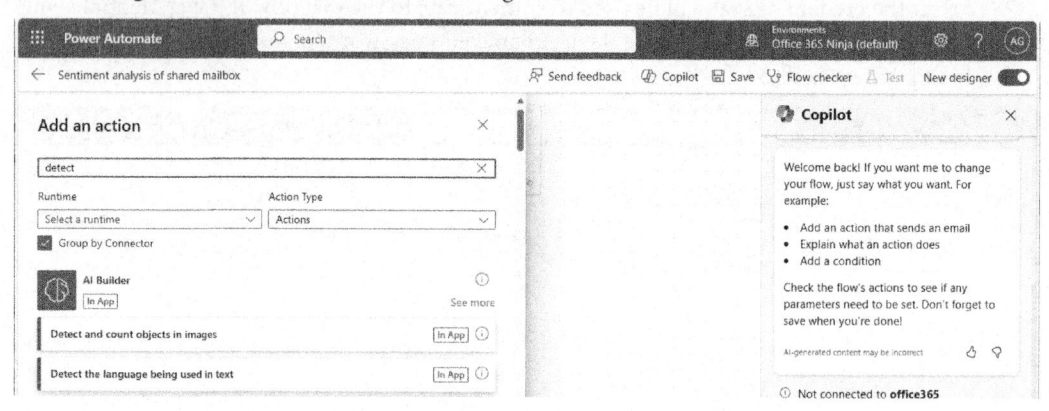

Figure 6.13 – Choosing the Detect the language being used in text action

Configuring a sentiment analysis flow   107

12. In the **Detect the language being used** flyout, click inside the **Text** box. Select the lightning bolt icon to expand the dynamic content picker:

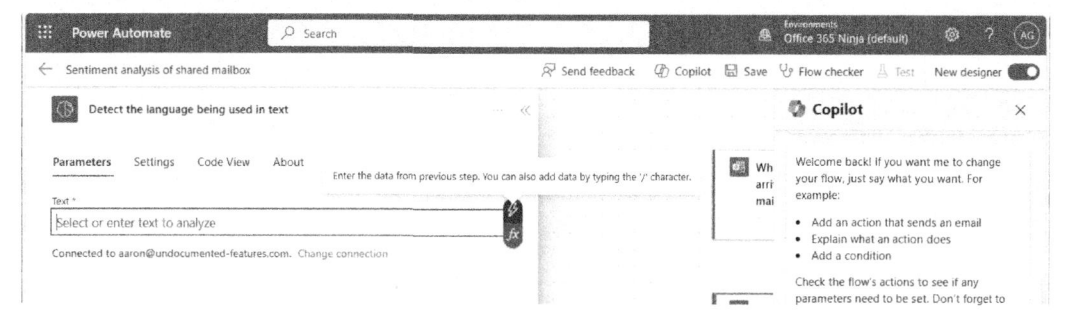

Figure 6.14 – Configuring the Detect the language being used in text action

13. Select the **Body** token:

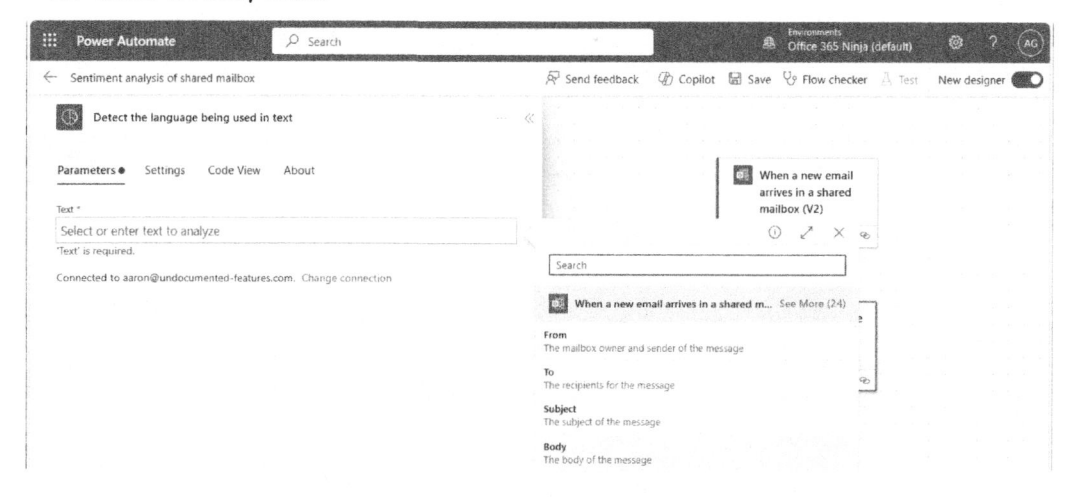

Figure 6.15 – Selecting the Body token

14. Collapse the flyout.
15. Click the + icon outside the **For each** loop component and select **Add an action**.
16. In the **Add an action** flyout, type `sentiment analysis` in the search box and select the **Analyze positive or negative sentiment in text** action.

Processing Data with Sentiment Analysis

17. On the **Analyze positive or negative sentiment in text** flyout, choose the **Language** dropdown and select **Enter a custom value**. Select the lightning bolt icon to display the dynamic content picker:

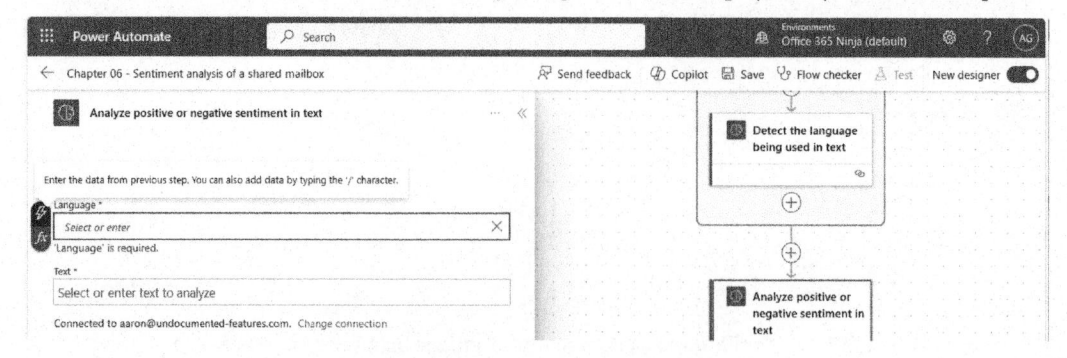

Figure 6.16 – Configuring the Language field

18. Select the lightning bolt icon to display the dynamic content picker.
19. In the dynamic content picker, under the **Detect the language being used in the text** action, select the **Language** dynamic content token:

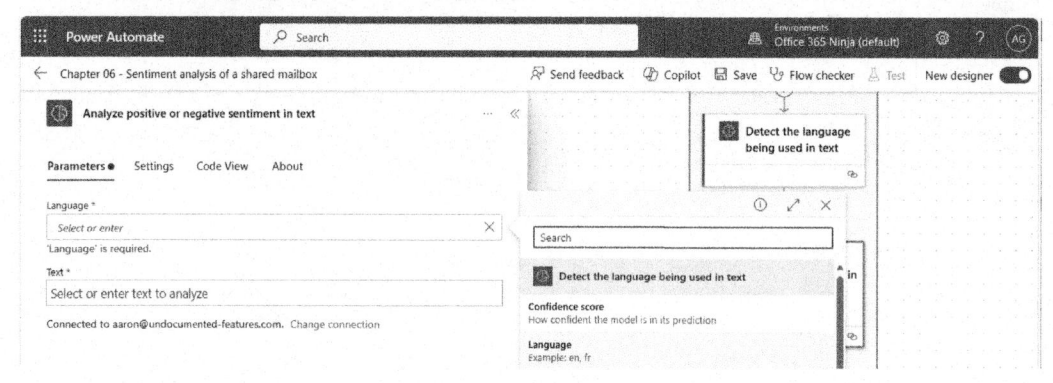

Figure 6.17 – Choosing the Language dynamic content token

20. Click inside the **Text** field and select the dynamic content picker.
21. In the dynamic content picker, under the **When a new email arrives in a shared mailbox (V2)** action, select the **Body** token.
22. Collapse the flyout.

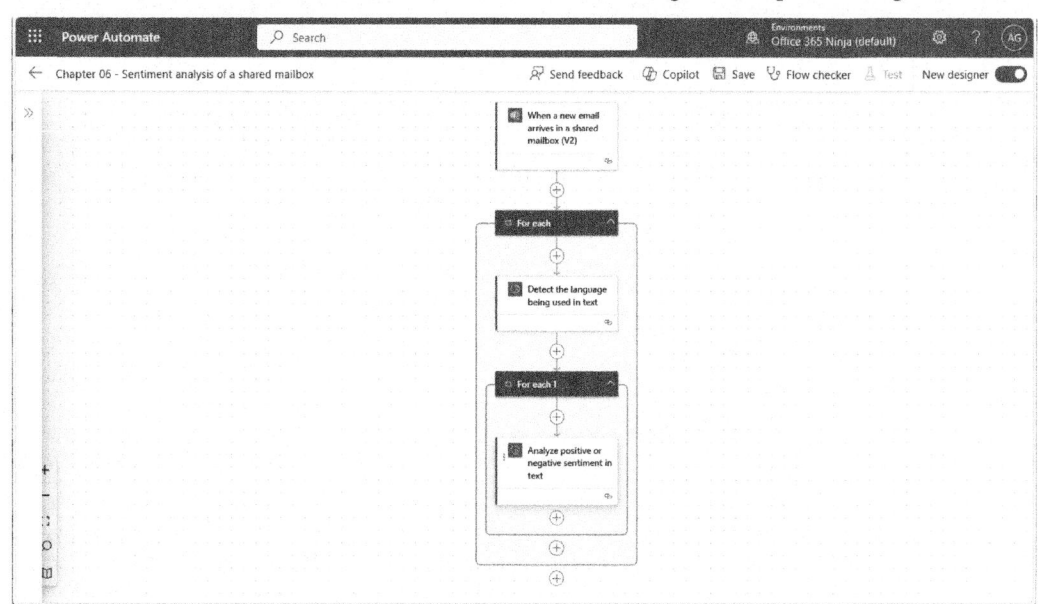

23. Review the flow so far. It should look similar to the arrangement depicted in *Figure 6.18*:

Figure 6.18 – Reviewing the current state of the flow

24. Inside the nested **For each** loop container containing the **Analyze positive or negative sentiment in text** action, click the + icon to **Add an action**.
25. In the **Add an action** flyout, enter `condition` in the search box and select the **Condition** action located under **Control**.
26. In the **Condition** flyout, click inside the left textbox and choose the dynamic content picker.
27. In the dynamic content picker, under **Analyze positive or negative sentiment in text**, choose the **Overall text sentiment** token. If that token doesn't display in the default list of choices, you may need to click **See more**:

Processing Data with Sentiment Analysis

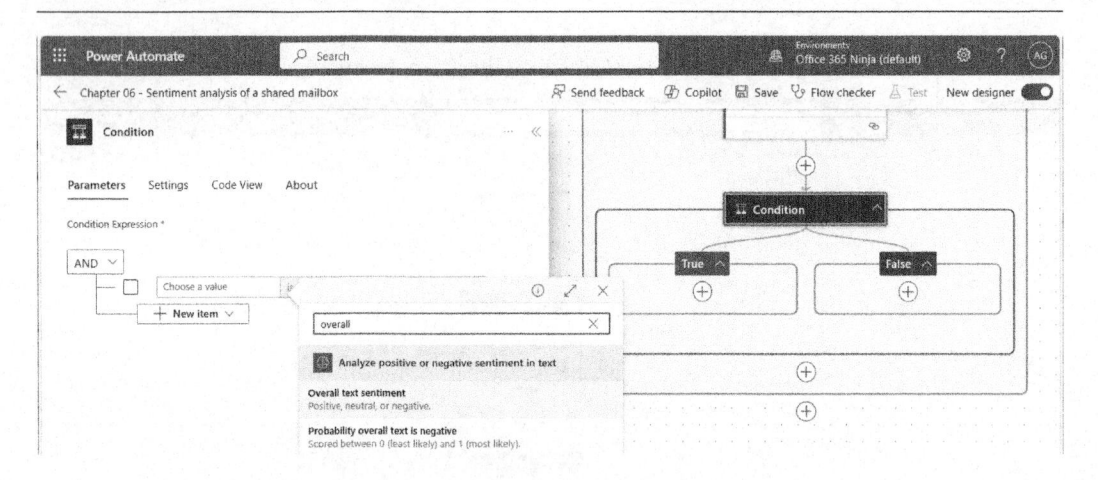

Figure 6.19 – Selecting the Overall text sentiment token

28. In the right textbox, enter `negative`:

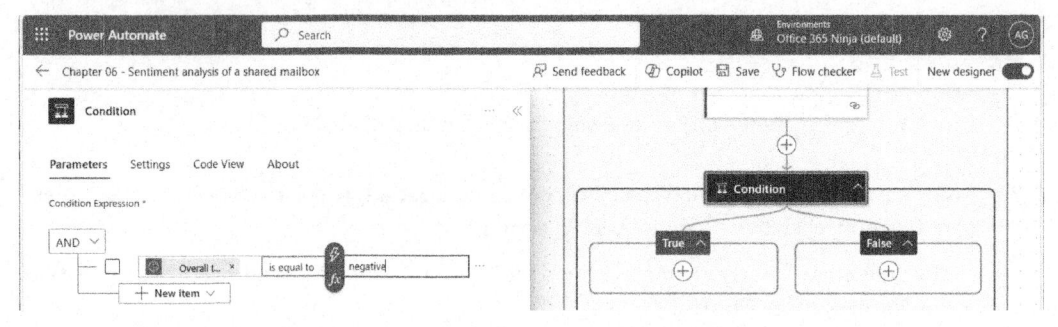

Figure 6.20 – Configuring the condition evaluation

29. Collapse the flyout.
30. In the **True** branch of the condition, click the + icon to **Add an action**.
31. In the search box, enter `post message` and select the **Post message in a chat or channel** Microsoft Teams action:

Configuring a sentiment analysis flow   111

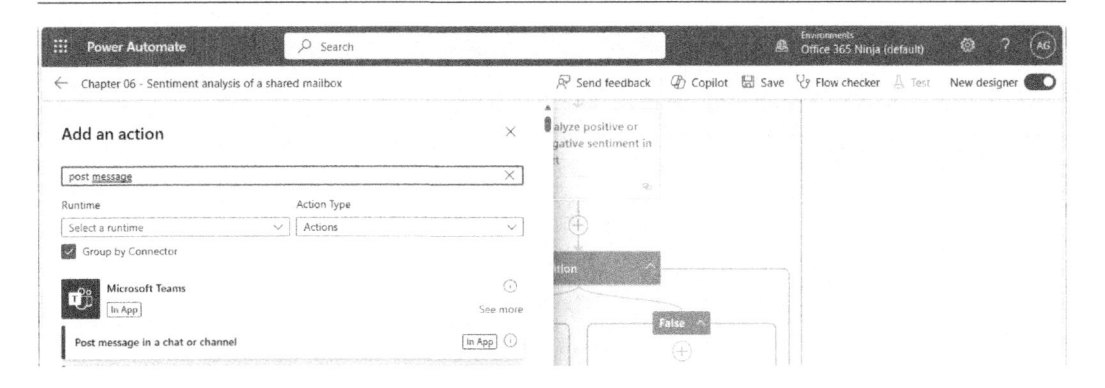

Figure 6.21 – Adding the Post message in a chat or channel action

32. On the **Post message in a chat or channel** flyout, click **Sign in** to create a connection. Provide credentials for the user account that will be used to post to Teams.
33. In the **Post As** dropdown, select **Flow bot**.
34. In the **Post In** dropdown, select **Channel**.
35. In the **Team** dropdown, search for the team you created in the *Licensing prerequisites* section.
36. In the **Channel** drop-down, select **General**.
37. In the **Message** textbox, add details for the message to be posted to the channel. You can use rich text formatting options, as well as select from dynamic content tokens. See *Figure 6.22*:

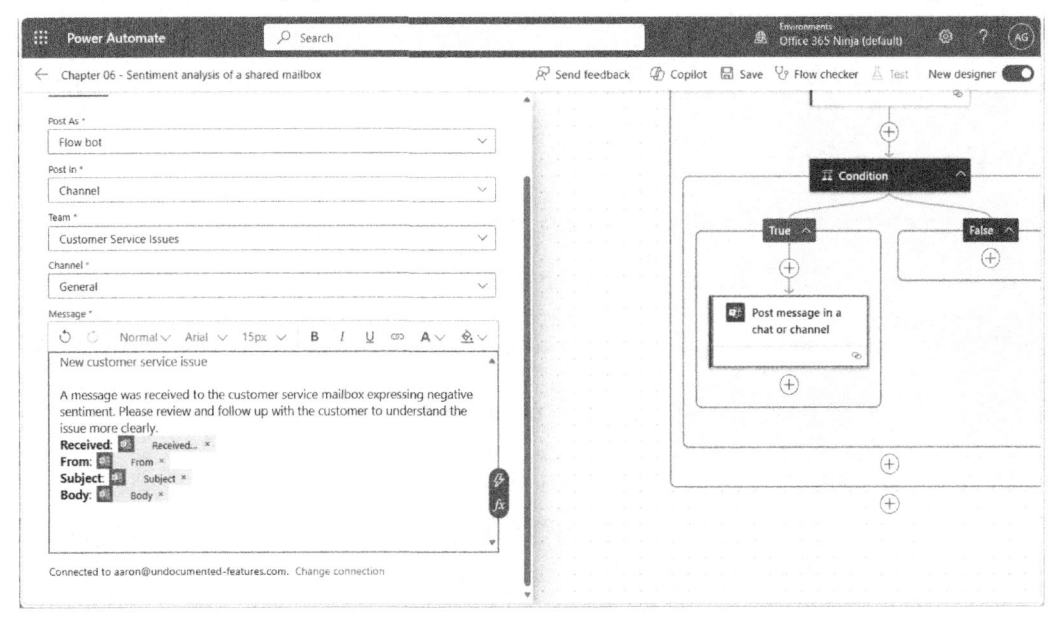

Figure 6.22 – Configuring the Post message in a chat or channel action

112   Processing Data with Sentiment Analysis

38. Collapse the flyout.
39. Review the flow's layout and check for any obvious errors. See *Figure 6.23*:

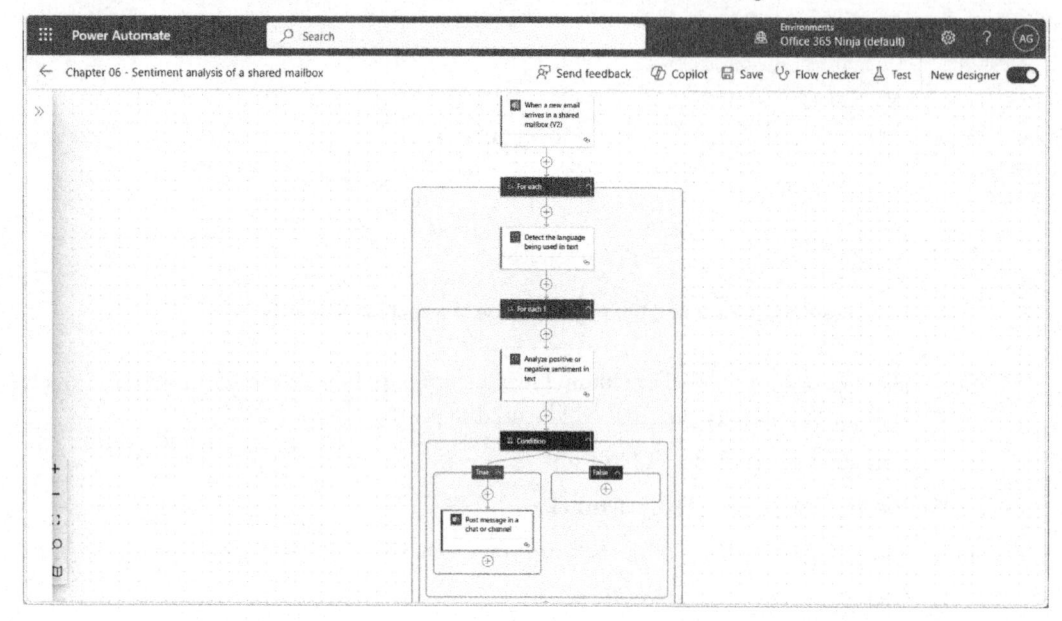

Figure 6.23 – Reviewing the overall flow

40. On the menu bar, click **Save** to save the flow.

Review the flow to make sure the steps have been configured. Once you're done, it's time to test it!

Testing the flow

Now, it's time to make sure everything works as anticipated:

1. From the menu bar, select the **beaker** icon (**Test**):

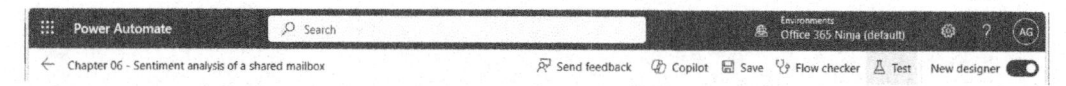

Figure 6.24 – Testing the flow

2. Select the **Manually** radio button and click **Test**.
3. Test your flow by sending an email to the configured shared mailbox. Be sure to word it strongly to ensure you are expressing disapproval:

Send	To	○ customerservice;
	Cc	
	Bcc	
	Subject	Recently purchased the Widget 2000

Hi,

I recently purchased the Widget 2000. The product arrived broken. I called customer support and was placed on hold for 2 hours, after which I was told to mail back my defective product. After exchanging it via mail for a replacement, that product was also defective. I am very disappointed with the overall experience and demand a refund.

Figure 6.25 – Composing a test email

4. After sending the email, the flow run history should begin to update in the Power Automate Maker Portal:

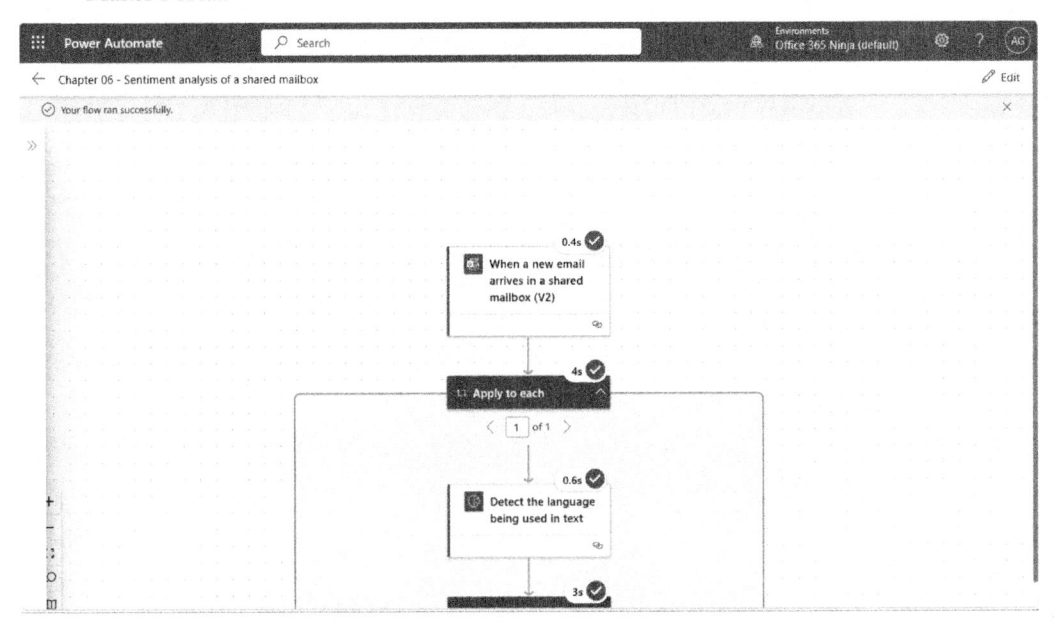

Figure 6.26 – Flow execution results

5. Open Microsoft Teams (or navigate to `https://teams.microsoft.com`) and validate that the channel post has been made:

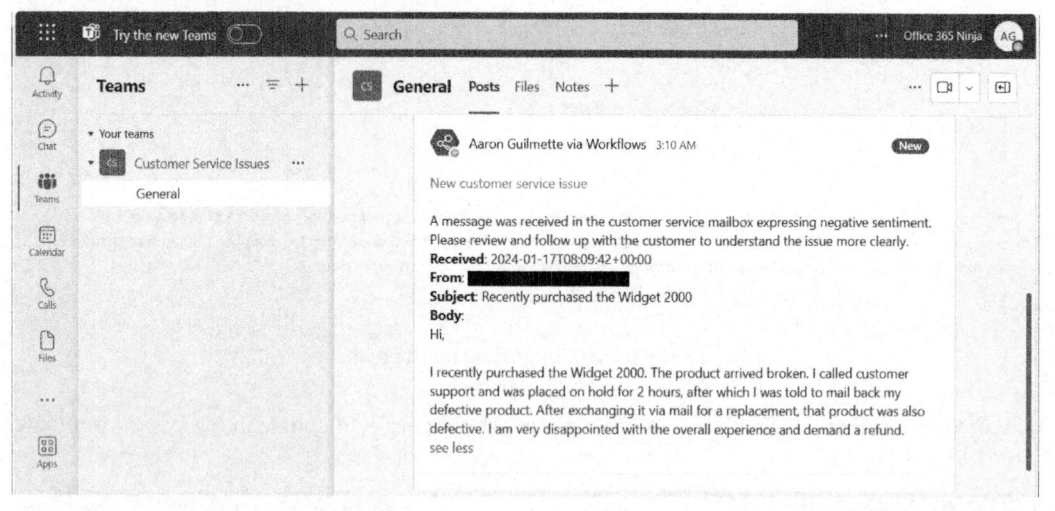

Figure 6.27 – Verifying the channel post

Further exploration

Depending on your requirements and other connected systems, you may be able to expand and enhance this solution, including workflows that do the following:

- Connect to an e-commerce platform and generate a coupon code for a discount on future purchases
- Respond to a customer via email and initiate a refund
- Integrate with a delivery carrier to generate a mailing label

With that covered, let's summarize what we learned in this chapter.

Summary

AI Builder models have a lot of capabilities out of the box. In this chapter, you learned how to leverage AI to process emails that are received in a customer service mailbox. With the sentiment analysis model, you were able to detect whether an email had an overall positive or negative tone and then trigger an additional action to post a notification in a Teams channel conversation.

In the next chapter, we'll explore using Power Automate with AI services to transform a simple Word document into a PowerPoint presentation.

7

Using Power Automate and AI to Build PowerPoint Presentations

If you've ever been faced with a last-minute requirement to prepare a presentation for your boss or an activity club, you're not alone. Whether it's familiar content or something you've never seen before, condensing information and making it accessible to an audience is no small task.

In this chapter, we'll start with everyone's favorite open source knowledge base, Wikipedia, and use ChatGPT to summarize sections of it and insert it into a PowerPoint deck.

With a little bit of tweaking, you can reuse this same type of summarization tooling on documents stored in SharePoint, internal corporate websites, or other digital content sources.

Licensing prerequisites

Using AI models and connectors in Power Platform has several prerequisites:

- A subscription that includes Microsoft Dataverse
- AI Builder capacity (or trial capacity)
- Power Apps or Power Automate premium licensing

If you haven't already enabled Dataverse and AI Builder capacity, see *Chapter 2, Configuring an Environment to Support AI Services*, and *Chapter 6, Processing Data with Sentiment Analysis*.

Since Power Automate does not have a native connector for PowerPoint, this particular solution requires a third-party connector product by software vendor **Encodian**. This connector allows you to transform standard Power Automate objects into PowerPoint content.

Encodian offers a free 30-day trial, including 500 credits, of the Flowr connector at `https://www.encodian.com/product/flowr/`:

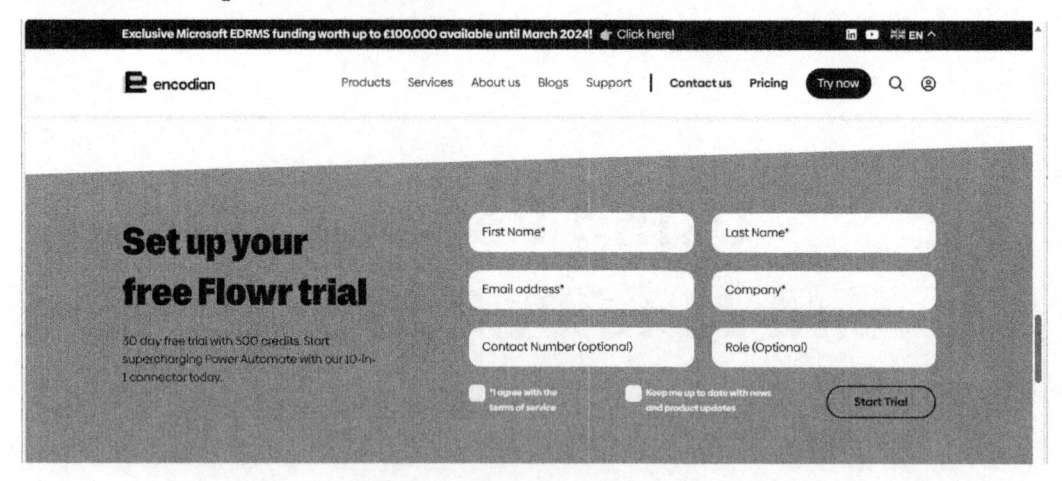

Figure 7.1 – Establishing a Flowr trial

After signing up, you will receive an API key (sample shown in *Figure 7.2*) that you can use to configure the Encodian connector in Power Automate:

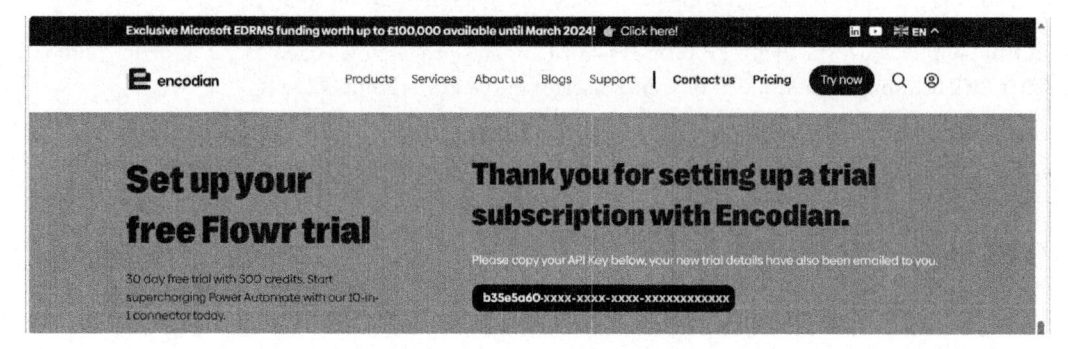

Figure 7.2 – Sample Encodian API key

Once that's activated, you'll want to build a generic PowerPoint template file that can be saved and reused whenever you need it!

Learning about the Encodian Flowr connector

Before you get started working on a flow, you'll need to understand how to use the Encodian Flowr connector and its actions. In this section, we'll look at the critical pieces that are needed to make this flow work. To successfully work with the connector and actions, you'll need to understand the following concepts, terminology, and actions:

- Input formatting
- Tokens
- The **Populate PowerPoint** action
- The **Merge Presentations** action

Let's take a quick look at each of these areas!

Input formatting

Many of Encodian's content manipulation actions require the use of structured data. In this case, structured data is typically supplied in the **JavaScript Object Notation (JSON)** syntax:

```
{
    "object1" : "value1",
    "object2" :  "value2—electric boogaloo"
}
```

As shown in this simple example, the JSON text is formatted as a **key/value** (think *term:definition*) pair. JSON, like many programming constructs, also has the concept of **arrays** or **collections**. An array or collection is a group of similar objects.

Let's say you wanted to list a collection containing various kinds of foods. It might look something like this when formatted as JSON:

```
{
  "foods": [{
    "category": "fruit",
    "data": [
      {"type": "orange","count": 1},
      {"type": "strawberry","count": 7},
      {"type": "apple","count": 3}]
    },
    {
    "category": "grain",
    "data": [
      {"type": "sorghum","count": 1},
```

```
        {"type": "wheat","count": 3}]
    }]
}
```

In the `foods` JSON object, you can see several examples of how data values are specified. There are both standard key/value pairs (as in `"category":"fruit"`), which identify a single object, as well as arrays (such as `"data": [ {"type": "sorghum","count":1"}, {"type":"wheat","count": 3}]`), which are used to identify groups of key/value pairs.

A JSON object can include a variety of data types, including **strings** (text), **integers** (numbers), **arrays** (collections of strings or key/value pairs), **Boolean** values (True or False), as well as other JSON objects.

> **Further reading**
>
> JSON is an extraordinarily flexible format for working with structured content since it's both human-readable as well as platform and language-agnostic. For more information on working with JSON objects and syntax, see `https://www.w3schools.com/JS/js_json_intro.asp`. You can also use tools such as `https://jsonformatter.org/` to help ensure your JSON is formatted correctly.

Tokens

Several of the Flowr actions work with specially formatted **tags** (or **tokens**, as Encodian refers to them), which the connector will use in a find-and-replace fashion with the content you supply.

Let's say, for example, you wanted Flowr to place the words or phrase "The quick brown fox did some things" inside a document. You might decide to assign that phrase to a token named `fox`. Inside the document template, you would indicate the locations you want this text to appear in by typing the token name surrounded by a series of square and angled brackets:

```
<<[fox]>>
```

See *Figure 7.3* for an example of a token inside a PowerPoint slide:

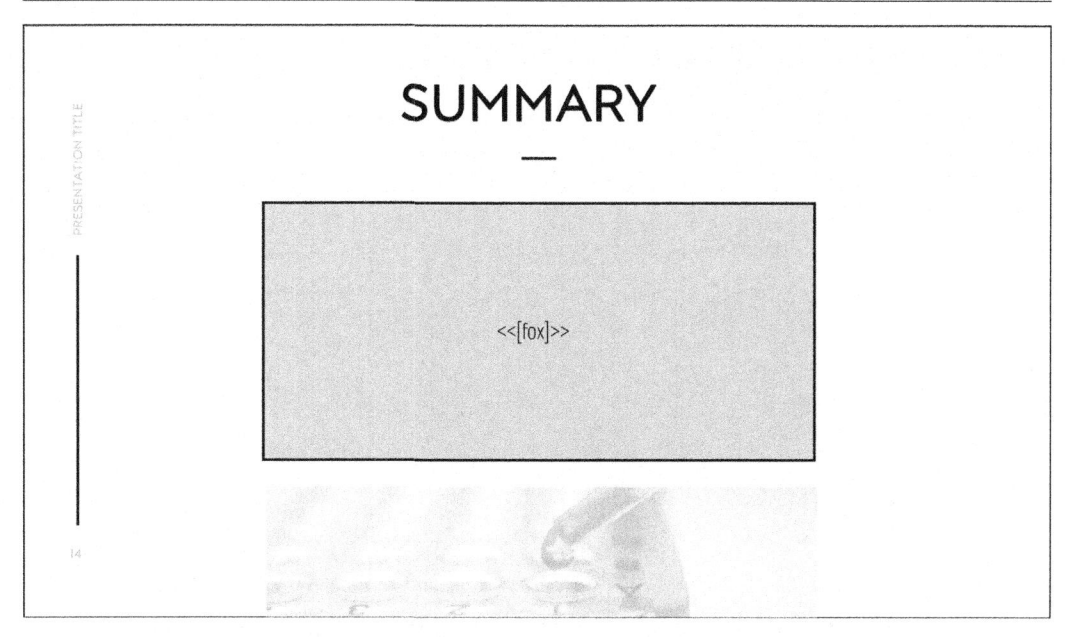

Figure 7.3 – Viewing the <<[fox]>> token inside a PowerPoint slide

Populate PowerPoint

The **Populate PowerPoint** action does just what it says – it's the primary action that's used to place content into a PowerPoint slide. After assigning values to the tokens, the **Populate PowerPoint** action will search the template files, replacing the tokens with the values. The inputs to this will be the token/content key/value pairs and any source PowerPoint template files. The output will be a completed PowerPoint slide.

Merge Presentations

Finally, the **Merge Presentations** action can be used to compile the modified PowerPoint pages into a single, cohesive document. The inputs will be the generated PowerPoint files (typically, one slide per file) and the output will be a single multi-slide PowerPoint deck.

Now that you're familiar with the core concepts that we'll be using during the flow, it's time to start working!

Interacting with Wikipedia articles

Since the source of our content for this example is going to be a Wikipedia article, it's important to understand how to gather the data. Wikipedia has an API endpoint (`https://en.wikipedia.org/w/api.php`) that returns the page content as JSON, as shown in *Figure 7.4*:

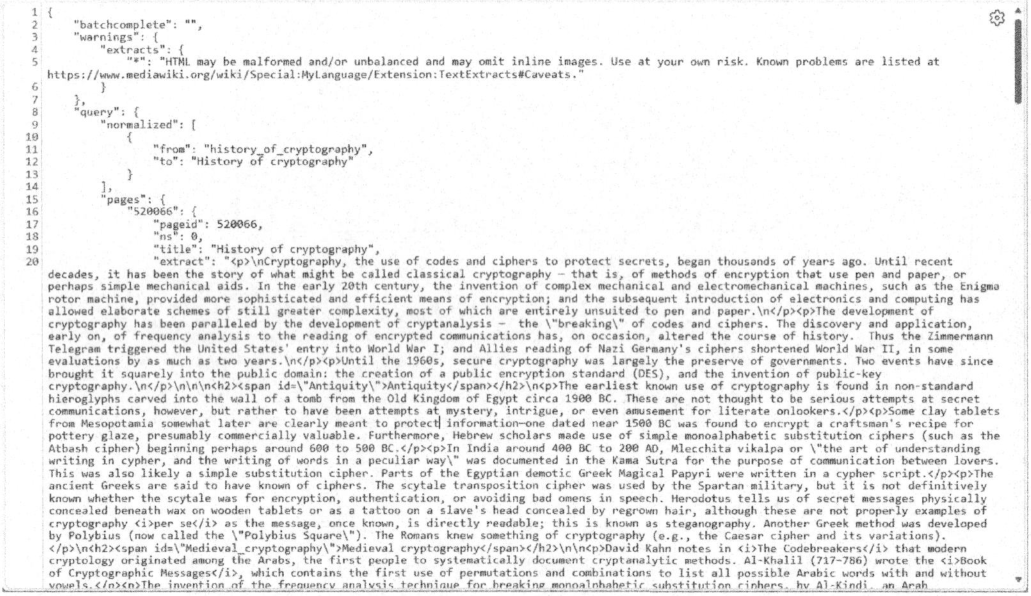


```
{
    "batchcomplete": "",
    "warnings": {
        "extracts": {
            "*": "HTML may be malformed and/or unbalanced and may omit inline images. Use at your own risk. Known problems are listed at https://www.mediawiki.org/wiki/Special:MyLanguage/Extension:TextExtracts#Caveats."
        }
    },
    "query": {
        "normalized": [
            {
                "from": "history_of_cryptography",
                "to": "History of cryptography"
            }
        ],
        "pages": {
            "520066": {
                "pageid": 520066,
                "ns": 0,
                "title": "History of cryptography",
                "extract": "<p>\nCryptography, the use of codes and ciphers to protect secrets, began thousands of years ago. Until recent decades, it has been the story of what might be called classical cryptography - that is, of methods of encryption that use pen and paper, or perhaps simple mechanical aids. In the early 20th century, the invention of complex mechanical and electromechanical machines, such as the Enigma rotor machine, provided more sophisticated and efficient means of encryption; and the subsequent introduction of electronics and computing has allowed elaborate schemes of still greater complexity, most of which are entirely unsuited to pen and paper.\n</p><p>The development of cryptography has been paralleled by the development of cryptanalysis -  the \"breaking\" of codes and ciphers. The discovery and application, early on, of frequency analysis to the reading of encrypted communications has, on occasion, altered the course of history.  Thus the Zimmermann Telegram triggered the United States' entry into World War I; and Allies reading of Nazi Germany's ciphers shortened World War II, in some evaluations by as much as two years.\n</p><p>Until the 1960s, secure cryptography was largely the preserve of governments. Two events have since brought it squarely into the public domain: the creation of a public encryption standard (DES), and the invention of public-key cryptography.\n</p>\n\n\n<h2><span id=\"Antiquity\">Antiquity</span></h2>\n<p>The earliest known use of cryptography is found in non-standard hieroglyphs carved into the wall of a tomb from the Old Kingdom of Egypt circa 1900 BC. These are not thought to be serious attempts at secret communications, however, but rather to have been attempts at mystery, intrigue, or even amusement for literate onlookers.</p><p>Some clay tablets from Mesopotamia somewhat later are clearly meant to protect information—one dated near 1500 BC was found to encrypt a craftsman's recipe for pottery glaze, presumably commercially valuable. Furthermore, Hebrew scholars made use of simple monoalphabetic substitution ciphers (such as the Atbash cipher) beginning perhaps around 600 to 500 BC.</p><p>In India around 400 BC to 200 AD, Mlecchita vikalpa or \"the art of understanding writing in cypher, and the writing of words in a peculiar way\" was documented in the Kama Sutra for the purpose of communication between lovers. This was also likely a simple substitution cipher. Parts of the Egyptian demotic Greek Magical Papyri were written in a cypher script.</p><p>The ancient Greeks are said to have known of ciphers. The scytale transposition cipher was used by the Spartan military, but it is not definitively known whether the scytale was for encryption, authentication, or avoiding bad omens in speech. Herodotus tells us of secret messages physically concealed beneath wax on wooden tablets or as a tattoo on a slave's head concealed by regrown hair, although these are not properly examples of cryptography <i>per se</i> as the message, once known, is directly readable; this is known as steganography. Another Greek method was developed by Polybius (now called the \"Polybius Square\"). The Romans knew something of cryptography (e.g., the Caesar cipher and its variations).</p>\n<h2><span id=\"Medieval_cryptography\">Medieval cryptography</span></h2>\n\n<p>David Kahn notes in <i>The Codebreakers</i> that modern cryptology originated among the Arabs, the first people to systematically document cryptanalytic methods. Al-Khalil (717-786) wrote the <i>Book of Cryptographic Messages</i>, which contains the first use of permutations and combinations to list all possible Arabic words with and without vowels.</p><p>The invention of the frequency analysis technique for breaking monoalphabetic substitution ciphers, by Al-Kindi, an Arab
```


Figure 7.4 – Viewing the JSON output of a Wikipedia article

The link is constructed using the following components:

- API URL: `https://en.wikipedia.org/w/api.php`
- **Action** parameter: Query
- **Format** parameter: JSON
- **Titles** parameter: The title of the Wikipedia article
- Properties (**Prop**) parameter: Extracts (the full content of the article)

The data itself that we'll be using is in the **extract** node, nested inside the **query** JSON object.

When reviewing Wikipedia articles, you might notice that the headings are a mix of heading level 2 (<H2>) tags, which are used as main topic headings, and heading level 3 (<H3>) tags, which denote subtopics. For this flow, we'll focus on treating the content inside a <H2> tag as one unit. *Figure 7.5* shows examples of text being displayed as <H2> headings:

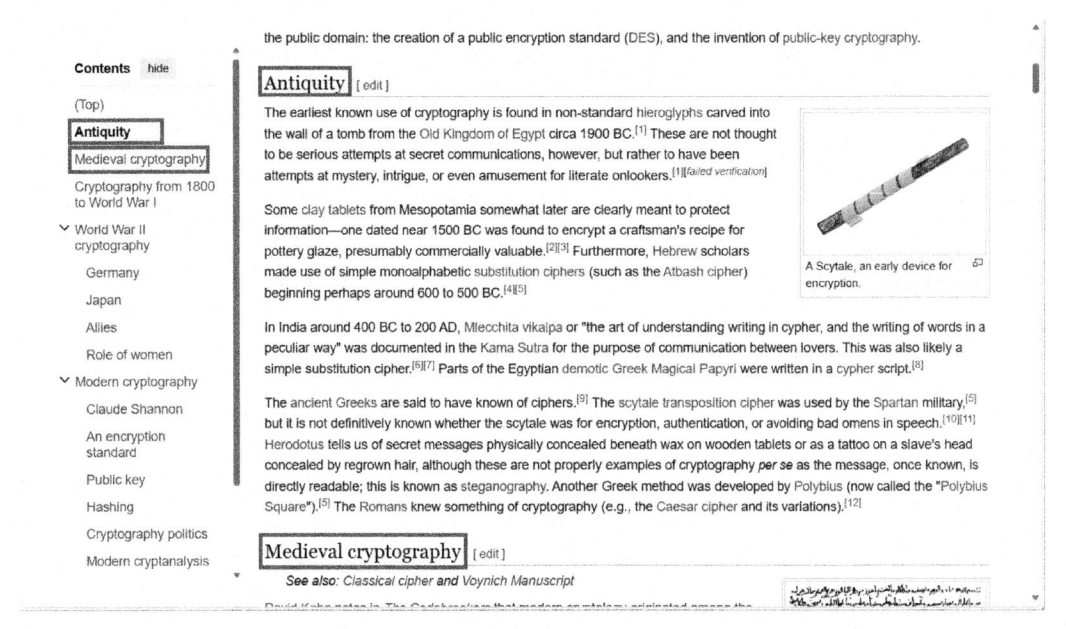

Figure 7.5 – Viewing a Wikipedia article

You can confirm this by viewing the document source in your chosen web browser, as shown in *Figure 7.6*:

Figure 7.6 – Viewing the source of a Wikipedia article

In terms of how we'll use this information, we'll be summarizing the content using the following structure:

```
{
    "title" : "value of the <H2> tag"
    "page" : "1 of number of <H2> tags"
    "content" : "AI-generated summary of the content following an <H2> tag"
}
```

Translating that to how the Flowr connector works, we'll create three tokens:

```
<<[title]>>
<<[page]>>
<<[content]>>
```

Now that you've got a basic understanding of how this is going to work, let's create a PowerPoint template to hold the generated content!

Creating a PowerPoint template

Before you execute any flows, you need to create a template so that the **Populate PowerPoint** action has something to manipulate. For this example, we'll just use a single slide in the template file.

To create a simple template file, follow these steps:

1. Launch PowerPoint and select **New**. You can either choose **Blank Presentation** or use a themed template file:

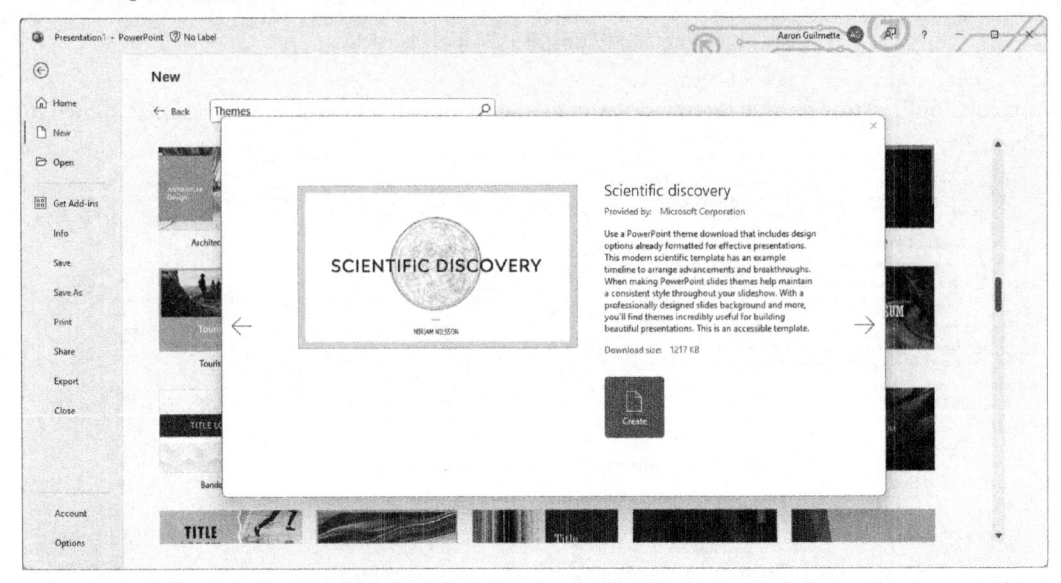

Figure 7.7 – Creating a new template file

2. Edit the content of the file, placing it in the tokens you identified earlier. You can apply formatting such as **bolding** or *italics* to the tokens:

Creating a PowerPoint template 123

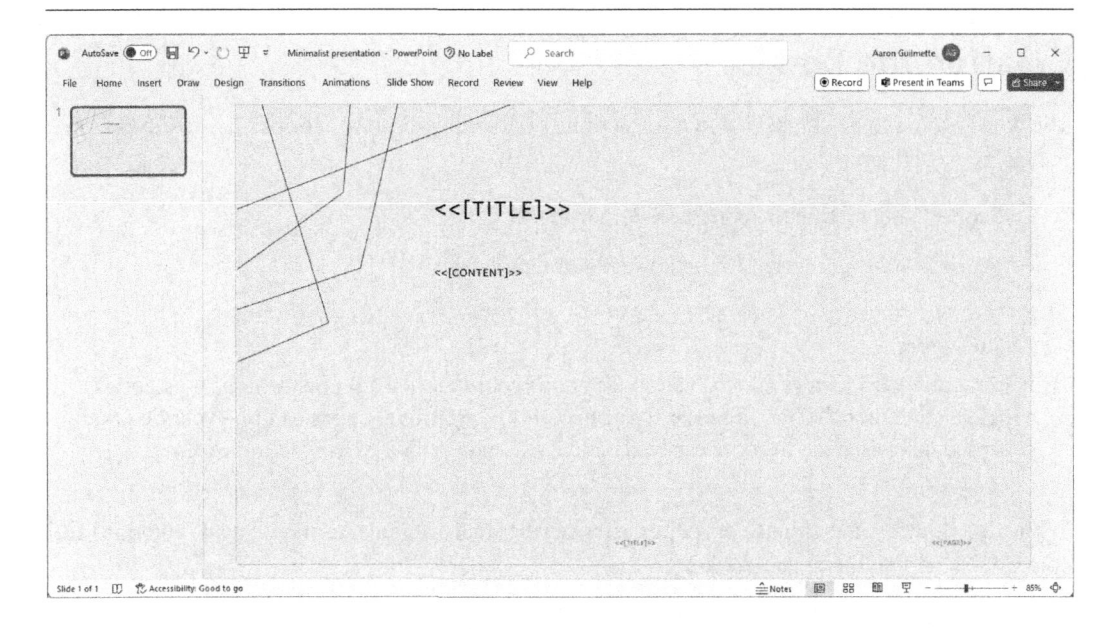

Figure 7.8 – Updating the template with the content tokens

3. Save the document in a SharePoint or OneDrive for Business site:

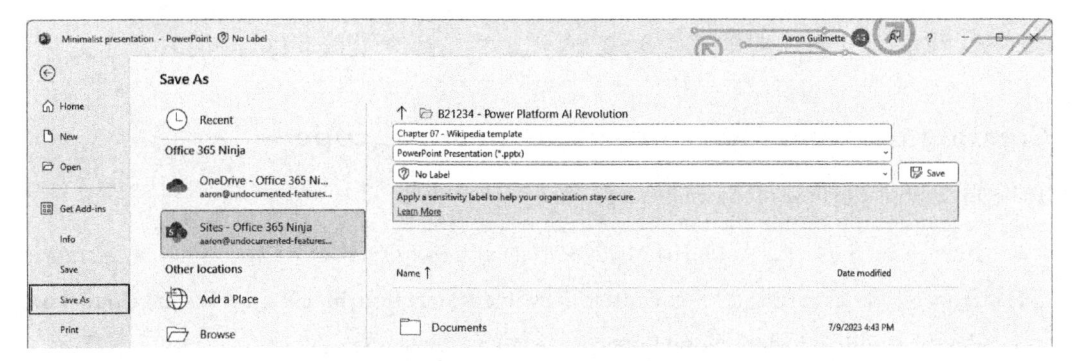

Figure 7.9 – Saving a PowerPoint template file

With that done, it's time to start building our flow!

Creating the flow

The flow is going to be comprised of two sections performing discrete actions, divided into scopes to help manage them:

- **Scope 1**: Generating the content summaries
- **Scope 2**: Adding content to the PowerPoint templates

> **About scopes**
>
> Power Automate includes an oft-overlooked control object called a **scope**. A scope is essentially a logical container that can be used to group actions together. Scopes can be expanded and collapsed, allowing you to more easily visualize and manipulate parts of complex flows.

While this flow features the use of scopes, they're essentially organization objects. If you don't feel comfortable adding them, you don't need to.

> **What do I do if I'm stuck?**
>
> If you run into a roadblock for some reason (can't find a feature, an option isn't showing up, or something is unclear), help is only a click away! You can download this chapter's artifacts from our GitHub site: `https://github.com/PacktPublishing/Power-Platform-and-the-AI-Revolution`.

Creating the Generate Content Summaries scope

To begin creating the flow, follow these steps:

1. Navigate to the Power Automate Maker Portal (`https://make.powerautomate.com`).
2. From the navigation pane, select **Create**. Then, under **Start from blank**, select **Instant cloud flow**.
3. On the **Build an instant cloud flow** page, enter a **Flow name** value.
4. Under **Choose how to trigger this flow**, select **Manually trigger a flow**. Then, click **Create**:

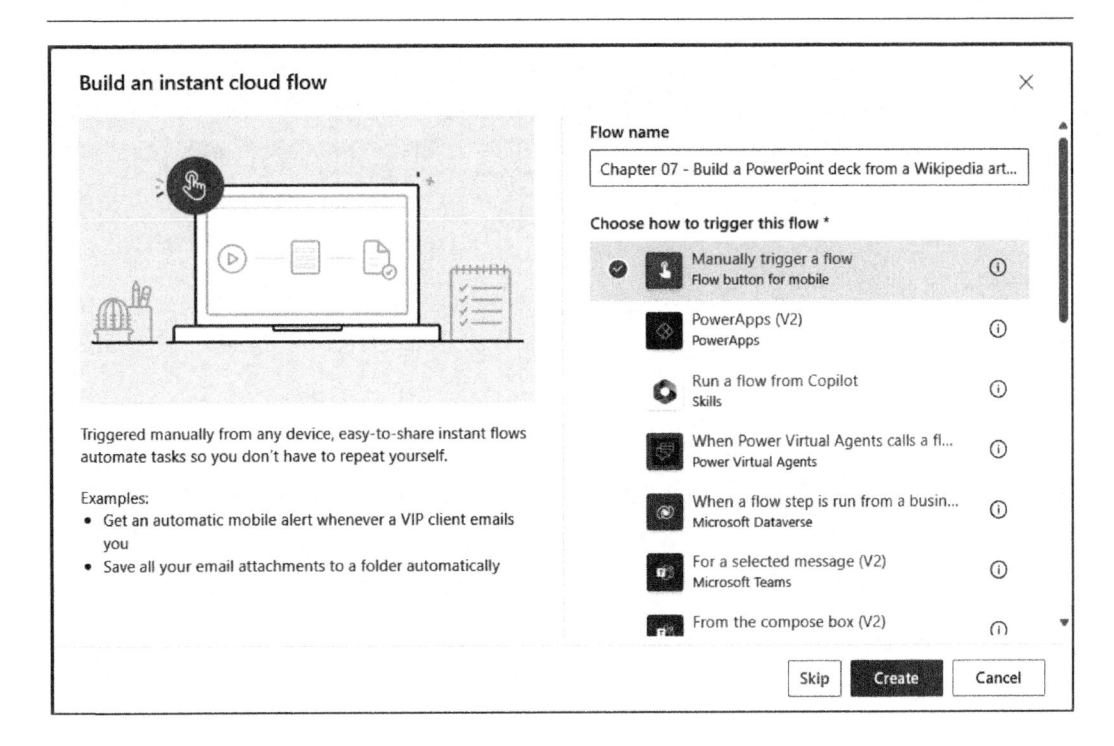

Figure 7.10 – Creating a new flow

5. Click the **Manually trigger a flow** action to expose the **Manually trigger a flow** flyout.
6. Select the **Parameters** tab and choose **Add an input**:

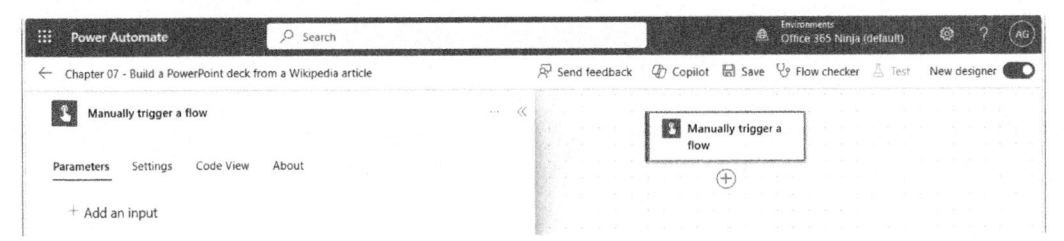

Figure 7.11 – Adding an input

7. For the **Choose the type of user input** prompt, select the **Text** input type.

126   Using Power Automate and AI to Build PowerPoint Presentations

8. If you wish, modify the input prompt with a description that describes the type of content that should be supplied – for example, `Enter Wikipedia article URL`:

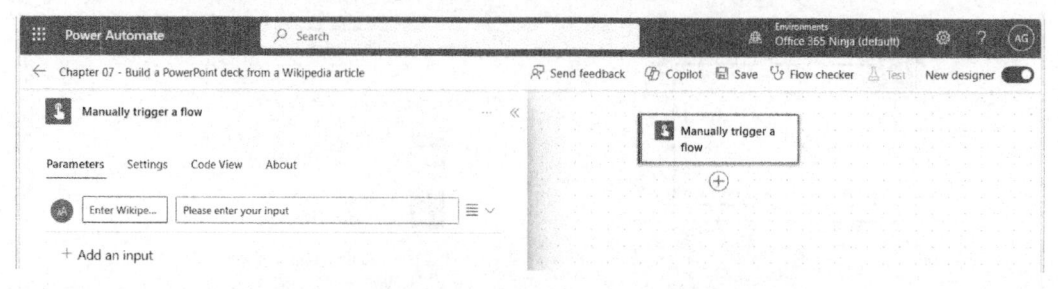

Figure 7.12 – Customizing the text entry prompt

9. Under the **Manually trigger a flow** card, click + and then **Add an action**.
10. In the **Search** box, type `Scope` and select the **Scope control** action:

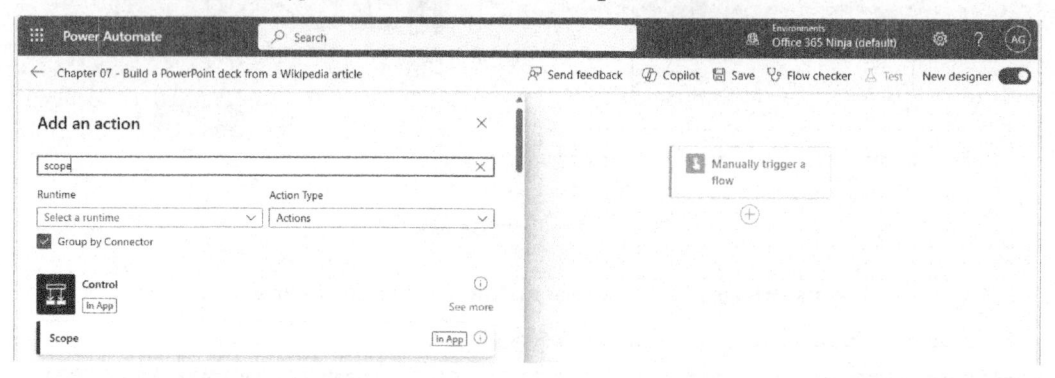

Figure 7.13 – Adding the Scope control action

11. Click the maroon **Scope** title bar to open the **Scope** flyout. Rename the scope to `Scope - Generate Summaries` by clicking on the word **Scope** and editing the field:

Creating the flow 127

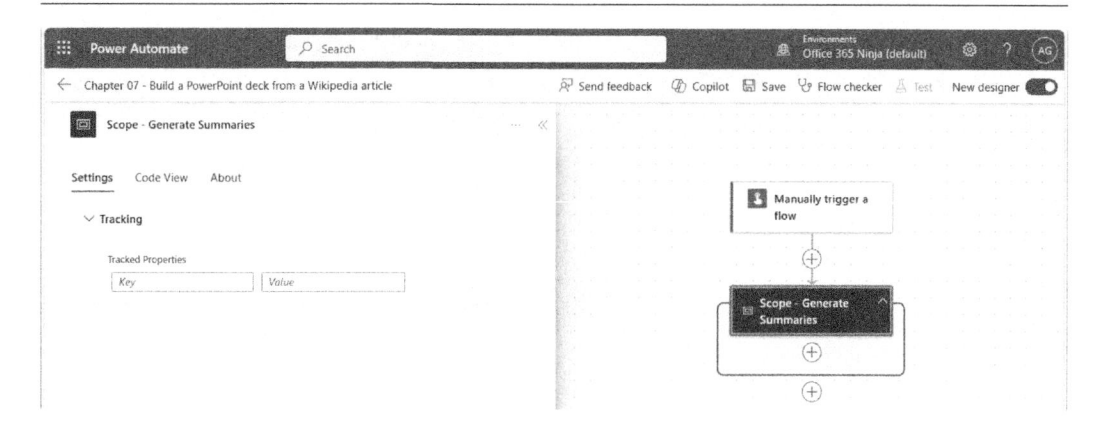

Figure 7.14 – Updating the scope's name

12. Inside the **Scope** card on the canvas, click the + icon and then select **Add an action**.

13. In the **Add an action** flyout, select the **Compose** action:

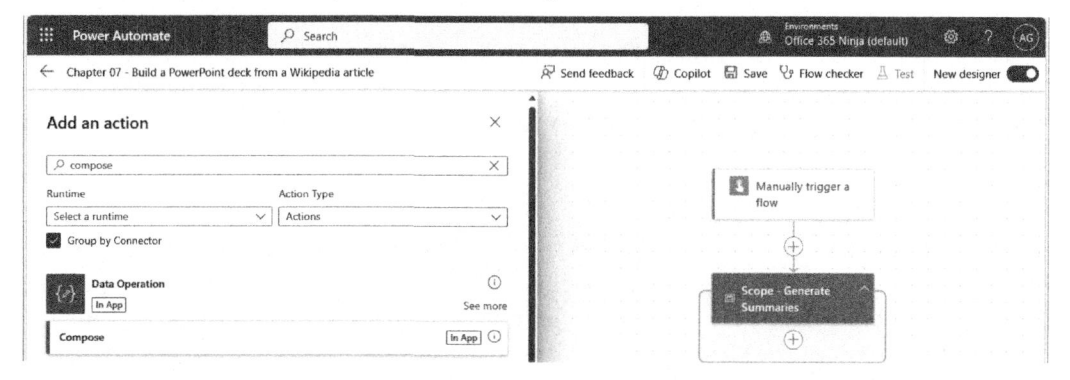

Figure 7.15 – Adding the Compose action

14. In the **Input** box, type a / character or click the *fx* icon to open the **Expression** flyout. In the flyout, enter `last(split(triggerBody()?['text'],'/'))` and click **Add**. Using the / character as a separator, the expression will take the last value from the text input string (from the **Manually trigger a flow** action) and extract the title of the supplied Wikipedia article. For example, when using `https://en.wikipedia.org/wiki/History_of_cryptography`, the expression will return `History_of_Cryptography`. See *Figure 7.13*:

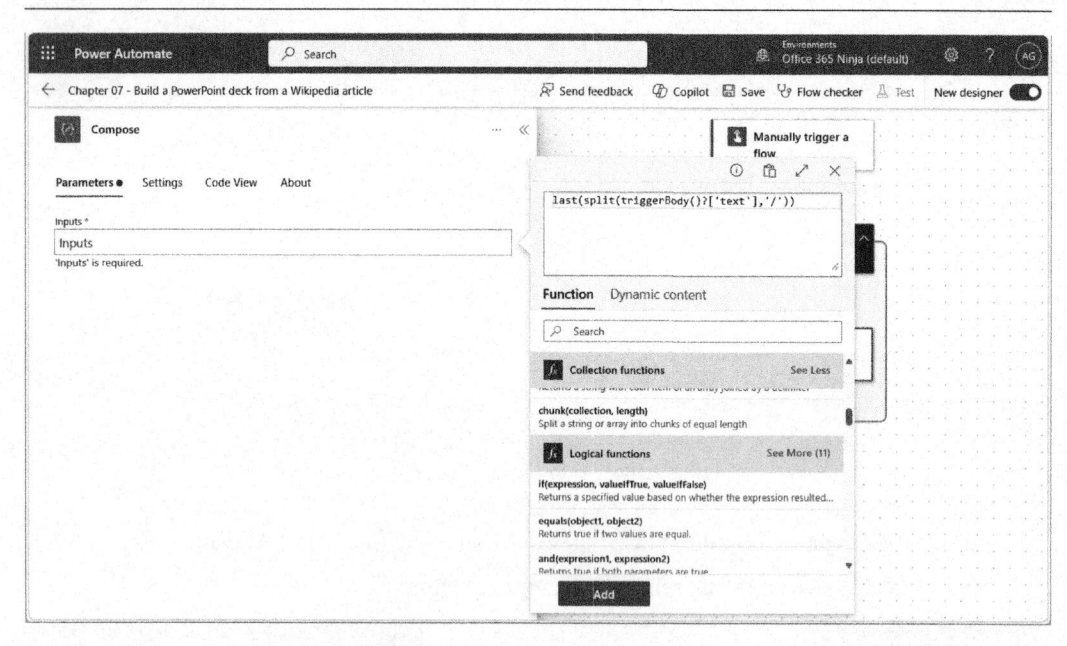

128 Using Power Automate and AI to Build PowerPoint Presentations

Figure 7.16 – Adding the expression

15. Inside the **Scope – Generate Summaries** control card, after the **Compose** card, click + and choose **Add an action**.
16. In the **Add an action** flyout, select the **HTTP** action.
17. On the **Parameters** tab, inside the URI, type a / character or click the *fx* icon to open the **Expression** flyout. In the flyout, enter concat('https://en.wikipedia.org/w/api.php?action=query&format=json&titles=',outputs('Compose'), '&prop=extracts') and click **Add**. This expression uses the CONCAT function to combine the Wikipedia API endpoint, the query and formatting parameters, and the extracted title value:

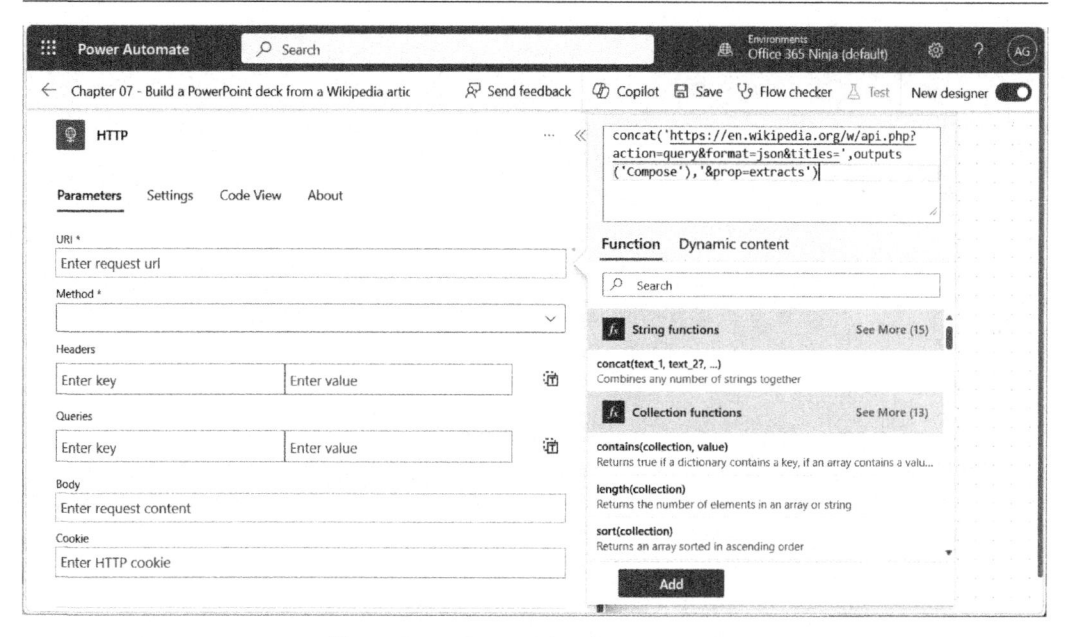

Figure 7.17 – Customizing the HTTP action

18. Under the **Method** dropdown, select **GET**.
19. Click **Save**. Do not exit the Power Automate flow canvas.

Next, we'll start configuring the content processing.

Configuring the JSON parameters

In this section, we'll import the JSON schema or definition of how the content is structured. To get the schema output, you'll need to manually construct the API endpoint with the necessary parameters and then insert an article name. Follow these steps:

1. Launch a new browser tab, navigate to https://en.wikipedia.org, and search for any article of your choosing. In this example, **History of Cryptography** has been selected. Copy (*Ctrl* + *C*) the last portion of the URL after the final / character – for example, History_of_cryptography. See *Figure 7.18*:

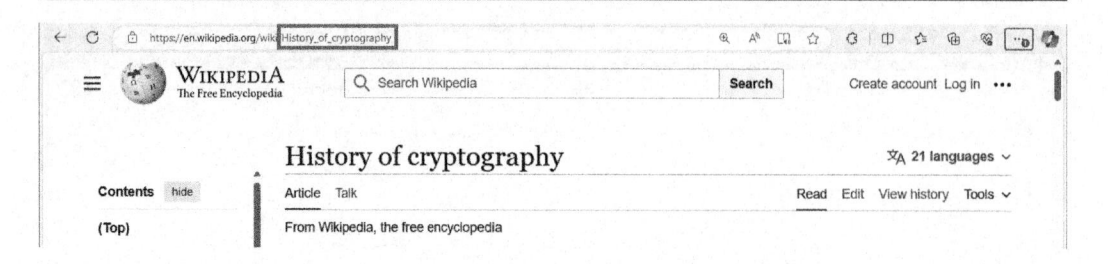

130   Using Power Automate and AI to Build PowerPoint Presentations

Figure 7.18 – Extracting the relative URL of a Wikipedia article

2. Open a new browser tab and navigate to the Wikipedia API endpoint: `https://en.wikipedia.org/w/api.php`.

3. At the end of the URL, append `?action=query&format=json&prop=extracts&titles=` and then paste the copied Wikipedia article value at the end of the URL bar – for example, `?action=query&format=json&prop=extracts&titles=History_of_cryptograpy`. The result should be a JSON-formatted object that contains the text of the Wikipedia article, as shown in *Figure 7.19*:

Figure 7.19 – Viewing the JSON output of the Wikipedia API

4. Select all the content (*Ctrl + A*) and copy it to the buffer (*Ctrl + C*).

5. Switch back to the browser tab containing the Power Automate flow.

Creating the flow | 131

6. Inside the **Scope – Generate Summaries** control card, after the **HTTP** card, click + and choose **Add an action**.
7. In the **Add an action** flyout, select the **Parse JSON** action:

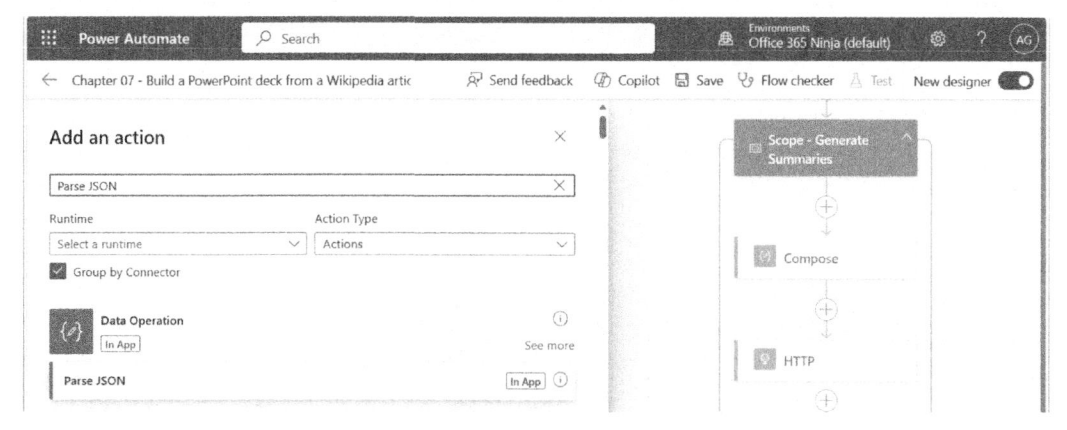

Figure 7.20 – Adding the Parse JSON action

8. In the **Parse JSON** flyout, select the **Parameters** tab.
9. Click inside the **Content** text area, select the dynamic content icon, and then choose the **Outputs** object of the **HTTP** action:

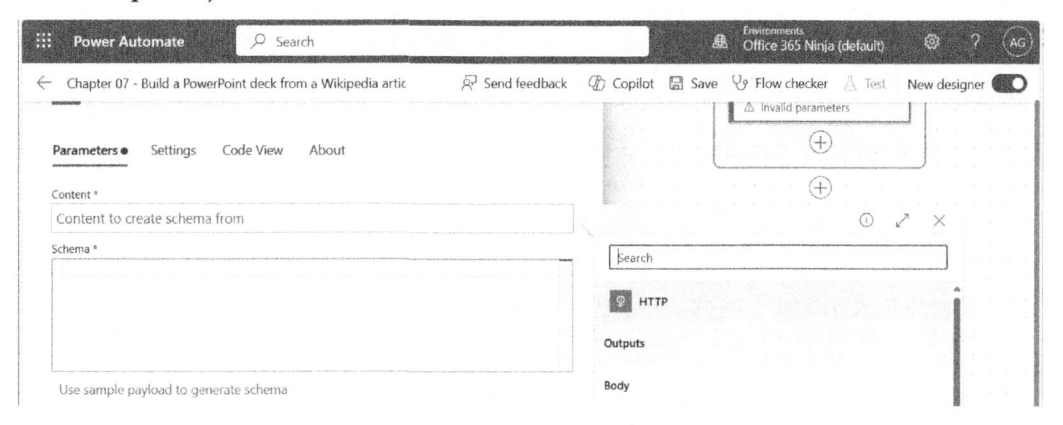

Figure 7.21 – Adding the HTTP Outputs object

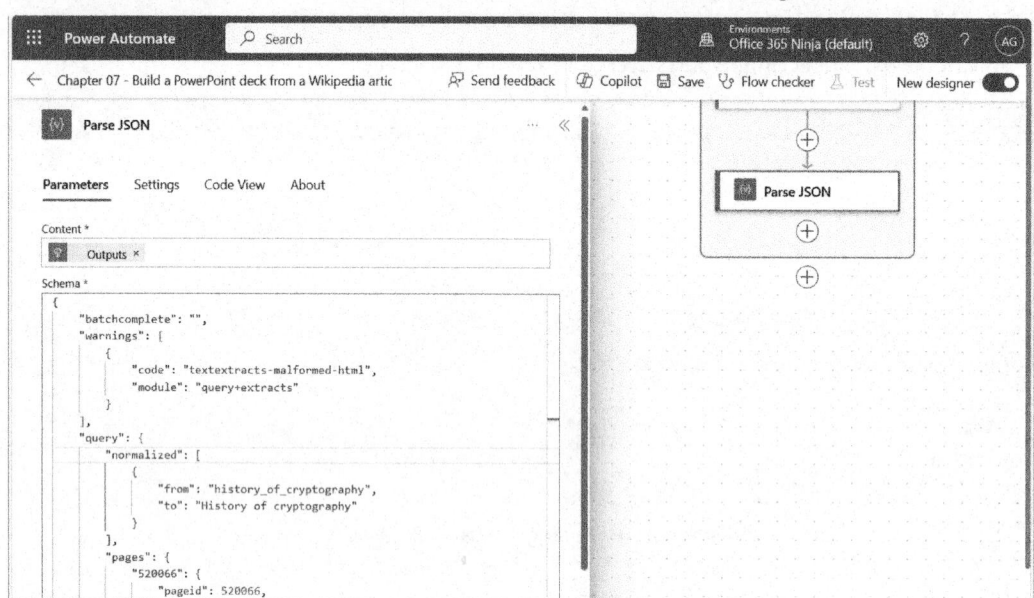

10. Paste the contents of the buffer into the **Schema** area, as shown in *Figure 7.22*:

Figure 7.22 – Populating Content with the Wikipedia API output

11. Click the **Save** icon. Do not exit the Power Automate flow canvas.

Customizing the GPT prompt

Working with completion prompts is as much about art as it is about science. It can take a lot of refinement to get consistently good results.

> **Prompt frameworks**
>
> As the old saying goes, "Garbage in, garbage out." AI models are becoming increasingly more sophisticated and can interpret instructions. To get good results, you need to provide good instructions. Just as people can mimic and learn through examples, so can AI models. Prompt frameworks are one way of helping explain the type of results that meet your expectations. For examples of common prompt frameworks, go to `https://www.undocumented-features.com/2023/12/15/chatgpt-patterns-practices-and-prompts/`.

In this section, you'll create a custom prompt that ChatGPT can use to build the data object. Follow these steps:

1. Inside the **Scope – Generate Summaries** control card, after the **Parse JSON** card, click + and choose **Add an action**.
2. In the **Add an action** flyout, select the **Create text with GPT using a prompt** action:

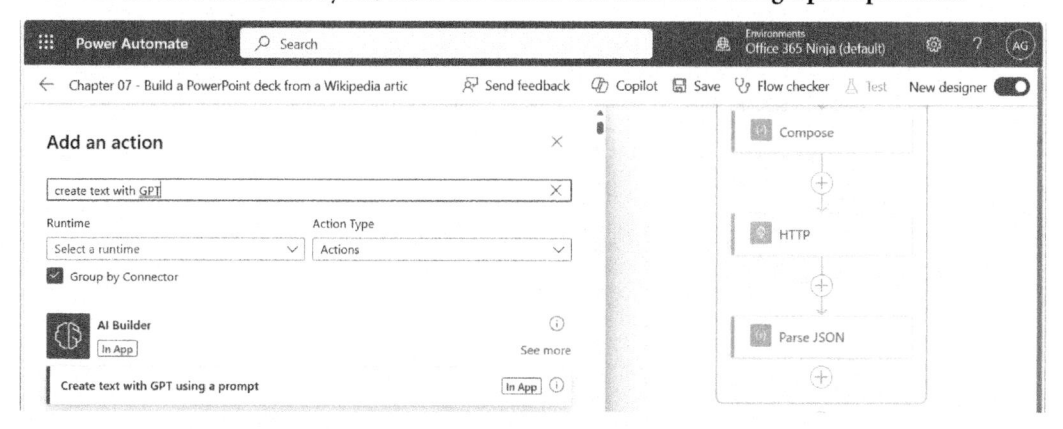

Figure 7.23 – Adding the Create text with GPT using a prompt action

3. In the **Prompt** dropdown, select **New custom prompt**:

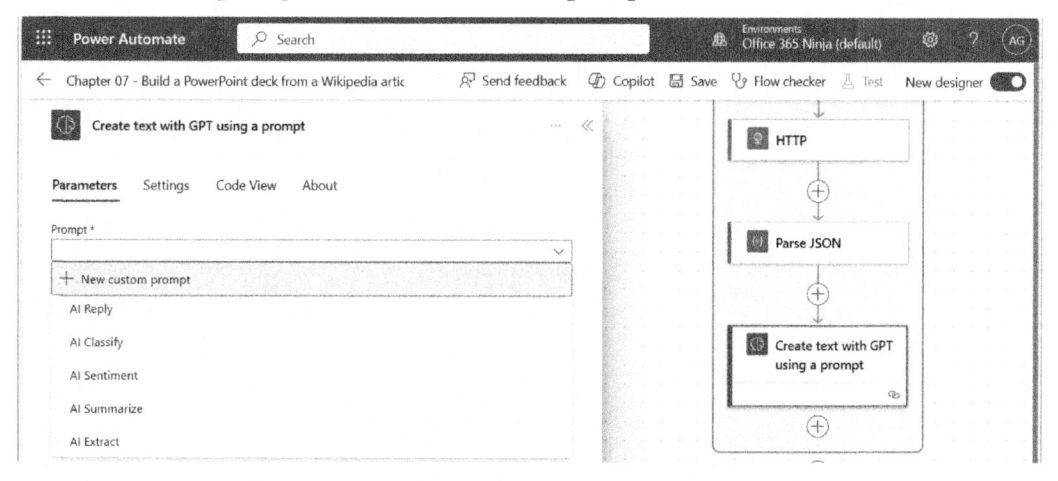

Figure 7.24 – Selecting the New custom prompt option

4. Give the prompt a name, such as `Summarize Wikipedia article`.

5. In the **Prompt** area, paste text similar to the following prompt:

   > You are generating content for a PowerPoint slide deck. Your input is a Wikipedia article. The output must be a well-structured JSON array and must adhere to the length requirement of 75 words or less. Each slide will be represented as an object inside the JSON array. Write a summary of the input body('Http').
   >
   > Data is divided into sections separated by use of the H2 HTML tag. Each H2 section should be summarized as a separate paragraph. For every H2 tag, generate only one paragraph. The content summarization paragraph must be limited to a maximum of 75 words long. Each section will be used as a separate page in a slide deck. Each paragraph should be represented as an individual JSON object. Each object must include the following components:
   >
   > Title: Use the text of the HTML H2 tag
   >
   > Page: Page information in the form of "x of y," where x is the current page or paragraph, and y is the total number of slides that will be generated
   >
   > Content: The formatted paragraph data from each H2 tag, limited to a maximum length of 75 words.
   >
   > Do not deviate from the provided JSON format:
   > [{
   > "title" : "Hanging gardens of Babylon",
   > "page" : "1 of 1"
   > "content" : "The hanging gardens of Babylon are one of the seven wonders of the ancient world. The exquisite, tiered gardens contained a wide variety of trees, shrubs, flowers, and vines. According to legend, the Hanging Gardens were built by King Nebuchadnezzar for his wife, Queen Amytis, because she missed the gardens and landscape from her homeland. The exact location of the Hanging Gardens has never been definitively established."
   > }]
   >
   > Ensure the output of the JSON array is well-formatted, with a separate object for each paragraph and the content keyword not to exceed 75 words.

The following screenshot shows this:

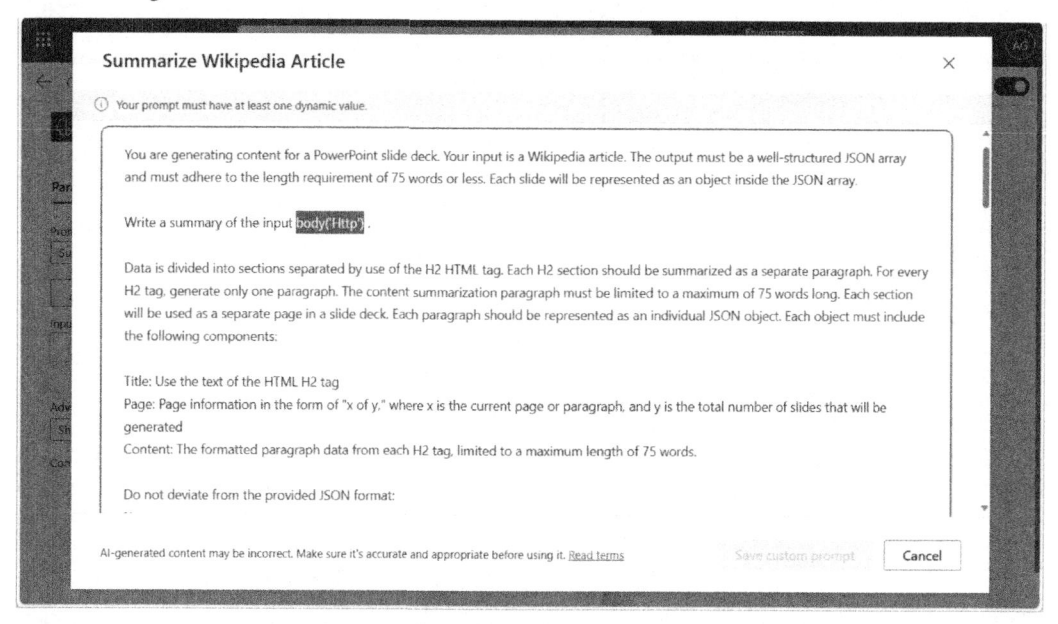

Figure 7.25 – Adding a prompt value

1. Notice the banner, indicating that a dynamic value is required. Copy the value highlighted in *Figure 7.20*, **body('Http')**, by pressing *Ctrl + C*. Then, click **Add dynamic value**. The highlighted portion of the prompt should be replaced with a dynamic value placeholder. See *Figure 7.26*:

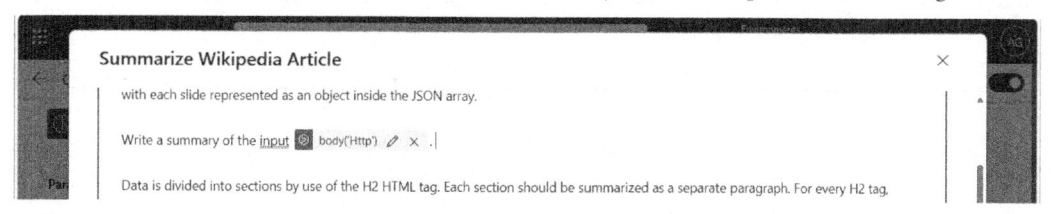

Figure 7.26 – Viewing the updated dynamic value token

2. To test the prompt, scroll to the bottom of the prompt customization area. Switch to the browser tab containing the Wikipedia API content, select it all, and copy it to your computer's buffer using *Ctrl + C*:

3. Switch back to the browser tab containing the customized AI prompt. In the **Test your prompt** area, paste the copied Wikipedia API output, as shown in *Figure 7.27*:

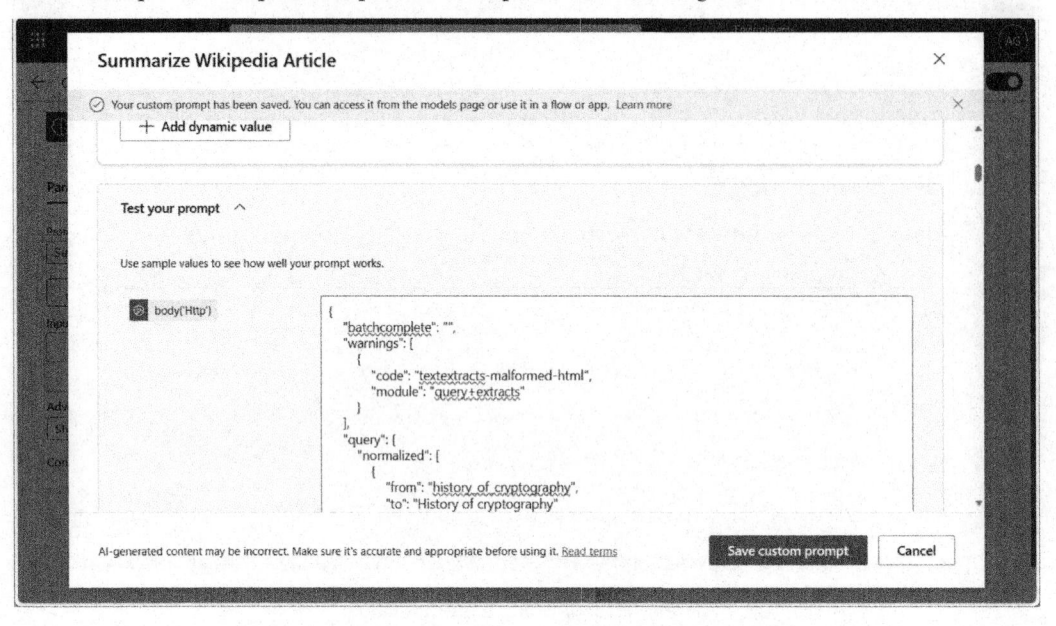

Figure 7.27 – Loading data into the Test your prompt area

4. Scroll to the bottom of the **Test your prompt** area and click **Test prompt**.
5. Wait while the AI Builder prompt generates a response. Review the response to make sure it adheres to your requirements:

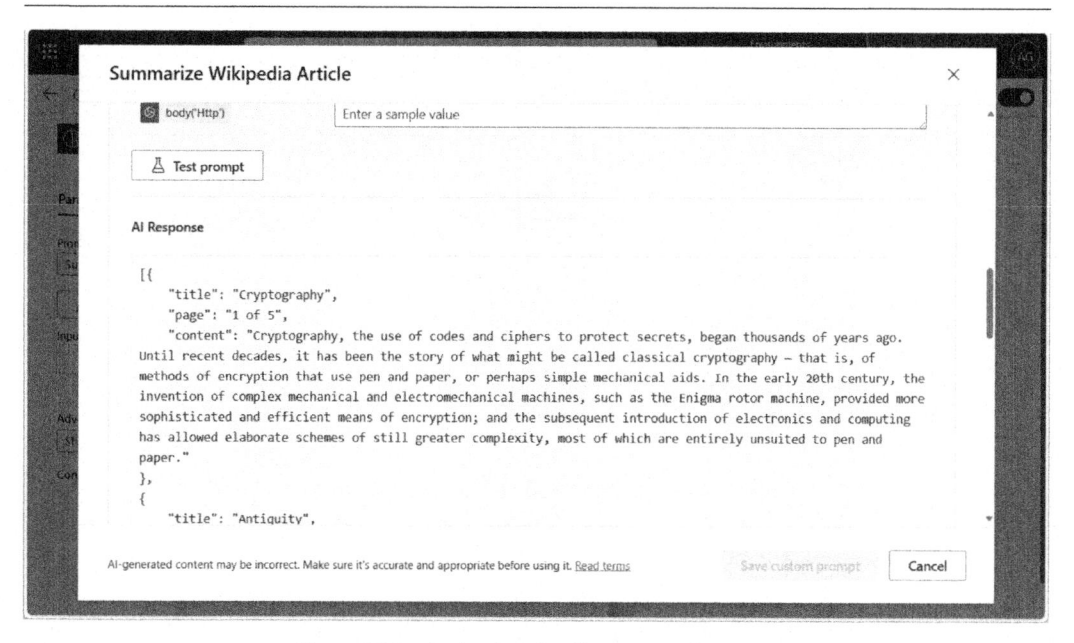

Figure 7.28 – Reviewing the AI-generated content

6. Click inside the **Input Body('Http')** field, select the dynamic content icon, and then select the **Body** object of the **Parse JSON** action:

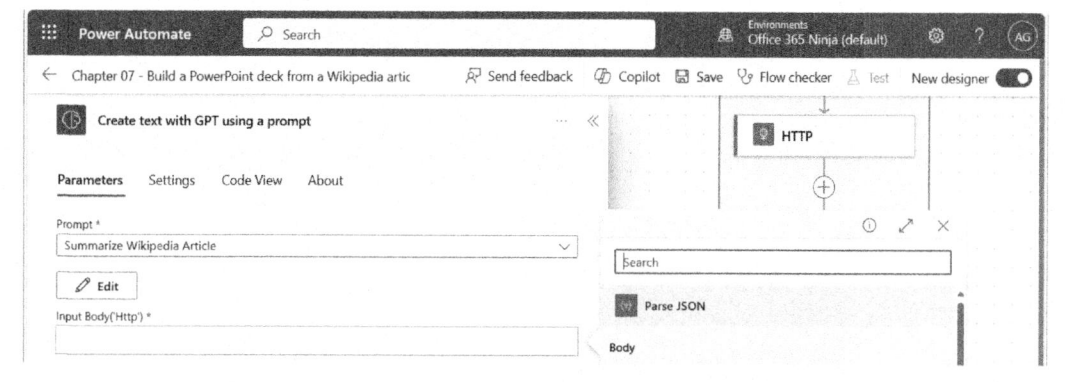

Figure 7.29 – Adding the Body object to the Input Body('Http') field

7. Click the + icon after the **Create text with GPT using a prompt** action and select **Add an action**.
8. Select the **Parse JSON** action. This action will convert the GPT output into an array object that can be iterated through later.
9. On the **Parse JSON** action flyout, rename the action **Parse JSON – Create Array**.

10. On the **Parameters** tab, click inside the **Content** field. Select the dynamic content icon and then choose the **Text** token under the **Create text with GPT using a prompt** action. See *Figure 7.30*:

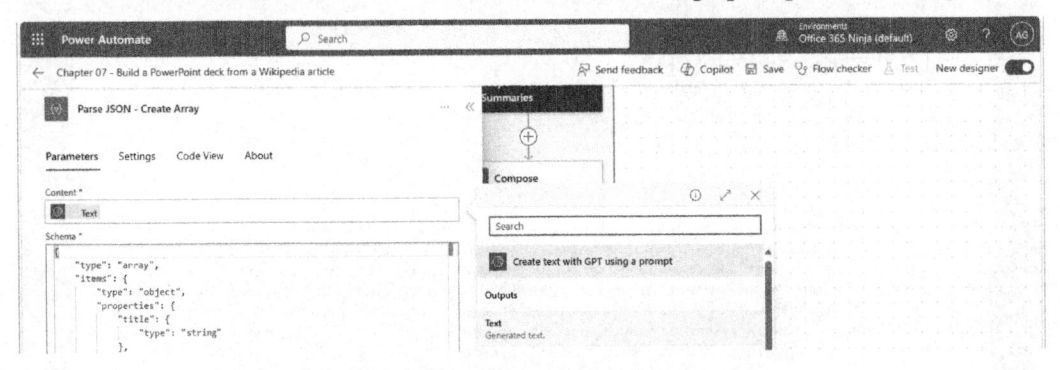

Figure 7.30 – Adding the text dynamic content token

11. In the **Schema** area, copy and paste the following content:

```
{
    "type": "array",
    "items": {
        "type": "object",
        "properties": {
            "title": {
                "type": "string"
            },
            "page": {
                "type": "string"
            },
            "content": {
                "type": "string"
            }
        },
        "required": [
            "title",
            "page",
            "content"
        ]
    }
}
```

This schema definition can be obtained by running the flow up to this point, copying the output, and then pasting it in the **Use sample payload to generate schema** popup on the **Parse JSON** flyout.

12. Click **Save**. Do not close the Power Automate flow canvas.

So far, you've created a flow that can take a Wikipedia article URL and summarize each H2 element into its own JSON object. Next, we'll work on sending that data to the PowerPoint template.

Creating the Generate Slides scope

In this section, we'll take the JSON object array and turn it into a PowerPoint slide deck. Follow these steps to process the AI-generated content:

1. Scroll to the bottom of the flow on the canvas and select the + icon outside the **Scope – Generate Summaries** control:

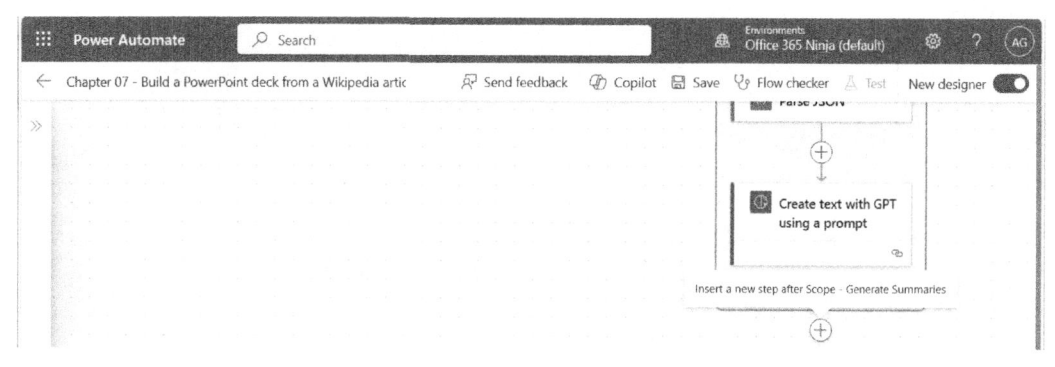

Figure 7.31 – Adding a new step

2. Add a new scope control and rename it `Scope - Generate Slides`.
3. Click the + icon and choose **Add an action** inside the **Scope - Generate Slides** card.
4. Choose the **Get file content using path** action for either SharePoint Online or OneDrive for Business, depending on where you saved your template file:

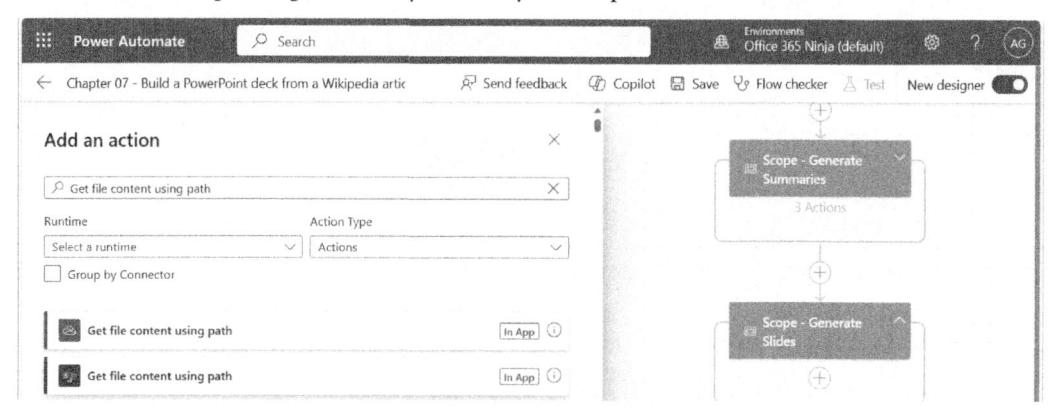

Figure 7.32 – Adding the Get file content using path action

5. On the **Get file content using path** flyout, locate the file. If you're using the OneDrive for Business action, select the **File Path** field using the folder browser. If you're using the SharePoint Online action, select the **Site Address** value where the file is located and then use the folder browser in the **File Path** field to select the file:

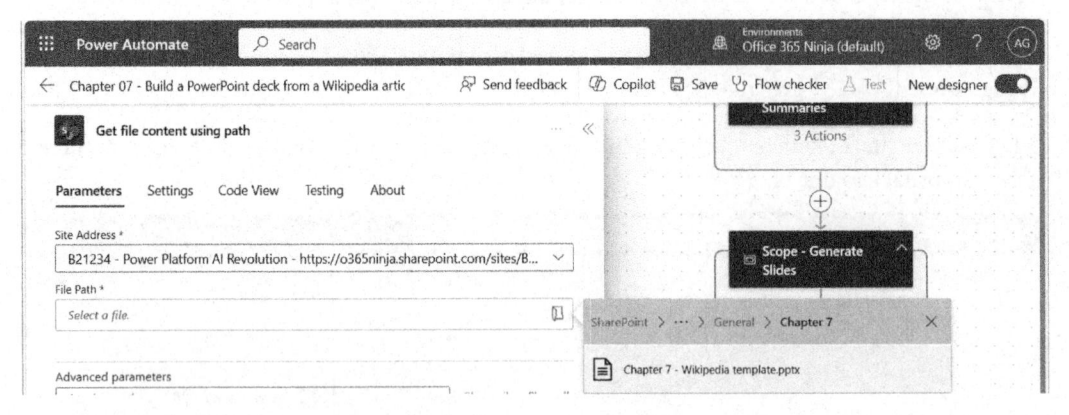

Figure 7.33 – Selecting the PowerPoint template file

6. Inside the **Scope - Generate Slides** card, click the + icon and select **Add an action**.
7. Add the **Apply to each** control.
8. On the **Apply to each** control flyout, select the **Parameters** tab.
9. In the **Select an Output From Previous Steps** field, add the **Body** output from the **Parse JSON – Create Array** action you created earlier:

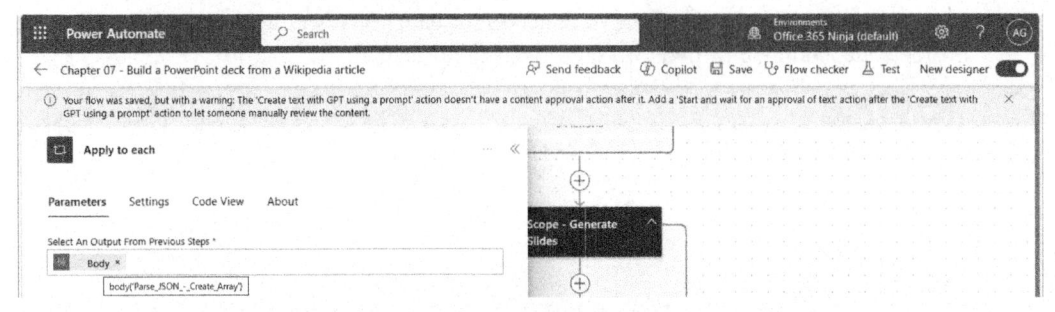

Figure 7.34 – Adding the Body output from the Parse JSON – Create Array action

10. Inside the **Apply to each** control card, click + and select **Add an action**.
11. Select the **Parse JSON** action.
12. Rename the **Parse JSON** action `Parse JSON - PPT Values`.
13. On the **Parameters** tab of the **Parse JSON – PPT values** flyout, click inside the **Content** field.

14. Select the **Current item** dynamic content token. See *Figure 7.35*:

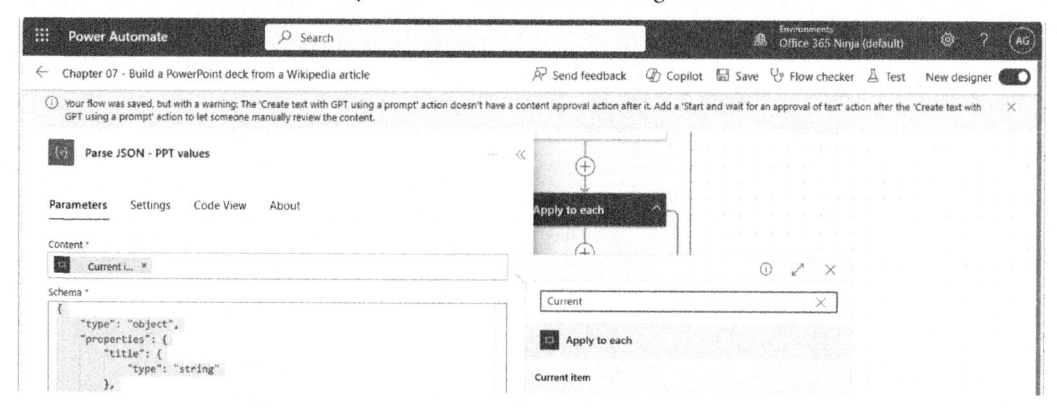

Figure 7.35 – Selecting the Current item dynamic content token

15. In the **Schema** area, copy and paste the following value:

    ```
    {
        "type": "object",
        "properties": {
            "title": {
                "type": "string"
            },
            "page": {
                "type": "string"
            },
            "content": {
                "type": "string"
            }
        }
    }
    ```

    This content can be derived by running the flow up to this point, viewing the **Run history** area, selecting the output of the **Create text with GPT using a prompt** action, and then pasting it into the **Use sample payload to generate schema** popup.

16. Click **Save**. Do not close the Power Automate flow canvas.

Next, we'll start sending data to the Encodian connector.

142   Using Power Automate and AI to Build PowerPoint Presentations

Working with Encodian Flowr

In this section, you'll start interfacing with the Flowr connector. It can be tricky to get it to work, so do the following:

1. Inside the **Apply to each** card, click the + icon following **Parse JSON – PPT values** and select **Add an action**.

2. Add the **Populate PowerPoint** action:

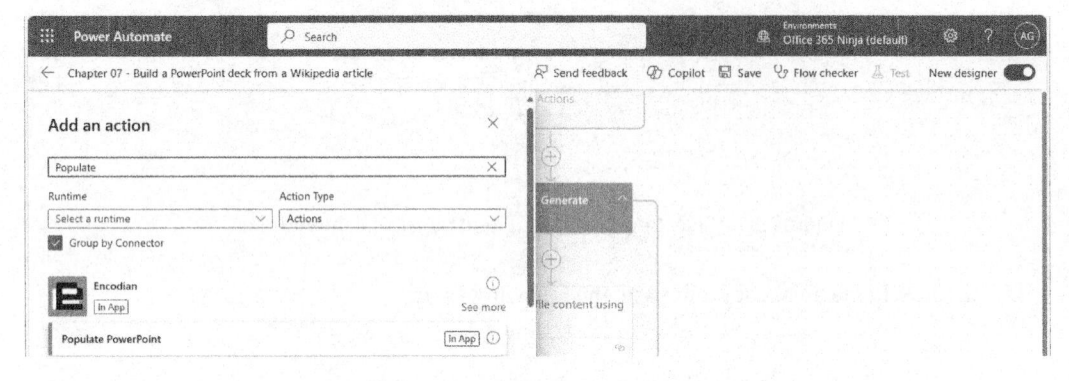

Figure 7.36 – Adding the Populate PowerPoint action

3. On the **Populate PowerPoint** flyout, enter a **Connection Name** value for the Encodian connection and add your **API Key**. Click **Create New** to finish the setup:

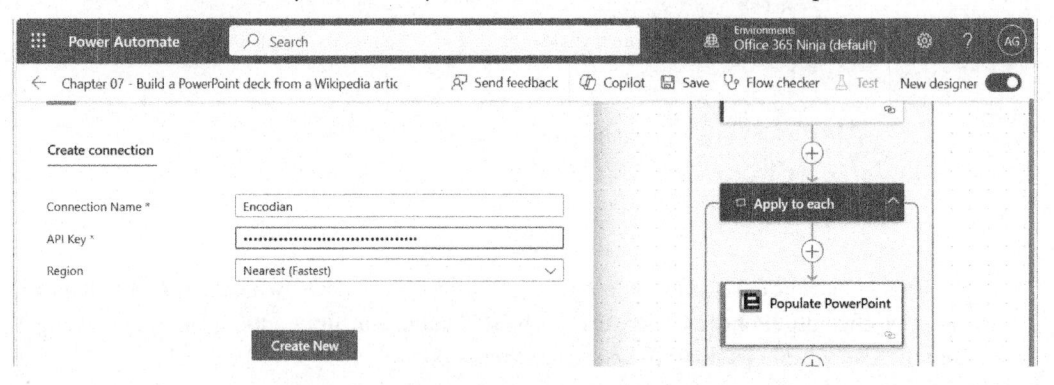

Figure 7.37 – Configuring the Encodian connection

4. On the **Populate PowerPoint** flyout, click **Show all** next to the **Advanced parameters** dropdown:

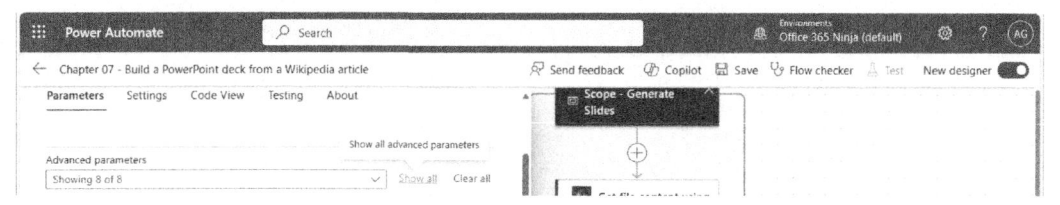

Figure 7.38 – Expanding all of the available parameters

5. Click inside the **File Content** field, select the dynamic content icon, and then choose the **File Content** token for the configured storage location (either **SharePoint Online** or **OneDrive for Business**):

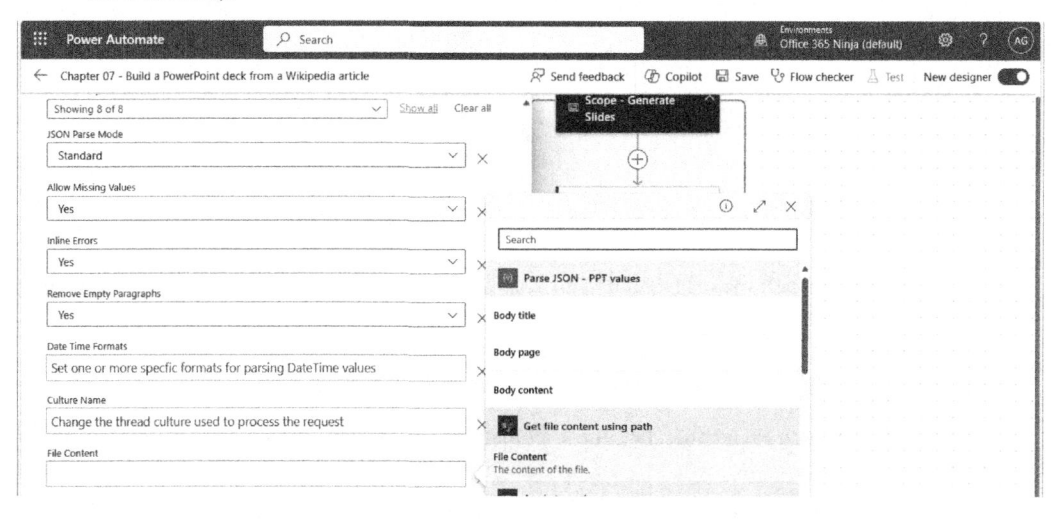

Figure 7.39 – Adding the File Content token

6. In the **JSON Data** field, define the JSON structure that the connector will use to replace the content tokens in your template file. For example, this exercise utilizes the **title**, **content**, and **page** tokens. The JSON definition should look similar to the following sample:

```
{
"title": "@{body('Parse_JSON_-_PPT_values')?['title']}",
"content" : "@{body('Parse_JSON_-_PPT_values')?['content']}",
"page": "@{body('Parse_JSON_-_PPT_values')?['page']}"
}
```

It should look like this:

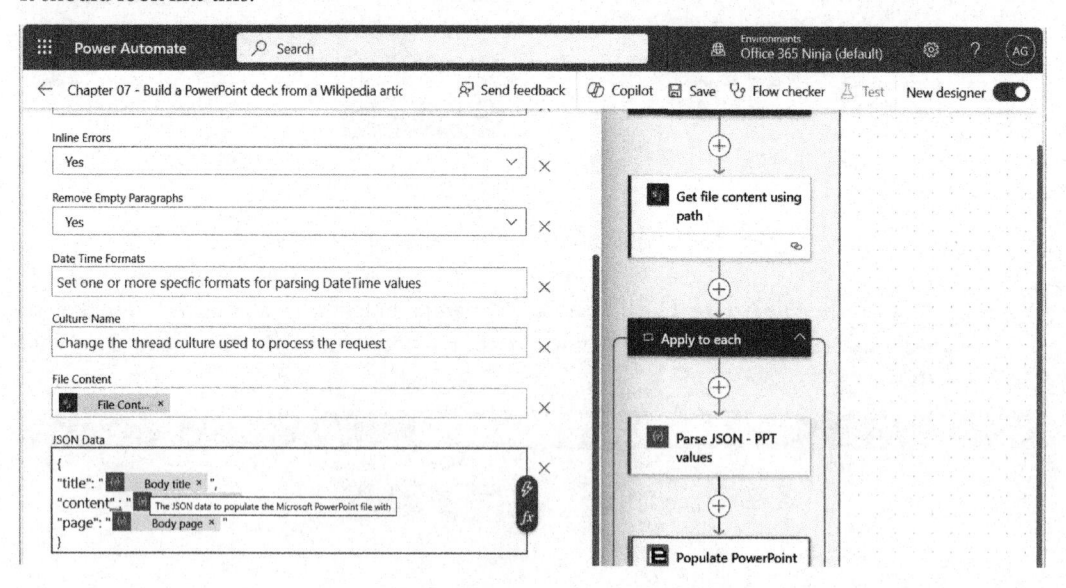

Figure 7.40 – Configuring the JSON data property

You can type the definitions (such as `"title" : " "`) and then choose the corresponding parameter values from the dynamic content token list. The outputs should be selected from the **Parse JSON – PPT Values** action. Alternatively, if you have renamed the actions to follow the exercise, you can copy and paste the entire JSON definition.

1. Inside the **Apply to each** card, click the + icon after the **Populate PowerPoint** action and select **Add an action**.
2. Select the **Compose** action.
3. On the **Compose** flyout, rename the action `Compose PowerPoint Slides`.
4. On the **Parameters** tab of the **Compose PowerPoint slides** flyout, click inside the **Inputs** field and paste the following content:

```
{
"fileName": ".pptx",
"fileContent": {
"$content-type": "application/vnd.openxmlformats-officedocument.presentationml.presentation",
"$content":
}
}
```

5. In the **Inputs** area, place the cursor before the . character on the **fileName** definition. Click the function icon and add the **guid()** function. The **Merge Presentation** action requires a **fileName** property later – and **guid()** is the simplest function to allow you to create random filenames that won't conflict with existing files anywhere. See *Figure 7.35* to refer to placement. Note that both the key and value parameters are enclosed with double quotation marks ("). Without the quotes, you will receive a JSON format error:

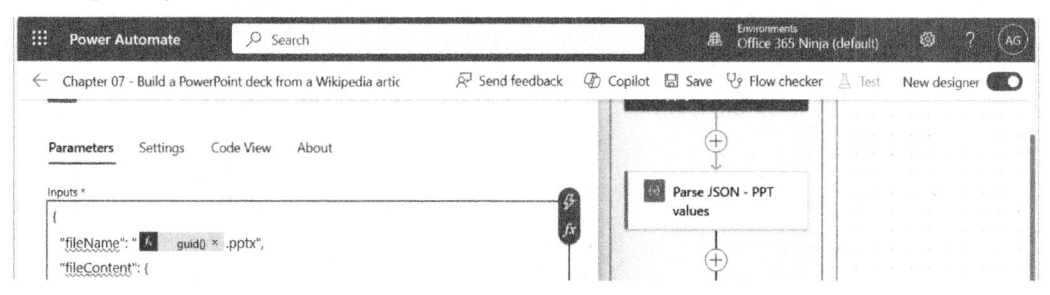

Figure 7.41 – Adding the guid() function to the filename

6. In the **Inputs** area, place the cursor after "$content" : and click the dynamic content icon. Choose the **File Content** dynamic content token. See *Figure 7.42*:

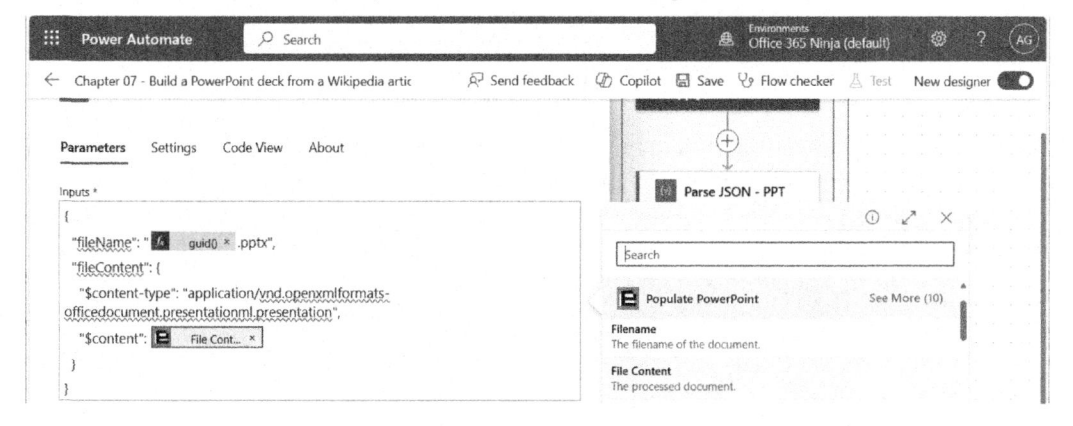

Figure 7.42 – Adding the File Content dynamic content token

7. Inside the **Apply each card**, click the + icon below the **Compose PowerPoint Slides** action and select **Add an action**.
8. Choose the **Merge Presentations** action.
9. Enter a **Filename** value if desired (the default filename is Presentation.pptx).
10. Under **Advanced parameters**, select **Show all**.

146 Using Power Automate and AI to Build PowerPoint Presentations

11. In the **Documents** section, click the T icon (**Switch to input entire array**). This will allow you to select the output of the **Compose PowerPoint Slides** action – the collection of files that were assigned <guid>.PPTX names:

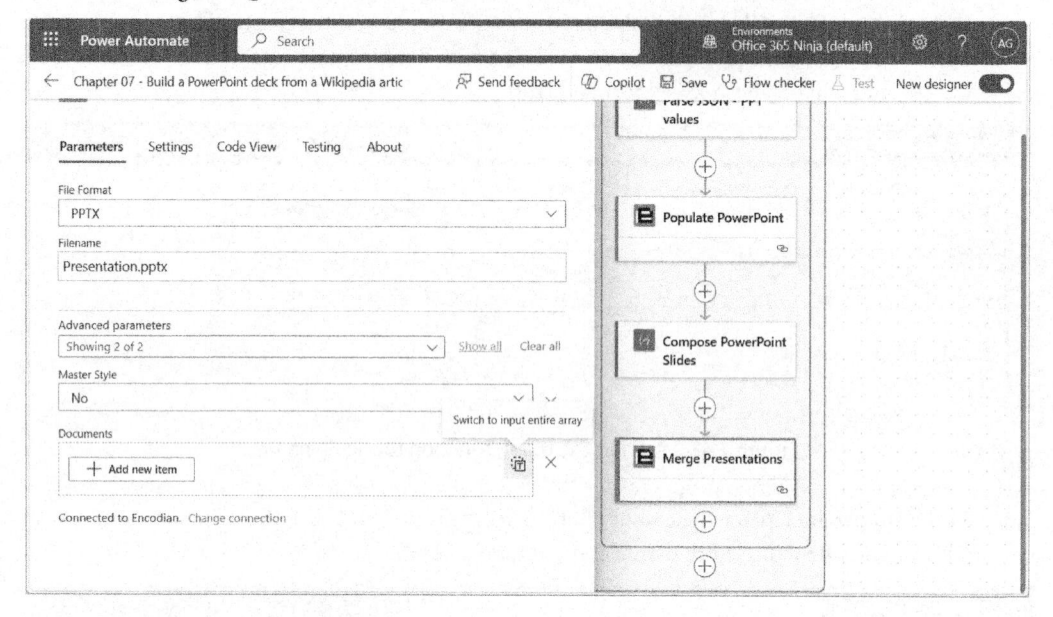

Figure 7.43 – Changing the input type

12. Click inside the **Documents Item** field and select the dynamic content token icon. Under **Compose PowerPoint Slides**, choose **Outputs**:

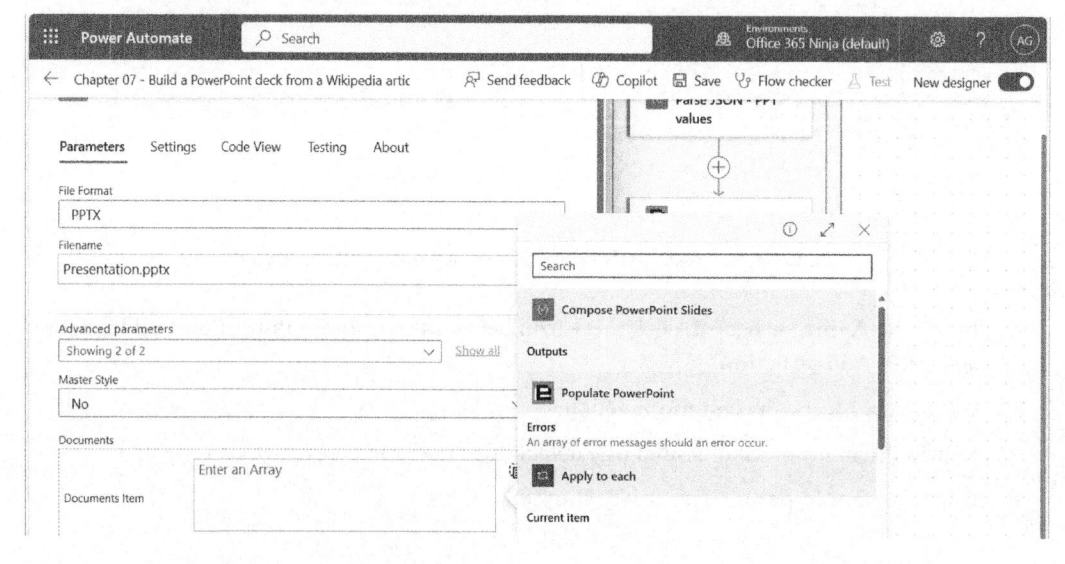

Figure 7.44 – Updating the Document Item field

Creating the flow 147

13. Collapse the **Merge Presentations** flyout.
14. Drag the **Merge Presentations** card outside of the **Apply to each** and **Scope – Generate Slides** cards and place it on the + icon below the scope card. See *Figure 7.45*:

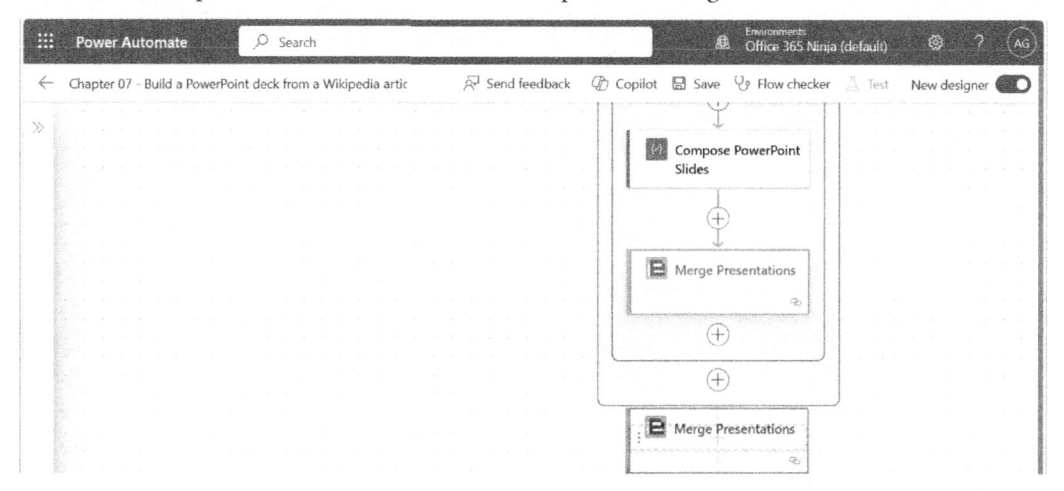

Figure 7.45 – Moving the Merge Presentations card

This order of steps is necessary to ensure that the **Compose PowerPoint Slides** output can be chosen from the dynamic content menu.

15. Click the + icon after **Merge Presentations** and then select **Add a step** to add it to the end of the flow.
16. Select the **Create file** action (either SharePoint or OneDrive for Business), depending on where you want the output. It does not have to be in the same location where the template file is stored.
17. On the **Create file** flyout, select the location (either a **Folder Path** location if you chose OneDrive for Business or a **Site Address** and **Folder Path** location if you chose SharePoint Online).
18. In the **File Name** field, add the **Filename** dynamic content token from the **Merge Presentations** action.

19. In the **File Content** field, add the **File Content** dynamic content token from the **Merge Presentations** action, as shown in *Figure 7.46*:

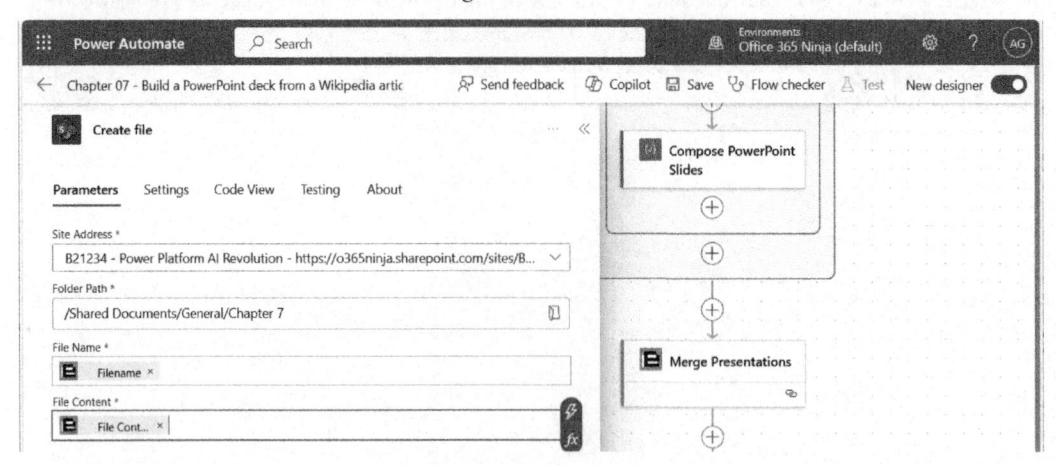

Figure 7.46 – Selecting the File Content dynamic content token

20. Click **Save**.

Click the **Flow checker** area to ensure your flow contains no obvious errors. When you're finished with that, it's time to test the flow!

Testing the flow

To test the flow, follow these steps:

1. Open a new browser tab. Navigate to Wikipedia (https://en.wikipedia.org) and search for an article of your choosing. For this example, you might try searching for Sailing or History of cryptography.
2. After the article loads, click the URL bar and copy the URL value using *Ctrl + C*.
3. Switch back to the browser tab that's running the Power Automate canvas.
4. Click the **beaker** icon labeled **Test**:

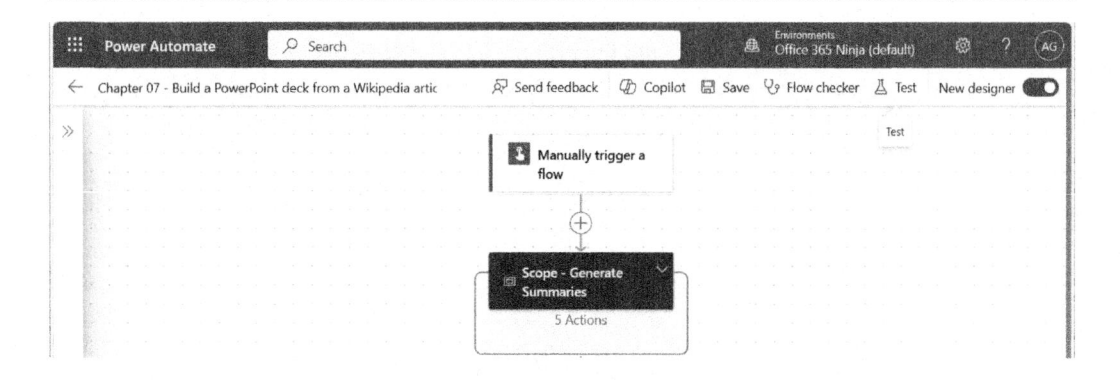

Figure 7.47 – Preparing to test the flow

5. On the **Test Flow** flyout, select the **Manually** radio button and click **Test**.
6. If prompted, confirm any permissions and click **Continue**:

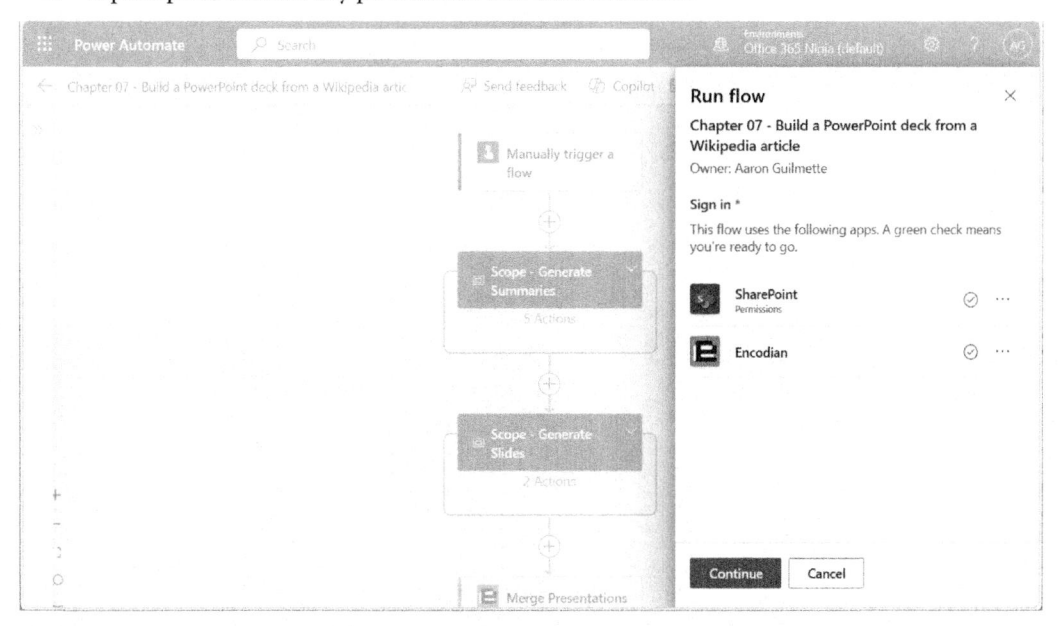

Figure 7.48 – Confirming permissions for the flow

150   Using Power Automate and AI to Build PowerPoint Presentations

7. Paste the copied Wikipedia URL into the prompt area and click **Run flow**:

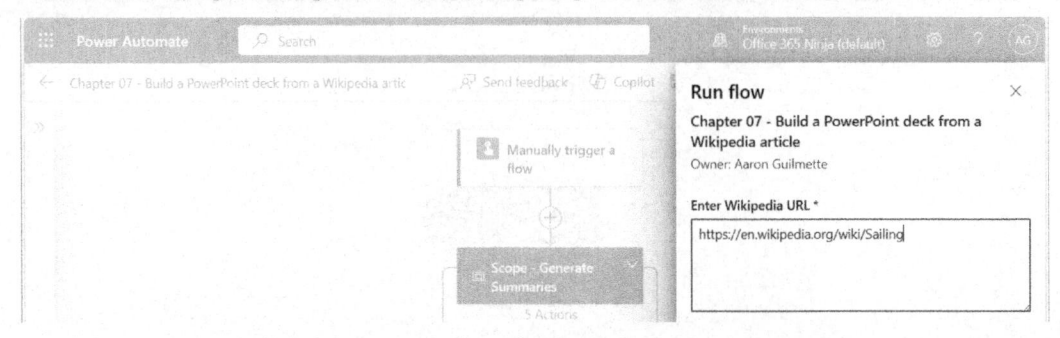

Figure 7.49 – Entering a URL

8. Click **Done** to return to the canvas and watch the flow run execute.
9. Wait while the flow executes:

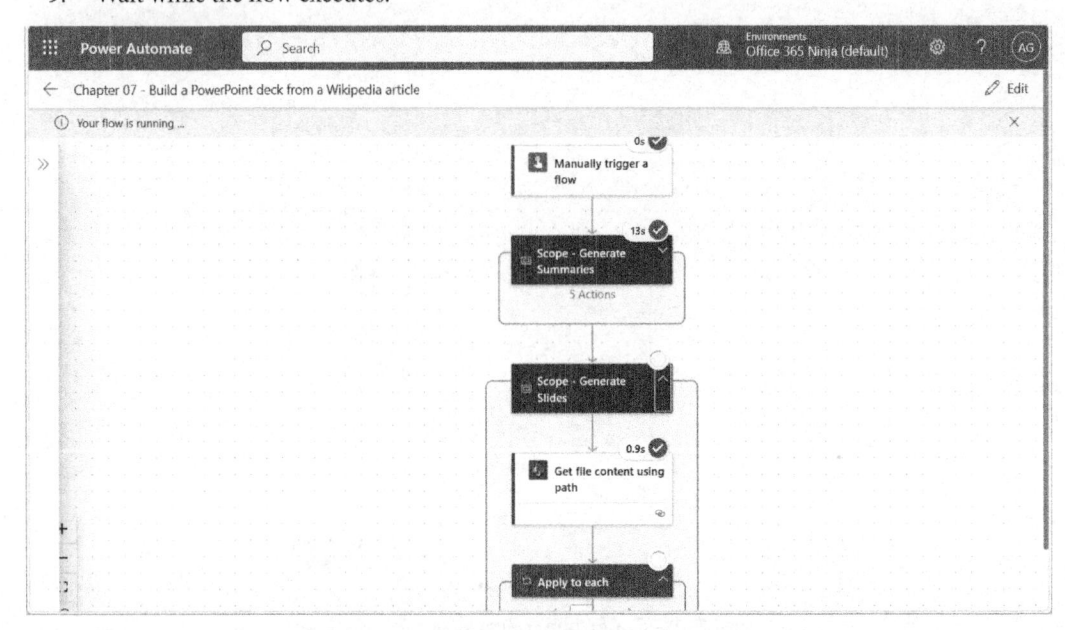

Figure 7.50 – Waiting for the flow to complete

10. After the flow has been completed, navigate to the location where you specified the completed presentation should be saved.

11. Open the presentation:

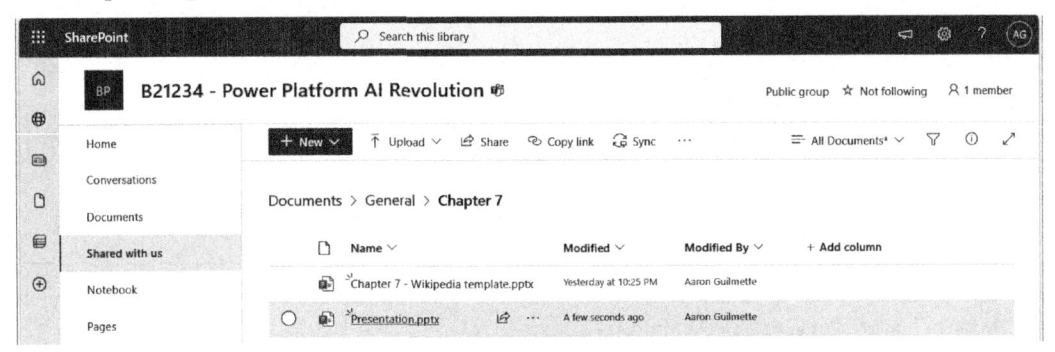

Figure 7.51 – Launching the presentation

12. Review the completed presentation, taking note of how the content tokens in the slide were replaced with the corresponding JSON values that were passed to the Encodian Flowr connector:

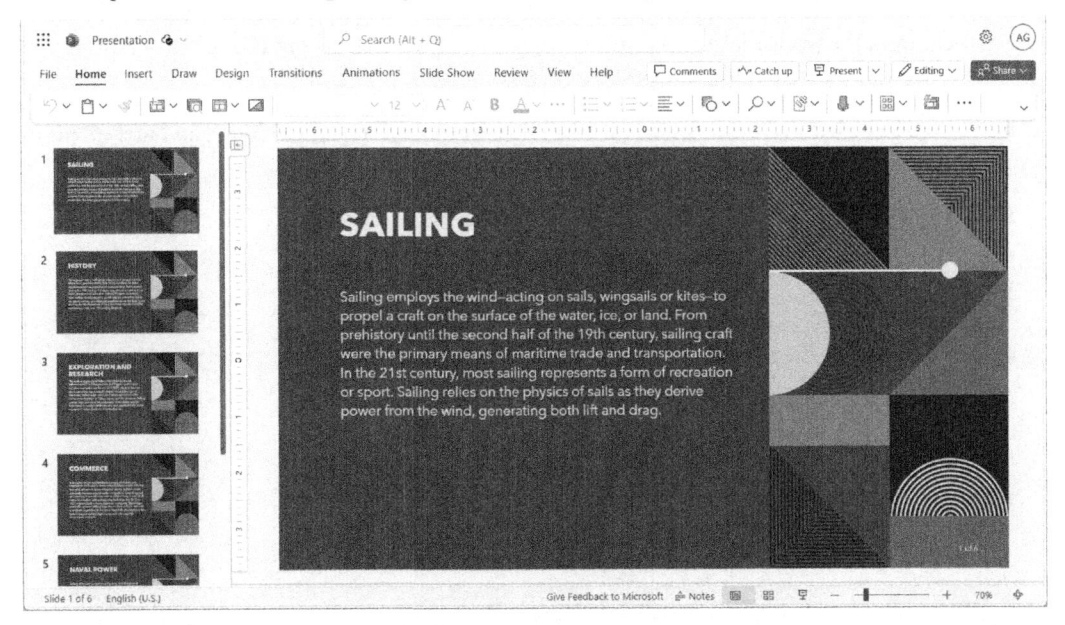

Figure 7.52 – Reviewing the completed presentation

That's it! You've now created an entire PowerPoint presentation just by scraping website content.

Further exploration

Think about all the ways you can further expand, reuse, or repurpose this type of solution to build slide decks from different types of content sources:

- Quarterly reports
- Executive summaries
- Sales reports

By combining the power of Generative AI with automation for common Microsoft 365 Apps document creation tools, you can create presentations in a snap!

Summary

This chapter demonstrated some of the incredible capabilities that are available by harnessing the power of Generative AI. By using the native AI Builder ChatGPT connector, you were able to ingest web content from the world's largest online encyclopedia, summarize it, and turn it into a PowerPoint presentation (with the help of the Encodian Flowr connector).

Using the skills you learned here, you could adapt this flow to pull together reports and presentations from content stored in SharePoint, OneDrive, or other websites and documents.

In the next chapter, we'll learn about using the AI Builder ID reader model.

8

Building an Event Registration App with Identity Verification

There are times when identity verification and validation are necessary to determine eligibility for a product or service. In this chapter, you'll be learning about the AI Builder capabilities surrounding identity document content extraction.

The AI Builder Identity Document reader is a pre-built model that recognizes content in identity documents such as passports, driver's licenses, and other forms of identification.

Designing a solution

When thinking about how to build a solution that would process identity, I immediately thought of some sort of an event registration app or scenario that would require identity verification or validation—and it seemed like a great idea.

Many organizations host events. While some event registrations may be internal (such as a large organization's yearly technical or sales conferences) and likely have little need for identity verification, many events are industry- or topic-focused, drawing in attendees from a myriad of companies. This seemed like a perfect target scenario.

I had an idea in my head of how I wanted this solution to work. However, when working with emerging technology products, sometimes the things you want to do don't exactly line up with the capabilities of the products. As a solution designer, it's important to be flexible and have a mindset that allows you to be able to pivot when you identify roadblocks.

When getting down to the details of the solution, I was faced with several challenges:

- **Power Apps**-based solutions require tenant identity and licensing, neither of which are ideal for external users.
- **Microsoft Forms** allows for file uploads, but only for internal (tenant) users—again, making it not ideal for external use cases.

Building an Event Registration App with Identity Verification

- **Power Pages** solutions can accept uploads, but a solution requires a pretty significant amount of permissions setup and management, in addition to designing an entire website interface and creating Dataverse tables. While there is a basic event registration app template available, it still requires a lot of customization and modification to apply this sort of validation logic.
- **SharePoint Online** can accept file uploads but is typically restricted to authenticated users. There is a request-a-file API that does allow anonymous upload, but it requires enablement by a SharePoint administrator and crafting a custom API file link for a record.

As you can see from the list of options, there are a lot of hurdles to overcome—whether it's licensing, coding challenges, or end-user ease of use. All of these things must be taken into consideration when choosing how to implement a solution—there may be limitations of the product in the box that you need to work around, especially if you're trying to minimize investment in third-party products or limit the amount of overall product development time.

In this solution, we're going to choose a path that allows for simple form design (using Microsoft Forms) and leverage the SharePoint Online API (even though it requires a little bit of custom development work).

Figure 8.1 depicts an overall workflow of how this solution will work:

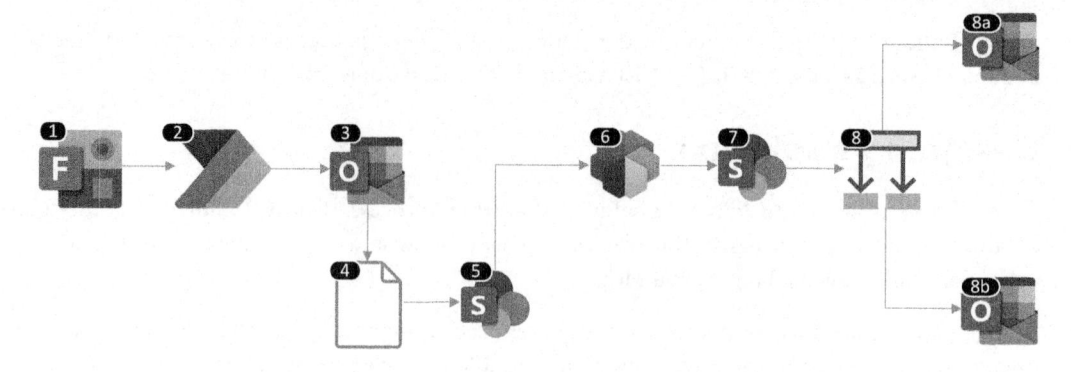

Figure 8.1 – Event registration and identity validation workflow

1. Let's break this down:
2. The user fills out an event registration form using the Microsoft Forms link.
3. Power Automate triggers and processes the form response, requesting data upload from the user.
4. The user receives an email with instructions to upload their identity document.
5. The user clicks the link in the generated email to upload the identity document.
6. The identity document is stored in SharePoint Online.

7. AI Builder is triggered to validate the identity document.
8. The SharePoint Online event registration list is updated to reflect whether document validation was successful or unsuccessful.
9. The Power Automate condition checks the identity verification status:

    I. If identity validation is successful, the user receives a confirmation email.

    II. If identity validation is unsuccessful, the user receives a failure notice.

Next, we'll look at the licensing prerequisites for this solution.

Licensing prerequisites

Using AI models and connectors in the Power Platform has several prerequisites:

- A subscription that includes Microsoft Dataverse
- AI Builder capacity (or trial capacity)
- Power Apps or Power Automate premium licensing
- A subscription that includes Microsoft Teams
- A subscription that includes Exchange Online
- Outlook desktop application

If you haven't already enabled Dataverse and AI Builder capacity, see *Chapter 2, Configuring an Environment to Support AI Services*, and *Chapter 6, Processing Data with Sentiment Analysis*.

Configuring solution prerequisites

Before you start the workflow configuration, you'll need to create a SharePoint list to hold registrants' information and a Teams meeting link that can be added to the confirmation email.

Configuring SharePoint Online

By default, SharePoint Online is restricted to authenticated users—whether they're in the same tenant or an external user who has previously redeemed a guest invitation. SharePoint does, however, allow anonymous sharing links as well as a feature for users to generate a file upload request and send it to an anonymous or otherwise unauthenticated user. We'll be taking advantage of the file request feature in a programmatic fashion to get SharePoint Online to allow anonymous uploads as part of a workflow.

> **Further reading**
>
> For more information on the file request feature, see `https://learn.microsoft.com/en-us/sharepoint/enable-file-requests` and `https://support.microsoft.com/en-us/office/create-a-file-request-f54aa7f8-2589-4421-b351-d415fc3b83af`. There are several caveats to getting this working (such as not restricting anonymous external access, anonymous or **Anyone** links enabled, and the appropriate permissions for **Anyone** links), so be sure your environment is configured.

Let's step through the requirements for making sure SharePoint Online is correctly configured.

Creating a SharePoint site

In order to receive file uploads, you'll want to set up a new SharePoint site. To configure a new SharePoint site, follow these steps:

1. Navigate to the SharePoint Online admin center (`https://admin.microsoft.com`), click **Show all…**, and then select **SharePoint** under **Admin centers**.
2. Expand **Sites** and select **Active sites**.
3. Click **Create**.
4. On the **Create a site: Select the site type** page, select **Team site**.
5. On the **Select a template** page, choose **Standard team**.
6. On the **Preview and use 'Standard team' template** page, click **Use template**.
7. On the **Give your site a name** page, enter a site name such as `Event Registration`.
8. Add a **Group owner** name and click **Next**.
9. Click **Create site**.
10. Click **Finish**.

After you've created the site, be sure to capture the full site URL—it will be needed later. The full URL will be in the format of `https://<tenant>.sharepoint.com/sites/<sitename>`. You can retrieve the site URL by selecting the site in the SharePoint admin setting to expand the site properties and copying the **View site** link, as shown in *Figure 8.2*:

Figure 8.2 – Copying the SharePoint site link

Next, you'll need to configure the **Anyone** links settings in the SharePoint admin center.

Enabling Anyone links

The first requirement is ensuring that **Anyone** links are enabled at the tenant level. To do that, follow these steps:

1. Navigate to the SharePoint Online admin center (`https://admin.microsoft.com`), click **Show all…**, and then select **SharePoint** under **Admin centers**.
2. Expand **Policies** and select **Sharing**. Ensure that the SharePoint access control slider is moved all the way to the top (**Anyone**). See *Figure 8.3*:

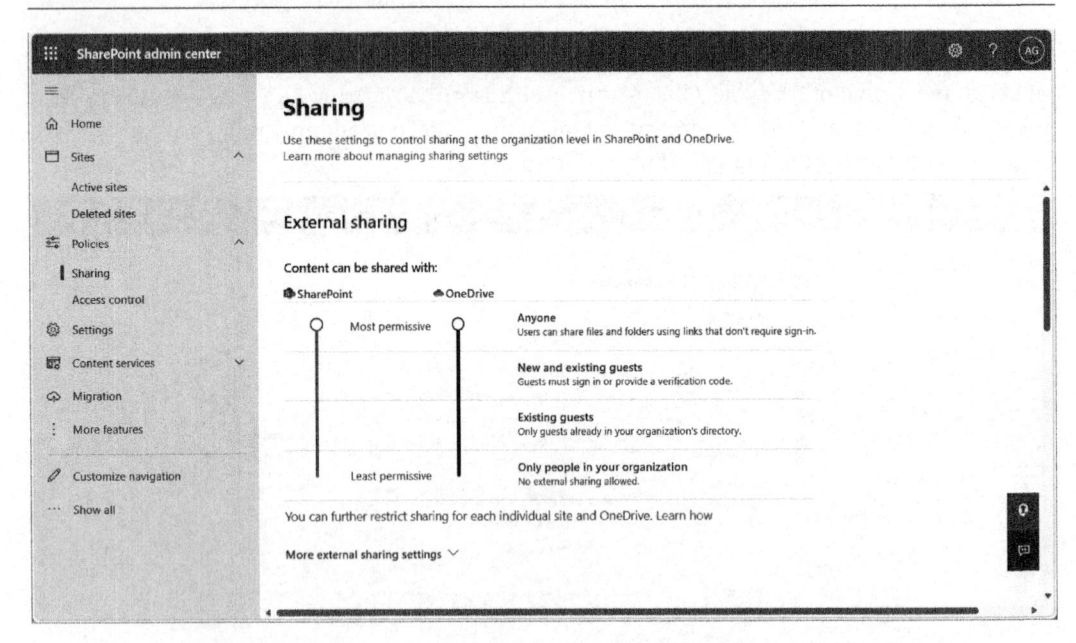

158　Building an Event Registration App with Identity Verification

Figure 8.3 – Configuring SharePoint external sharing access control level

3. Expand the **More external sharing settings** dropdown.
4. Ensure the **Allow only users in specific security groups to share externally** checkbox is cleared (not checked):

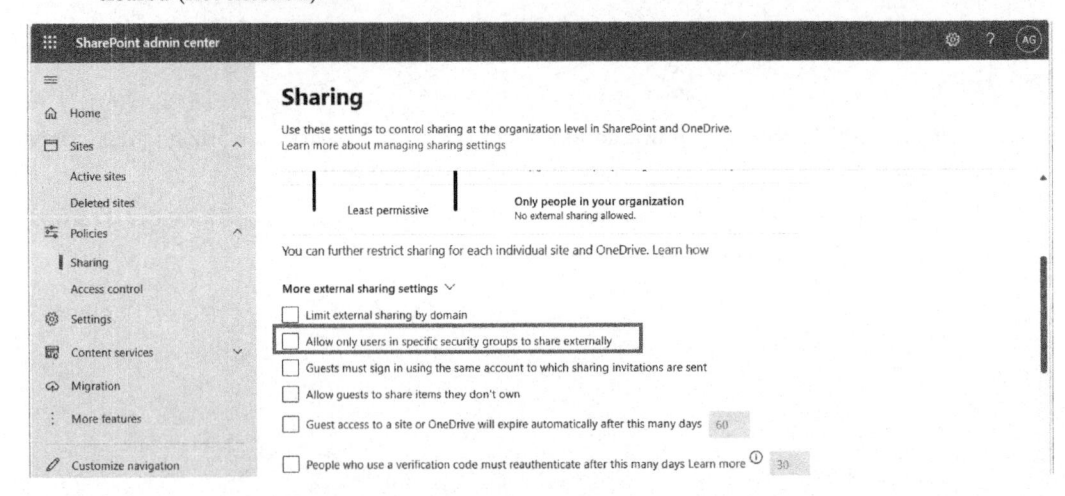

Figure 8.4 – Configuring More external sharing settings

Configuring solution prerequisites   159

5. Under **Choose expiration and permissions options for Anyone links**, ensure that **Folders** is set to **View, edit, and upload**:

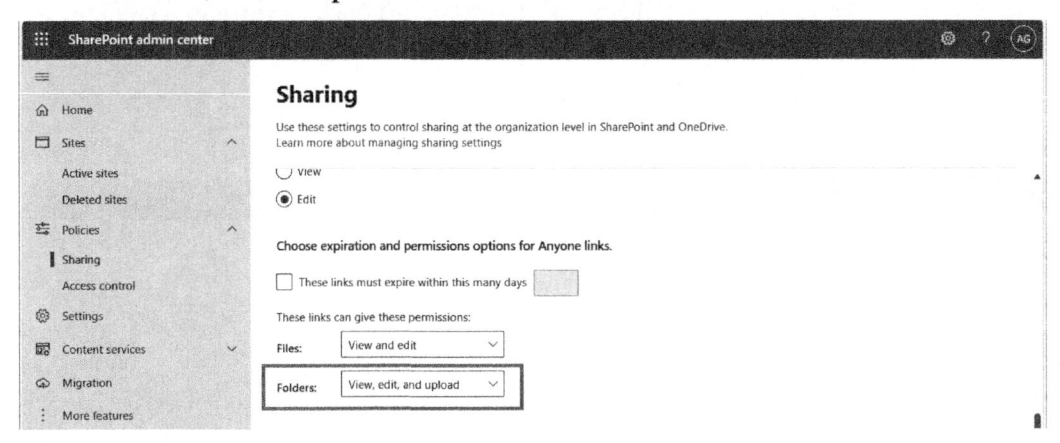

Figure 8.5 – Configuring additional SharePoint settings

6. Click **Save**.

The next step is to create a document library that will hold attendees' identity documents.

Provisioning a SharePoint document library

This solution requires a storage location to hold the uploaded identity document. While you can use the default document library, it tends to lead to more troubleshooting as the library's display name (**Documents**) is different than its actual name (**Shared Documents**).

To create a new SharePoint document library, follow these steps:

1. Navigate to the **Event Registration** SharePoint site.
2. Click **New** and then select **Document library**.
3. On the **Create new document library** page, select **Blank library**.
4. Enter Uploads in the **Name** field and click **Create**.

That's it! Next, we'll create a SharePoint list for attendees.

Provisioning a SharePoint list

The final piece of configuring the SharePoint list. The list will be used to store registrant information as well as track the identity validation status. Follow these steps:

1. Navigate to the **Event Registration** SharePoint site.
2. Click **New** and then select **List**:

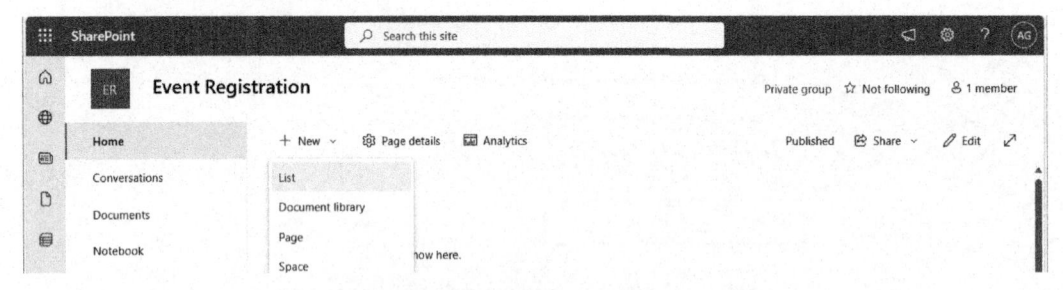

Figure 8.6 – Creating a new list

3. On the **Create a list** page, select **Blank list**.
4. Enter a **Name** value for the list, such as `Attendees`, and click **Create**.
5. On the **Attendees** list, click **Add column**. Select **Text** as the type and click **Next**:

Figure 8.7 – Configuring a new column

6. Name the column `First name` and click **Save**.

Configuring solution prerequisites   161

7. Repeat adding a column using the column names and types in *Table 8.1*:

Column name	Column type
Last name	Text
Phone number	Text
DOB	Text
Email	Text
Validation status	Choice: Pending submission, Passed, Failed
Valid through	Text
Identity data	Text

Table 8.1 – SharePoint list column information

Updating SharePoint Online settings

Next, you'll need to configure the SharePoint Online tenant to display the **Request file** action. Follow these steps:

1. Launch an elevated PowerShell prompt.

2. Install the latest version of the SharePoint Online Management PowerShell module:

   ```
   Install-Module Microsoft.Online.SharePoint.PowerShell -Force
   ```

3. Connect to the SharePoint Online management interface using `<tenant>-admin` to reference your site. See *Figure 8.8*, where the tenant name is `o365ninja`. Your tenant name was established during the Microsoft 365 setup and is in the form of `tenant.onmicrosoft.com`:

   ```
   Connect-SPOService -Url https://<tenant>-admin.sharepoint.comhttps://<tenant>-admin.sharepoint.com
   ```

```
PS C:\> Install-Module Microsoft.Online.SharePoint.PowerShell -Force
PS C:\> Connect-SPOService -Url https://o365ninja-admin.sharepoint.com
PS C:\>
```

Figure 8.8 – Connecting to SharePoint Online

4. Next, you'll need to enable the **Request files** feature on the SharePoint site you created earlier. Use the following cmdlet in the SharePoint Management Shell:

```
Set-SpoSite -Identity <SiteURL> -RequestFileLinkEnabled $True
```

Figure 8.9 – Enabling the file request feature

5. Once the setting has been updated, navigate to the SharePoint Online site URL for the event registration solution. Select **Uploads** to display the document library created earlier.
6. Create a new folder called `RegistrationData`. Right-click on the new folder and search for the **Request files** option, as shown in *Figure 8.10*. If it is visible, everything has been configured properly:

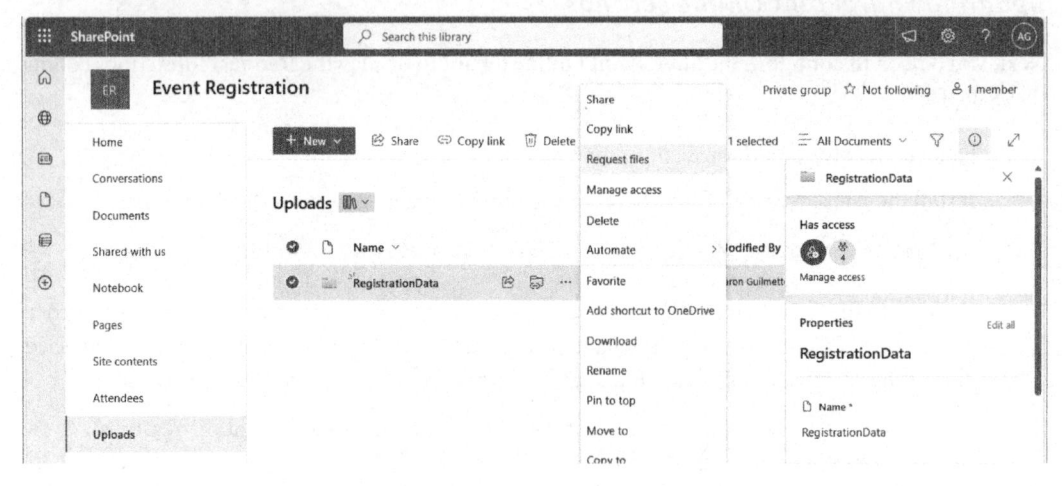

Figure 8.10 – Viewing the availability of the Request files option

Next, it's time to configure a Teams meeting.

Establishing a Teams meeting

This optional step can be performed if your event is going to be online and conducted through Microsoft Teams. In this process, you'll create a meeting and export it as an ICS file. While you can generate an ICS file manually, it's far easier just to export one from Outlook. To create a meeting, follow these steps:

1. Navigate to Microsoft Teams and select **Calendar** from the left rail to open the Calendar app.
2. Click the dropdown next to **New meeting** and select **Town hall**. While webinars do have registration, it's integrated into the app, and there currently isn't a way to inject a flow into the native webinar registration process. Live events are scheduled to be retired in 2024, and meeting organizers should schedule either webinars or **Town hall** events. See *Figure 8.11*:

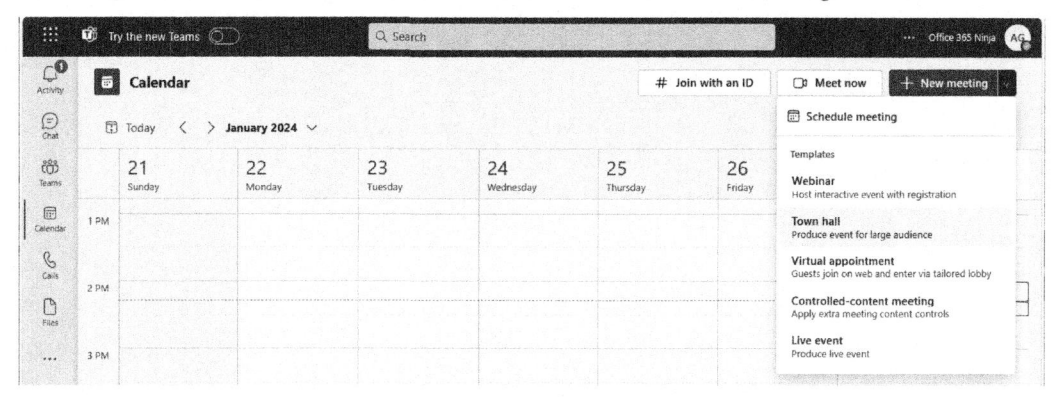

Figure 8.11 – Creating a new Town hall meeting

3. Configure the details of the meeting, including **Title**, **Start date**, **End date**, and **Description** values.
4. Scroll to the bottom of the invitation and select **Public** under **Attendees**:

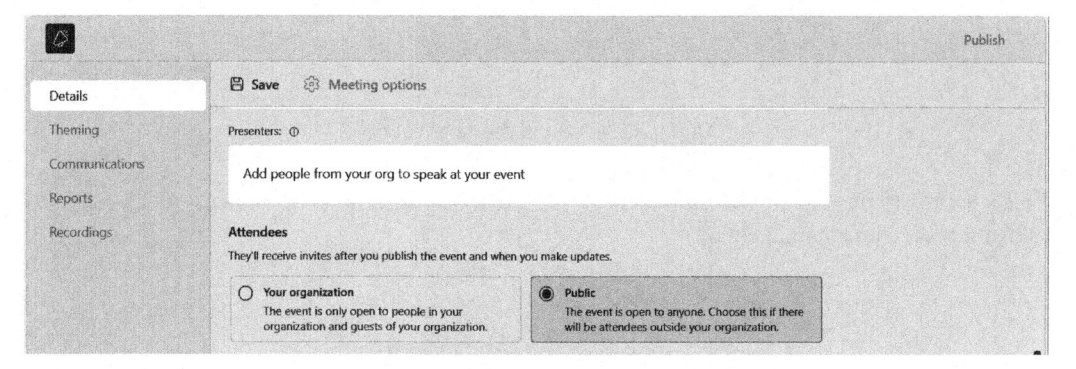

Figure 8.12 – Configuring the meeting settings

5. Click **Save**.
6. Click **Publish** to publish the meeting.
7. Launch the Outlook desktop client.
8. Navigate to the calendar event that was created by the Teams meeting wizard. Open the meeting.
9. Click **File** to open the **Backstage** tab, then select **Save As**.
10. Navigate to a OneDrive for Business or SharePoint Online site where you can save the ICS file. Ensure the **Save Selected Appointment** radio button is selected and click **Save**:

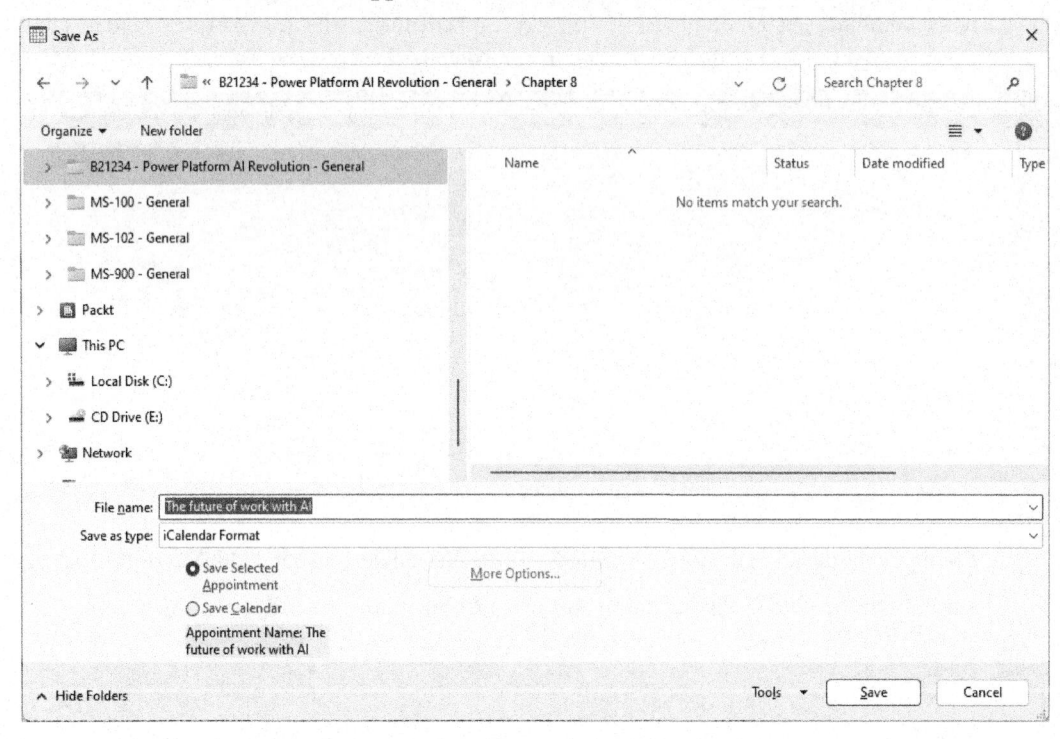

Figure 8.13 – Saving the calendar file

Once the registration is complete and identity validated, this calendar appointment will be delivered with a success confirmation email.

Building an input form

The final preparation step is building a Microsoft form that will be used by event participants to register. To configure the form, follow these steps:

1. Navigate to Microsoft Forms (https://forms.microsoft.com) and click **New Form**:

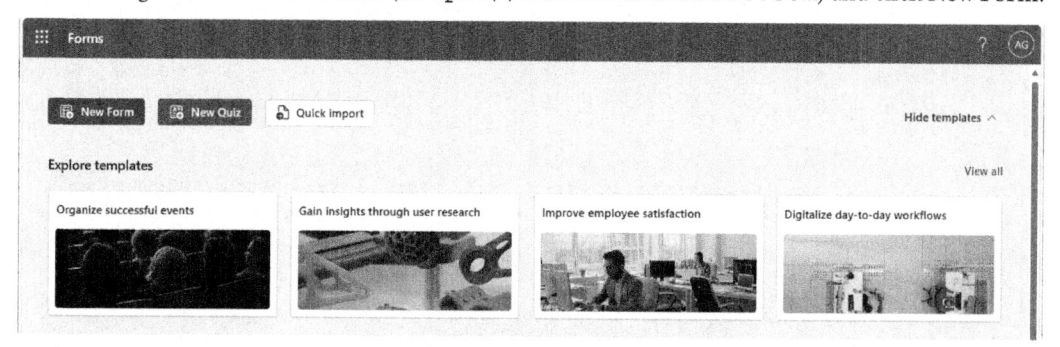

Figure 8.14 – Creating a new Microsoft form

2. Name the form, and add text fields for **First name**, **Last name**, **Email**, and **Phone number**:

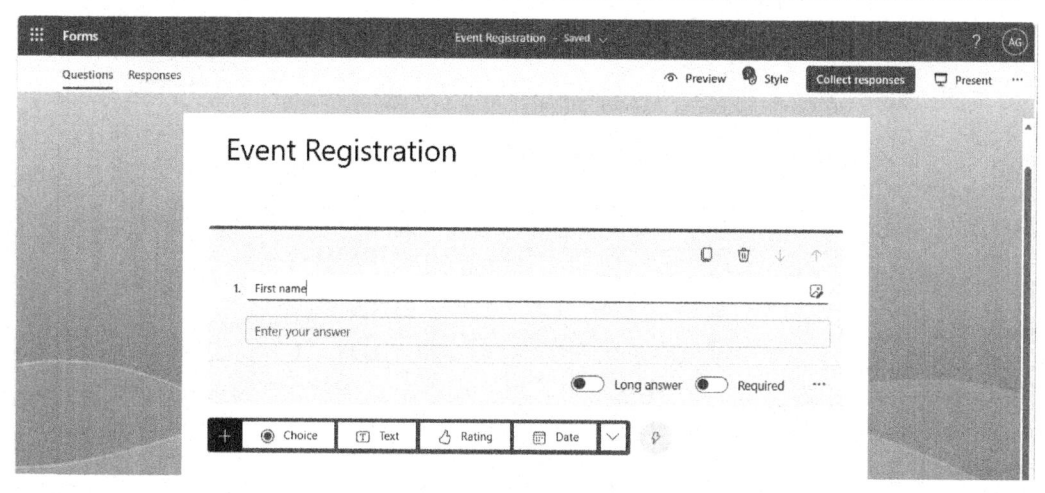

Figure 8.15 – Adding fields

3. Expand the ellipsis and select **Settings**, as shown in *Figure 8.16*:

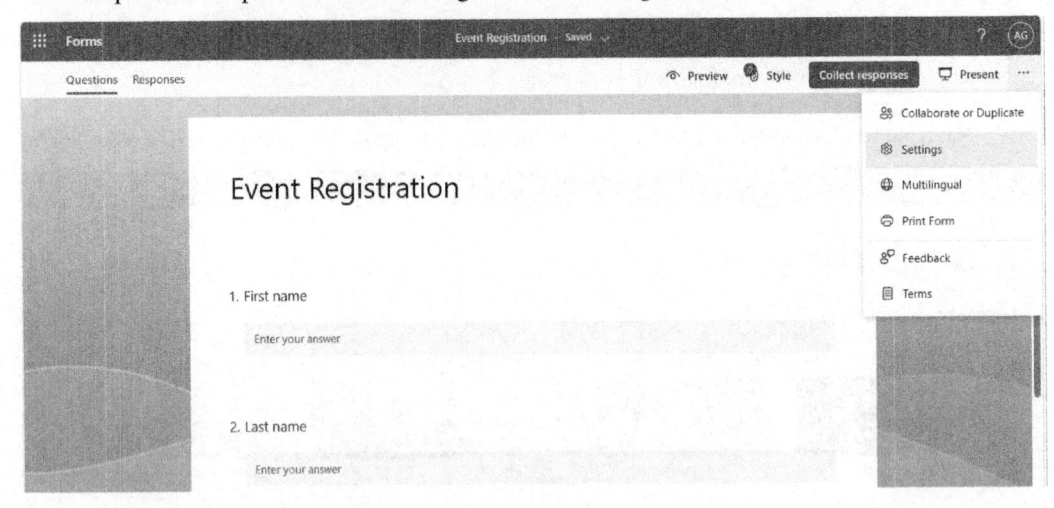

Figure 8.16 – Configuring form settings

4. Under **Who can fill out this form**, ensure that the **Anyone can respond** radio button is selected:

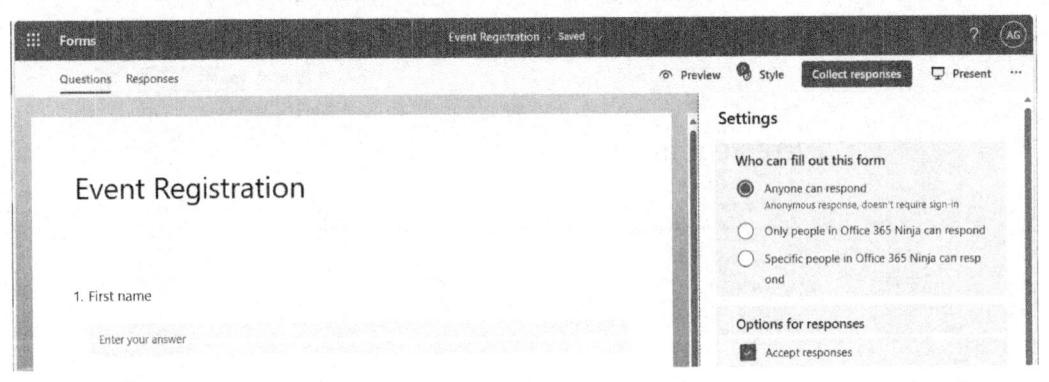

Figure 8.17 – Updating form settings

5. Click **Collect responses** and then copy the form link to a text file for later use during the testing phase.

Figure 8.18 – Copying the form link

With the prerequisites configured, it's time to start working on some automation!

Creating flows

This solution has two flows—one that is triggered on the form response and another that is triggered when the identity document is uploaded to SharePoint.

> **What do I do if I'm stuck?**
>
> If you run into a roadblock for some reason (can't find a feature, an option isn't showing up, or something is unclear), help is only a click away! You can download this chapter's artifacts from our GitHub site: `https://github.com/PacktPublishing/Power-Platform-and-the-AI-Revolution`.

Let's get started with the first flow!

Configuring a flow to handle form submission

This flow is triggered on the submission of a form. After the form has been processed, the registrant will receive an email prompting them to upload their identity document. As mentioned earlier, Forms does allow a file upload natively, but it requires the user to be authenticated to the Microsoft 365 tenant (which isn't ideal for external users).

Processing the form

In this first section, you'll start by processing the Microsoft Form data. Follow these steps:

1. Open a browser and navigate to the Power Automate maker portal (`https://make.powerautomate.com`), select **Create**, and then click **Automated cloud flow**.

2. On the **Build an automated cloud flow** page, enter a **Flow name** value and then select the **When a new response is submitted** trigger. Click **Create**.

3. On the canvas, click the **When a new response is submitted** trigger. If necessary, click **Change connection** to log in to Microsoft 365:

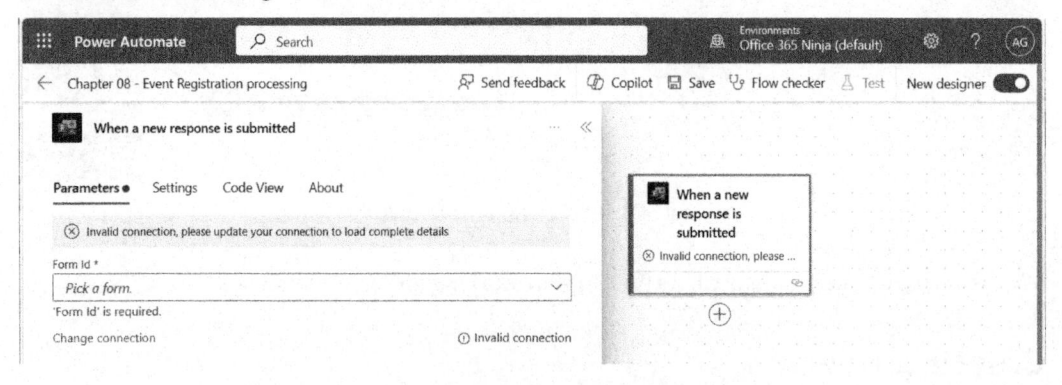

Figure 8.19 – Updating the trigger with credentials

4. Click the **Form Id** dropdown and select the **Event Registration** form:

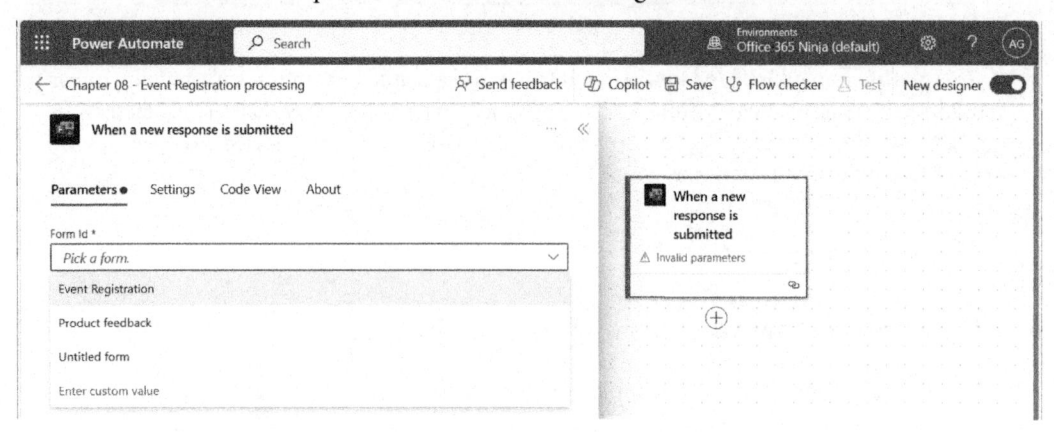

Figure 8.20 – Selecting a form

5. Click the + sign to add an action and select the **Scope** control.

Creating flows 169

6. Rename the scope control to Processing the form. See *Figure 8.21*:

Figure 8.21 – Updating the scope name

7. Inside the **Scope** control, click **Add an action**.
8. In the **Add an action** flyout, select the **Get response details** action.
9. Under **Form Id**, select the **Event Registration** form.
10. Under **Response Id**, select the dynamic content token for **List of response notifications Response Id**. The action will be inserted into an **Apply each** or a **For each** wrapper (depending on if you are using **Classic designer** or **New designer**):

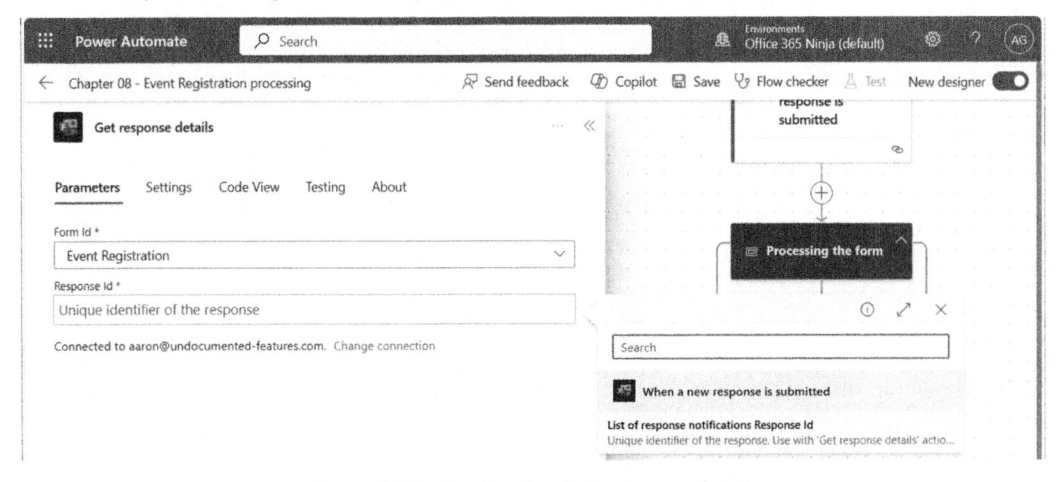

Figure 8.22 – Configuring Get response details

11. In the **For each** wrapper, after **Get response details**, click **Add an action**.

170　Building an Event Registration App with Identity Verification

12. Select the **Compose** action. Rename the action to `ComposeUnique`. The **Compose** action will be used to generate a unique ID that will be used to name the evidence submitted by the **Request files** action later.

13. In the **Inputs** textbox, add an expression. On the **Function** tab, paste the following content:

    ```
    concat(utcNow('yyyyMMddHHMMss'),'_',)
    ```

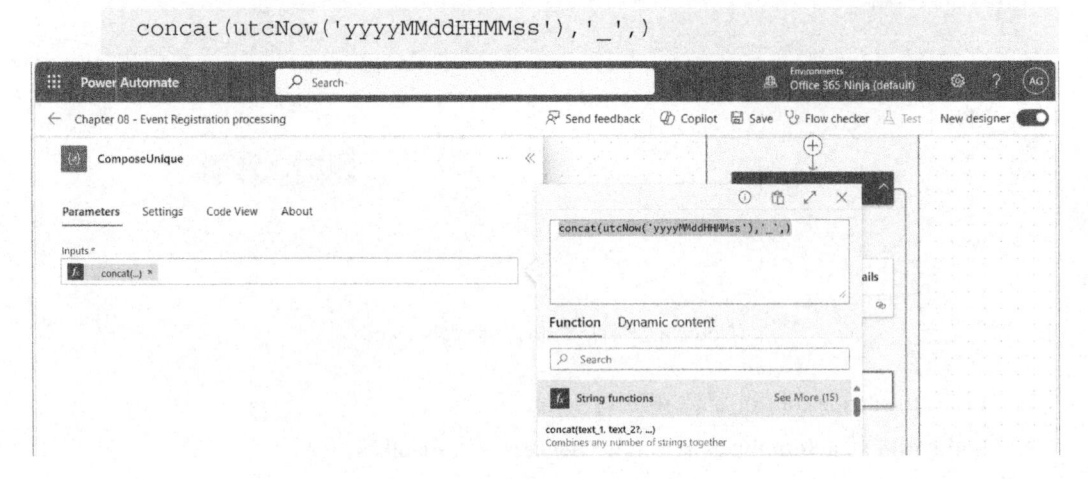

Figure 8.23 – Configuring the Compose action

14. Click in the text area between the last comma (,) and the closing parenthesis ()). Click the **Dynamic content** tab and then add the **Email** dynamic content token from the **Get response details** action. See *Figure 8.24*:

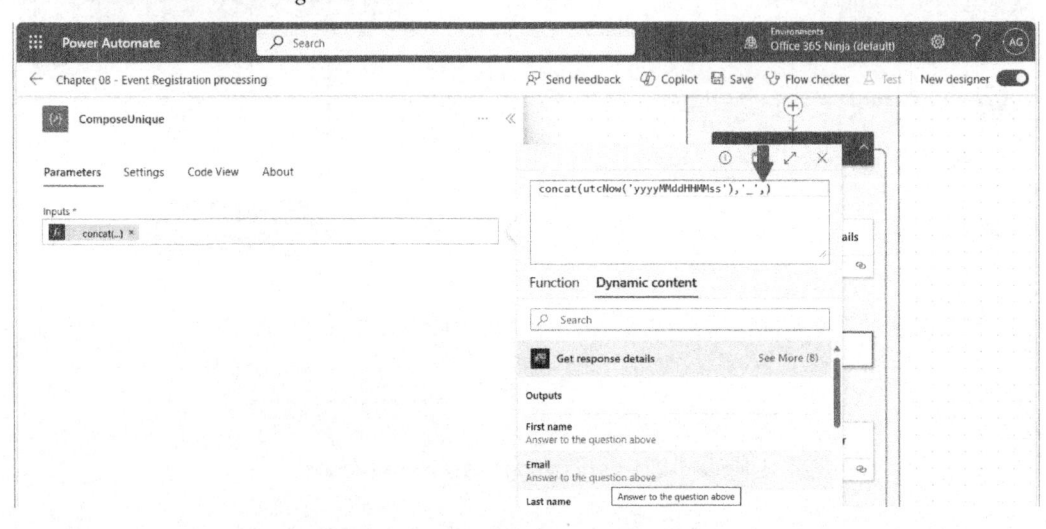

Figure 8.24 – Updating the Compose action with the Email token

When completed, the function value should look similar to the following example:

```
concat(utcNow('yyyyMMddHHMMss'),'_',body('Get_response_
details')?['r05e4d4be0beb4bb7b64c3b502b312d63'])
```

This is used to compose a value that is comprised of the current date and time the flow executes plus the responder's submitted email address to provide a unique value. You can't copy and paste this whole value, as it directly corresponds to the specific form object in this environment.

> **Further reading**
>
> For more information on the Concat function, see https://learn.microsoft.com/en-us/power-platform/power-fx/reference/function-concatenate. For more information on the UtcNow function, see https://learn.microsoft.com/en-us/power-platform/power-fx/reference/function-now-today-istoday.

15. Inside the **Apply to each** wrapper, click **Add an action** after the **ComposeUnique** action. Select the **Create new folder** SharePoint action.
16. In the **Create new folder** flyout, select the **Event Registration** site under **Site Address**.
17. Under **List or Library**, select the **Uploads** document library you created earlier.
18. Under **Folder Path**, add the **Outputs** dynamic content token from the **ComposeUnique** action, as shown in *Figure 8.25*:

Figure 8.25 – Configuring the Create new folder action

19. Inside the **Apply to each** wrapper, click **Add an action** after the **Create new folder** action. Select the **Create item** SharePoint action.
20. In the **Create item** flyout, under **Site Address**, select the **Event Registration** site.

21. Under **List name**, select the **Attendees** list.

22. Under **Advanced parameters**, under **Title**, select the **Outputs** dynamic content token from the **ComposeUnique** action.

23. Under **First name**, add an expression to convert the **First name** value to uppercase letters. In the **Function** text area, enter `toUpper()`.

24. Place the cursor between the `(` and `)` characters. Select the **Dynamic content** tab and then add the **First name** dynamic content token from the **Get Response Details** action. The output should look similar to the following:

```
toUpper(body('Get_response_
details')?['rd5fe1d483e4d4f23ac7a55bbbed1c004'])
```

Identity documents use *UPPERCASE* formatting. Attendees may not enter their details in all uppercase, so conversion is necessary to ensure any compare operations are successful.

25. Under **Last name**, add an expression to convert the **First name** value to uppercase letters. In the **Function** text area, enter `toUpper()`.

26. Place the cursor between the `(` and `)` characters. Select the **Dynamic content** tab and then add the **Last name** dynamic content token from the **Get Response Details** action. The output should look similar to the following:

```
toUpper(body('Get_response_
details')?['rfd1546de5f714c8da504d988e5c692ec'])
```

27. Under **Phone number**, select the **Phone number** dynamic content token from the **Get Response Details** action.

28. Under **Email**, select the **Email** dynamic content token from the **Get Response Details** action.

> **Caution**
>
> Do not select the **Responders' Email** dynamic content token from the **Get response details** action. The **Responders' Email** dynamic content token is linked to the authenticated user that submits the form. If the form is submitted by someone outside your Microsoft 365 tenant (which is the goal of this solution), this token value will be *anonymous*.

29. Under **Validation Status Value**, select the **Pending submission** option. See *Figure 8.26* for the completed **Create item** action configuration:

Creating flows 173

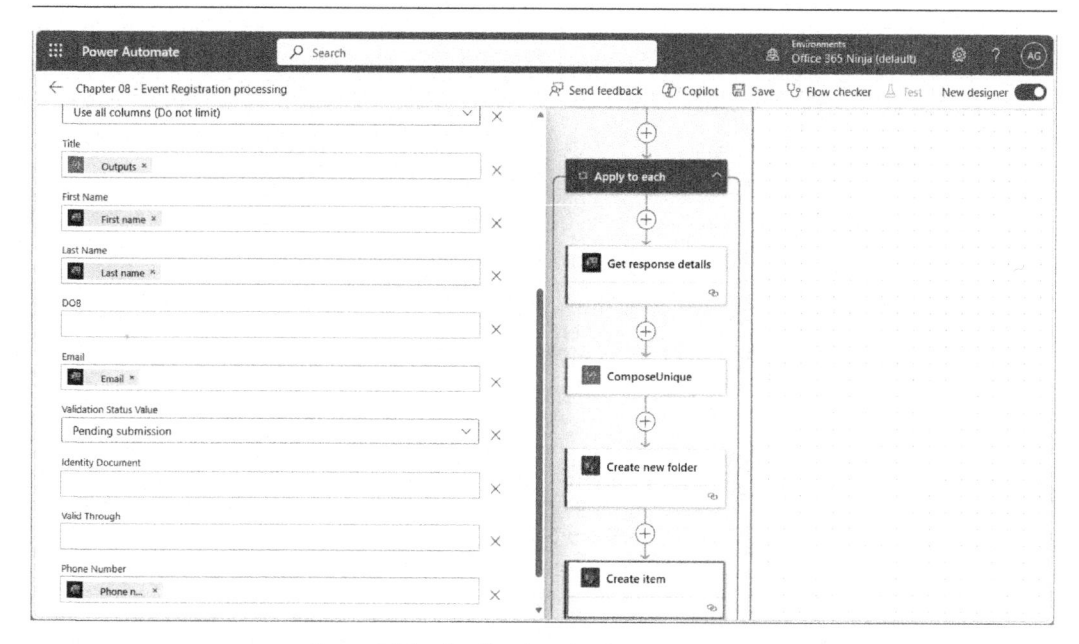

Figure 8.26 – Configuring the Create item action

30. Click **Save**.

Next, you'll generate a SharePoint Online file request using the SharePoint Online REST API.

Generating a file request link

In this section, you'll create a new scope nested inside the **Processing the form** scope. This will help you group tasks related to generating the link and sending the email. Follow these steps:

1. Click the + sign outside the **Apple to each** wrapper and inside the **Processing the form** scope control. Select **Add an action** and select the **Scope** control.
2. Update the name of the new scope to `Generating the SharePoint Online file request`.
3. Inside the **Generating the SharePoint Online file request scope**, click **Add an action**.
4. Select the **Send HTTP request to SharePoint** action.
5. Under **Site Address**, select the **Event Registration** site.
6. Under **Method**, select **POST**.

7. Under **URI**, enter the following data (where `'Uploads'` is the document library that contains the **RegistrationData** folder created in the prerequisites section):

   ```
   _api/web/Lists/GetByTitle('Uploads')/GetItemById('@
   {body('Create_new_folder')?['ID']}')/ShareLink
   ```

   This special URI path locates the `Uploads` document library and then adds in the unique identifier of the folder that was created in the previous section.

8. Under **Advanced parameters**, click **Show all** to display the **Body** area.

9. Paste the following data into the **Body** area:

   ```
   {
   "request": {
    "createLink" : true,
    "settings" : {
       "allowAnonymousAccess" : true,
       "linkKind" : 6,
       "restrictShareMembership": false,
       "updatePassword": false,
       "password" : "",
       "description": "@{outputs('ComposeUnique')}",
       "role" : 8,
       "applicationLink" : false,
       "limitUseToApplication" : false
       }
      }
   }
   ```

   This JSON value will be sent to SharePoint Online to trigger the file request.

> **Further reading**
>
> For more on the structure of the SharePoint Online REST API function for requesting a file, see `https://learn.microsoft.com/en-us/graph/api/driveitem-createlink?view=graph-rest-1.0&tabs=http`.

Creating flows 175

10. Verify the settings in the action configuration. See *Figure 8.27*:

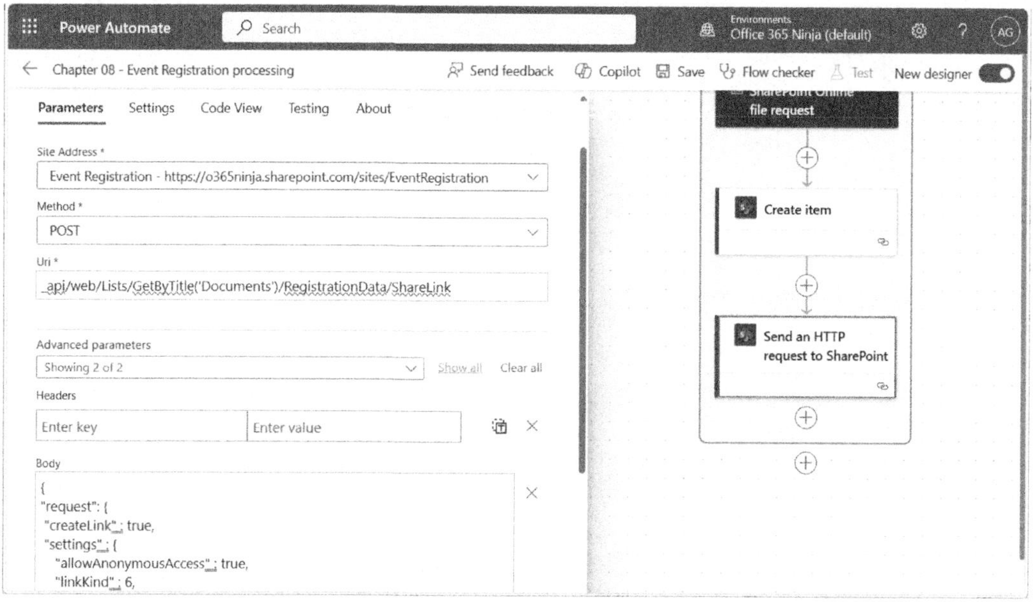

Figure 8.27 – Configuring the Send an HTTP request to SharePoint action

11. In the **SharePoint Online file request** scope, click **Add an action** after the **Send an HTTP request to SharePoint** action.
12. Select the **Compose** action.
13. Rename the **Compose** action to `ComposeURL`.
14. In the **Inputs** field, insert an expression, and enter the following value:

```
body('Send_an_HTTP_request_to_SharePoint')?['body']?['d/
ShareLink/sharingLinkInfo/url']
```

This action takes the output of the **Send an HTTP request to SharePoint** action and extracts the dynamically created SharePoint URL.

This expression is derived from looking at a previous flow run to determine what properties are available from the **Send an HTTP request to SharePoint** action's output. See *Figure 8.28*:

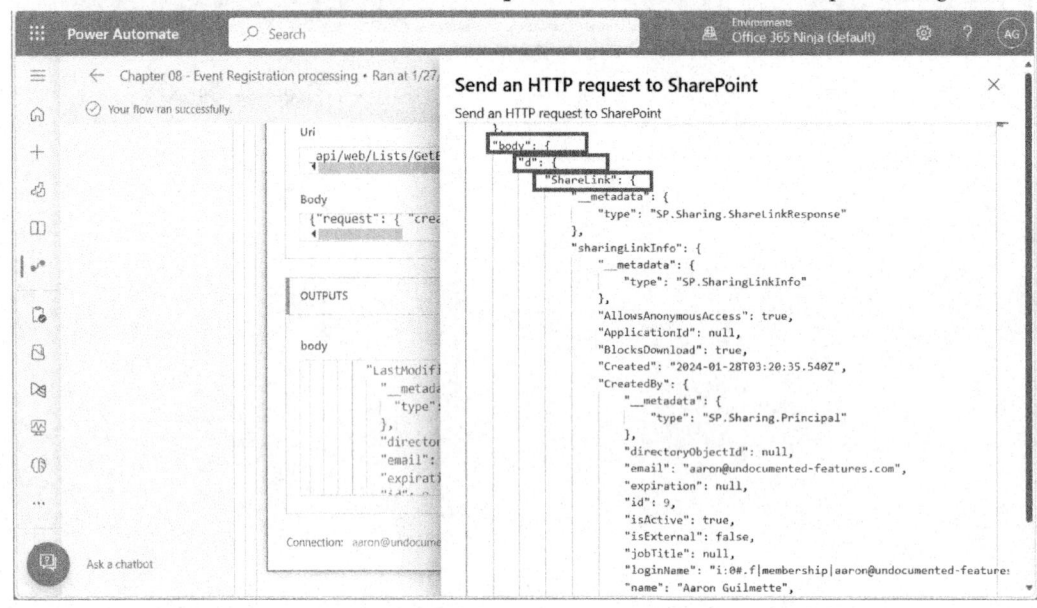

Figure 8.28 – Reviewing the output of a successful Send an HTTP request to SharePoint action

From a JSON output perspective, the structure is the following:

```
{
    "statusCode": 200,
    "headers": {
        "Cache-Control": "no-store, max-age=0, private"
    },
    "body": {
        "d": {
            "ShareLink": {
                "sharingLinkInfo": {
                    "AllowsAnonymousAccess": true,

                    "Description": "20240128030134_user@domain.com",
                    "IsCreateOnlyLink": true,
                    "IsDefault": true,
                    "IsEditLink": true,
                    "LimitUseToApplication": false,
                    "LinkKind": 6,

                    "RequiresPassword": false,
```

```
                    "RestrictedShareMembership": false,
                    "SharingLinkStatus": 1,
                    "Url": "https://o365ninja.
sharepoint.com/:f:/s/EventRegistration/
EmlH2cOzMrRLsLRK6AjhXUwB97IiZxGyd2hQOv9GySxTSA"
                }
            }
        }
    }
}
```

The property that's needed for the attendee to upload their identity document is stored in the `Url` key/value pair. Power Automate allows you to navigate levels of the JSON structure using a / character. Traversing the JSON object from the `Url` node reveals the hierarchy that's needed to reference the URL:

Url > sharingLinkInfo > ShareLink > d > body

When translating this to the Power Automate syntax, it becomes the following:

```
body('Send_an_HTTP_request_to_SharePoint')?['body']?['d/
ShareLink/sharingLinkInfo/url']
```

Click **Add**.

15. In the **SharePoint Online file request** scope, click **Add an action** after the **ComposeURL** action.
16. Select the **Send an email V2** Outlook action.
17. In the **Send an email (V2)** action flyout, populate the **To** field using the **Email** dynamic content token from the **Get response details** action.
18. Enter a **Subject** name and create a basic email message in the **Body** area. Be sure to include the **Outputs** dynamic content value from the **ComposeURL** action (since it contains the URL necessary for the attendee to upload their identity document), as shown in *Figure 8.29*:

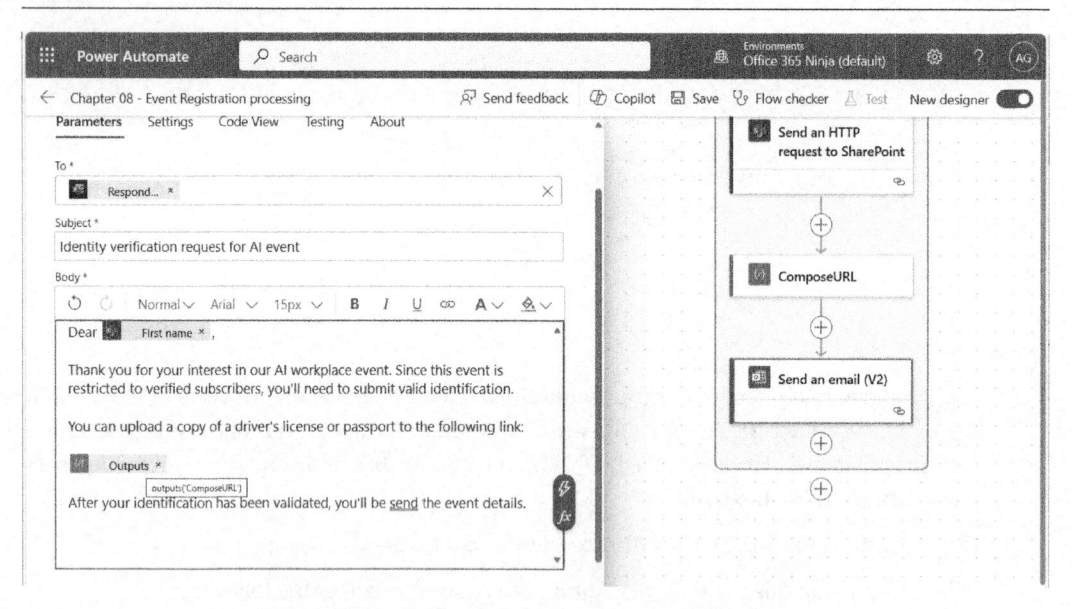

Figure 8.29 – Configuring the Send an email (V2) action

19. Click **Save**.

At this point, you can test the flow by submitting a form and seeing if a message arrives in the registrant's email. Otherwise, let's get creating the second flow!

Processing the identity document

Up to this point, you've created a flow that processes a Microsoft Forms response and uses the data inside to generate a custom file upload link to the registrant. In this next flow, you'll use the AI Builder Identity Document reader to extract data from the uploaded file and update the corresponding attendee registration row in the **Attendees** SharePoint list.

Let's go!

1. From the Power Automate maker portal (https://make.powerautomate.com), click **Create** and select **Automated cloud flow**.

2. Enter a **Flow name** value and select the **When a file is created (properties only)** SharePoint trigger, as shown in *Figure 8.30*:

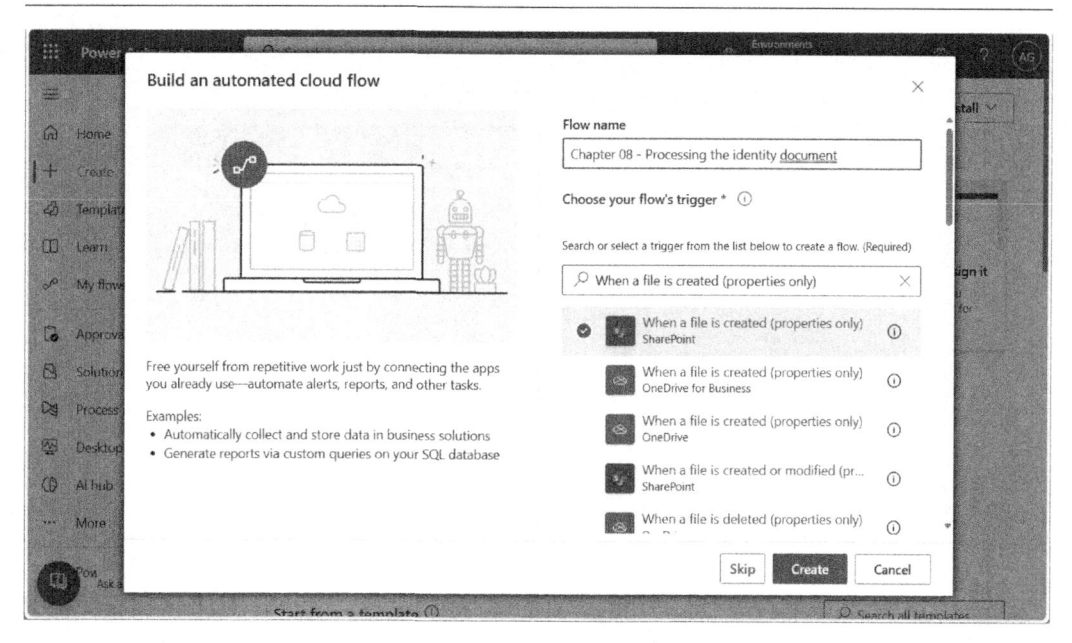

Figure 8.30 – Creating a new flow

3. Click **Create**.
4. Select the **When a file is created (properties only)** trigger to bring up the flyout.
5. Under **Site Address**, select the **Event Registration** site.
6. Under **Library Name**, select **Uploads**.
7. Since the **When a file is created (properties only)** action is also triggered upon folder creation, it's important to exclude folder creation activities from the trigger. Select the **Settings** tab of the action. Under **Trigger conditions**, click **Add**.

8. In the field, enter `@equals(triggerOutputs()?['body/{IsFolder}'],false)` to filter out events that involve folder creation. See *Figure 8.31*:

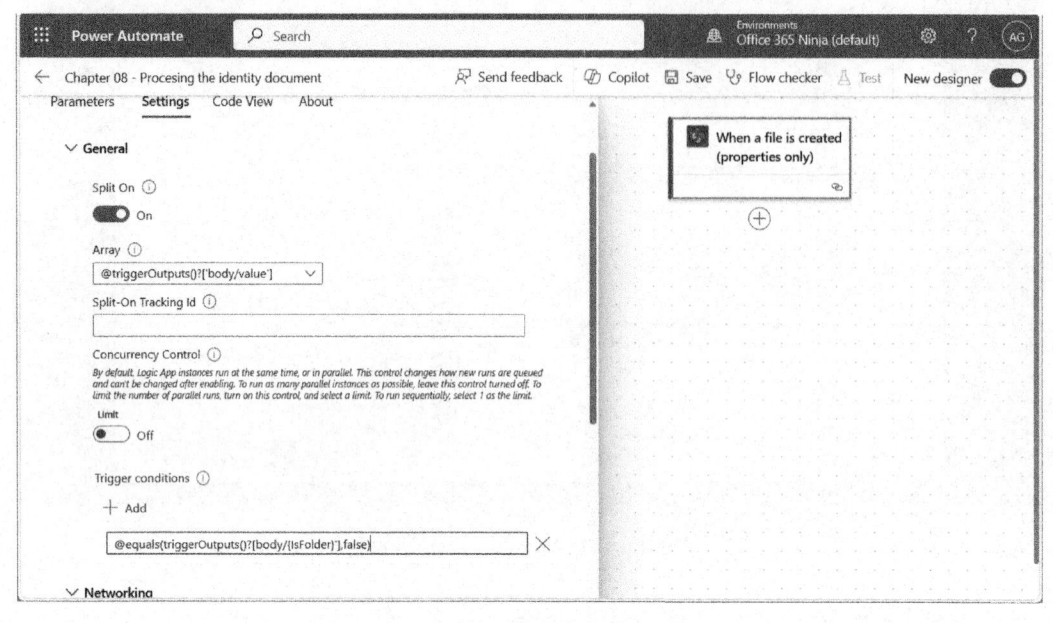

Figure 8.31 – Adding a trigger condition

9. Next, bring the content of the uploaded file into the flow by adding a **Get file content** action. Click **Add an action** and then select the **Get file content using path** action. We're using this action because both the folder name value and the row entry in the **Attendees** list were generated previously using an expression: `(concat(utcNow('yyyyMMddHHMMss'),'_',body('Get_response_details')?['value'])`.

10. In the **Get file content using path** flyout, under **Site Address**, choose the **Event Registration** site.

11. In the **File path** field, select the **Full Path** dynamic content token under the **When a file is created (properties only)** action.

   Power Automate may add a **For each** or **Apply to each** control since more than one new document may be present when the flow runs. If one isn't automatically added, click + and then select **Add an action**. Select the **Apply to each** control and drag the **Get file content** action into it.

> **Note**
> If the **Dynamic content** control doesn't show any dynamic content values, you may try switching to the Classic Power Automate designer and re-add the **Get file content using path** action. If desired, you can save and switch back to **New designer** afterward.

12. After the **Get file content using path** action, click **Add an action** and select the **Extract information from identity documents** AI Builder action, as shown in *Figure 8.32*:

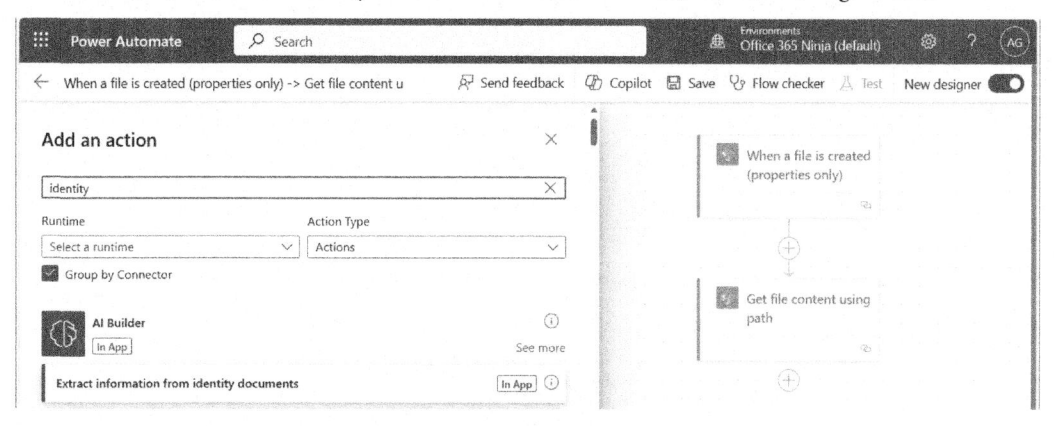

Figure 8.32 – Adding the AI Builder action

13. In the **Extract information from identity documents** flyout, add the **File Content** dynamic token from the **Get file content using path** action:

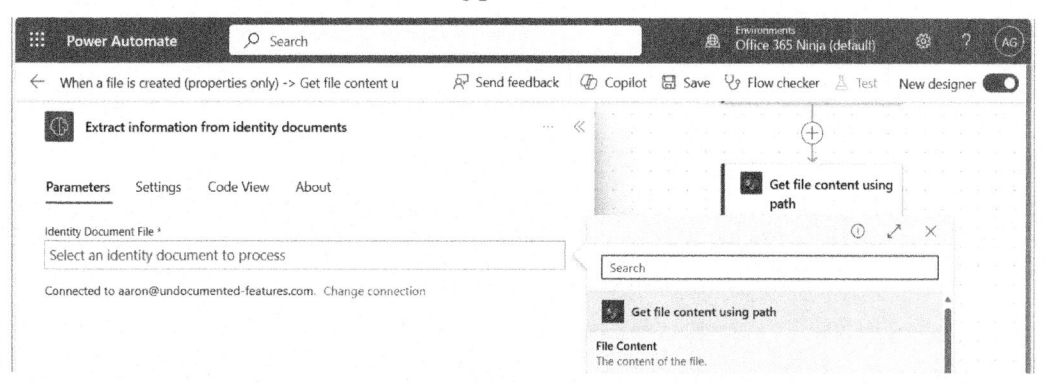

Figure 8.33 – Selecting the file content to use with AI Builder

14. After the **Extract information from identity documents** action, click **Add an action** and select the **Get items** SharePoint action.
15. Under **Site Address**, select the **Event Registration** site.
16. Under **List Name**, select the **Attendees** list.
17. In the **Advanced parameters** dropdown, select the **Filter Query** parameter.
18. In the **Filter Query** field, enter `Title eq'`.
19. Click inside the **Filter Query** field and add an expression.

182   Building an Event Registration App with Identity Verification

20. Enter `split(triggerOutputs()?['body/{Path}'],'/')?[1]` in the text area and click **Add**. Add a closing ' character to the **Filter Query** string. The completed value should resemble the following:

    ```
    Title eq '@{split(triggerOutputs()?['body/{Path}'],'/')?[1]}'
    ```

    The expression manipulates the SharePoint item path, extracting the value after the / character. This path value is the same as the item name value of the corresponding item in the SharePoint list.

21. After the **Get items** action, click **Add an action** and choose the **Get item** action:

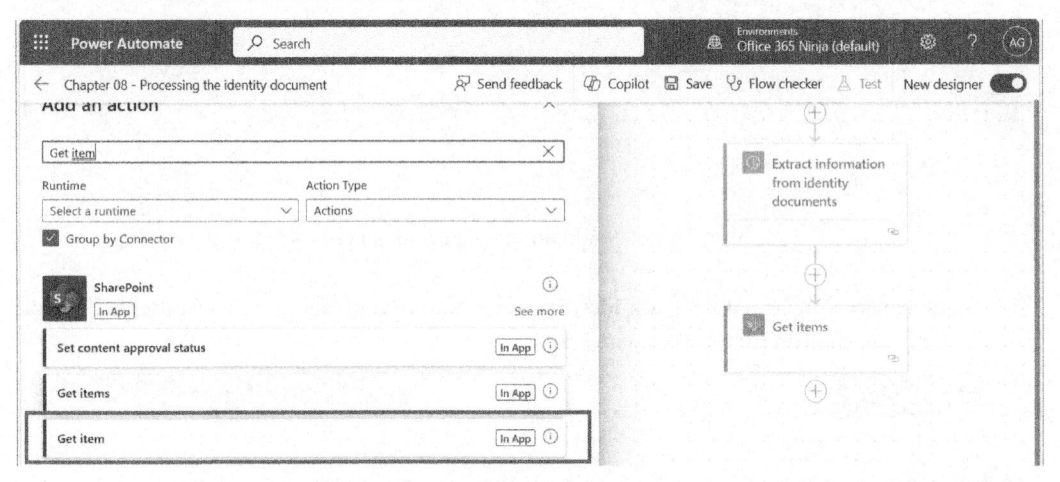

Figure 8.34 – Choosing the Get item action

Be sure to get the **Get item** action (and not the **Get items** action). **Get items** returns a collection of items, while **Get item** returns a single item.

22. Under **Site Address**, select the **Event Registration** site.

23. Under **List Name**, select the **Attendees** list.

24. Click in the **Id** field area. Select the expression icon.

25. On the **Function** tab, enter `first(outputs('Get_items')?['body/value'])?['id']`. Click **Add**:

Creating flows | 183

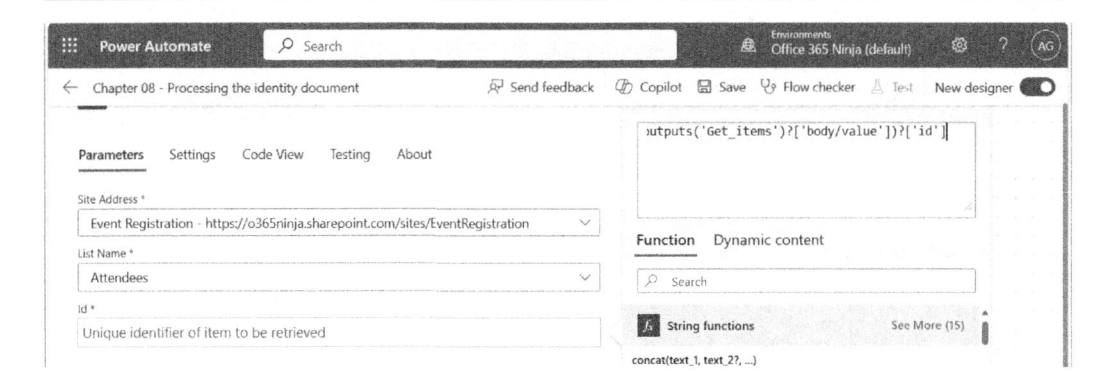

Figure 8.35 – Configuring the item expression

The previous expression used a filter query to return a single item. This expression builds on that by looking up the `id` property of the **Get items** action using the output of the expression in *step 20*.

26. After the **Get item** action, select **Add an action** and choose the **Condition** control.
27. Configure the **Condition** control flyout. In the **Condition expression** area, configure the conditions based on *Table 8.2*:

Condition	Operation	Condition
First name from **Extract information from identity documents** AI Builder action	**Contains**	**First name** from **Get item** SharePoint action
Last name from **Extract information from identity documents** AI Builder action	**Contains**	**Last name** from **Get item** SharePoint action

Table 8.2 – Configuring Condition control values

28. Review the **Condition** control configuration. See *Figure 8.36*:

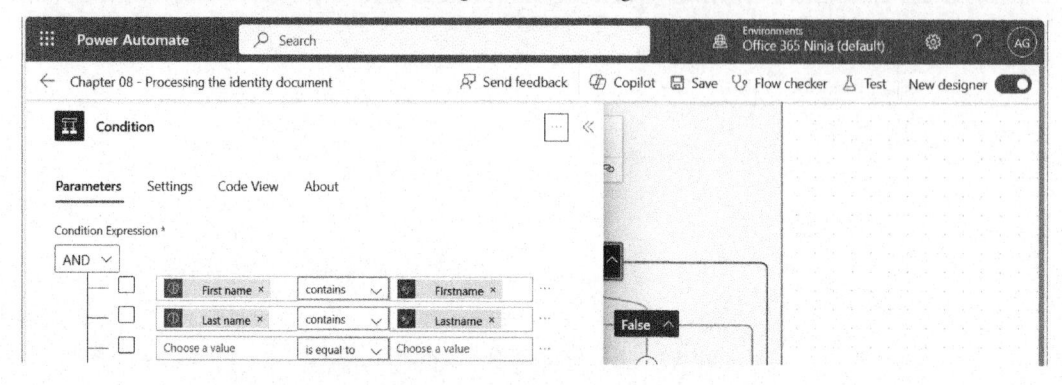

Figure 8.36 – Reviewing the Condition control

29. In the **True** branch of the **Condition** control, click **Add an action**. Select the **Update item** SharePoint action.
30. On the **Update item** flyout, under **Site Address**, choose the **Event Registration** site.
31. Under **List Name**, select the **Attendees** list.
32. In the **Id** field, add the **ID** dynamic content token from the **Get item** (not **Get items**) action. See *Figure 8.37*:

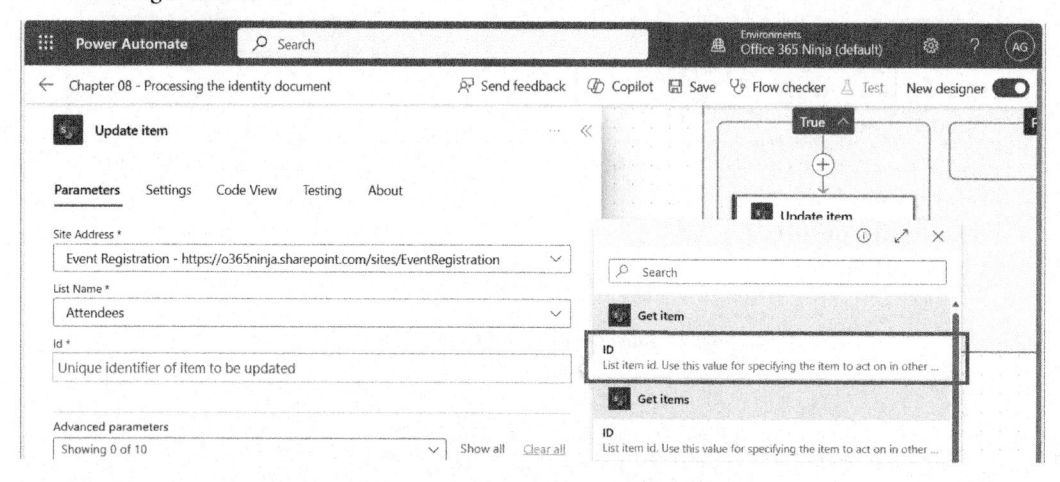

Figure 8.37 – Configuring the Update item action

33. Under **Advanced parameters**, click **Show all**.
34. In the **DOB** field, add the **Date of Birth** dynamic content value from the AI Builder **Extract information from identity documents** action.

Creating flows   185

35. In the **Validation Status Value** dropdown, select **Passed**.
36. In the **Identity Document** field, select the **Document Number** dynamic content value from the AI Builder **Extract information from identity documents** action.
37. In the **Valid Through** field, select the **Date of Expiration** dynamic content value from the AI Builder **Extract information from identity documents** action. See *Figure 8.38*:

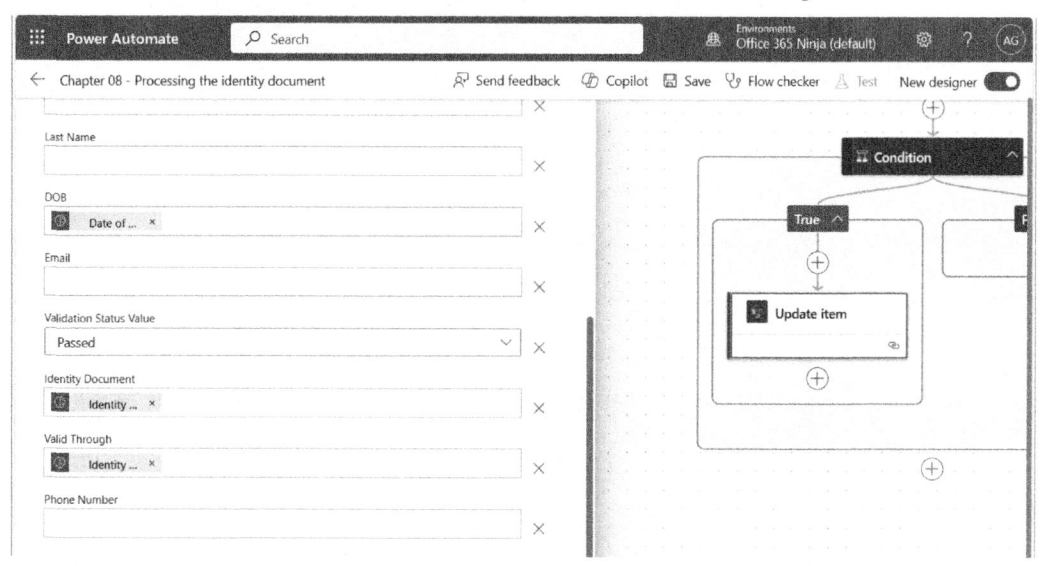

Figure 8.38 – Configuring the Update item action

38. Click **Save**.

To finish up this flow, we'll configure the notification emails.

Sending confirmation messages

Follow these steps:

1. In the **True** branch of the **Condition** control, click **Add an action** after the **Update item** action. Select the **Get file content** action.
2. Rename the **Get file content** action to `Get calendar invitation`.
3. In the **Site Address** dropdown, select the site where you saved the ICS calendar file from the *Establishing a Teams meeting* prerequisite step.

4. In the **File Path** field, click the folder icon and browse to the saved ICS file. See *Figure 8.39*:

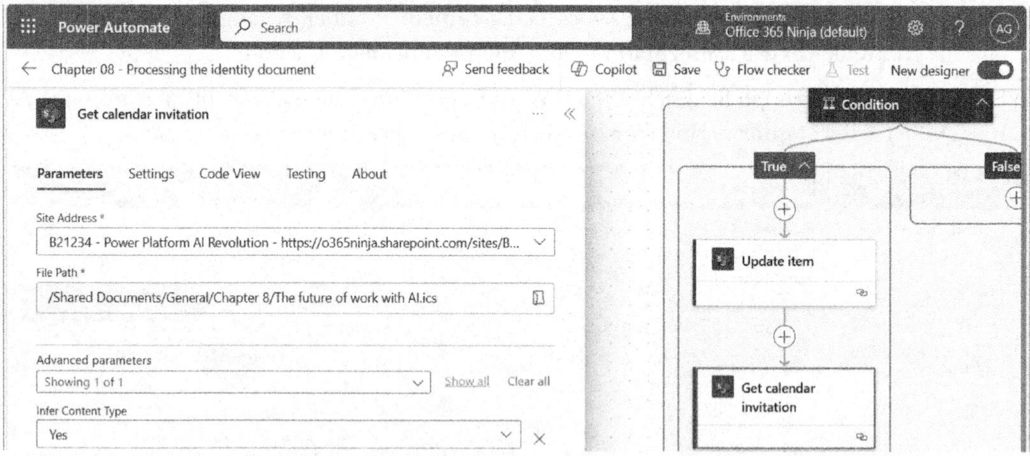

Figure 8.39 – Getting the ICS calendar file for the meeting invitation

5. In the **True** branch of the **Condition** control, click **Add an action** after the **Get calendar invitation** action. Select the **Send an email (V2)** action.

6. Select the **Send an email (V2)** action.

7. In the **To** field, select the **Email** dynamic content token from the **Get item** action.

8. In the **Subject** field, enter a message such as `Congratulations! Your event registration is complete!`.

9. In the **Body** area, enter a message.

10. Under **Advanced parameters**, select the checkbox to enable the **Attachments** parameter.

11. In the **Attachments** area, enter a **Name** value (such as `Meeting.ics`) for the attachment.

12. In the **Content** field, add the **File Content** dynamic content token from the **Get calendar invitation** action:

Creating flows 187

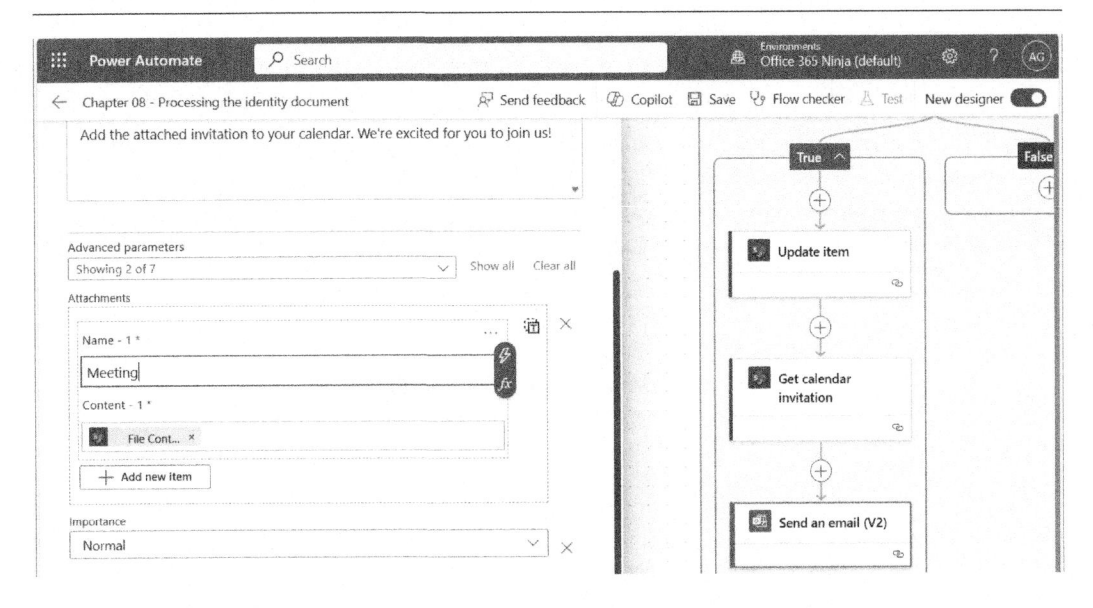

Figure 8.40 – Adding an attachment to the email message

13. In the **Attachments** area, click on the **Switch to input entire array** icon.
14. Remove the quotation marks surrounding the **File Content** dynamic object. See *Figure 8.41*:

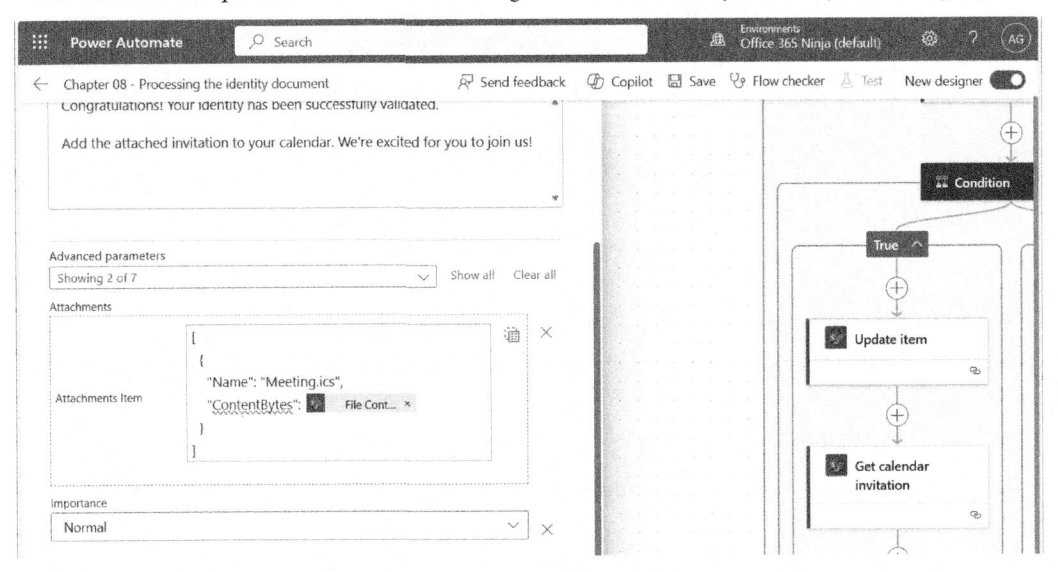

Figure 8.41 – Updating the attachment area

188   Building an Event Registration App with Identity Verification

15. It's important to remove the quotation marks surrounding the dynamic content token here—otherwise, the attachment shows up as a base64-encoded file and cannot be added to the calendar.
16. Under the **True** branch of the **Condition** control, right-click the **Update item** action and select **Copy action**, as shown in *Figure 8.42*:

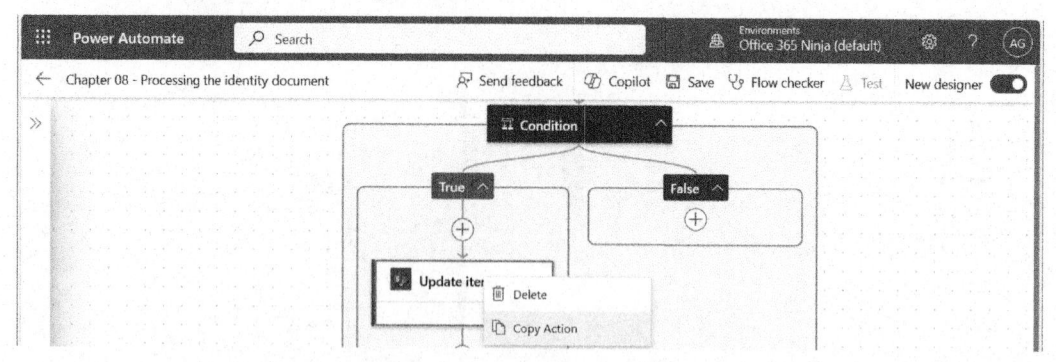

Figure 8.42 – Copying an action

17. In the **False** branch of the **Condition** control, click + and then select **Paste an action**:

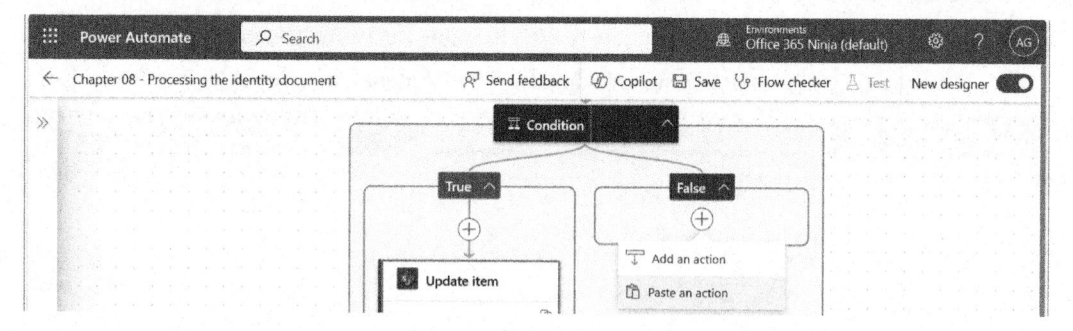

Figure 8.43 – Pasting an action

18. Rename the action to `Update item - Failed`.
19. Under **Advanced parameters**, delete the dynamic content tokens for **DOB**, **Identity document**, and **Valid through**.
20. Under the **Validation Status Value** dropdown, select **Failed**.
21. Under the **True** branch of the **Condition** control, right-click the **Send an email (V2)** action and select **Copy action**.
22. In the **False** branch of the **Condition** control, click the + sign after the **Update item – Failed** action and click **Paste an action**.
23. Rename the action to `Send an email (V2) - Failed`.
24. Update the **Subject** value with a message indicating an incomplete registration.

25. Update the **Body** value with instructions for resolving the issue.
26. Under **Advanced parameters**, click the **X** sign to remove the configured attachment:

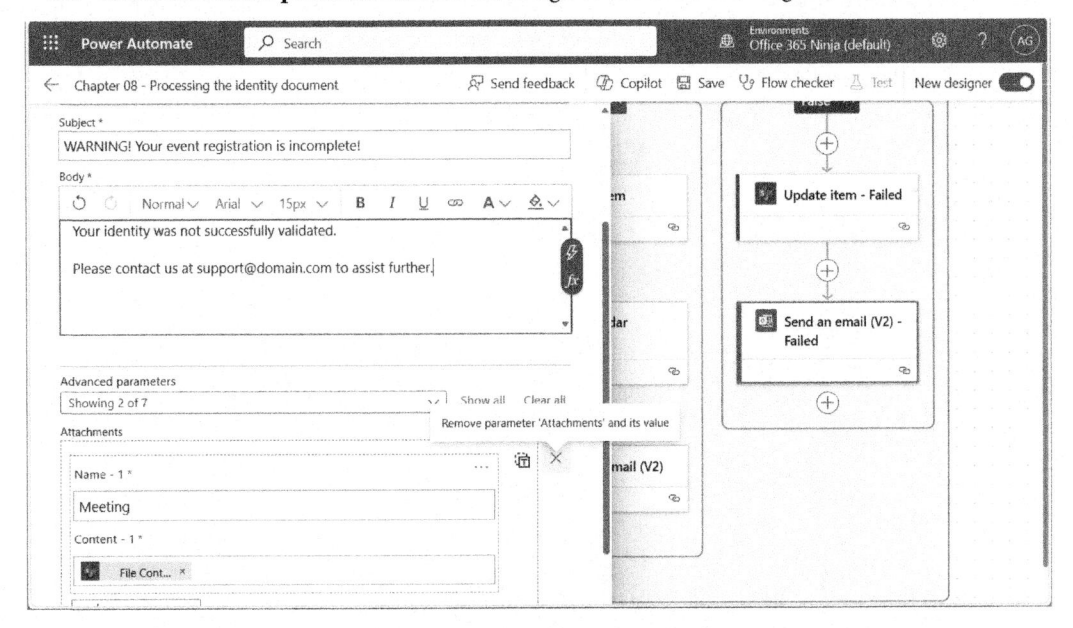

Figure 8.44 – Removing the attachment

27. Click **Save**.

Now for the moment of truth!

Testing the flow

You may have been tempted to test this flow while you were building it—and that's totally fine. It's part of the learning process and an important step to verify that your syntax is correct and that you have chosen the correct dynamic content tokens.

To test the flow, you'll need a few things:

- An email account where you can receive confirmation messages
- A driver's license or passport (either real or samples from the internet) that features a full name, date of birth, expiration date, and document number
- A phone or tablet device with a camera (or an already digitized identity document)

To execute the flow, follow these steps:

1. Navigate to the Microsoft form you created in the prerequisite section. You should have captured the form URL in *step 5* of the *Building an input form* section.

2. Fill out the form using a name that matches the identity document you'll be submitting. Make sure you use an email address that you have access to. In this example, we'll be using the following sample passport card for HAPPY TRAVELER:

Figure 8.45 – Reviewing the identity document data

> **Testing tip**
> Enter the name in mixed case (such as `Happy Traveler`) to ensure you're also testing the `toUpper()` function that converts the **First name** and **Last name** values to uppercase.

3. Check your email for the automated response. The response should have an upload link:

Testing the flow | 191

[Screenshot of an Outlook email window]

Identity verification request for AI event

Aaron Guilmette
To: ○ aaronguilmette
Sun 1/28/2024 12:38 PM

Dear Happy,

Thank you for your interest in our AI workplace event. Since this event is restricted to verified subscribers, you'll need to submit valid identification.

You can upload a copy of a driver's license or passport to the following link:

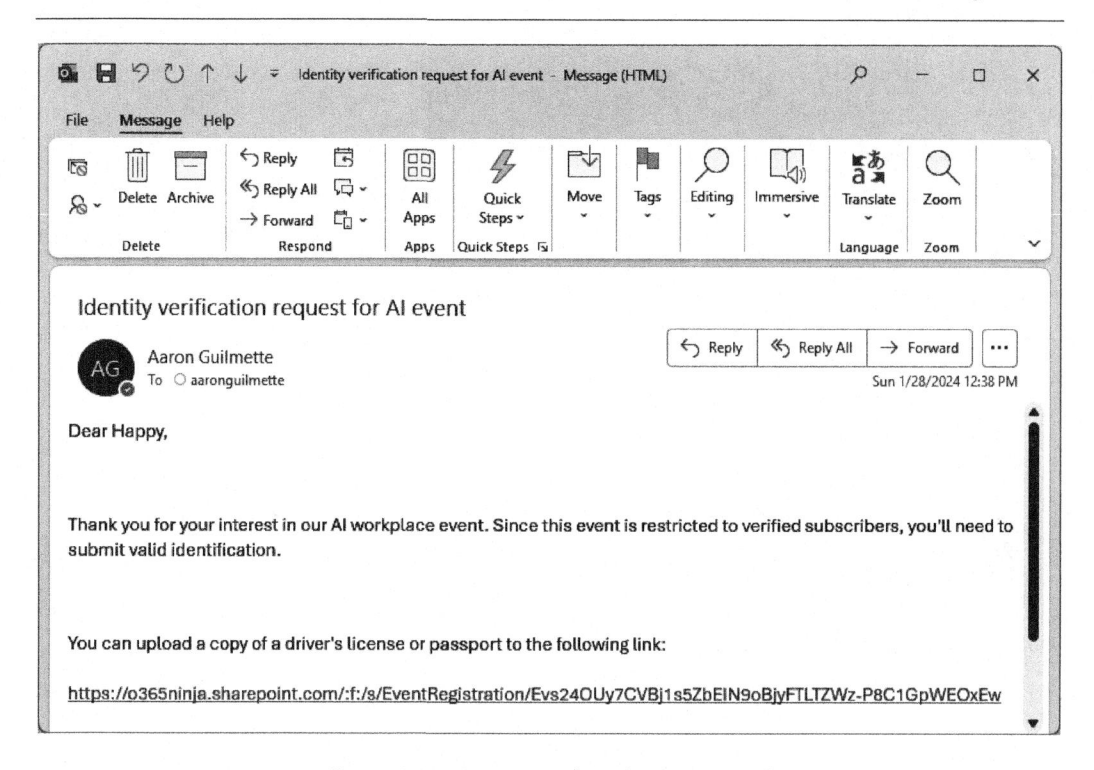

https://o365ninja.sharepoint.com/:f:/s/EventRegistration/Evs24OUy7CVBj1s5ZbEIN9oBjyFTLTZWz-P8C1GpWEOxEw

Figure 8.46 – Reviewing the submission email

4. Click on the link. You should be redirected to a page where you can upload a file:

[Screenshot of OneDrive file upload page]

Microsoft

A member of "Event Registration" is requesting files for:

20240128170149_redactedemail@gmail.com

Select files

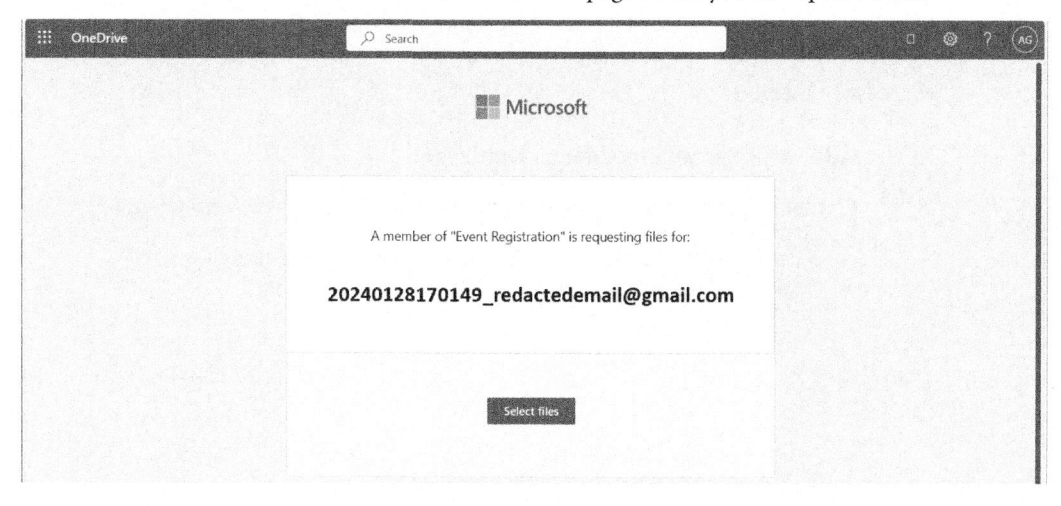

Figure 8.47 – Navigating to the file upload page

5. Click **Select files**. Browse to a previously saved image file or take a picture of a new one using the photo application on your mobile device.

6. Click **Upload**.

7. Wait for a confirmation message with the ICS calendar attachment:

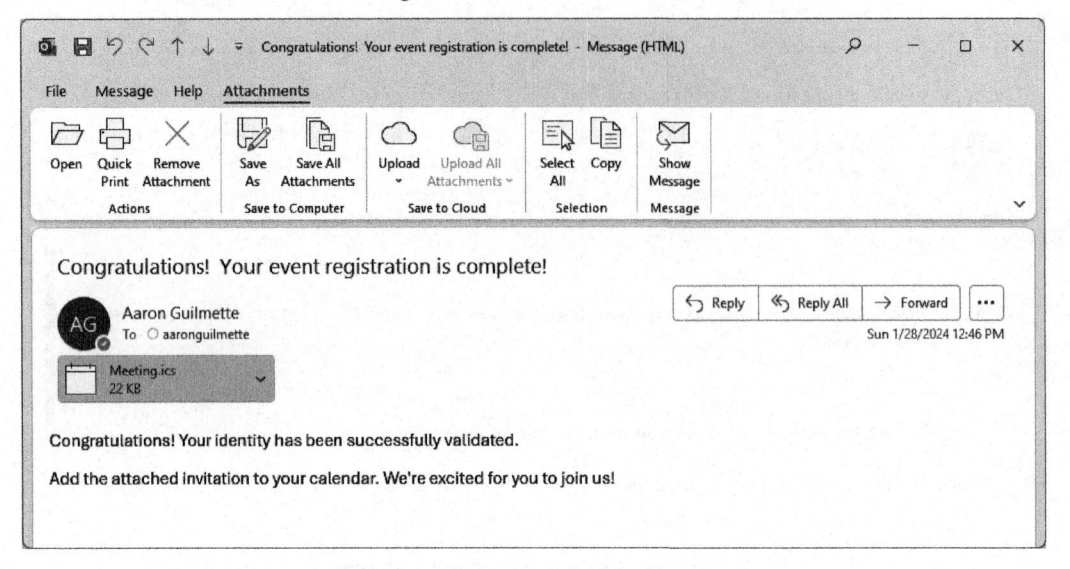

Figure 8.48 – Reviewing the success confirmation

8. Double-click the attachment to add it to your calendar:

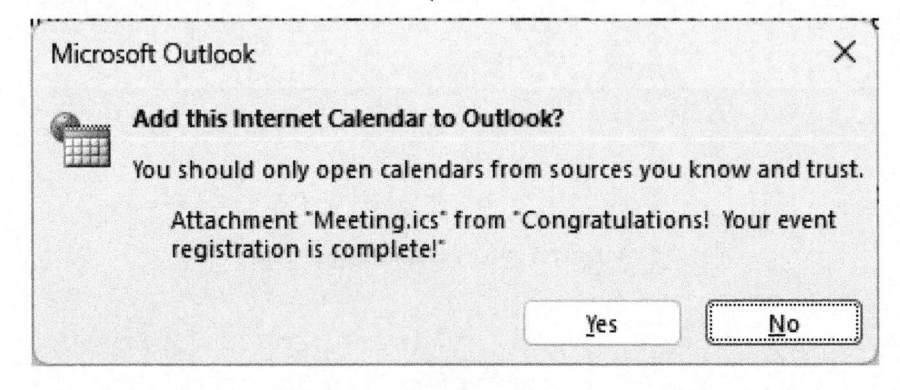

Figure 8.49 – Adding the invitation to the calendar

9. View the meeting information, complete with the join link:

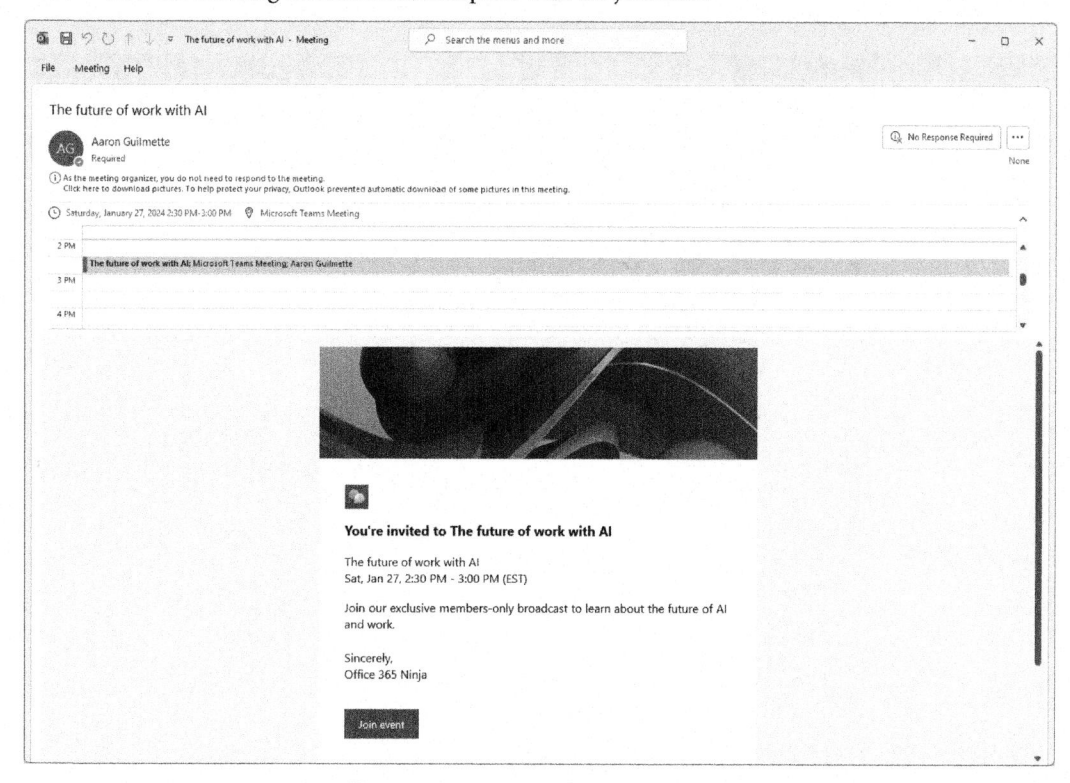

Figure 8.50 – Viewing the calendar item

10. Navigate to the **Event Registration** site and select the **Attendees** list. Click the entry to view the extracted information:

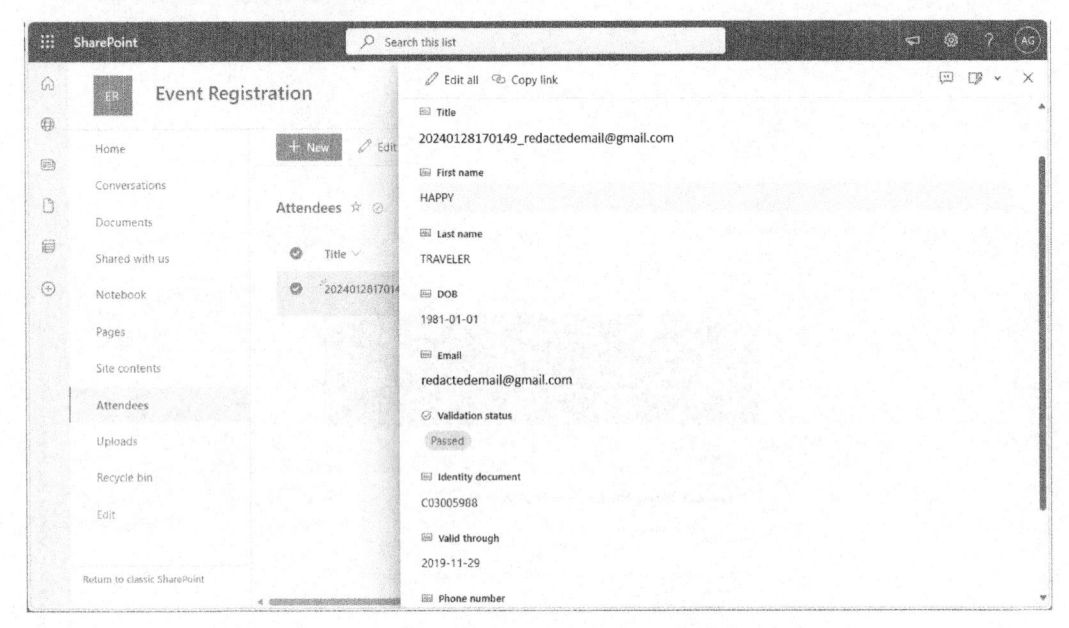

Figure 8.51 – Viewing the attendee information

Congratulations! You've successfully verified the flow!

You can also try submitting different combinations of identity documents and names to test the failure scenarios.

Further exploration

There are quite a few different ways to take this solution. One idea might be using a Zoom meeting instead of a Microsoft Teams meeting. To do so, you'll need the Zoom client and calendar client. Instead of generating an ICS file manually, you'll be able to download an ICS file directly through the Zoom interface. See `https://support.zoom.com/hc/en/article?id=zm_kb&sysparm_article=KB0060791`.

Another idea might be implementing more robust validation mechanisms for the identity document, such as verifying that the document is still valid or that it has a document identification number associated with it.

Summary

The exercises in this chapter demonstrated a lot of advanced capabilities of the Power Automate and SharePoint Online tools. You were able to successfully accept uploads from anonymous users, process identity using the native AI Builder document reader, and generate emails with meeting attachments—all in less than an hour!

With the skills gained in this chapter, you can further enhance your identity processing requirements.

In the next chapter, we'll learn about using another AI Builder model for text extraction.

9
Implementing an AI-Enabled Resume Screener

At some point, you may be responsible for hiring someone—or, at a minimum, reviewing a stack of resumes and trying to separate out the good candidates.

If you make a popular job posting, you could be faced with dozens, hundreds, or even thousands of resumes. How can you filter through those effectively?

Keyword matching might be one tactic you can employ. What about getting help from AI? Is there something an AI model might be able to do? Let's find out!

Designing a solution

This solution is going to build on some of the skills already learned in this book, including working with Power Automate flows and AI Builder capabilities. In this solution, you'll be using AI to process candidate resumes, extract key information, and compare the candidates against a list of job descriptions to see if they're qualified. Candidates that the AI model determines are qualified will be posted to a Teams channel.

The following diagram represents the logical process behind the solution:

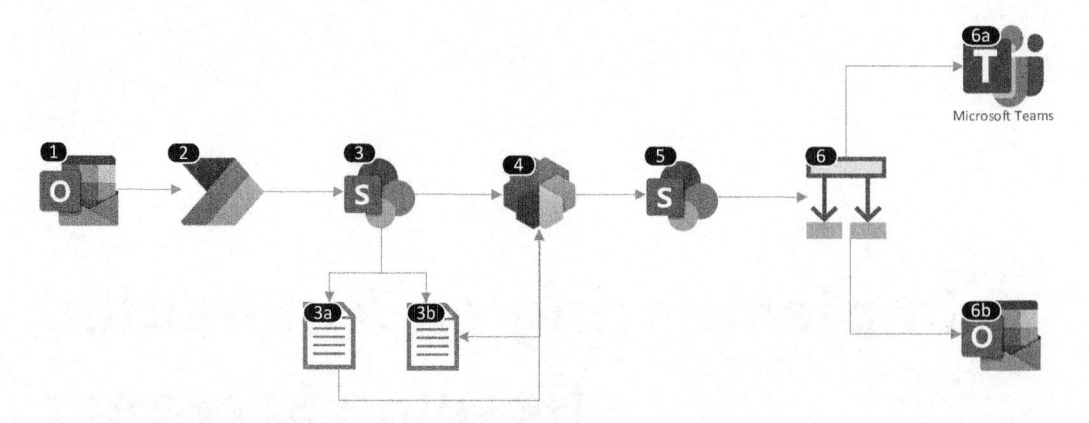

Figure 9.1 – Reviewing the solution workflow

Let's break this down:

1. Resume is received by a shared mailbox.
2. Power Automate retrieves the document and sends it to SharePoint.
3. SharePoint is used to maintain the status information of the applicant:

    I. The resume document itself is stored in a SharePoint library.

    II. A reference to the candidate is stored as an item in a SharePoint list.

4. AI Builder processes the resume and updates the SharePoint list with the extracted candidate information.
5. AI Builder also evaluates the candidate against a job description stored in SharePoint.
6. The output of AI Builder determines how the flow proceeds:

    I. If the candidate is a potential match, a notification is sent to the Teams channel.

    II. If the candidate is not a match, a declination email is sent back to the candidate's email address.

This solution uses AI in two ways:

- To extract **entity** information (such as a person's name and email address)
- To reason over the text to determine the meaning of the content

There are a lot of moving pieces in this project, so let's get going!

Licensing prerequisites

Using AI models and connectors in the Power Platform has several prerequisites:

- A subscription that includes Microsoft Dataverse
- AI Builder capacity (or trial capacity)
- Power Apps or Power Automate premium licensing
- A subscription that includes Microsoft Teams
- A subscription that includes Exchange Online so that you can provision a shared mailbox
- A Cloudmersive Free Tier account

If you haven't already enabled Dataverse and AI Builder capacity, see *Chapter 2, Configuring an Environment to Support AI Services*, and *Chapter 6, Processing Data with Sentiment Analysis*.

Configuring solution prerequisites

Before you start the workflow configuration, you'll need to set up a few prerequisites, such as Microsoft Teams, as well as a few SharePoint lists and a document library. Since all teams in Microsoft Teams include a SharePoint site, you can just leverage the SharePoint site component of that team—saving you (and your IT environment) from sprawl.

Creating a shared mailbox

Creating a shared mailbox is a relatively straightforward task. This mailbox is going to be used by candidates submitting their resumes. To configure a shared mailbox, follow these steps:

1. Navigate to the Microsoft 365 admin center (`https://admin.microsoft.com`).
2. From the navigation menu, expand **Teams & groups** and select **Shared mailboxes**.
3. Click **Add a shared mailbox**.
4. Enter a **Name** value, such as `resumes`. Confirm the entry for the **Email** address and click **Save changes**.
5. After the mailbox has been created, select **Add members to your shared mailbox**, as shown in *Figure 9.2*:

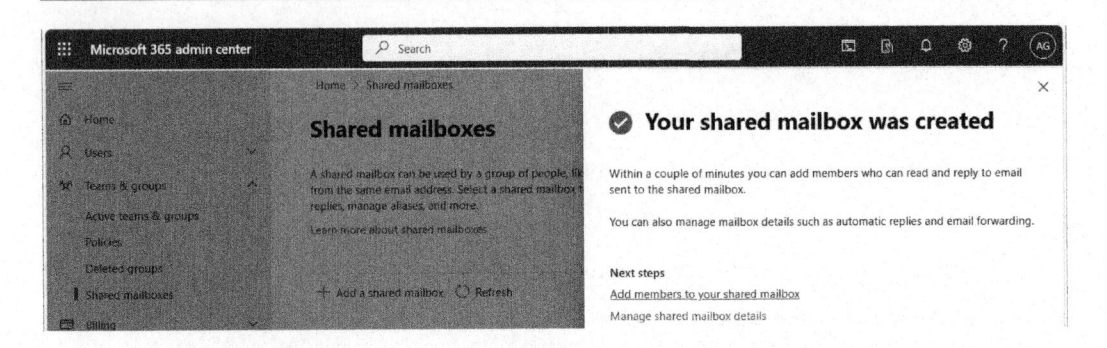

Figure 9.2 – Adding members to a shared mailbox

6. On the **Shared mailbox members** flyout, select **Add members**.
7. Select one or more users (such as yourself) and click **Add**.

Next, you'll create a team that will be used for storing resumes and candidates' information (since one of the components of a team is a SharePoint site), as well as notifying other people that a potential candidate has submitted their resume for a role.

Creating a team

Creating a team is similarly straightforward. You can create one from either Microsoft Teams or the Microsoft 365 admin center. Since we're already in the Microsoft 365 admin center, we'll just use that interface. Follow these steps:

1. From the Microsoft 365 admin center (`https://admin.microsoft.com`), expand **Teams & groups** and then select **Active teams & groups**.
2. On the **Active teams and groups** page, select **Add a team**.
3. On the **Basics** page, enter a value for **Name of team**, such as `Jobs and candidates`, and click **Next**.
4. On the **Owners** tab, add at least one owner (such as yourself) and click **Next**.
5. On the **Members** tab, optionally add extra team members. Click **Next**.
6. On the **Settings** page, add a value for **Team email address** (such as `jobsandcandidates`). Select **Public** for the **Privacy level** and click **Next**.
7. Validate the settings and click **Add team** to finish.
8. Click **Close**.

Once the team has provisioned, it's time to move on to SharePoint.

Configuring SharePoint Online

As mentioned earlier, every Microsoft Teams team gets a SharePoint site. For this solution, we'll be using some SharePoint lists and a document library.

> **Further reading**
>
> For more information on the components that make up a Microsoft Teams team object, see `https://www.undocumented-features.com/2021/07/05/a-deeper-dive-into-teams-architecture/`.

Let's step through the requirements for making sure SharePoint Online is correctly configured. The first step is to create a document library that will hold candidates' application documents.

Provisioning a SharePoint document library

This solution requires a storage location to hold a candidate's resume. While you can use the default document library, it tends to lead to more troubleshooting as the library's display name (**Documents**) is different than its actual name (**Shared Documents**).

To create a new SharePoint document library, follow these steps:

1. From the Microsoft 365 admin center (`https://admin.teams.microsoft.com`), expand **Teams & groups** and select **Active teams & groups**.
2. Select the team you created in the previous section.
3. On the flyout, click **View site** to navigate to the team's connected SharePoint site. See *Figure 9.3*:

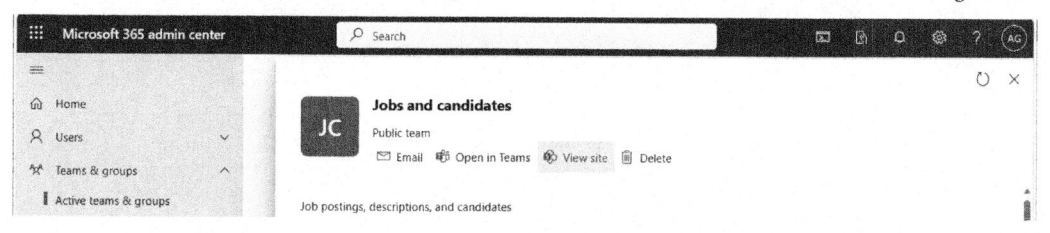

Figure 9.3 – Navigating to the team's connected SharePoint site

4. Click **New** and then select **Document library**.
5. On the **Create new document library** page, select **Blank library**.
6. Enter `Resumes` in the **Name** field and click **Create**.

That's it! Next, we'll create some SharePoint lists.

Provisioning SharePoint lists

In this section, you'll be creating two SharePoint lists—one that lists role names and descriptions, and one that is used to store candidate information. Follow these steps:

1. Navigate to the **Jobs and candidates** SharePoint site home page.
2. Click **New** and then select **List**.
3. On the **Create a list** page, select **Blank list**.
4. Enter a **Name** value for the list, such as `Roles`, and click **Create**.
5. On the **Roles** list, click **Add column**. Select **Multiple lines of text** as the type and click **Next**.
6. **Name** the column `Job descriptions` and click **Save**.
7. Click **Home** to navigate back to the home page for the site.
8. Click **New** and then select **List**.
9. On the **Create a list** page, select **Blank list**.
10. Enter a **Name** value for the list, such as `Candidates`, and click **Create**.
11. Repeat the process of adding a column to the **Candidates** list using the column names and types in *Table 9.1*:

Column name	Column type
First name	Text
Last name	Text
Phone number	Text
Email	Text
Current company	Text
Current role	Text
Candidate summary	Multiple lines of text
Resume link	Text
AI-screened	Yes/No; default value No
Service Desk Technician	Choice: Yes/No/Maybe (You can also use Text as the column type)
Reason	Multiple lines of text

Table 9.1 – SharePoint list column information

> **Neat trick**
>
> Later on, we're going to create a flow to populate the **Resume link** column with the URL of the file. If you want to make it clickable, you can customize the field formatting. Select the **Resume link** column, point to **Column settings**, and click **Format this column**. Paste the following JSON into the textbox and click **Save**:
>
> `{ "$schema": "https://developer.microsoft.com/json-schemas/sp/v2/column-formatting.schema.json", "elmType": "a", "txtContent": "@currentField", "attributes": {      "target": "_blank", "href": "=@currentField" } }`

Configuring job descriptions

One of the goals of this resume screening solution is to be able to determine if a candidate is a good fit for a role. In order to do that, you need to define the role information. There are many ways to import the job description data; in this example, we're going to use the **Roles** SharePoint list that we created earlier.

> **Finding good sample job descriptions**
>
> In order for the AI model to determine if a resume matches a job, you'll need good job descriptions (preferably ones that you can also find corresponding resumes for). You can use a site such as `https://resources.workable.com/job-descriptions/` to retrieve sample job descriptions.

To add job descriptions, follow these steps:

1. Navigate to the **Roles** SharePoint list you created earlier in the **Jobs and candidates** site.
2. Click **New**.
3. Enter the role or job title in the **Title** field.
4. Enter a job description in the **Job Description** text area field.
5. Click **Save**.

Repeat the process, adding several job titles and descriptions. In this chapter, we're just going to focus on matching a single job description (such as an IT service desk technician).

> **Online content**
>
> You can download sample resumes from this book's GitHub site: `https://github.com/PacktPublishing/Power-Platform-and-the-AI-Revolution`

Configuring the AI model

To this point, you've used a few different kinds of AI technologies:

- Prompts, such as the AI Builder **generative AI (GenAI)** prompting or Open AI's ChatGPT
- Copilot for Power Platform
- Pre-built AI Builder models such as the sentiment analysis model

In each of these examples, you've supplied the content you want to be analyzed or processed at runtime (that is, in the context of the flow or app). In this solution, however, you're going to use an AI model that requires training.

Training, in this context, means showing the model a sample dataset and then highlighting what data is important and how to map the recognized data to fields. Since we're building a resume screener, the training data should be representative of resumes you might expect to process. You can obtain samples from searching sources such as LinkedIn or the internet. You could ask co-workers, family, or friends for resumes as well. The model will do best by seeing lots of different kinds of samples.

> **Finding good sample data**
>
> The reason you need several examples is so that you can train the AI model on how to identify certain fields. Key item or entity extraction works best when the AI model has learned what kinds of data are associated with certain fields. For example, if a human sees *123 Main Street, Chicago, IL*, they're easily able to determine that it's an address. An AI model, unless trained otherwise, just sees numbers and letters. To help bolster your training data, you can download example resumes from a site such as `https://www.beamjobs.com/resumes`. Be sure to seek out resume templates that include the types of roles and job descriptions you added to the **Roles** list earlier.

Training an AI model

To train the AI model, follow these steps:

1. Navigate to the Power Automate maker portal (`https://make.powerautomate.com`).
2. From the navigation menu, select **AI hub**.
3. Select **AI models**:

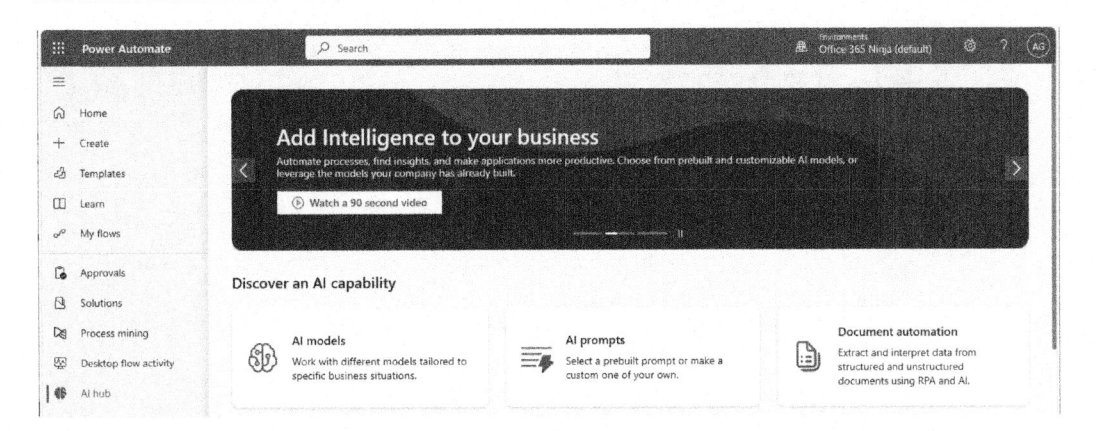

Figure 9.4 – Exploring the AI hub

4. From the top navigation bar, select **Documents** and then choose the **Extract custom information from documents** custom model:

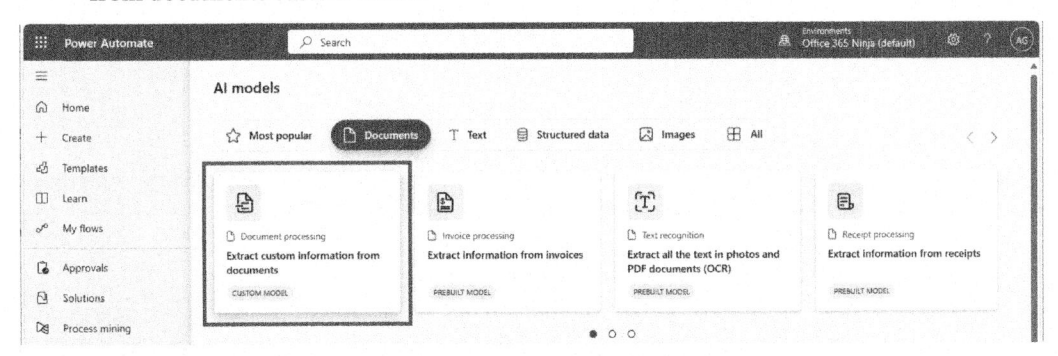

Figure 9.5 – Selecting the custom model

5. On the **Extract custom information from documents** page, select **Create custom model**, as shown in *Figure 9.6*:

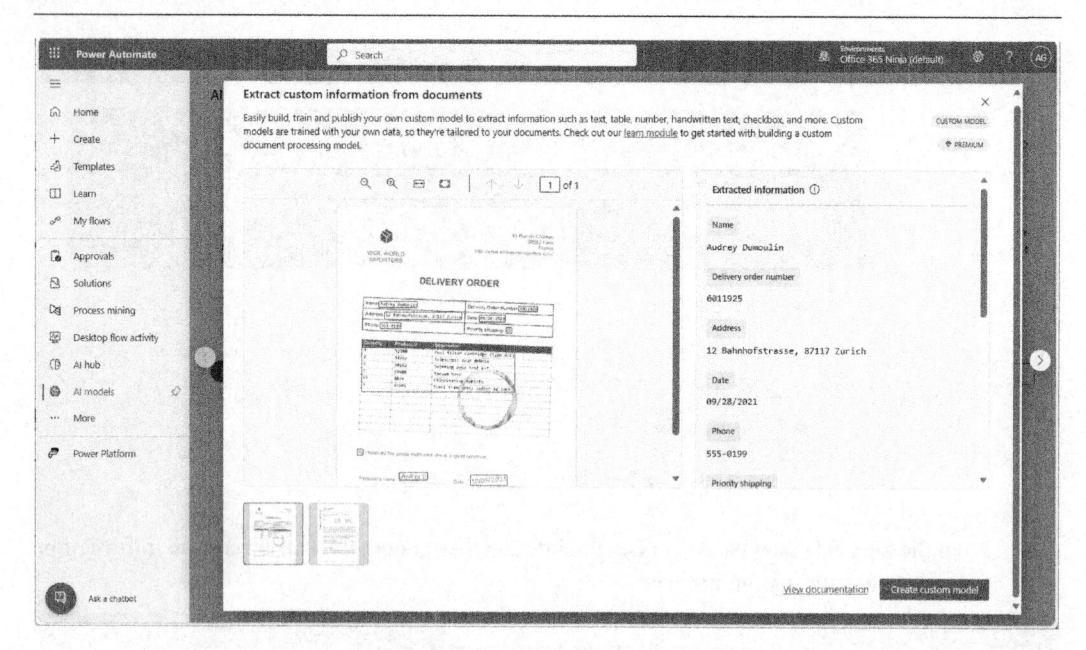

Figure 9.6 – Creating a custom model

6. On the **Choose document type** page, select **Unstructured documents**:

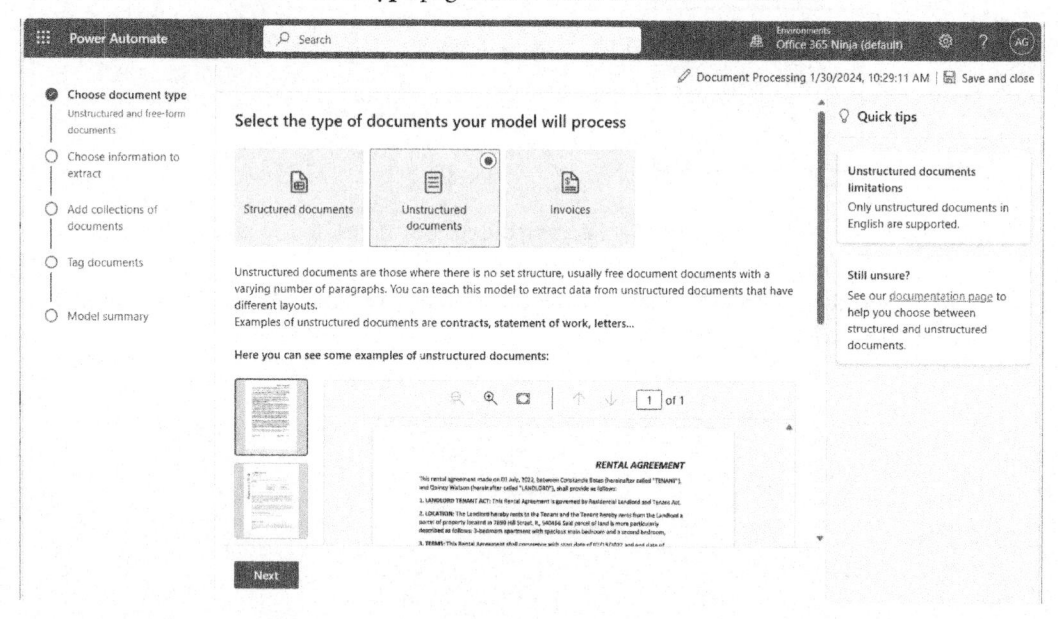

Figure 9.7 – Selecting Unstructured documents

Configuring solution prerequisites   207

7. Click **Next**.
8. On the **Choose information to extract** page, click **Add** and select **Text**:

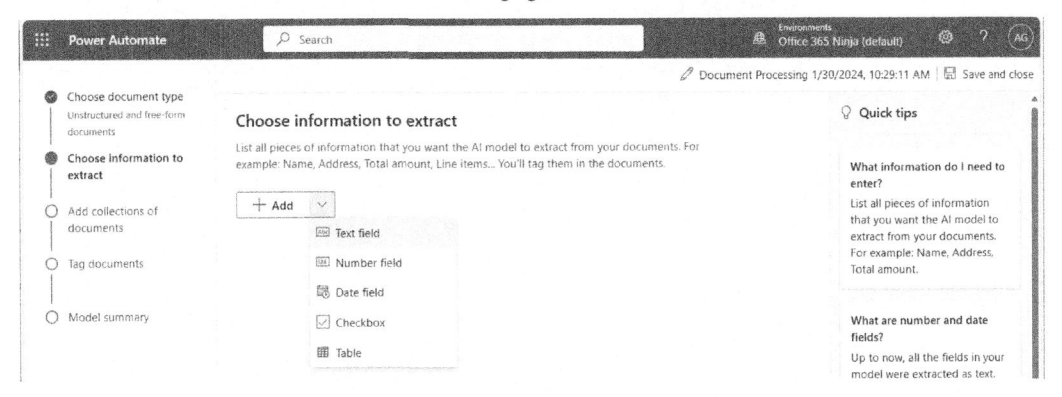

Figure 9.8 – Choosing information to extract

9. In the **Text field** flyout, enter **First name** for the field. Click **Done**.
10. Add additional text fields for **Last name**, **Email**, **Phone number**, **Current role**, and **Current company**. Click **Next** when finished.
11. On the **Add collections of documents** page, click **New collection**, as shown in *Figure 9.9*:

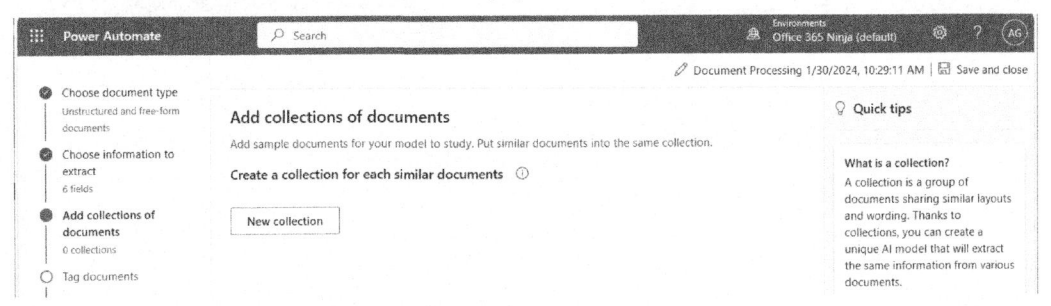

Figure 9.9 – Adding a collection of documents

12. Click the + sign to add documents to the collection.
13. On the **Collection 1** flyout, click **Add documents**:

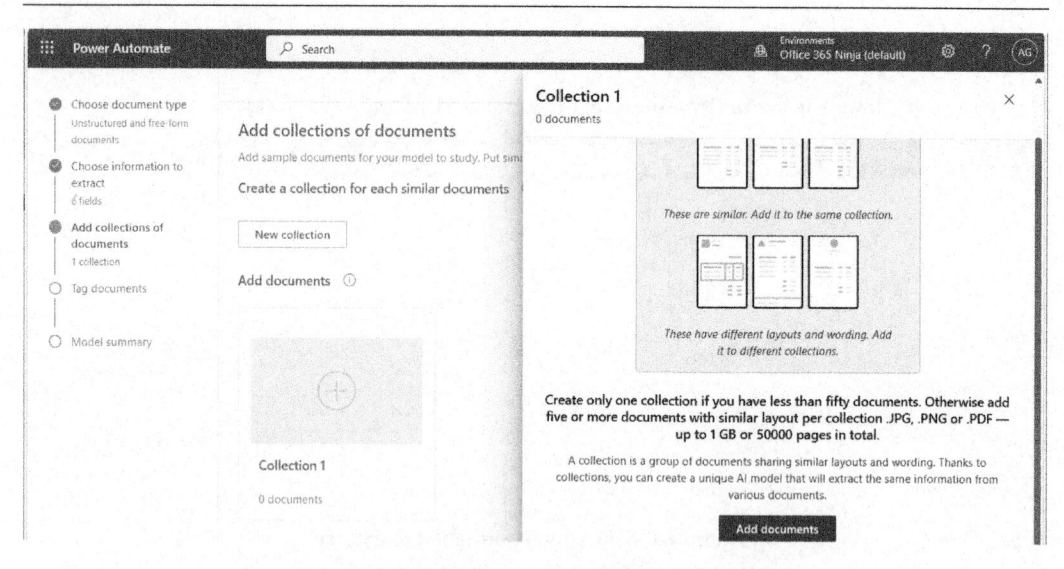

208   Implementing an AI-Enabled Resume Screener

Figure 9.10 – Adding documents to the collection

14. Select the location where your sample data is stored.
15. Choose documents to include in the collection and click **Add**:

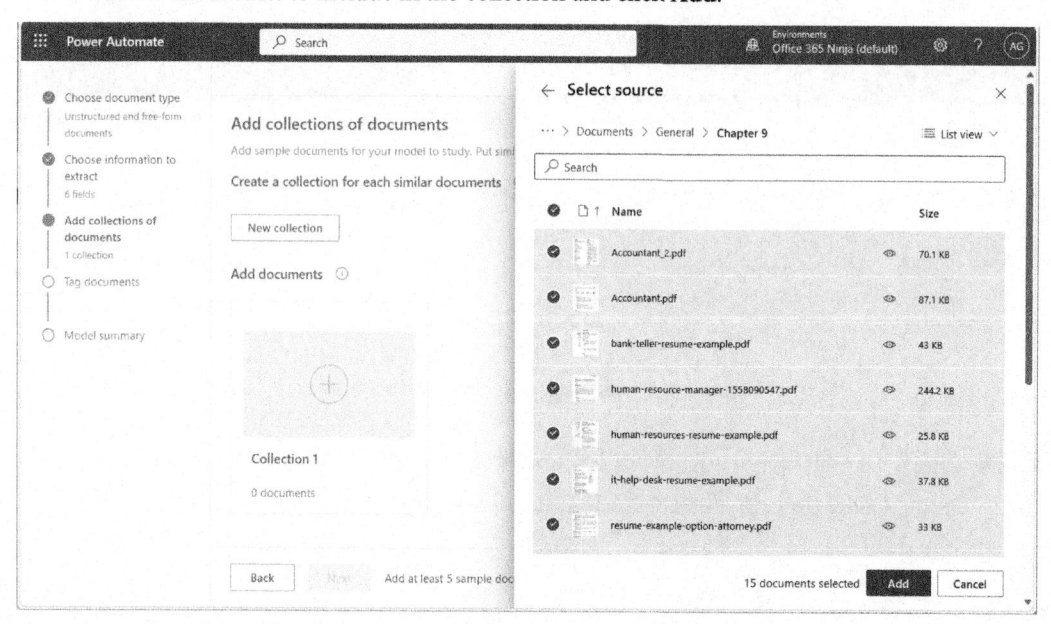

Figure 9.11 – Selecting documents for the collection

Configuring solution prerequisites · 209

16. On the **Upload documents** page, click **Upload documents**.
17. Click **Done** after the upload has completed.
18. Click **Next**.
19. For each document in the collection, select text in the document that corresponds to one of the **Text** fields (**First name**, **Last name**, **Email**, **Phone number**, **Current role**, **Current company**). After selecting the text for a field, choose the appropriate field to map this item to. See *Figure 9.12*:

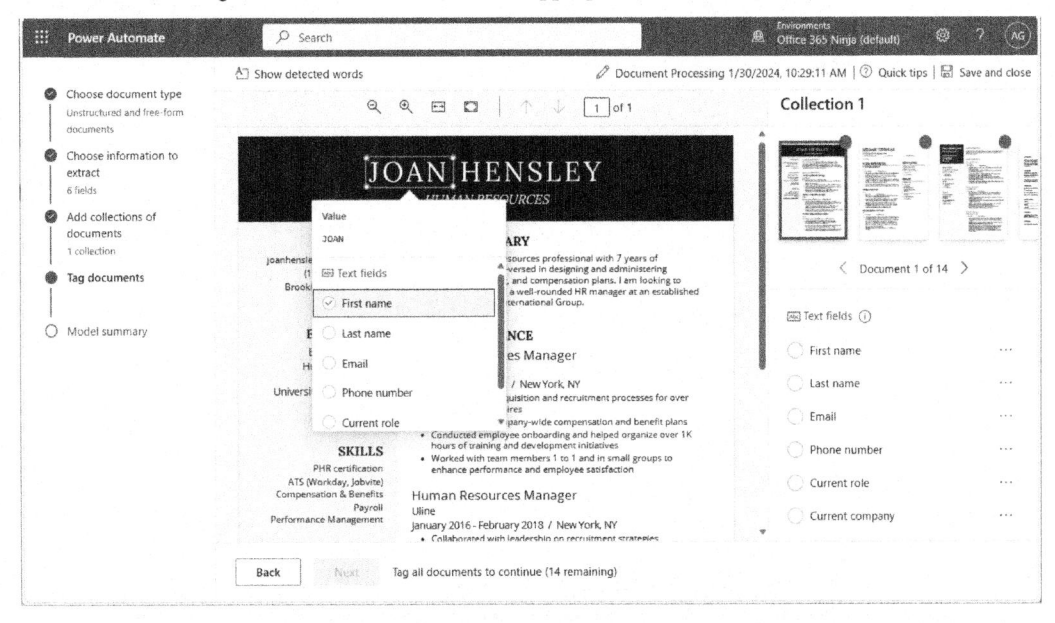

Figure 9.12 – Tagging fields

20. After you've tagged all the fields for the selected document, use the navigation arrows in the collection pane to move to the next document in the collection. Repeat the selection and tagging process for each document. After tagging each field in a document, the document thumbnail will be updated with a checkmark indicating completion. If a sample document does not have a field present, select the ellipsis next to the field and choose **Not available in document**. See *Figure 9.13*:

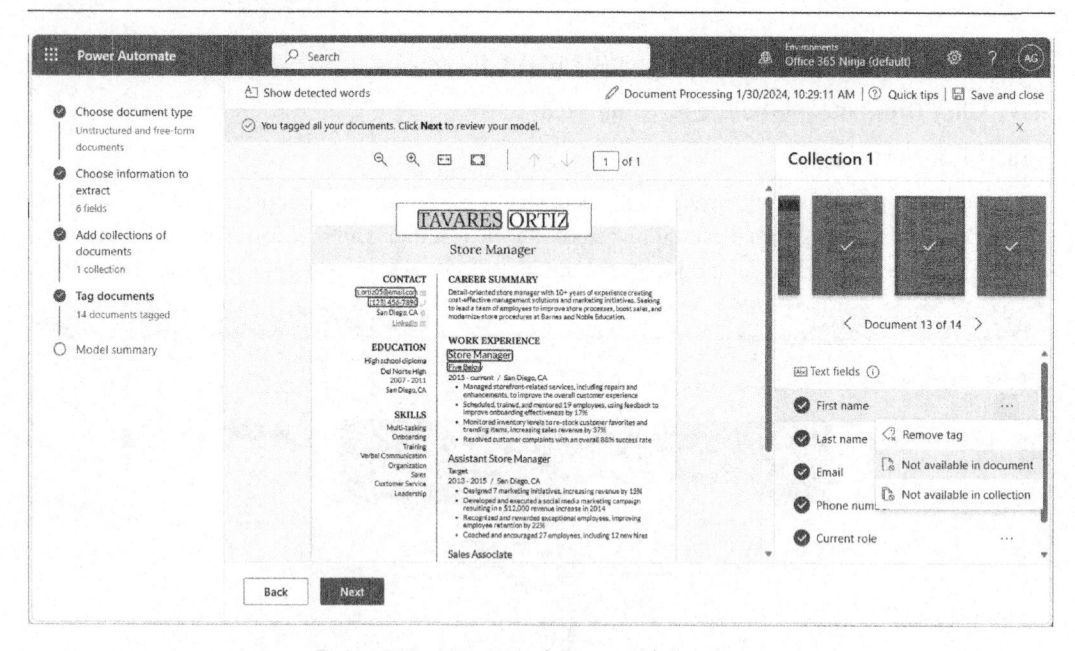

210　Implementing an AI-Enabled Resume Screener

Figure 9.13 – Viewing a fully tagged document

21. When all documents have been tagged, click **Next**.
22. On the **Model summary** page, click **Train**. The model training may take anywhere from a few minutes to a few hours. Click **Go to models** after the training job has been submitted.

You can review the status on the **AI models** > **My models** page, as shown in *Figure 9.14*:

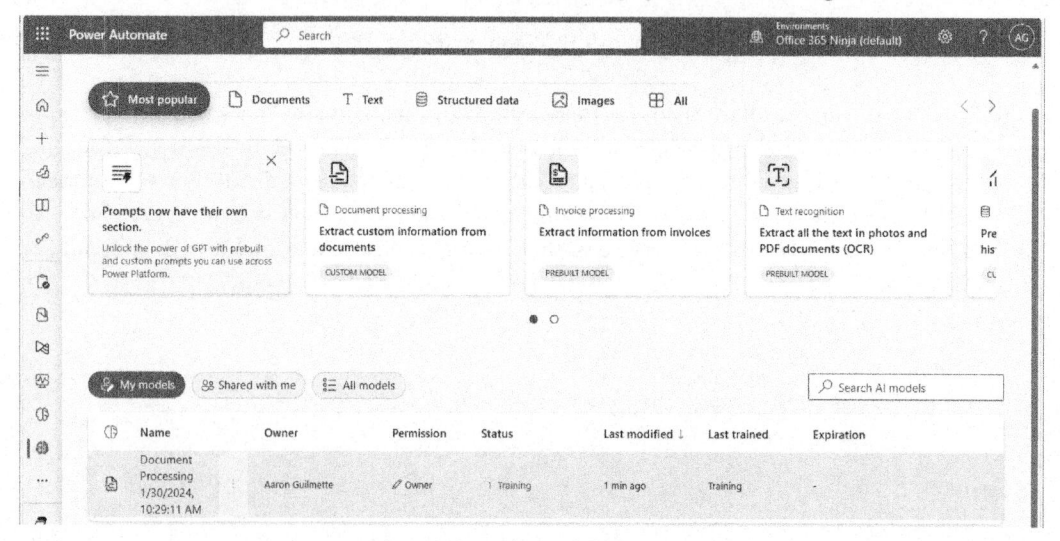

Figure 9.14 – Viewing the model training

If desired, you can modify the **Settings** field of the model and rename it to something such as `Resume identification`. If your environment has multiple AI models trained, this will help you easily identify it.

Testing the model

After the model has completed training, you should test it to make sure it returns the desired results.

To test a model, follow these steps:

1. From the **AI hub** setting, open the model by clicking on its name.
2. Under **Training document**, select **Quick test**:

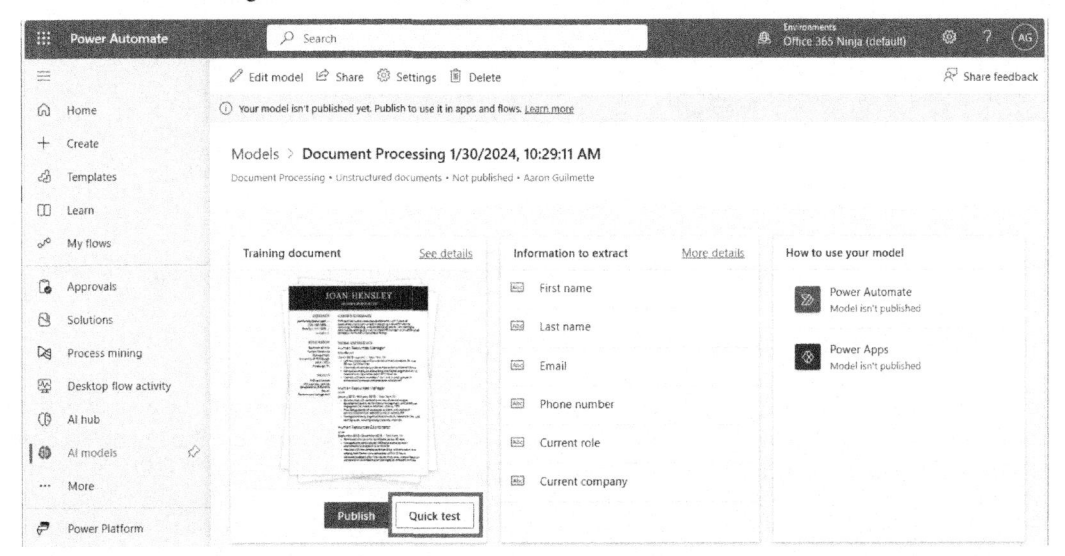

Figure 9.15 – Running a quick test

3. On the **Quick test** page, click **Upload from my device** and browse to a sample resume document (preferably one that you didn't use for training).
4. If it doesn't recognize certain fields or you discover that it's mapping data to the wrong fields, you may need to update the model by adding more reference documents to the collection and rerunning the training.

Publishing the model

After you are satisfied with the model's data recognition, you need to make it available to the Power Platform by **publishing** it. To publish a model, click on a trained model and then select **Publish**:

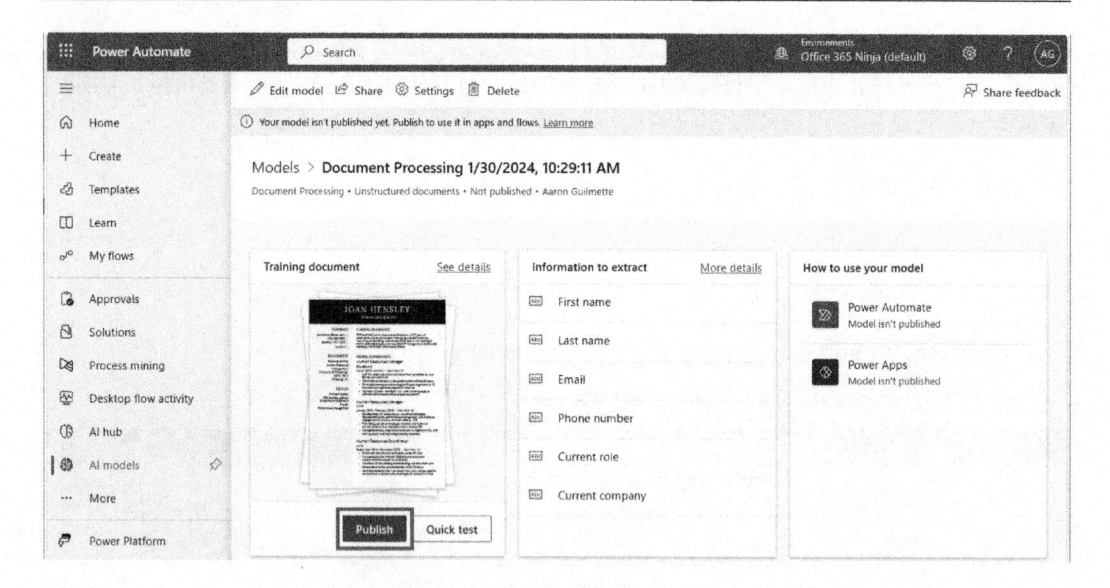

Figure 9.16 – Publishing the model

Next, let's go sign up for a connector to make some of the text manipulation a bit easier.

Enabling the Cloudmersive connector

Some AI Builder actions require you to specify a document-type parameter or only take input in the form of text. Since end users may email in a variety of document types (such as Word documents or PDFs), you'll need to be able to format data accordingly.

While you could do some of this with some condition controls and compose statements, why not use tools to make your job easier? Cloudmersive's connector makes converting content a snap! And, with 800 free API calls per month forever, it's a pretty good deal, too.

To sign up, follow these steps:

1. Navigate to `https://portal.cloudmersive.com/signup`.
2. Fill out the form and click **Sign Up Now**.
3. On the **Select Plan** page, choose **Free Tier**.
4. On the **Select your role to finish account setup** page, select a role that represents your job type.
5. On the **Which API do you wish to start with?** page, select **Document and Data Conversion API**.
6. On the **Which programming language do you wish to use?** page, select **Microsoft Flow / Power Automate**.
7. On the **API Keys** page, click **Create Key**.

8. Copy the value in the **API Key** area under **Free Tier Keys** to a location that you can easily access later. The API key is a 36-character code consisting of the letters a through f and numerals 0-9.

Now, it's time to start working with the automation!

Creating a flow

With all of the prerequisites out of the way, it's time to start working with some automation! This flow will be broken into several sections to help you conceptualize the actions.

Configuring the trigger and variables

In the *Designing a solution* section, we identified a shared mailbox as the way resume content will be ingested. In the real world, that might only be one way you choose to receive resumes. You might also have a website where candidates can upload their resumes or even a third-party job posting service that you may configure to store or forward resumes. In any case, the processes will be very similar. The triggers will depend on what access, polling, or notification methods you have available to you.

For simplicity's sake, this example will use a shared mailbox.

This flow will make use of **variables**—essentially, placeholders that can be used to hold temporary content or values in memory throughout the flow. There will be four variables constructed:

- `RoleFitJson`: Used to store the JSON output of the AI Builder action evaluating the candidate's resume.
- `RoleFit`: One-word answer for whether the candidate is a good fit. The example flow will output one of three potential values—**Yes**, **Maybe**, and **No**.
- `RoleFitSummary`: Brief description or reasoning behind AI Builder's evaluation. This helps your organization map to Microsoft's Responsible AI principle of transparency.
- `CandidateSummary`: Brief summary of the candidate's resume.

Throughout the flow, we'll update these with the values generated by our various AI solutions.

> **What do I do if I'm stuck?**
>
> If you run into a roadblock for some reason (can't find a feature, an option isn't showing up, or something is unclear), help is only a click away! You can download this chapter's artifacts from our GitHub site: `https://github.com/PacktPublishing/Power-Platform-and-the-AI-Revolution`.

214　Implementing an AI-Enabled Resume Screener

To configure the flow, follow these steps:

1. Navigate to the Power Automate maker portal (`https://make.powerautomate.com`) and select **Create**.

2. Under **Start from blank**, select **Automated cloud flow**.

3. On the **Build an automated cloud flow** page, provide a **Flow name** value (such as `Process resumes`) and select the **When a new email arrives in a shared mailbox (v2)** trigger. Click **Create**.

4. Select the **When a new email arrives in a shared mailbox (V2)** trigger. In the flyout, enter the email address of the shared mailbox you created in the prerequisites as a **custom value**.

5. Under **Advanced parameters**, select the **Only With Attachments** and **Include Attachments** parameters. For both parameters, select **Yes**. See *Figure 9.17*:

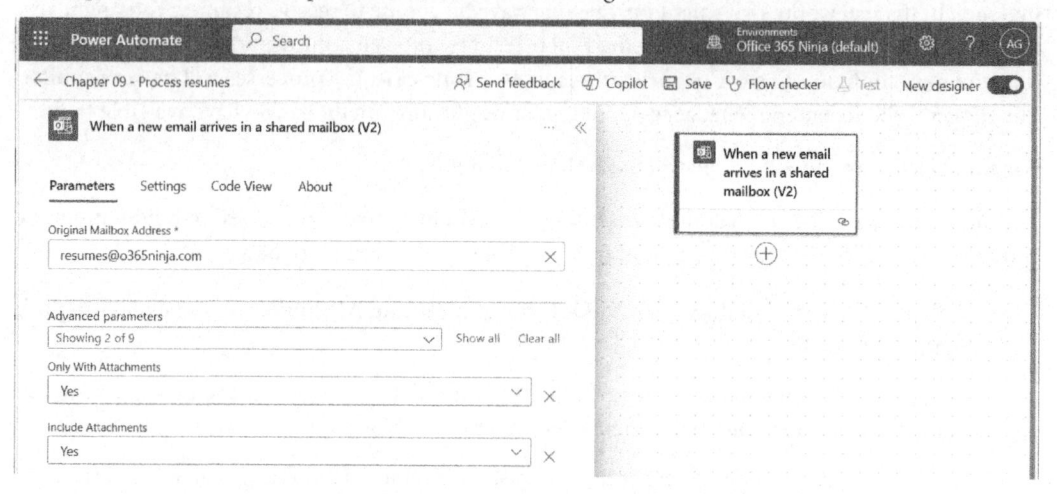

Figure 9.17 – Configuring the trigger

6. Click **Add an action** and select the **Initialize variable** variable action.

7. Update the **Name** value of the variable by appending - `RoleFitJson` to the action name. In the **Parameters** field, enter the **Name** value as `RoleFitJson` and select the **Type** value of **String**. See *Figure 9.18*:

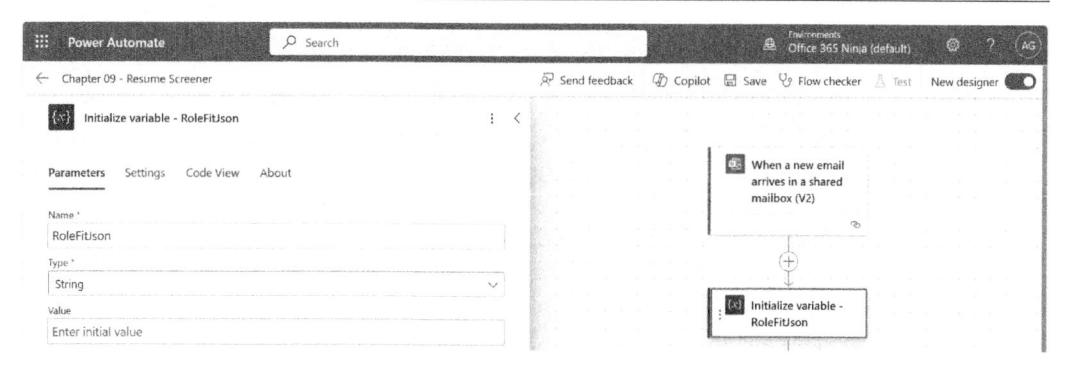

Figure 9.18 – Adding an Initialize variable action

8. Click **Add an action** and select the **Initialize variable** variable action.

9. Update the **Name** value of the variable by appending - `RoleFit` to the action name. In the **Parameters** field, enter the **Name** value as `RoleFit` and select the **Type** value of **String**.

10. Click **Add an action** and select the **Initialize variable** variable action.

11. Update the **Name** value of the variable by appending - `RoleFitSummary` to the action name. In the **Parameters** field, enter the **Name** value as `RoleFitSummary` and select the **Type** value of **String**.

12. Click **Add an action** and select the **Initialize variable** variable action.

13. Update the **Name** value of the variable by appending - `CandidateSummary` to the action name. In the **Parameters** field, enter the **Name** value as `CandidateSummary` and select the **Type** value of **String**.

Now, we'll work on saving the attachment and adding a SharePoint list item for the candidate.

Processing the attachment and candidate record

In this section, we'll configure the steps necessary to save the attachment and then add a SharePoint list item for candidates who send in their resumes. Follow these steps:

1. After the **Initialize variable CandidateSummary** action, add the **Create file** SharePoint action.

2. Update the **Name** value of the action by appending – `Add resume to SharePoint library` to the action name.

3. Under **Site Address**, choose the **Jobs and candidates** SharePoint site.

4. Under **Folder Path**, select the **Resumes** document library.

5. In the **File Name** field, add an expression. Add the following expression:

6. `concat(utcNow('yyyyMMddHHmmss'),'_',triggerOutputs()?['body/from'],'_',item()?['name'])`.

   This will construct a new name for the file according to the current date (Year-Month-Day-Hours-Minutes-Seconds), the sender's email address, and the original attachment name, each separated by an underscore character. For example, a filename of `20240326140005_sender@domain.com_MyResume.pdf` would indicate a file received on March 26, 2024, at 14:00:05 hours from `sender@domain.com` with the original filename of `MyResume.pdf`. While it's not wholly necessary, it does help track individual resume files to make sure they're individually identifiable easily.

7. In the **File Content** field, add the **Attachments Content** dynamic token under the **When a new email arrives in a shared mailbox (V2)** action. See *Figure 9.19*:

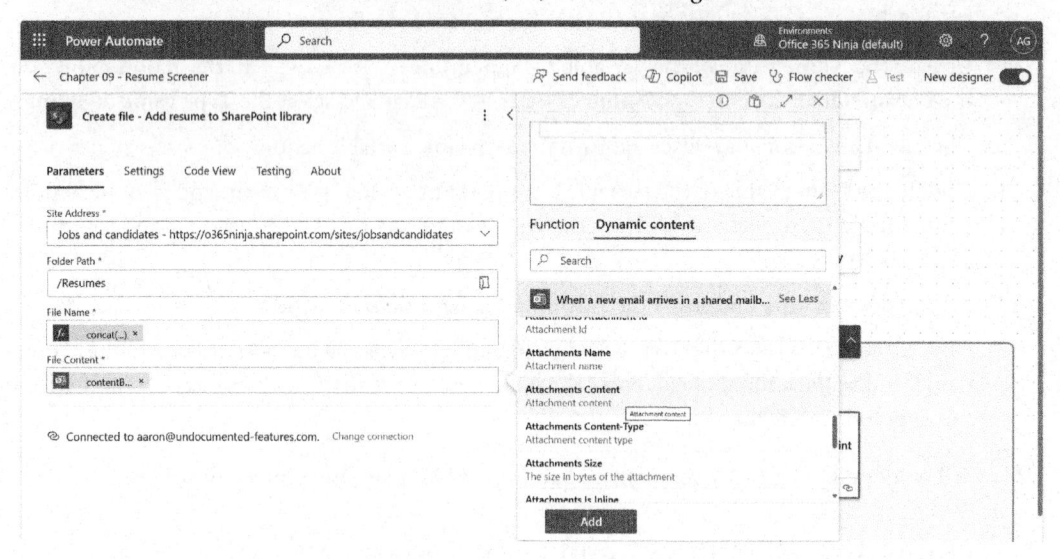

Figure 9.19 – Adding the SharePoint Create file action

8. Add the **Get file properties** SharePoint action and append `- Get properties of uploaded file` to the action name.

9. Under **Site Address**, select the site associated with the team created earlier. In this example, the team was named **Jobs and candidates** and has a SharePoint Online URL of `https://<tenant>.sharepoint.com/sites/jobsandcandidates`, as shown in *Figure 9.20*:

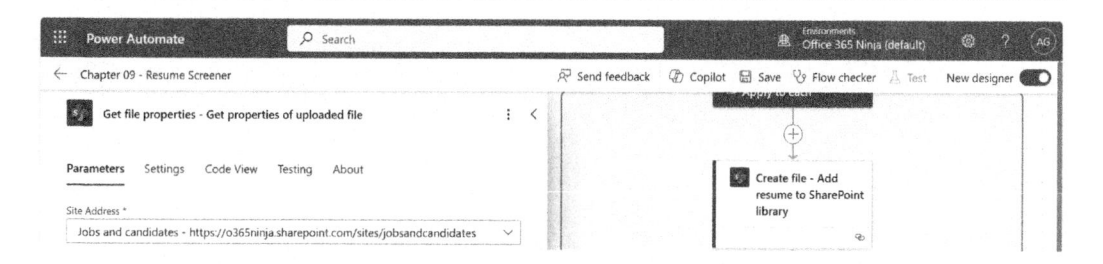

Figure 9.20 – Selecting the SharePoint site associated with the team

10. Under **Library Name**, select the **Resumes** document library.
11. Under **Id**, choose the **Id** or **ItemId** dynamic content token from the **Create file Add resume to SharePoint library** action. It also may be displayed as the **body/ItemId** token (depending on it you're using the **New designer** or **Classic designer** view), as depicted in *Figure 9.21*:

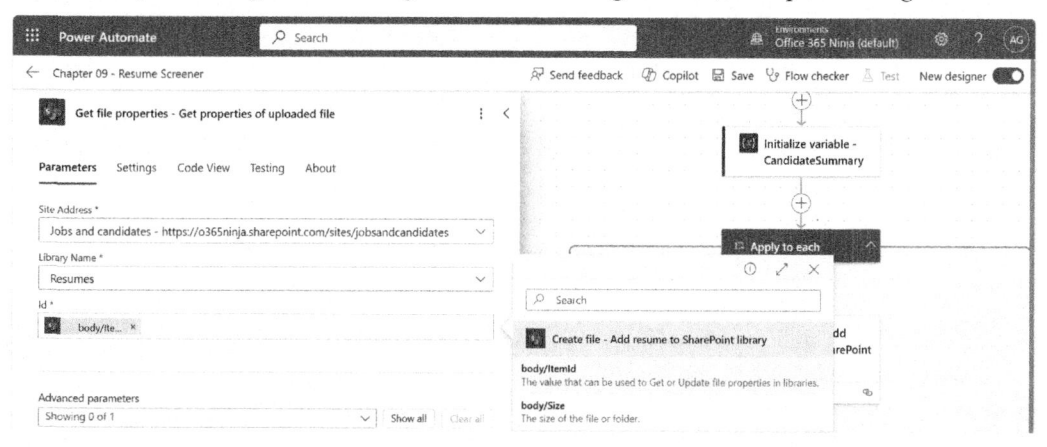

Figure 9.21 – Adding the ItemId dynamic content token

12. Next, add the **Get file content using path** SharePoint action and append – `Import resume data` to the action name.
13. Under **Site Address**, select the SharePoint site associated with the **Jobs and candidates** team. This should be the same site you chose for *step 8* previously.
14. Under **File Path**, add the **body/Path** dynamic content token under the **Create file Add resume to SharePoint library** action. See *Figure 9.22*:

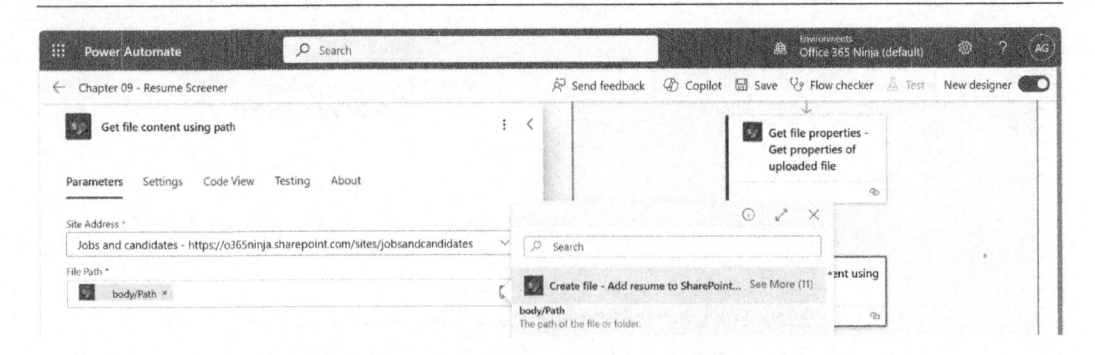

218 Implementing an AI-Enabled Resume Screener

Figure 9.22 – Adding the body/Path dynamic content token

15. After the **Get file content using path** SharePoint action, add the **Create item** SharePoint action. Append – `Candidate list entry` to the action name.

All right! Time to click **Save** to preserve your progress! Next, we'll introduce a new AI Builder action using the model that you trained earlier.

Extracting information from a resume and updating a candidate record

This next process will leverage the document extraction model. Since the model is already trained, there's nothing you really need to do other than send the document to the model. Follow these steps:

1. After the **Create item Candidate list entry** action, add the **Extract information from documents** AI Builder action:

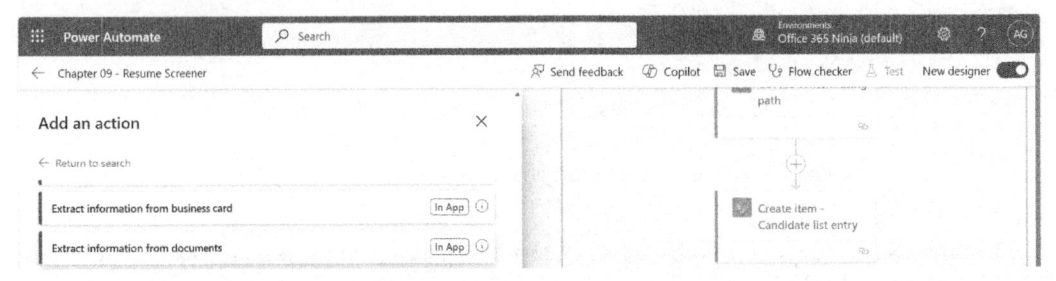

Figure 9.23 – Adding an AI Builder action

2. Append – `Extract candidate information from resume` to the action name.
3. Under **AI Model**, select the **Resume identification** model that you trained.
4. Under **Form Type**, select **PDF**.
5. Under **Form**, select the **File Content** dynamic content token under the **Get file content using path Import resume data** action:

Creating a flow   219

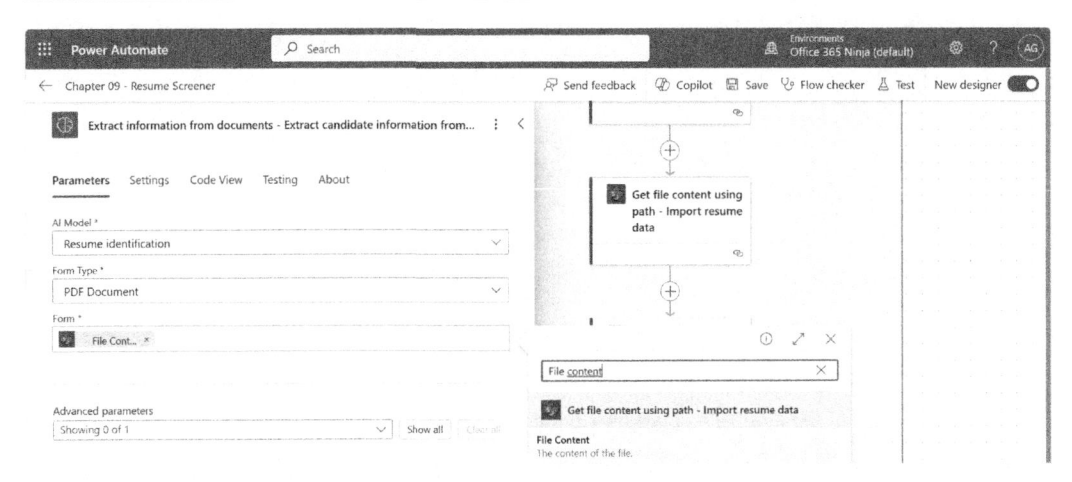

Figure 9.24 – Configuring the Extract information from documents action

6. Add an **Update item** SharePoint action. Append - `Update candidate personal data` to the action name.
7. Under **Site Address**, select the SharePoint site associated with the **Jobs and candidates** team.
8. Under **List Name**, select the **Candidates** list.
9. Under **Id**, select the **ID** dynamic content token under the **Create item - Candidate list entry** SharePoint action. See *Figure 9.25*:

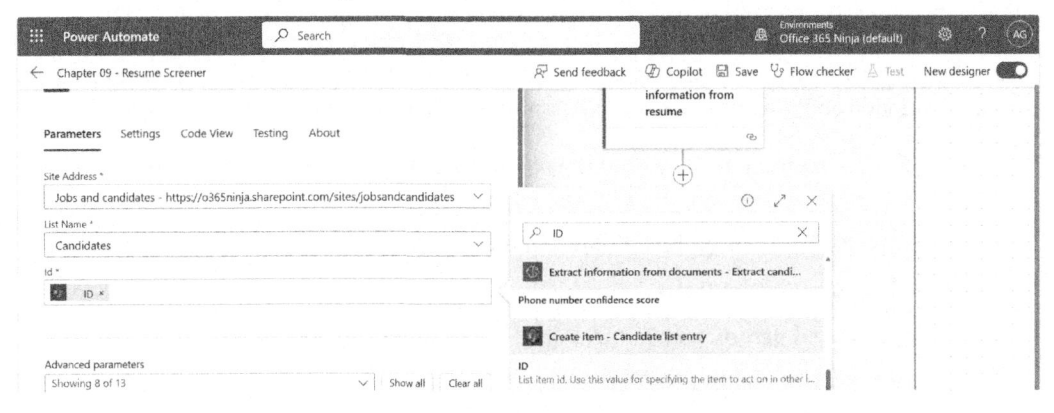

Figure 9.25 – Selecting the ID associated with the candidate entry

10. Under **Advanced parameters**, click **Show all**.
11. In the **First Name**, **Last Name**, **Phone Number**, **Email**, **Current Role**, and **Current Company** fields, add the corresponding dynamic content token under the **Extract data from documents - Extract candidate information** from resume action, as shown in *Figure 9.26*:

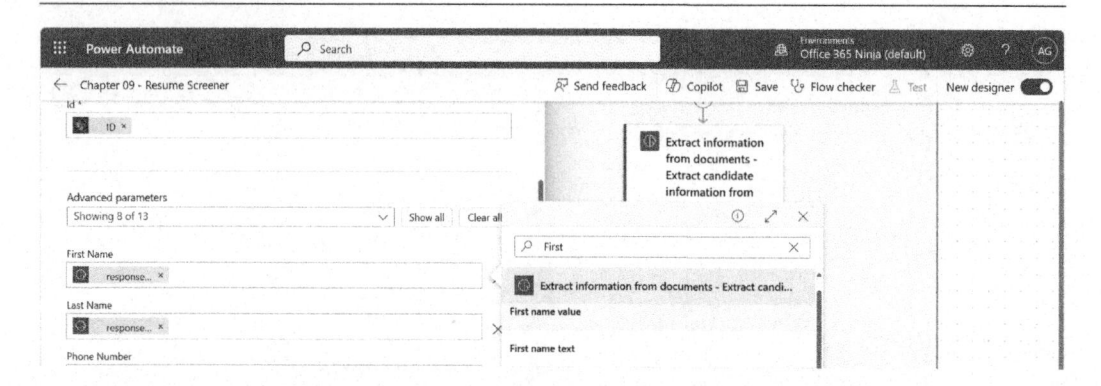

220　Implementing an AI-Enabled Resume Screener

[Screenshot of Power Automate interface showing field mapping with dynamic content tokens]

Figure 9.26 – Mapping dynamic content tokens to fields

You can use either the *<Field name> value* or *text* dynamic content tokens. For consistency's sake, use the same token type for all of the fields.

12. In the **Resume Link** field, add the **Link to item** dynamic content token under the **Get file properties Get properties of uploaded file** action.

It's time to click **Save** again! Up to this point, you've processed a resume to the point where you've extracted key details from the document and inserted them into the candidate record. Next, you'll evaluate the resume against the job description.

Evaluating the resume with a prompt

In this section, we'll configure actions to import one of the job descriptions and send the text of both the job description and the resume to a GenAI prompt. Follow these steps:

1. After the **Update item Update candidate personal data** action, add the **Get items** SharePoint action. Append `- Import job descriptions` to the description of the action.
2. Under **Site Address**, select the **Jobs and candidates** site.
3. Under **List Name**, select **Roles**.
4. Under **Advanced parameters**, in the dropdown, select **Filter Query**.
5. In the **Filter Query** field, enter `Title eq 'Service Desk Technician'`:

Creating a flow 221

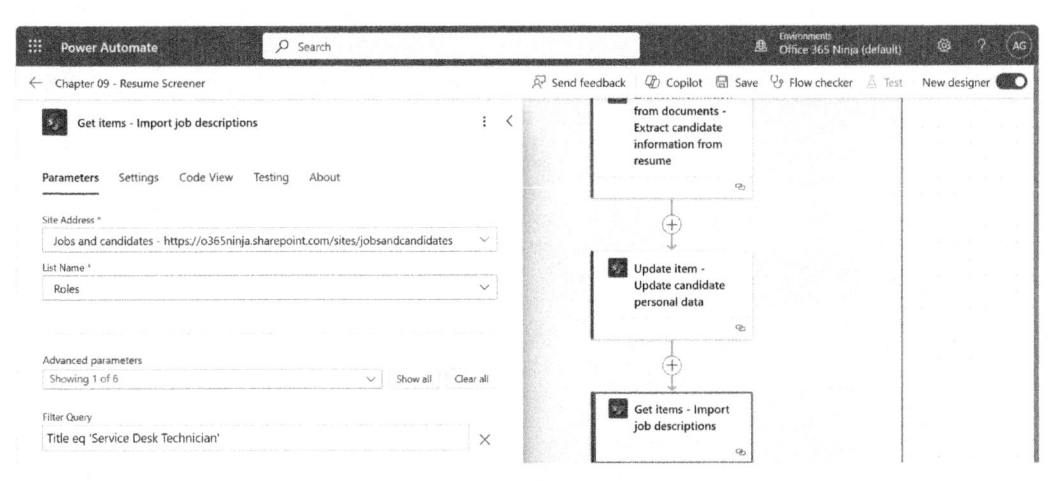

Figure 9.27 – Editing the filter query

6. In this example, the filter query is used to select the list row containing the job description for the *service desk technician*. Change the text between the single quotes to match the role description you're testing for.

7. Add the **Convert PDF Document to Text (txt)** Cloudmersive action:

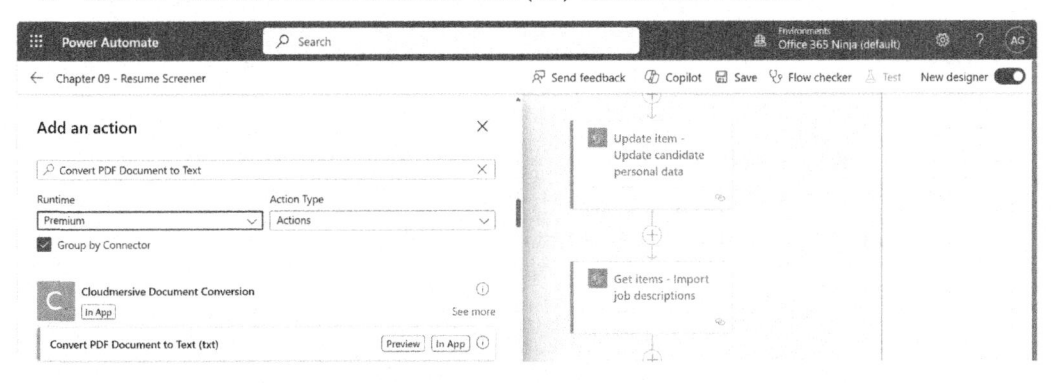

Figure 9.28 – Adding the Cloudmersive PDF document conversion action

8. On the **Create Connection** flyout, specify a **Connection Name** value and then enter the **API Key** value you obtained when you set up in the *Enabling the Cloudmersive connector* section. Click **Create new** when finished. See *Figure 9.29*:

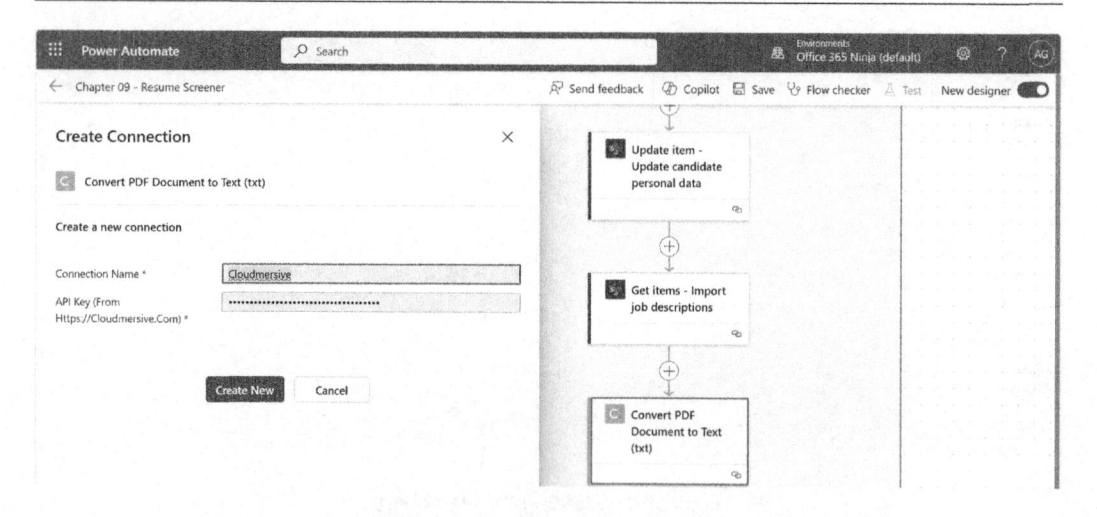

222   Implementing an AI-Enabled Resume Screener

Figure 9.29 – Configuring a connection

9. In the **Input File To Perform The Operation On** field, add the **File Content** dynamic content token under the **Get file content using path Import resume data** action.

10. In the **Input File to Perform the Operation On (File Name)** field, add the **File name with extension** dynamic content token under **the Get file properties Get properties of uploaded file** action.

    This will result in the resume PDF file being converted to text for processing with the GenAI prompt.

11. Add a **Create text with GPT using a prompt** AI Builder action. Append `- Evaluate candidate against job descript` to the description of the action.

12. Under **Prompt**, select **New custom prompt**:

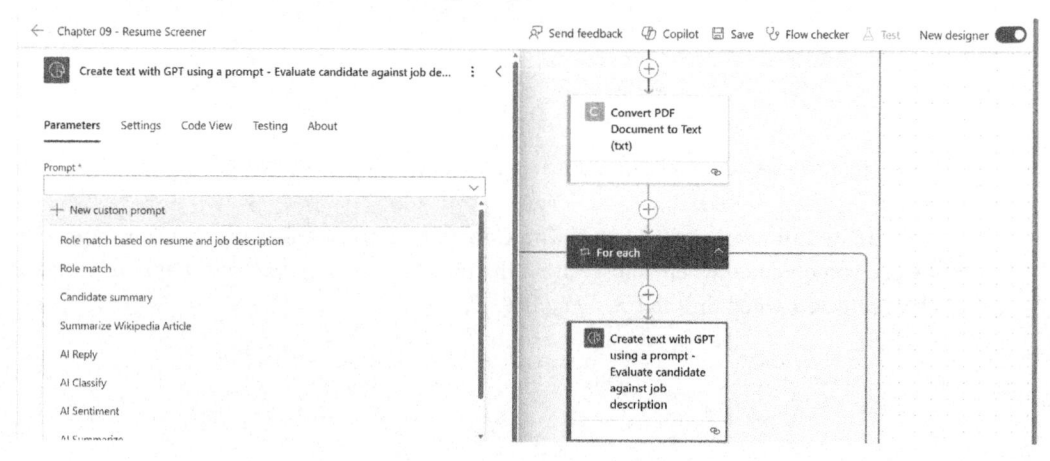

Figure 9.30 – Configuring the AI Builder GPT prompt

13. In the prompt area, paste the following text:

    > You are an HR professional screening candidate resumes. A candidate has submitted the following resume: *CandidateResume*
    >
    > You are trying to fill the position *RoleTitle* that has the following job description: *RoleDescription*
    >
    > Based only on the information in the supplied role description and the information in the candidate's resume, is this candidate a good fit for the position?
    >
    > Output must be structured in a JSON output. The JSON object must have three name value pairs:
    >
    > RoleFit: Evaluation of whether candidate is a fit for the role. Possible answers are Yes, No, Maybe.
    >
    > RoleFitSummary: Short summary of why candidate was or was not a fit. Limit to 50 words.
    >
    > CandidateSummary: Short summary of candidate skills, experience, and work history. Limit to 100 words.
    >
    > Only Yes, No, or Maybe answers are accepted for the RoleFit name value pair. Use the following information to determine good fit:
    >
    > The resume and the role description should have at least an 80% confidence match to be considered a good fit (Yes).
    >
    > If the resume and role description have between and 70% and 80% confidence match, then answer Maybe.
    >
    > If the resume and the role description is less than a 70% confidence rating, consider the candidate not a fit (No). You must limit your answers to either Yes, No, or Maybe for the RoleFit name value pair.
    >
    > The output data must be a properly formatted JSON object and should be ordered based on the following sample:
    >
    > {
    >
    > "RoleFit" : "yes",
    >
    > "RoleFitSummary" : "50 word description explaining reasoning.",
    >
    > "CandidateSummary" : " 100 word summary of candidate skills and experience."
    >
    > }

14. Add a **Name** value for the prompt, such as `Role match based on resume and job description`.

15. Replace the highlighted words, denoted by asterisks (*CandidateResume*, *RoleTitle*, and *RoleDescription*), with dynamic values. You can type a forward slash (/) character or use the **Add dynamic value** button to insert a dynamic content token. See *Figure 9.31* for an example of a completed prompt:

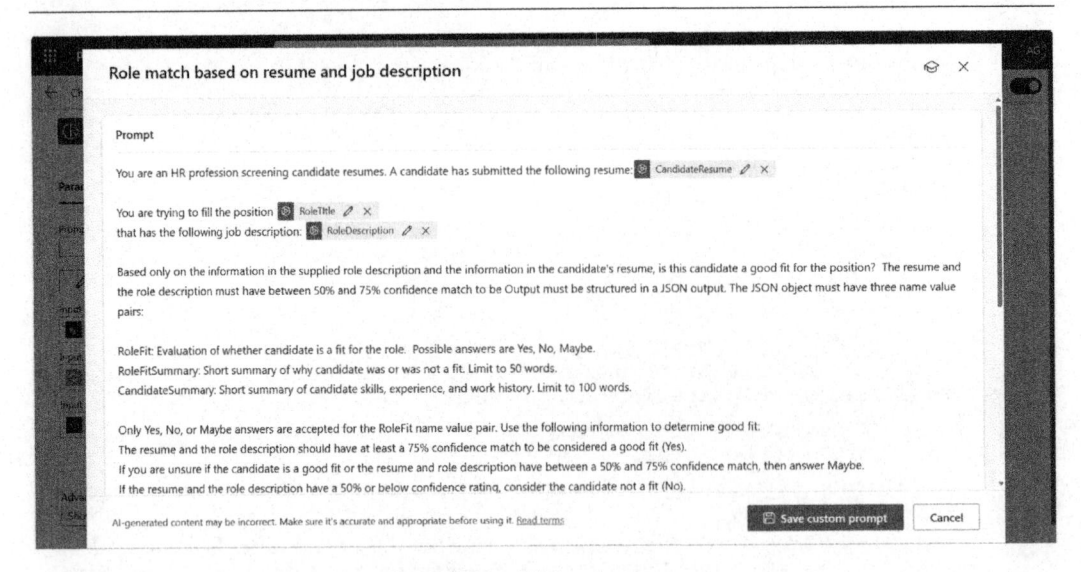

224 Implementing an AI-Enabled Resume Screener

Figure 9.31 – Editing the prompt

16. Click **Save custom prompt**.
17. In the **InputRoleTitle** field, select the **Title** dynamic content token under the **Get items Import job descriptions** action.
18. In the **Input CandidateResume** field, add the **body/TextResult** dynamic content token under the **Convert PDF Document to Text (txt)** action:

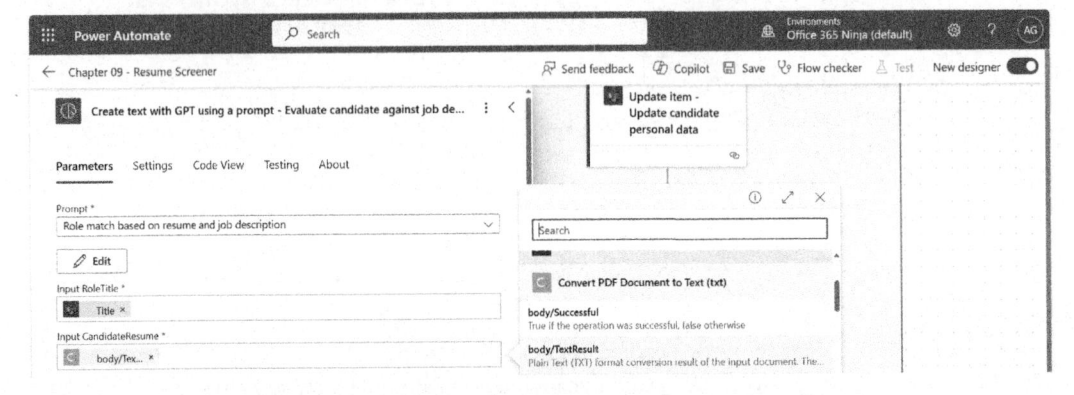

Figure 9.32 – Adding the Cloudmersive Convert PDF Document to Text (txt) action

19. In the **Input RoleDescription** field, add the **JobDescription** dynamic content token under the **Get items Import job descriptions** action.
20. Click **Save**.

You've only got a few sections left! Next, we'll update some variables that we can use for updating the candidate's record in the SharePoint list and generating messages to post to Teams or send via email.

Updating the candidate record

In this section, we'll take the generated data elements from the GPT action and add them back to the candidate record. Follow these steps:

1. After the **Create text with GPT using a prompt Evaluate candidate against job description** action, add a **Set variable** action. Append - `RoleFitJson` to the action name.
2. In the **Name** field, select **RoleFitJson**.
3. In the **Value** field, select the **Text** dynamic content token under the **Create text with GPT using a prompt Evaluate candidate against job description** action.

   This dynamic content token contains the JSON structure we specified in the prompt:

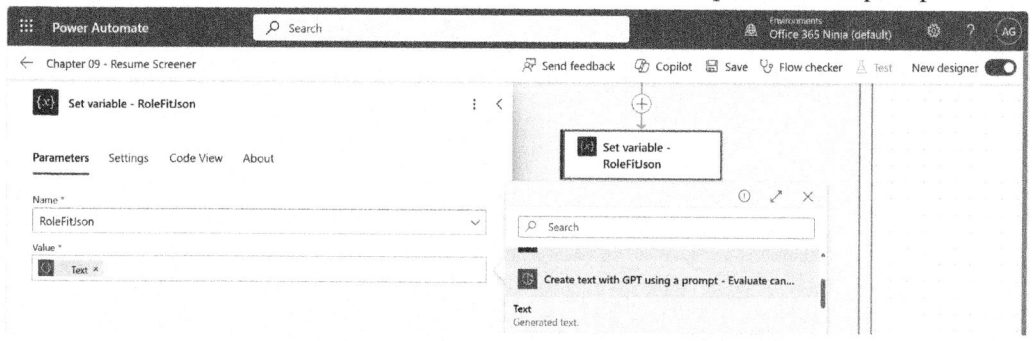

Figure 9.33 – Adding the text output of the GPT prompt

4. Add a **Parse JSON** data operations action. Append - `Extract generated RoleFit data` to the action name.
5. In the **Content** field, add the **RoleFitJson** variable dynamic content token.
6. In the **Schema** area, paste the following definition:

   ```
   {
       "type": "object",
       "properties": {
           "RoleFit": {
               "type": "string"
           },
           "RoleFitSummary": {
               "type": "string"
           },
           "CandidateSummary": {
   ```

```
                    "type": "string"
                }
            }
        }
```

This schema is used to define the structure of the JSON array. Notice the name/value pair definitions along with their content type. The **Parse JSON** action will extract the results of the prompt and allow you to save the results into their own variables.

7. Add a **Set variable** action. Append `- RoleFit` to the action name.
8. In the **Name** field, select the **RoleFit** variable.
9. In the **Value** field, add the **Body RoleFit** dynamic content token under the **Parse JSON Extract generated RoleFit data** action:

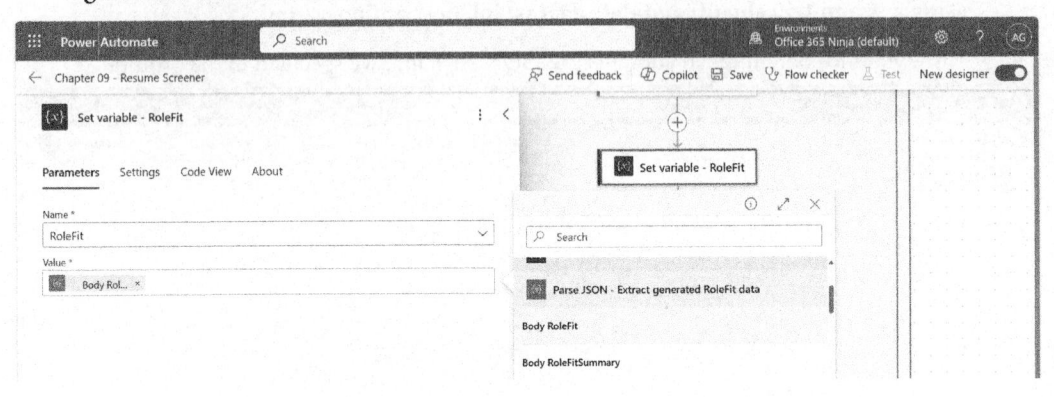

Figure 9.34 – Selecting the RoleFit content

10. Add a **Set variable** action. Append `- RoleFitSummary` to the action name.
11. In the **Name** field, select the **RoleFitSummary** variable.
12. In the **Value** field, add the **Body RoleFitSummary** dynamic content token under the **Parse JSON Extract generated RoleFit data** action.
13. Add a **Set variable** action. Append `- CandidateSummary` to the action name.
14. In the **Name** field, select the **CandidateSummary** variable.
15. In the **Value** field, add the **Body CandidateSummary** dynamic content token under the **Parse JSON Extract generated RoleFit data** action.
16. Add an **Update item** SharePoint action. Append `- Update Candidate Status` to the action name.
17. Under **Site Address**, select the SharePoint site containing the candidate resumes and list.
18. Under **List Name**, select **Candidates**.

19. In the **Id** field, add the **ID** dynamic content token under the **Create item Candidate list entry** action:

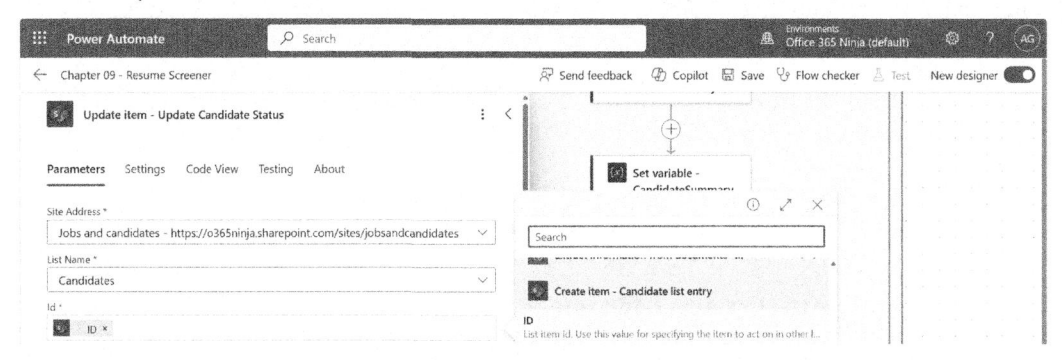

Figure 9.35 – Configuring the Update item action – Update Candidate Status

20. Under **Advanced Parameters**, click **Show all**.
21. In the **Candidate Summary** field, add the **CandidateSummary** variable.
22. In the **Service Desk Technician** field, add the **RoleFit** variable.
23. In the **Reason** field, add the **RoleFitSummary** variable. See *Figure 9.36*:

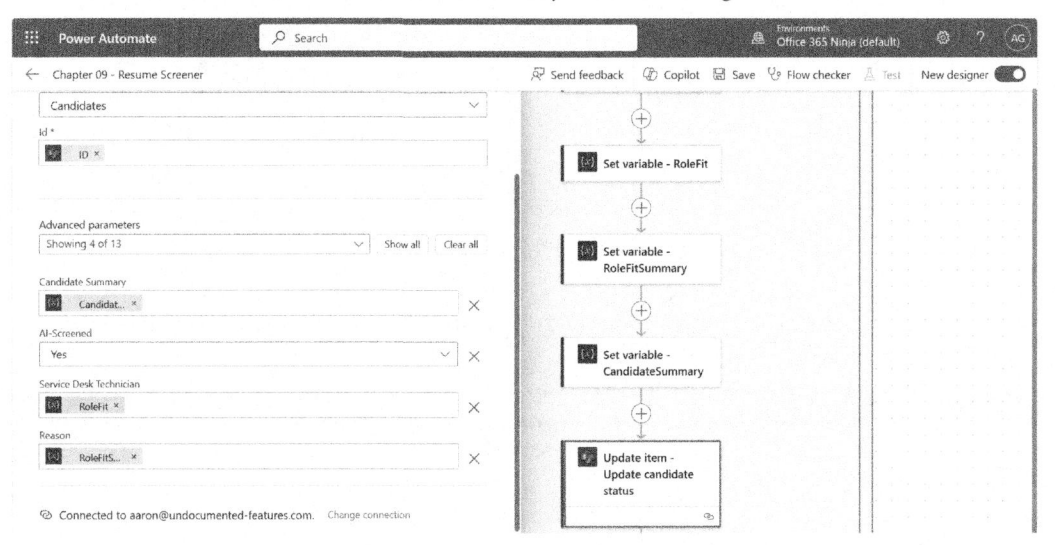

Figure 9.36 – Adding the output variables

Click **Save** to save the progress on the flow. In the final section, we'll add some notifications.

Sending confirmation messages

After updating the candidate's **RoleFit** status as either **Yes**, **No**, or **Maybe**, it's time to send some notifications! Follow these steps:

1. After the **Update item** action (where you updated the candidate's status), click **Add an action** and select the **Condition** control.
2. Change the expression evaluation from **AND** to **OR**.
3. In the first box, add the dynamic content token for the **RoleFit** variable, set the operator to **is equal to**, and then enter the text value Yes.
4. Click **New item** and then select **Add row**.
5. In the first box of the new row, add the dynamic content token for the **RoleFit** variable, set the operator to **is equal to**, and then enter the text value Maybe. See *Figure 9.37*:

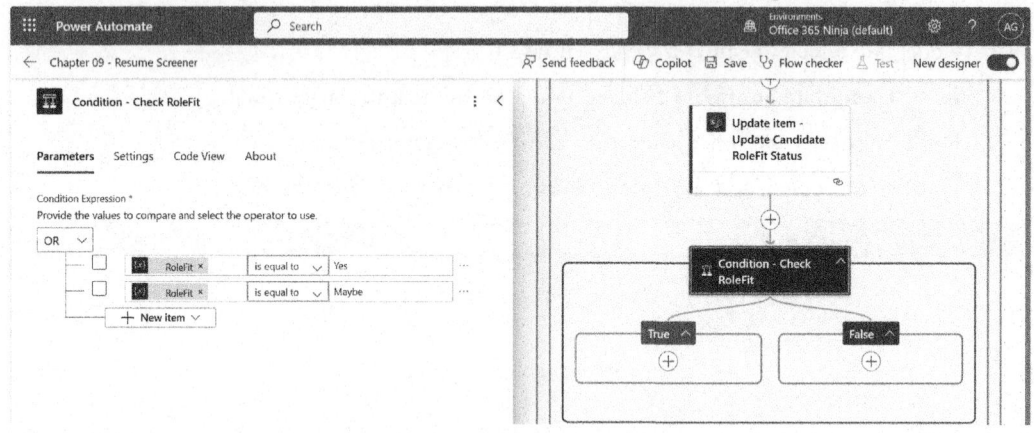

Figure 9.37 – Adding a Condition control for RoleFit

6. In the **True** branch of the **Condition** control, add the **Post message in a chat or channel** Teams action, as shown in *Figure 9.38*:

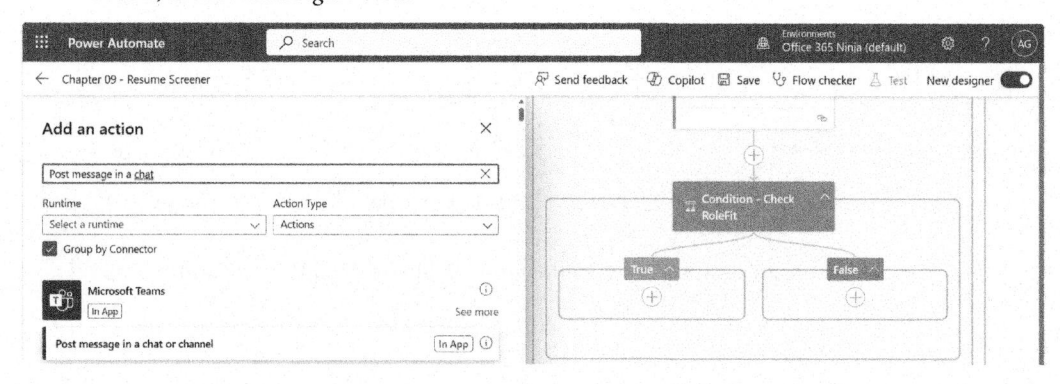

Figure 9.38 – Adding the Teams post message action

7. Under **Post As**, select **Flow bot**.
8. Under **Post In**, select **Channel**.
9. Under **Team**, select the **Jobs and candidates** team.
10. Under **Channel**, select **General**.
11. Customize the message area using tokens, such as *Candidate Summary*, *Role Fit*, and a link to the resume:

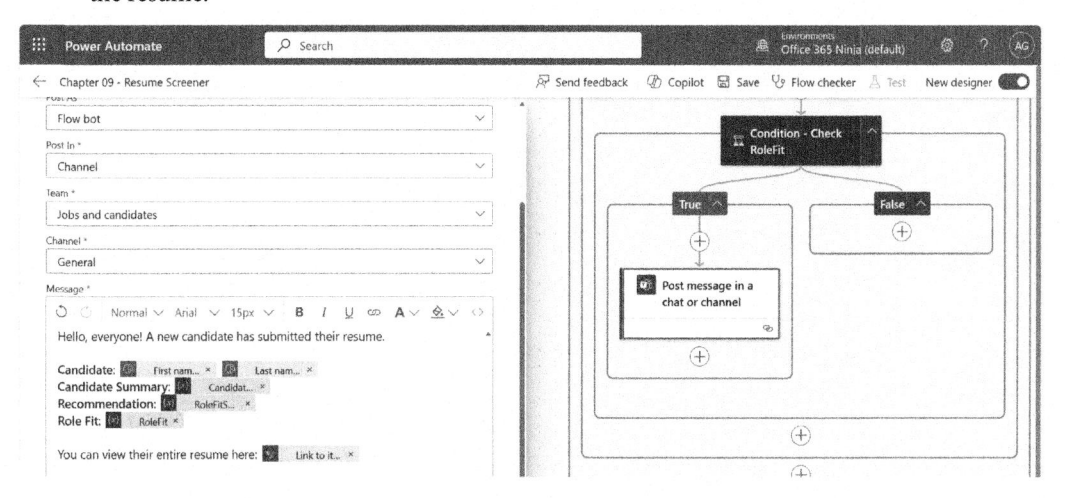

Figure 9.39 – Creating a Teams channel notification

12. In the **False** condition branch, add the **Send an email from a shared mailbox (V2)** Office 365 Outlook action.
13. In the **Original Mailbox Address** field, select **Enter custom value** and then add the email address of the shared mailbox configured earlier in this chapter.
14. In the **To** field, add the **Email value** dynamic content token from the **Extract information from documents Extract candidate information from resume** AI Builder action. This will select the email address specified in the resume.
15. In the **Subject** field, enter a message.
16. In the **Body** text area, enter a message to send back to a candidate, using any of the dynamic content tokens that you find appropriate for the message (such as the **First name value** token from the **Extract …** AI Builder action:

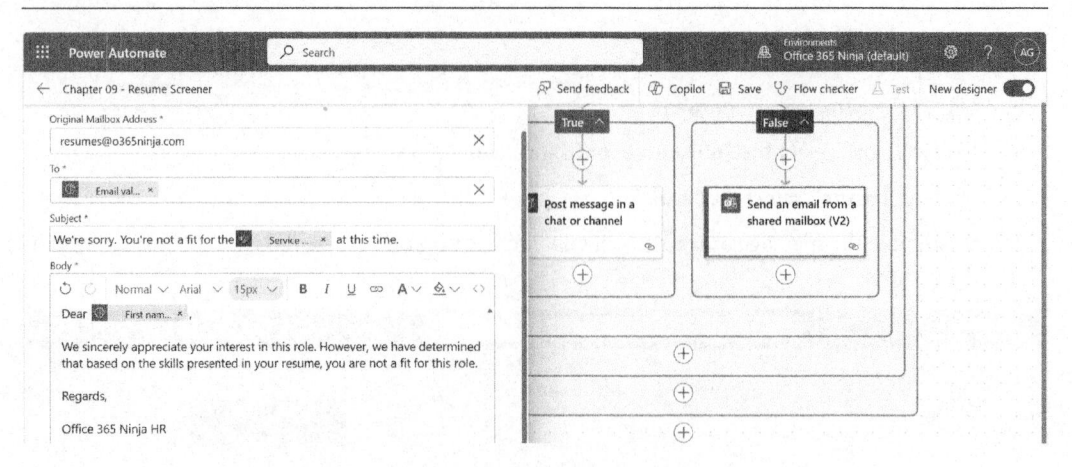

230　Implementing an AI-Enabled Resume Screener

Figure 9.40 – Customizing the email message

17. Click **Save**.

Now for the moment of truth!

Testing the flow

To test the flow, you'll need a few things:

- A few sample resumes (one that should match the job description and one that shouldn't)
- An email account to send the resumes from

To test the flow, follow these steps:

1. From the flow designer, click **Test**.
2. Select the **Manually** radio button and then click **Test**.
3. Launch your email client and send an email with a sample resume to the shared mailbox configured.
4. Review the flow run history as it is updated in the flow designer:

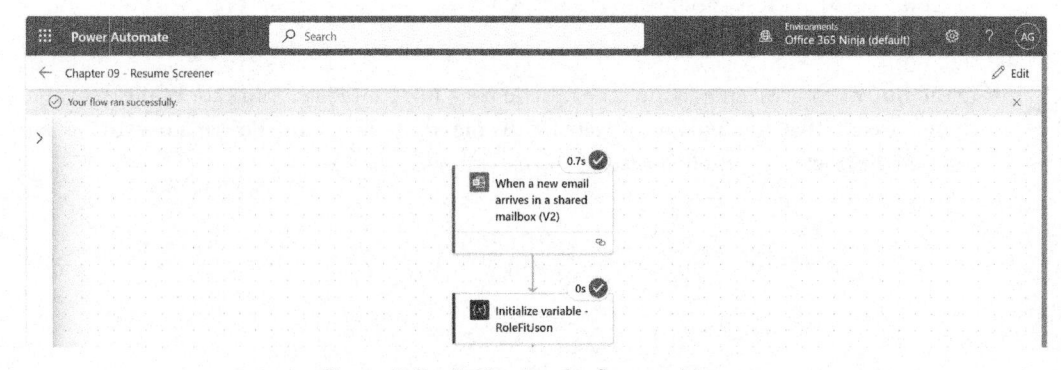

Figure 9.41 – Reviewing the flow run history

Testing the flow   231

5. Launch Microsoft Teams and navigate to the **Jobs and candidates** team. Check the channel you specified in the **Post message** action to see how the resume was evaluated:

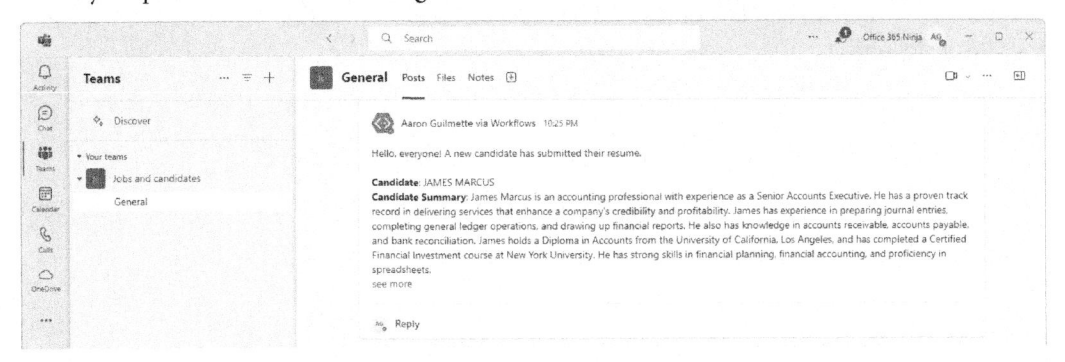

Figure 9.42 – Reviewing the Teams channel post

6. Next, navigate to the **Jobs and candidates** SharePoint site and select the **Candidates** list to see your resume submissions:

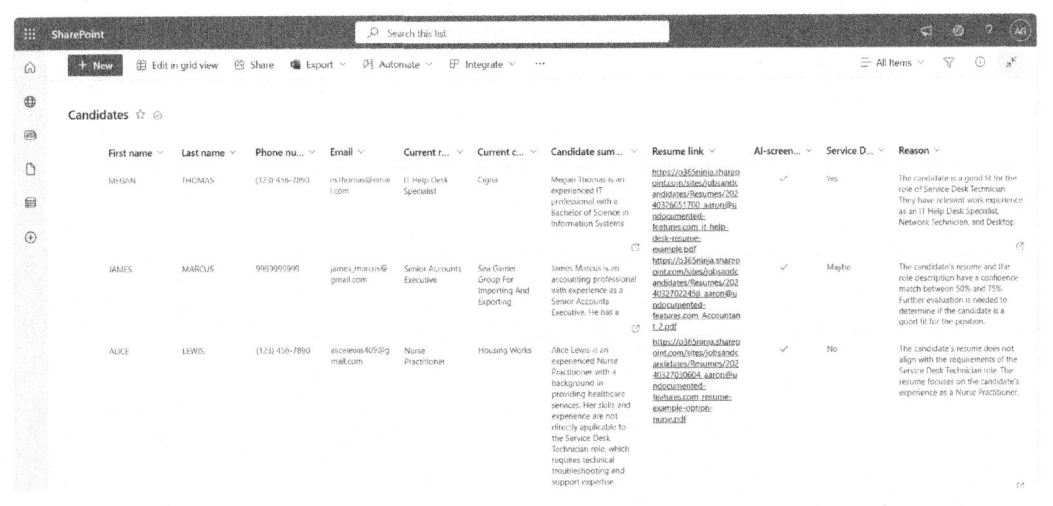

Figure 9.43 – Reviewing resume submissions

Congratulations! You've successfully verified the flow!

If the flow mis-categorizes resumes, you can easily go back and adjust the prompt to raise or lower the confidence requirements.

Further exploration

The foundation that this flow lays opens up a lot of possibilities for workflow automation. Possibilities include the following:

- Branching to allow checking against other role descriptions in the same flow
- Conditions to filter the subject of the message to route to other flows
- Document validation using a Cloudmersive action to ensure the submitted resumes can be read
- Conditions to reject attachments that are not PDFs
- Interview scheduling

Summary

In this chapter, we introduced two powerful AI Builder concepts: data extraction modeling and using GenAI to summarize and evaluate content.

With the skills gained in this chapter, you can adapt GenAI to a myriad of business challenges.

In the next chapter, we'll build on the GenAI text summarization capabilities from this chapter to craft executive summaries of documents.

10
Crafting an Executive Summary with GPT

Many of us have to put together proposals of some sort—whether it's responding to an RFP, delivering a statement of work, proposing a solution to a customer, or presenting a quarterly business report. The executive report is a key feature of each of those kinds of documents—bringing the key points together in a high-level, digestible overview.

In this chapter, we'll look at how we can leverage the power of generative AI to reason over content, build an executive summary, and insert it back into the document. We'll use some familiar tools (such as the Encodian and Cloudmersive connectors) to make it happen!

Designing a solution

If you went through the exercises in *Chapter 7, Using Power Automate to Build PowerPoint Presentations*, and *Chapter 9, Implementing an AI-Enabled Resume Screener*, you're already familiar with the Encodian Flowr and Cloudmersive connectors. This solution builds on both of those and combines it with the power of OpenAI ChatGPT.

Licensing prerequisites

Using AI models and connectors in the Power Platform has several prerequisites:

- Power Automate premium licensing
- An OpenAI subscription
- An Encodian free trial
- A Cloudmersive Free Tier account

If you haven't already enabled Dataverse and AI Builder capacity, see *Chapter 2, Configuring an Environment to Support AI Services*, and *Chapter 6, Processing Data with Sentiment Analysis*.

Configuring solution prerequisites

Before you start the workflow configuration, you'll need to get a few prerequisites out of the way—namely, to obtain free, trial, or paid subscriptions to OpenAI, Encodian, and Cloudmersive, set up a template document, and ensure you have a storage location for the finished document.

Let's quickly look at getting these ready.

Enabling subscriptions

If you've already got those, great! If not, you can refer to *Chapter 2* for information on the configuration of an OpenAI subscription, *Chapter 7* for obtaining an Encodian trial, and *Chapter 9* for signing up for a free Cloudmersive subscription.

Preparing a document template

If you've already completed the exercise in *Chapter 7*, you're familiar with the **Populate** action that we'll be using from the Encodian Flowr connector. Essentially, you edit a document (in this case, a Word document containing your statement of work or another document that has content that needs an executive summary) and insert a **token** that indicates where you want Flowr to place your content. The token is formatted as a keyword, surrounded by << [ ] >>, as shown in *Figure 10.1*:

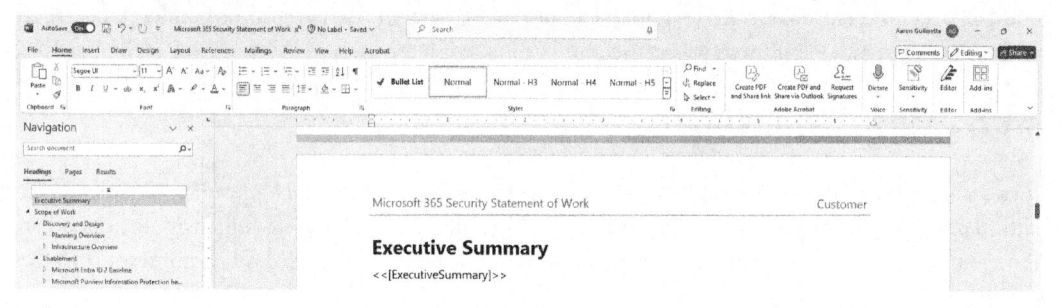

Figure 10.1 – Placing a token in a document

In *Figure 10.1*, the <<[**ExecutiveSummary**]>> token represents the location where Flowr will insert the executive summary content that the GPT service generates.

Setting up a cloud storage provider

In this chapter, we'll be using the OneDrive for Business service that comes with an Office 365 or Microsoft 365 subscription. You can use another solution (such as DropBox or Google Drive), but you'll have to configure those separately and use the appropriate connector.

Creating the flow

With all of the prerequisites out of the way, it's time to start working with some automation!

> **What do I do if I'm stuck?**
> If you run into a roadblock for some reason (you can't find a feature, an option isn't showing up, or something is unclear), help is only a click away! You can download this chapter's artifacts from our GitHub site at `https://github.com/PacktPublishing/Power-Platform-and-the-AI-Revolution`.

We'll start with the trigger.

Configuring the trigger

This flow works best with a manual trigger, where you will supply the document that will be used as the basis for the executive summary.

GPTs, as you already know, utilize prompts to provide instruction on the types of tasks to be performed. You have the option of supplying the entire prompt upfront in the trigger or moving the base of the prompt language to later on and allowing for customizations or tweaks in the trigger.

In this flow, we'll take the latter approach. This trigger will employ four input variables:

- A list of document sections that you want to include in the summary
- A list of document sections that you want to exclude from the summary
- A place where you can input additional instructions to tailor the response
- A file upload input

To configure the flow, follow these steps:

1. Navigate to the Power Automate maker portal (`https://make.powerautomate.com`) and select **Create**.
2. Under **Start from blank**, select **Instant cloud flow**.
3. On the **Build an automated cloud flow** page, provide a **Flow name** (such as `Generate executive summary`) and select the **Manually trigger a flow** trigger. Click **Create**.
4. Select the **Manually trigger a flow** trigger. In the flyout, select **Add an input**.
5. Select **Text**:

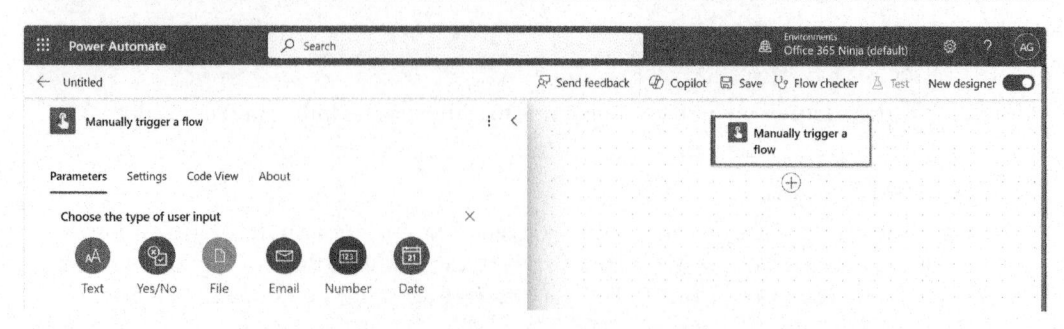

Figure 10.2 – Selecting the Text input

6. Replace **Input text** with `Inclusions`. This will be the text area where you can describe the document sections or components to include in your flow. In the text area, you can replace **Please enter your input** with suggestions on sections that may be important to include (such as `scope of work and project deliverables`), as shown in *Figure 10.3*:

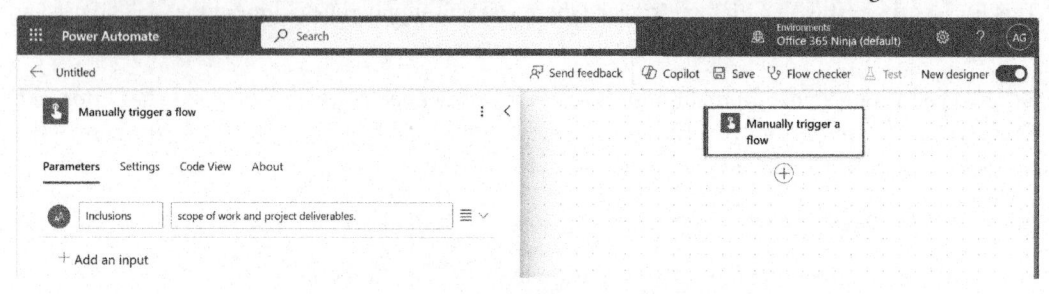

Figure 10.3 – Customizing the input

> **Note**
> It's important to note that the text you use as a suggestion is not the same as **default text** (text that will be automatically included if no customization is given). Power Automate currently does not support default text. You'll have to fill in this text during the flow run.

Depending on how your organization's scopes of work are constructed and what your typical executive summaries look like, you may want to customize this further.

7. Click **Add an input**.

8. Replace **Input text** with `Inclusions`. This will be the text area where you can describe the document sections or components to include in your flow. In the text area, you can replace **Please enter your input** with suggestions on sections that may be important to exclude (such as `project governance, project management, period of performance, resource planning, customer resource commitments, and pricing`). Depending on how your organization's scopes of work are constructed and what your typical executive summaries look like, you may want to customize this further.

Creating the flow | 237

9. Click **Add an input**.
10. Replace **Input text** with `Additional Instructions`. This will be the text area where you can provide any other relevant instructions, such as what types of things may be important to a particular customer. In the text area, you can replace **Please enter your input** with a suggestion such as `Focus on the positive outcomes and partnership opportunity with the customer`.
11. Click **Add an input** and select **File**.
12. Replace **File Content** with `Upload`.

With the trigger configured, it's time to start processing the document.

Converting the document

Since GPT can only process content in text form (and not the binary format of the Word document), it's necessary to convert it. This next set of steps will send the document to the Cloudmersive connector to convert it to plaintext:

1. After the trigger, click + and select **Add an action**.
2. In the **Add an action** flyout, type `Cloudmersive`, scroll to the **Cloudmersive Document Conversion** connector, and click **See more**:

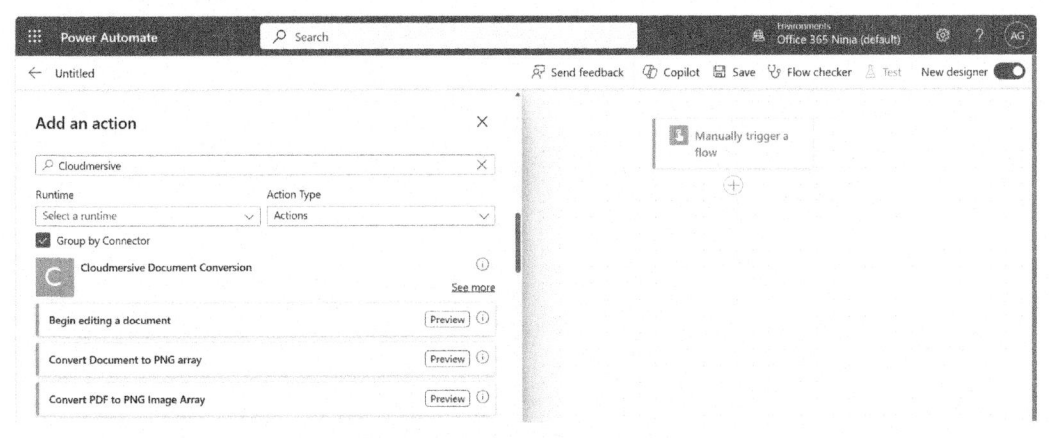

Figure 10.4 – Selecting the connector

3. Select the **Convert Word DOCX Document to Text (txt)** action, as shown in *Figure 10.5*:

238 Crafting an Executive Summary with GPT

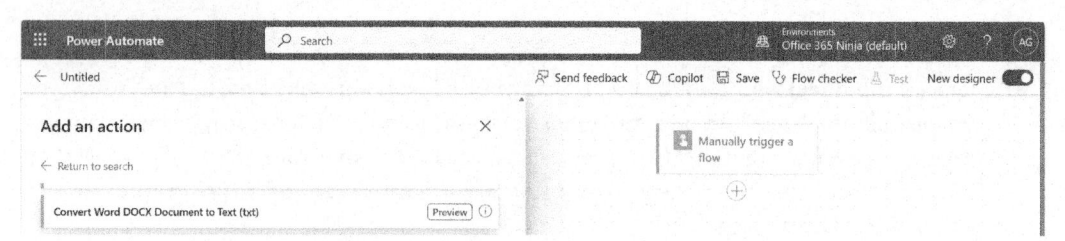

Figure 10.5 – Selecting the Convert action

4. The **Convert Word DOCX to Document to Text (txt)** flyout appears. In the **Input File to Perform the Operation On** box, add the dynamic content token for **File Content contentBytes** under the **Manually trigger a flow** action:

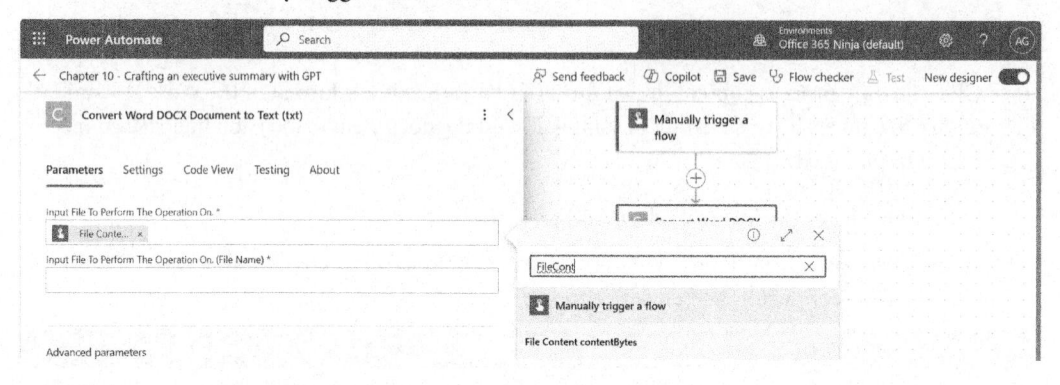

Figure 10.6 – Adding the File Content contentBytes dynamic content token

5. In the **Input File to Perform The Operation On (File Name)** box, add the **File Content name** dynamic content token under the **Manually trigger a flow** action.

Now, we'll send the data over to OpenAI's ChatGPT for processing!

Sending the content to GPT

In this section, we'll configure the steps necessary to save the attachment and then add a SharePoint list item for candidates who send in their resumes. We'll use the HTTP premium connector for this section.

Before we do that, though, let's explore the JSON payload that will be sent to OpenAI. This payload contains information about the model that will be used, the prompt information, and the parameters that will control how the model responds:

```
{
  "model": "gpt-4",
  "messages": [
    {
```

```
            "role": "system",
            "content": "You are a system architect collaborating with
    an account executive on a statement of work for a new customer."
        },
        {
            "role": "user",
            "content": "Generate an executive summary for the
    included content. Focus on the following areas of the document:
    **Inclusions** Exclude the following sections from the executive
    summary: **Exclusions** Use the following additional information
    to write a compelling closing statement: **Additional
    Instructions** The completed executive summary should be between
    225 and 350 words."
        }
    ],
    "max_tokens": 5000,
    "temperature": 0,
    "n": 1,
    "stream": false,
    "logprobs": null,
    "stop": null
}
```

When reviewing this code sample, there are several key areas:

- `model`: In this example, we'll be using **gpt-4**. You can use other models, but GPT-4 is the most advanced that OpenAI currently offers.

- `messages`: This object defines two roles, **system** and **user**, each with an associated **content** key/value pair. The **system** role represents internal instructions that you, as the developer, are giving to the GPT. The related content key is where you can supply the instructions to the system role. In this case, you're instructing the GPT to act as a system architect. The **user** role is the person or service asking the GPT to perform a task. Its content key/value pair is used to supply the request context and instructions.

- `max_tokens`: This is the maximum number of tokens you want the service to consume. As you may recall from *Chapter 3, Talking to ChatGPT*, tokens are the chunks of content (words or parts of words) that the GPT breaks down the request into. Each document may vary, but 5,000 tokens is approximately equivalent to a 10-15 page double-spaced document. You can use OpenAI's Tokenizer (`https://platform.openai.com/tokenizer`) to estimate how many tokens your source document contains:

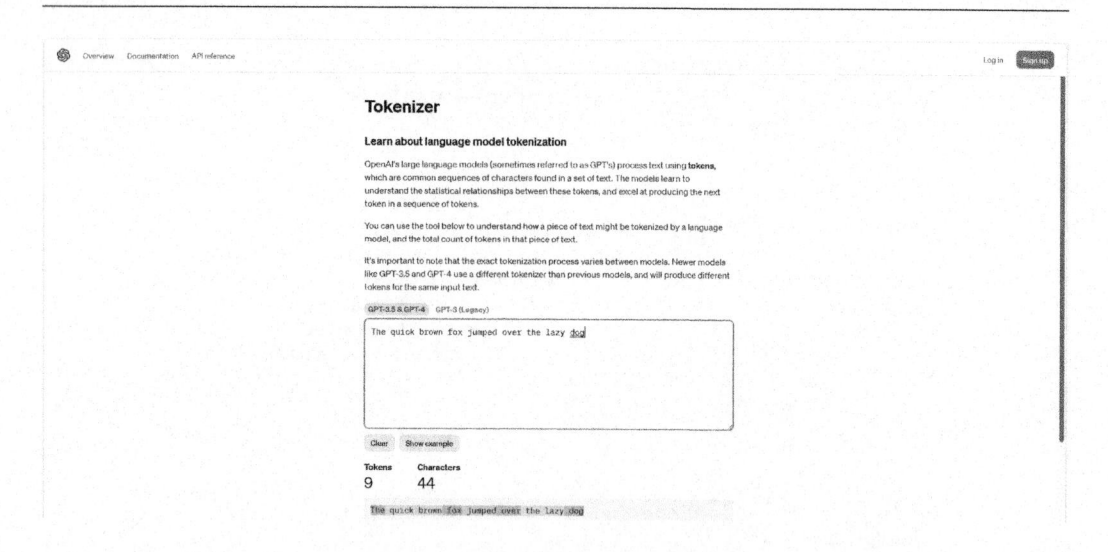

Figure 10.7 – Using the OpenAI Tokenizer

- `temperature`: This is a parameter (value between 0 and 1) that governs the randomness and creativity exhibited in the response. Closer to zero is more deterministic, while closer to 1 is more creative.
- `n`: How many completion choices to provide.
- `stream`: This allows partial message content to be sent. In this case, we want the full body of the response as a single entity.

You'll also notice some content that is surrounded by asterisks, such as **Inclusions** and **Exclusions**. These are simply placeholders that you will replace with dynamic content tokens.

Let's go!

1. After the **Convert Word DOCX Document to Text (txt)** action, add the **HTTP** action under the **HTTP** connector:

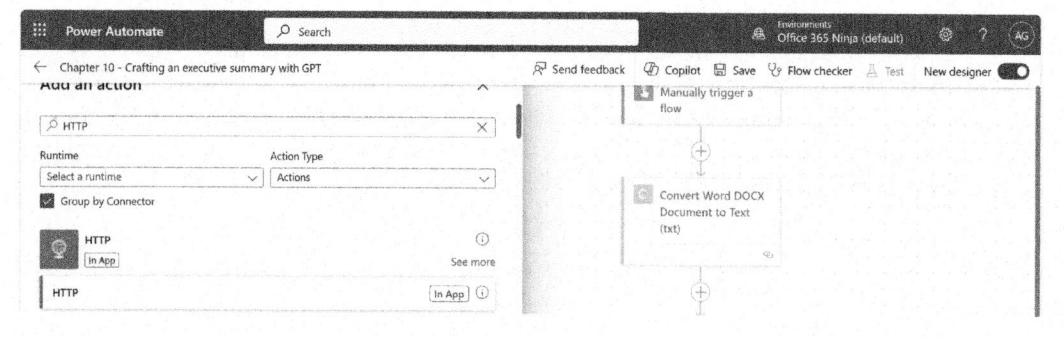

Figure 10.8 – Adding the HTTP action

2. In the **HTTP** action flyout, enter the following endpoint into the **URI** field: `https://api.openai.com/v1/chat/completions`

    This is the OpenAI service endpoint for chat completions.

3. Under **Method**, select **POST**.

4. Under **Headers**, enter the value `Authorization` in the **Key** field.

5. Next, you'll need your OpenAI API key. Under **Headers**, enter `Bearer <OpenAI AI key>` in the **Value** field. For example, if your OpenAI API key is *sk-qztnj1CoTtoXFsXXlFYnT3ClbkFJqOOBf7gFcn9ErCKqeYbV*, you'll enter the value `Bearer sk-qztnj1CoTtoXFsXXlFYnT3ClbkFJqOOBf7gFcn9ErCKqeYbV` in the **Value** field. See *Figure 10.9*:

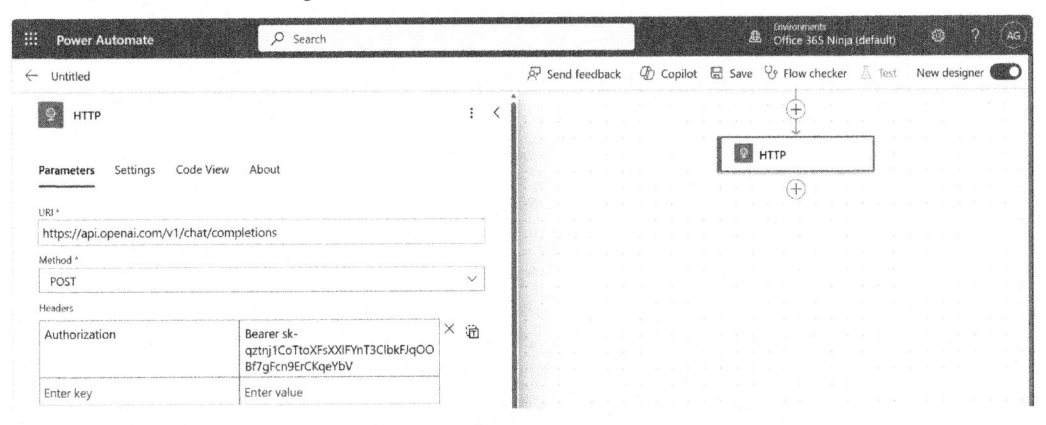

Figure 10.9 – Configuring the HTTP authorization

No, that's not a real key, so don't try to use it. It just looks like one.

6. The **Body** field is where we'll be sending the request to GPT. The request that we'll send will be structured as a JSON payload. You can copy the following payload (repeated from the beginning of the section):

```
{
  "model": "gpt-4",
  "messages": [
    {
      "role": "system",
      "content": "You are a system architect collaborating with an account executive on a statement of work for a new customer."
    },
    {
      "role": "user",
      "content": "Generate an executive summary for the included content. Focus on the following areas of the document:
```

Crafting an Executive Summary with GPT

```
    **Inclusions** Exclude the following sections from the executive
summary: **Exclusions** Use the following additional information
to write a compelling closing statement: **Additional
Instructions** The completed executive summary should be between
225 and 350 words."
    }
  ],
  "max_tokens": 5000,
  "temperature": 0,
  "n": 1,
  "stream": false,
  "logprobs": null,
  "stop": null
}
```

7. Select the text ****Inclusions**** and replace it with the **Inclusions** dynamic content token from the **Manually trigger a flow** action.

8. Select the text ****Exclusions**** and replace it with the **Exclusions** dynamic content token from the **Manually trigger a flow** action.

9. Select the text ****Additional Instructions**** and replace it with the **Additional Instructions** dynamic content token from the **Manually trigger a flow** action. See *Figure 10.10*:

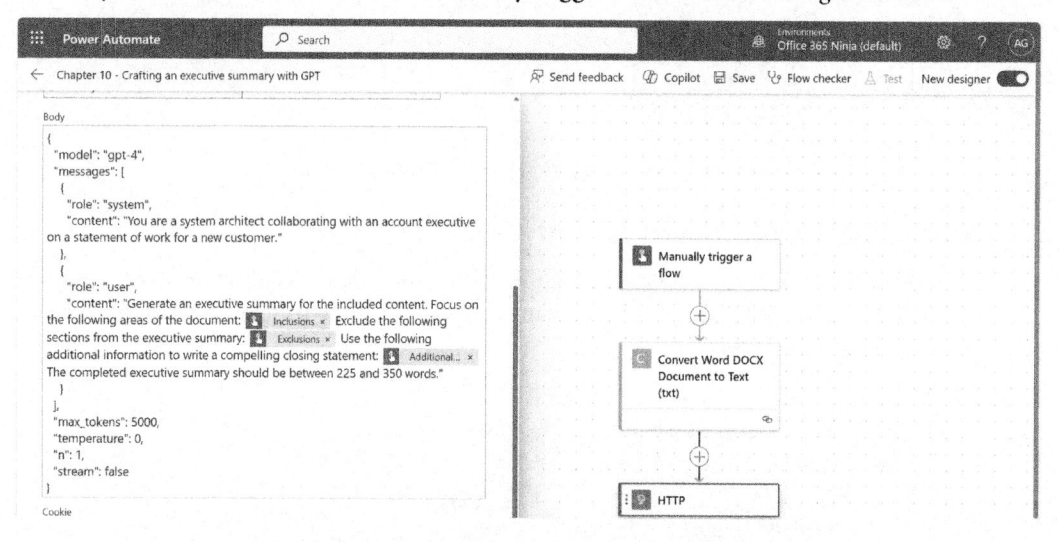

Figure 10.10 – Configuring the body of the HTTP action

10. After the **HTTP** action, add a **Parse JSON** action.

11. In the **Content** field, select the **Body** dynamic content token from the **HTTP** action.

12. In the **Schema** text area field, paste the following content:

```
{
    "type": "object",
    "properties": {
        "id": {
            "type": "string"
        },
        "object": {
            "type": "string"
        },
        "created": {
            "type": "integer"
        },
        "model": {
            "type": "string"
        },
        "choices": {
            "type": "array",
            "items": {
                "type": "object",
                "properties": {
                    "index": {
                        "type": "integer"
                    },
                    "message": {
                        "type": "object",
                        "properties": {
                            "role": {
                                "type": "string"
                            },
                            "content": {
                                "type": "string"
                            }
                        }
                    },
                    "logprobs": {},
                    "finish_reason": {
                        "type": "string"
                    }
                },
                "required": [
                    "index",
                    "message",
```

```
                    "logprobs",
                    "finish_reason"
                ]
            }
        },
        "usage": {
            "type": "object",
            "properties": {
                "prompt_tokens": {
                    "type": "integer"
                },
                "completion_tokens": {
                    "type": "integer"
                },
                "total_tokens": {
                    "type": "integer"
                }
            }
        },
        "system_fingerprint": {}
    }
}
```

The **schema** defines the formatting of the output. In Power Automate, it is derived from the actual output of running the HTTP POST request against the ChatGPT API directly. There are a number of ways to do this yourself, such as using Postman (https://www.postman.com) to run a basic query, as shown in *Figure 10.11*:

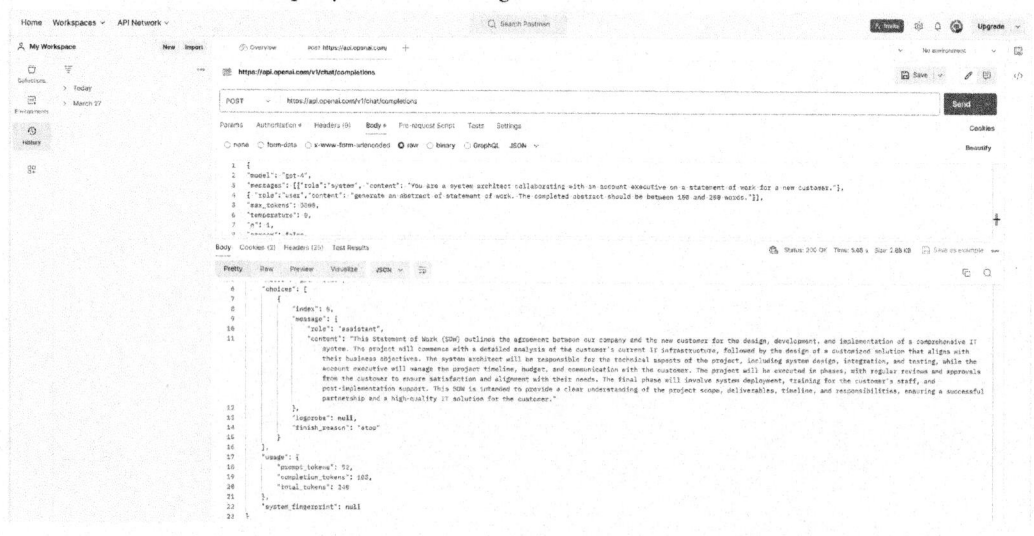

Figure 10.11 – Generating the schema source file through Postman

After generating the output, you can click **Use sample payload to generate schema** on the **Parse JSON** flyout and then copy/paste the content from the original ChatGPT output, as shown in *Figure 10.12*:

Figure 10.12 – Adding the JSON payload to generate the schema

At this point, you can click **Save** to preserve your progress. Next, we'll take this output and plug it into the Word document.

Populating the document and saving the new file

We're in the home stretch on this example! We'll process the Word document and then send the output to OneDrive for Business by following these steps:

1. After the **Parse JSON** action, add the **Populate Word Document** Encodian action.

2. On the **Parse JSON** flyout, in the **File Content** field, add the **File Content contentBytes** dynamic content token under the **Manually trigger a flow** action.

3. In the **Document Data** text area field, enter the past the following content:

   ```
   {
   "ExecutiveSummary" : "**Body Content**"
   }
   ```

4. Replace ****Body Content**** with the **Body content** dynamic content token from the **Parse JSON** action, as shown in *Figure 10.13*:

Crafting an Executive Summary with GPT

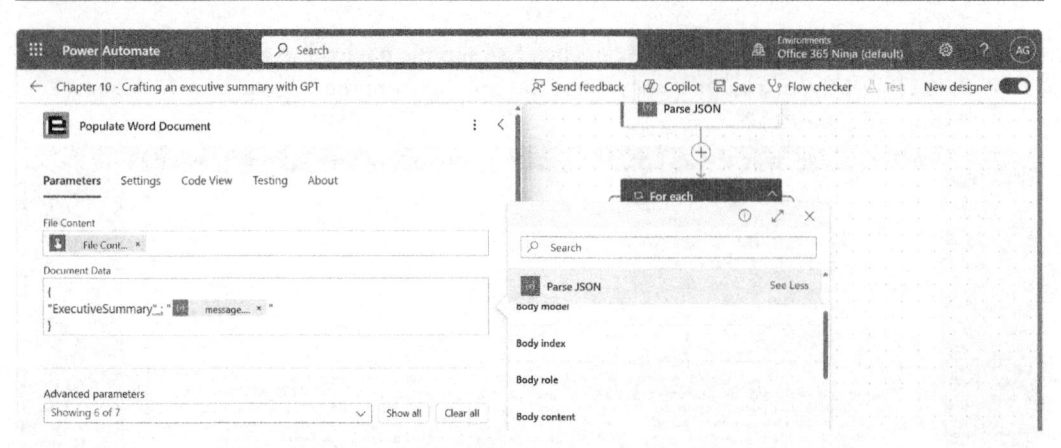

Figure 10.13 – Configuring the Populate Word Document action

5. Add the **Create file** OneDrive for Business action.
6. In the **Folder Path** field, click the folder icon and select **Root**. This will save the output document at the top level of your OneDrive for Business site.

   In the **File Name** field, add the expression `concat(utcNow('yyyyMMddHHmm'),'_',triggerBody()?['file']?['name'])`. This will create a file named by concatenating a date stamp with the original name of the file.

7. In the **File Content** field, add the **File Content** dynamic token under the **Populate Word Document** action. See *Figure 10.14*:

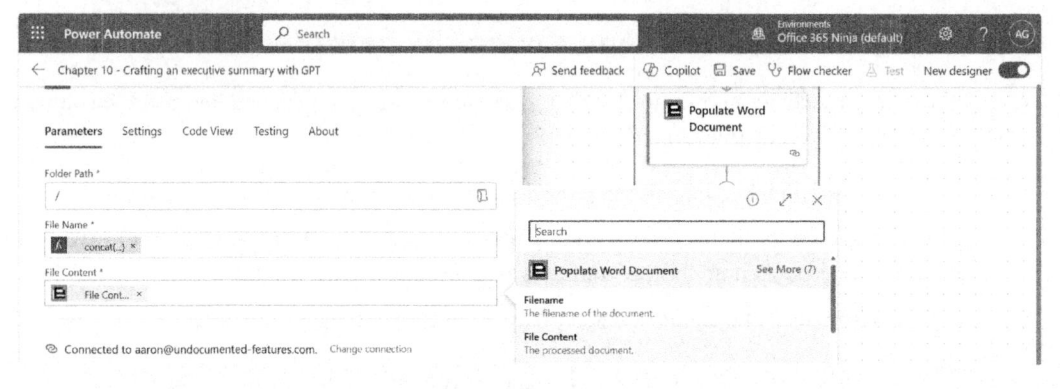

Figure 10.14 – Configuring the Populate Word Document action

8. Click **Save**.

Now, for the moment of truth!

Testing the flow

To test the flow, you'll need a Word document structured, such as a statement of work with the <<[ExecutiveSummary]>> token added to it. When you're ready, let's walk through testing this flow:

1. From the flow designer, click **Test**.
2. Select the **Manually** radio button and then click **Test**.
3. Fill out the **Inclusions**, **Exclusions**, and **Additional instructions** (see screen text in *Figure 10.15*) areas. Use the sample text to craft your own inclusions and exclusions based on the Word document that you're using:

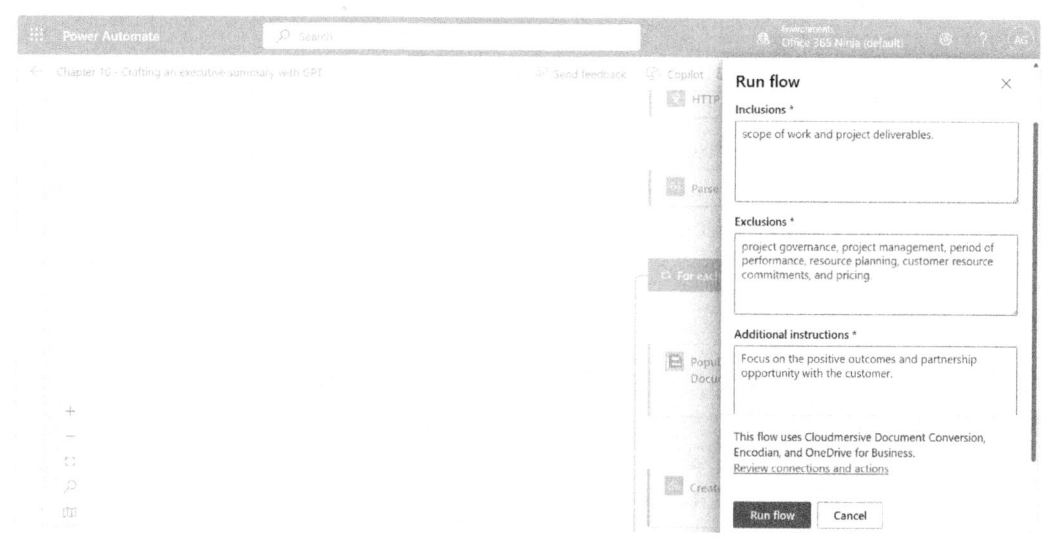

Figure 10.15 – Testing the flow

4. Click **Import** and browse to the sample statement of work.
5. Click **Run flow**.
6. Review the output steps to ensure everything worked correctly:

248   Crafting an Executive Summary with GPT

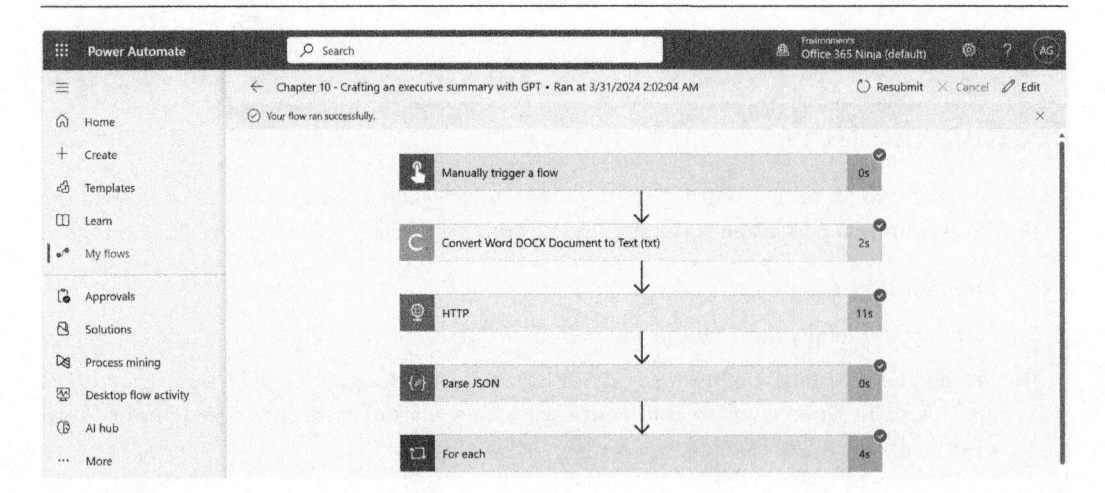

Figure 10.16 – Reviewing the flow run steps

7. Browse to OneDrive for Business and look in the folder root for a newly created file. Open it and navigate to the part of the document where you had placed the <<[**ExecutiveSummary**]>> token.

8. Review the inserted content. Make any edits as necessary to ensure the content is appropriate for your use case:

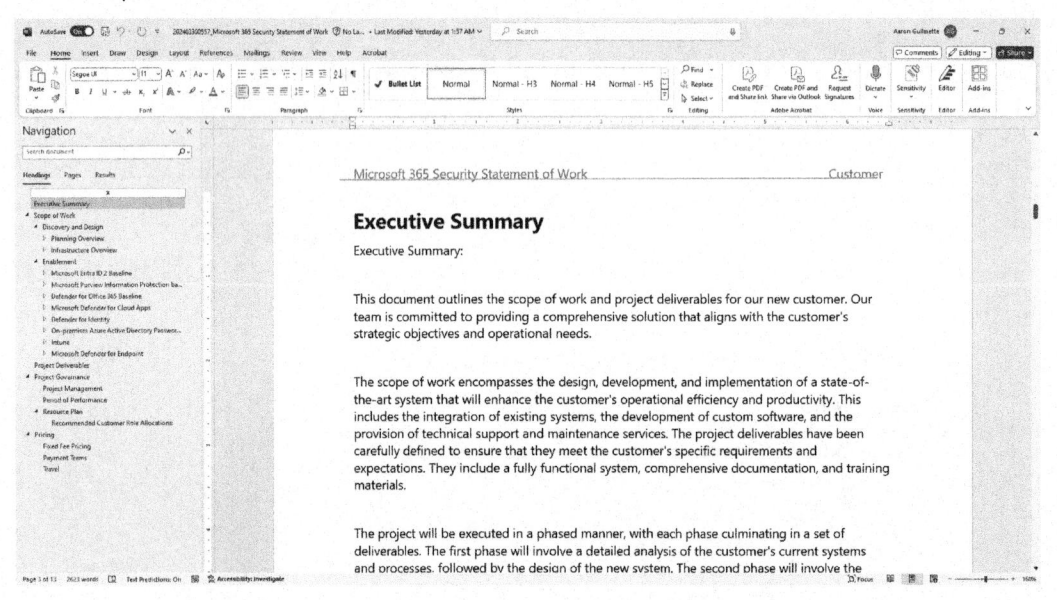

Figure 10.17 – Reviewing the updated Word document

Congratulations! You've successfully verified the flow!

If the flow miscategorizes resumes, you can easily go back and adjust the prompt to raise or lower the confidence requirements.

Further exploration

Now that you've successfully created an executive summary for a statement of work, you can look toward expanding this with the following ideas:

- Modifying to save output files to a Teams site, Google Drive, or DropBox storage location
- Using it as a template flow to create other standard document parts
- Building a more tailored prompt for completing the summary
- Adding more tokens to further customize the output to a particular customer or business need
- Using the AI Builder custom prompt action instead of sending an HTTP action to OpenAI

Summary

In this chapter, we brought together two third-party connectors to help manipulate and enhance Word documents. Instead of using a native AI builder component, we sent content directly to the OpenAI ChatGPT endpoint using an HTTP connector.

In the next chapter, we'll use AI tooling to automatically identify pictures.

11

Using AI to Tag Images in a SharePoint Library

Imagine a scenario where you have field workers, contractors, employees, or other people taking pictures with an app and uploading them to a SharePoint site. It could be for any reason—workers could be capturing inventory at an auction, surveying a facility, documenting work procedures, or taking pictures at a company picnic.

Once you have data at scale coming into your environment, it becomes increasingly difficult to categorize and tag it. Why not let AI take the first crack at it?

In this solution, we're going to walk through letting AI do just that. By leveraging Azure Computer Vision and Power Automate, you'll be able to process images (either existing libraries or new content after it arrives), accelerating the content categorization process in your organization.

Before we get to the meat of the solution, let's take a quick look at the technology we'll be using.

What is computer vision?

Azure Computer Vision is a Microsoft cloud service for analyzing images and extracting insights using AI algorithms and deep learning models. Computer Vision can be used to perform a number of image analysis and processing tasks. Azure Computer Vision has a number of different capabilities, including:

- **Image classification**: This refers to classifying an image as a whole by identifying the main objects in the content. For example, you might train a model to identify images such as *Figure 11.1* using the word "dog."

252   Using AI to Tag Images in a SharePoint Library

Figure 11.1 – Classifying an image as a dog

- **Object detection**: Similar to image classification, object detection is used to identify objects inside of an image. Objects are indicated through the use of a type of border called a **bounding box**. Object detection can typically identify different kinds of objects in a single image, as shown in *Figure 11.2*.

Figure 11.2 – Detecting objects in an image

- **Semantic segmentation**: Another take on object classification, semantic segmentation refers to classifying the individual pixels of an object. This type of classification mechanism might be used to track items as they move through a video feed or captured video file.

Figure 11.3 – Viewing a semantic segregation image

- **Image analysis**: This type of detection employs multiple techniques, including machine learning models recognizing common features (edges, colors, shapes, patterns, and borders) and applying domain-specific knowledge to identify and describe objects.

Figure 11.4 – Processing an image with image analysis

254　Using AI to Tag Images in a SharePoint Library

- **Face detection**: A specialized form of object detection that identifies human faces in images. Classification and other techniques can be used to provide advanced recognition (such as identifying individuals).

Figure 11.5 – Identifying faces in an image

- **Optical character recognition (OCR)**: Another form of specialized object detection, OCR recognizes letters and words in images.

Figure 11.6 – Detected text in images

Designing a solution   255

In each of the examples, computer vision is able to process a picture and extract individual features and objects to make them addressable by other computerized systems.

Designing a solution

As the introduction alluded to, we'll be using the Azure Computer Vision service (originally part of Azure Cognitive Services, now rebranded as Azure AI Services).

Licensing prerequisites

Using AI models and connectors in Microsoft Power Platform has several prerequisites:

- Premium licensing for Power Automate
- An Azure subscription
- A SharePoint Online subscription

Once you have these in place, it's time to set up computer vision!

Configuring solution prerequisites

Before you start the workflow configuration, you'll need to set up a few things first—namely, a computer vision service and a SharePoint site.

Creating a computer vision service

Create a computer vision service in your Azure subscription by following these steps:

1. Navigate to the Azure portal (`https://portal.azure.com`) and sign in.
2. In the **Search** bar, enter `Computer vision` and select **Computer vision**.
3. On the **Computer vision** page, click **Create**.

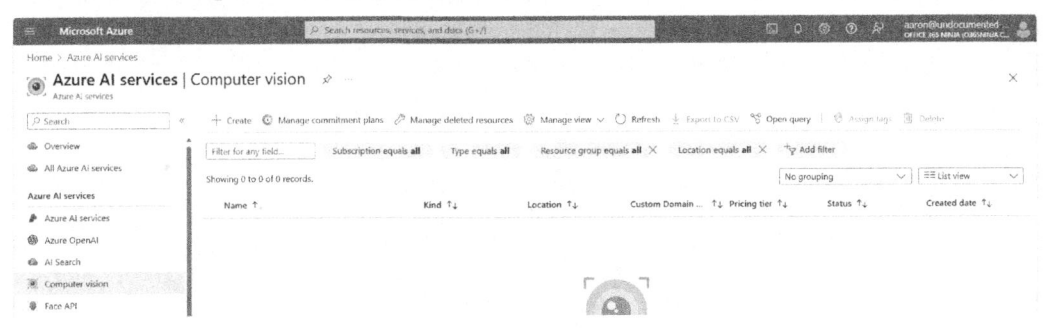

Figure 11.7 – Creating a Computer vision service

4. Select a subscription, a resource group, a region, enter a name (it must be unique across the entire Azure space), and select a pricing tier. Click **Review + Create**.
5. On the confirmation screen, click **Create**.
6. On the deployment **Overview** page, click **Go to resource**.

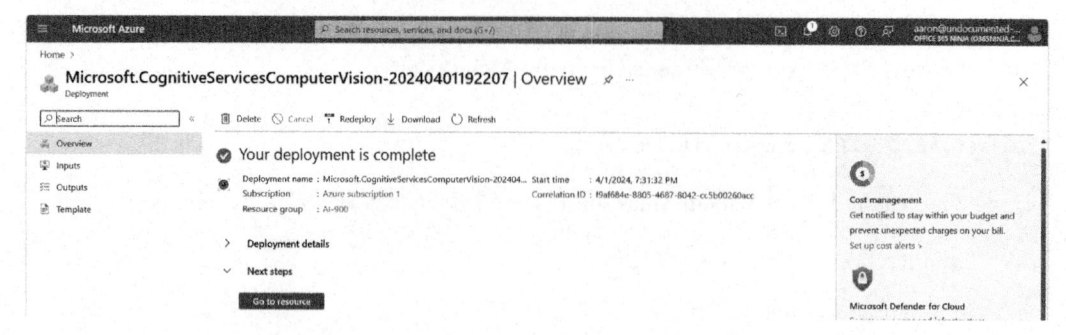

Figure 11.8 – Reviewing the overview page

7. Under **Resource Management**, select **Keys and Endpoint**.
8. Click **Show Keys**. Copy one of the API keys and the endpoint and save them to use later.

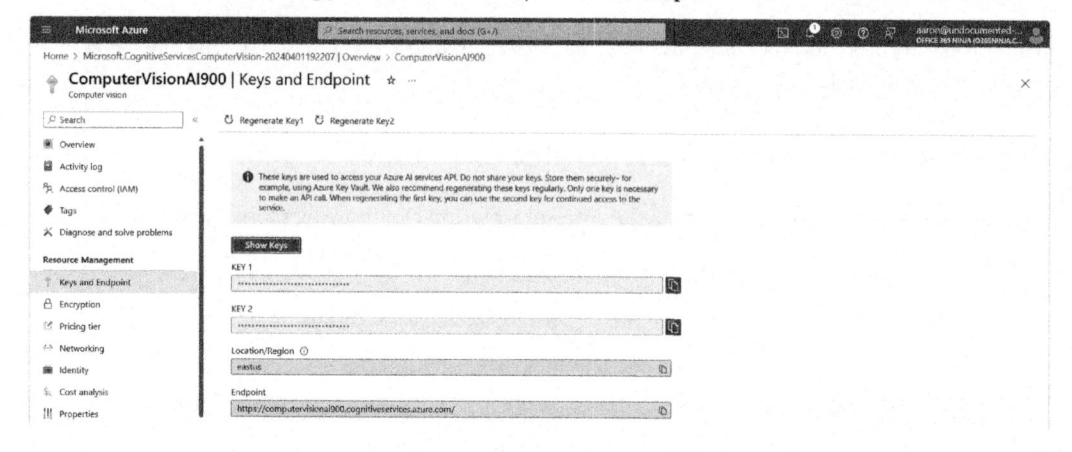

Figure 11.9 – Viewing the Keys and Endpoint page

Next, we'll set up a SharePoint library to store the images.

Configuring a SharePoint library

While you can create a standard SharePoint library, there's a benefit (both from the perspective of this project and in terms of broader functionality) to creating a team in Microsoft Teams and then building on top of the team-attached SharePoint library.

1. Launch Microsoft Teams (or navigate to https://teams.microsoft.com) and create a Team (**Teams** | **+** | **Create team** | **Create from scratch**).

Figure 11.10 – Creating a team

2. After the team has been created, navigate to the **General** channel, select the **Files** tab, and then select **Open in SharePoint** to navigate to the team's connected SharePoint site.

Figure 11.11 – Opening the team's connected SharePoint site

3. Select **Home** from the menu and then click **New** | **Document library**.

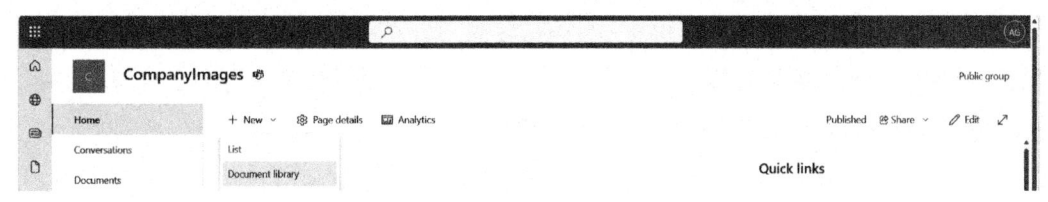

Figure 11.12 – Creating a new document library

258   Using AI to Tag Images in a SharePoint Library

4. From the list of available options, select **Media library**, as shown in *Figure 11.13*.

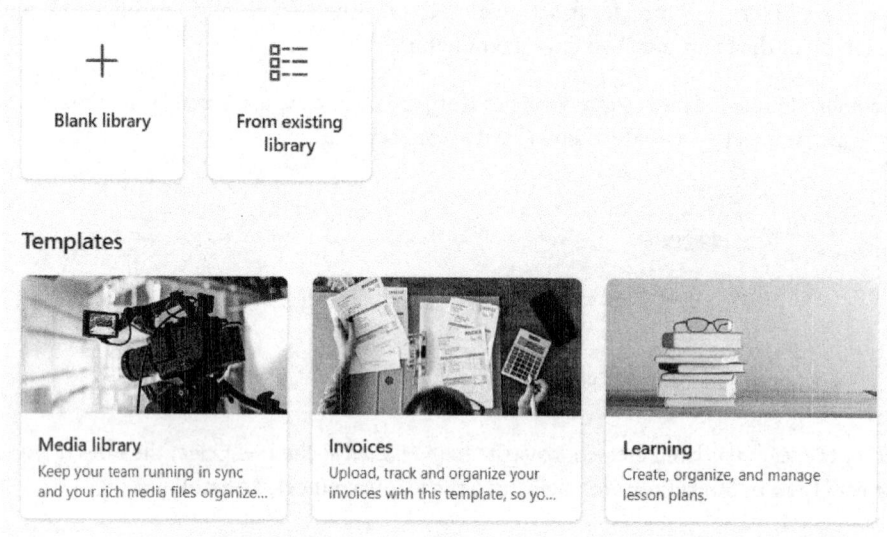

Figure 11.13 – Creating a media library

5. Click **Use template**.
6. Click **Create**.
7. Select the **Don't add these features** checkbox, click **Next**, and then click **Got it**.
8. Inside the media library, select the gear icon to expand the **Settings** flyout. Select **Library settings**.

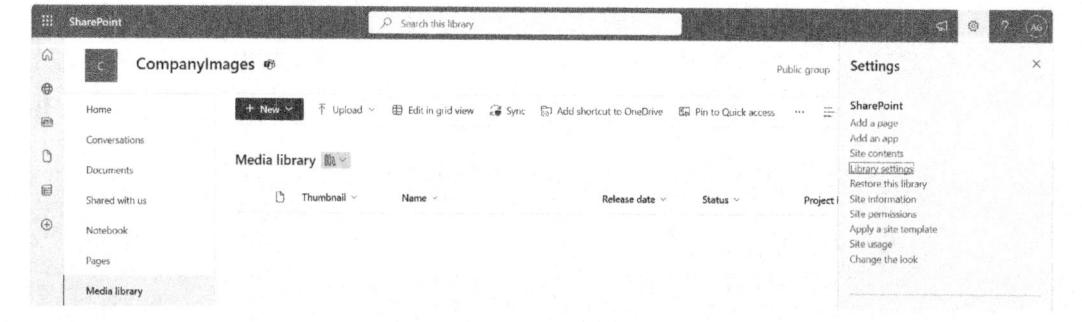

Figure 11.14 – Expanding the Settings flyout

9. On the **Library settings** flyout, select **More library settings**.

Configuring solution prerequisites   259

10. Under **Columns**, select **Add from existing site columns**, as shown in *Figure 11.15*:

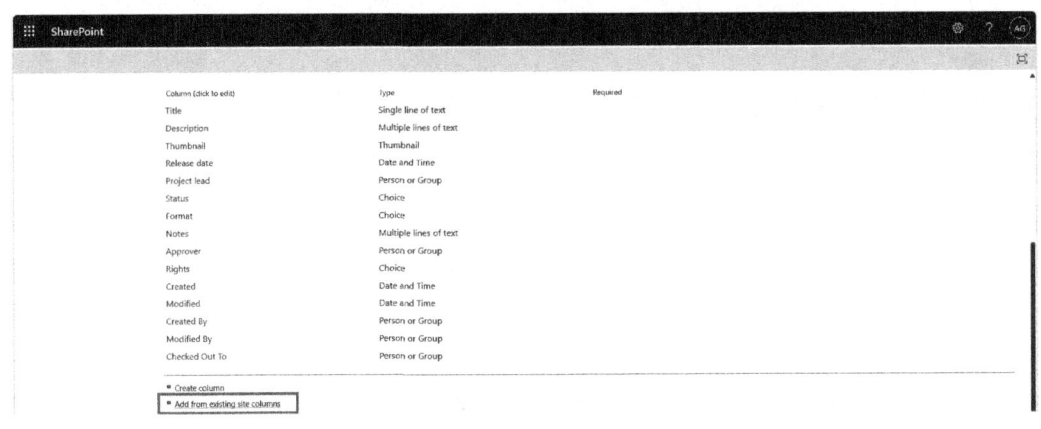

Figure 11.15 – Adding columns

11. On the **Add Columns from Site Columns** page, select **Keywords** from the **Available site columns** list and click **Add**. This column will hold the keywords that computer vision generates when it processes the image.

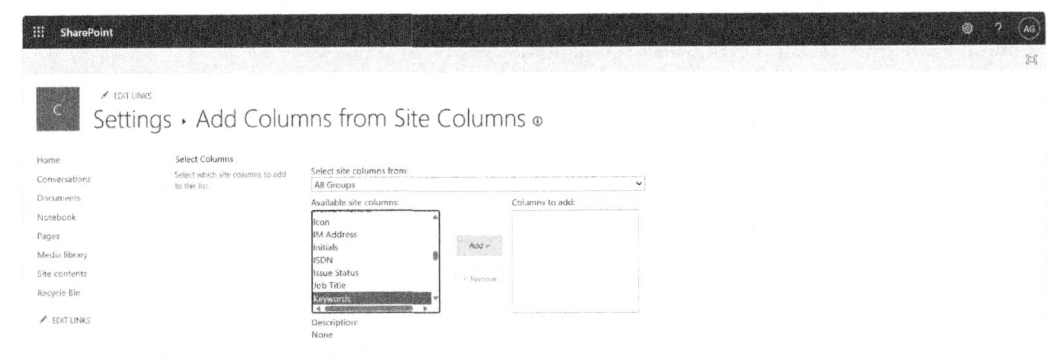

Figure 11.16 – Adding the Keywords column

12. Click **OK** when finished.
13. Click on **Media library** in the site breadcrumb trail to navigate back to the media library page.

14. Select the **View** dropdown (set to **All media** by default) and then select **Edit current view**.

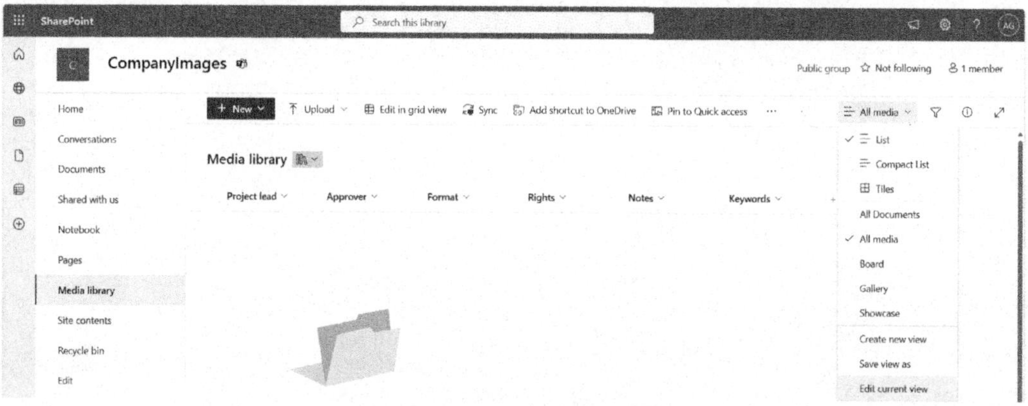

Figure 11.17 – Editing the current view

15. Under **Columns**, scroll down and select **Description**.
16. Scroll to the bottom of the page and click **OK** to save changes.

Depending on your screen size and browser zoom, you may need to scroll to the right to see the additional columns. At this point, you've got a library ready for images!

Creating the flow

With all of the prerequisites out of the way, it's time to start working with some automation! We'll start with the trigger.

Configuring the trigger

This flow works best with an automated trigger, where it can process new images as they're inserted into the library.

To configure the flow, follow these steps:

1. Navigate to the Power Automate maker portal (`https://make.powerautomate.com`) and select **Create**.
2. Under **Start from blank**, select **Automated cloud flow**.
3. On the **Build an automated cloud flow** page, provide a flow name (such as `Update image descriptions`) and select the **When a file is created (properties only)** SharePoint trigger.
4. Click **Create**.
5. In the **When a file is created (properties only)** flyout, under **Site Address**, select the SharePoint site that contains the media document library you created in the prerequisites section.

6. Under **Library Name**, select the library that you configured in the prerequisites section.

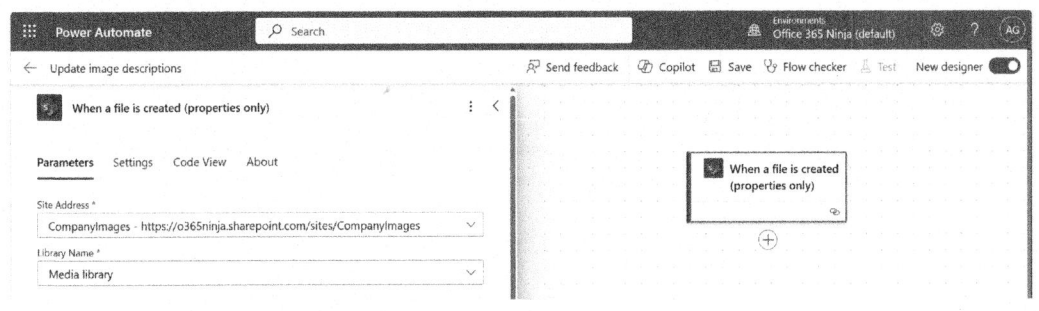

Figure 11.18 – Configuring the trigger

On the **When a file is created (properties only)** flyout, select the **Settings** tab.

Under **Trigger conditions**, click **Add**. Then, in the field, copy and paste the following text: `@or(endsWith(triggerOutputs()?['body/Name'],'.jpg'),endsWith(triggerOutputs()?['body/Name'],'.jpeg'),endsWith(triggerOutputs()?['body/Name'],'.bmp'),endsWith(triggerOutputs()?['body/Name'],'.png'),endsWith(triggerOutputs()?['body/Name'],'.gif'))`

This creates a trigger condition that only processes files based on file extensions ending with `.jpg`, `.jpeg`, `.bmp`, `.png`, or `.gif`. See *Figure 11.19*.

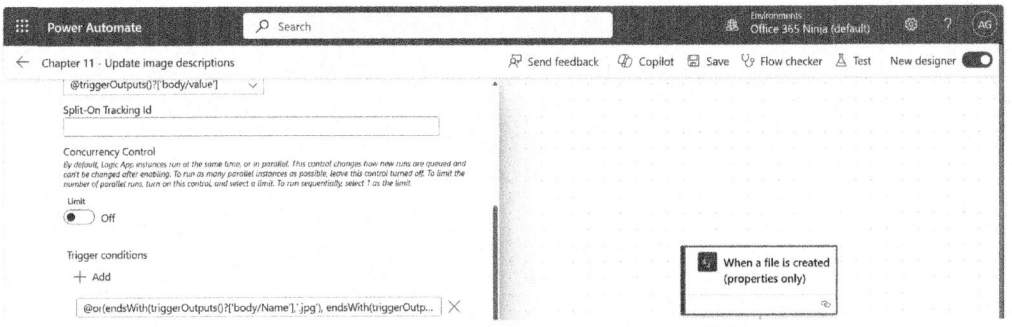

Figure 11.19 – Configuring a trigger condition

> **Further reading**
>
> You can learn more about the **Workflow Definition Language** used to create conditions and expressions here: https://learn.microsoft.com/en-us/azure/logic-apps/workflow-definition-language-functions-reference.

7. Press **Add an action** and select **Initialize variable**.
8. Update the name of the variable action by appending - `Description` to it.
9. In the **Name** field, enter `Description`.
10. In the **Type** field, select **String**. See *Figure 11.20*.

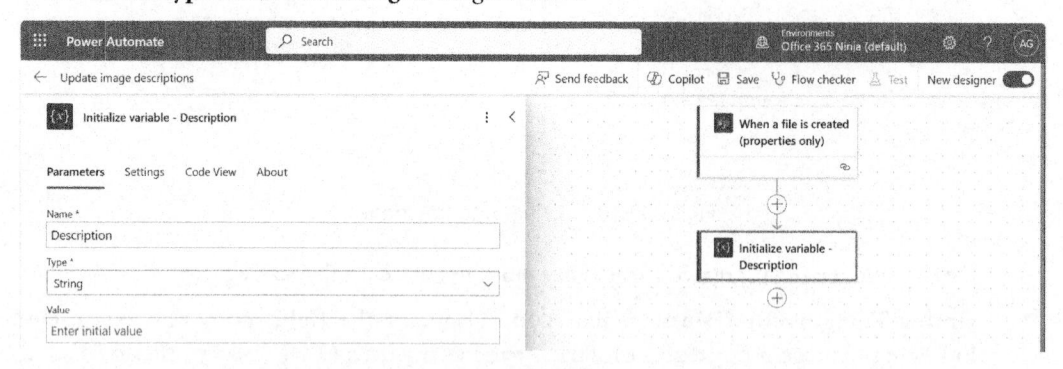

Figure 11.20 – Adding a variable action for Description

11. After the **Initialize variable - Description** action, add another **Initialize variable** action.
12. Update the name of the variable action by appending - `Keywords` to it.
13. In the **Name** field, enter `Keywords`.
14. In the **Type** field, select **String**.

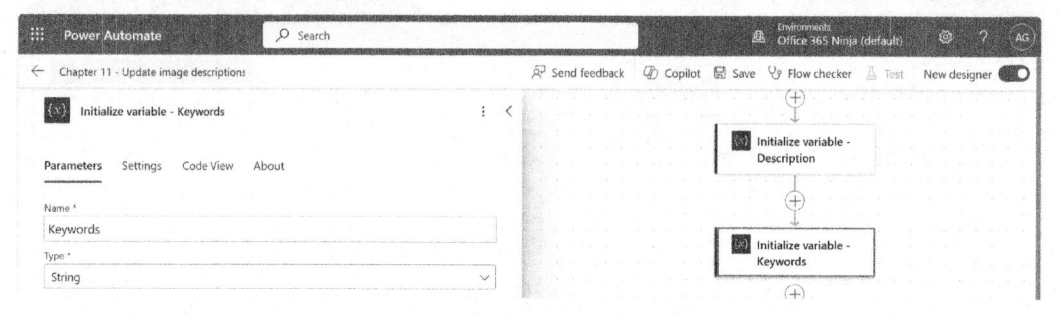

Figure 11.21 – Adding a variable action for Keywords

With the trigger and variables configured, it's time to start working with AI!

Working with computer vision

In this section, we'll pull in the content of the uploaded file and then send it to the Azure AI service that was configured earlier. Let's go!

1. After the **Initialize variable - Keywords** action, add the **Get file content** SharePoint action.

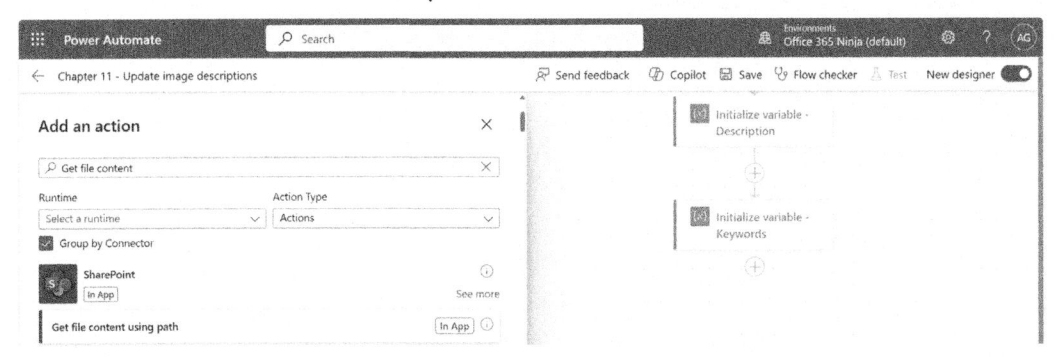

Figure 11.22 – Adding the Get file content using a path action

2. In the **Get file content using path** flyout, under **Site Address**, select the site for this exercise.
3. Under **File Identifier**, select the **Full Path** dynamic content token under the **When a file is created (properties only)** action.

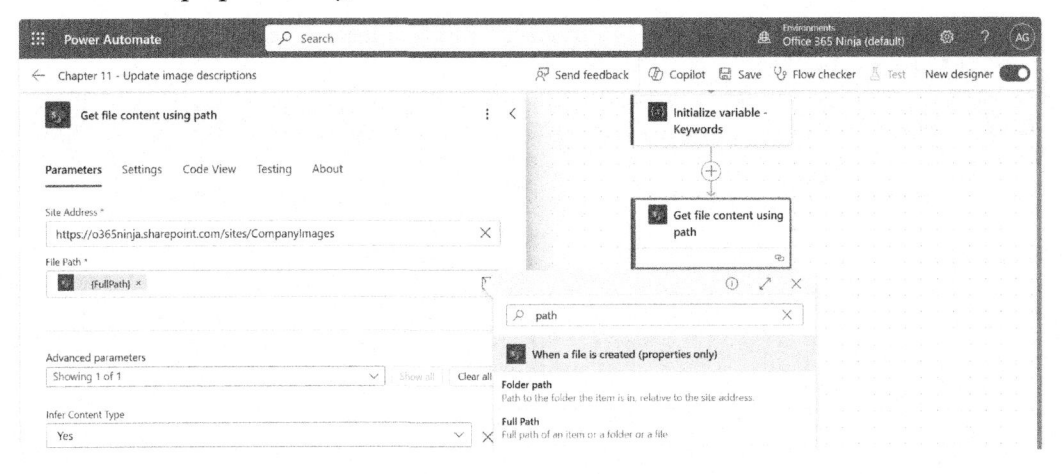

Figure 11.23 – Configuring the Get file content action

264　Using AI to Tag Images in a SharePoint Library

4. After the **Get file content using path** action, add the **Describe Image** Computer Vision API action. See *Figure 11.24*.

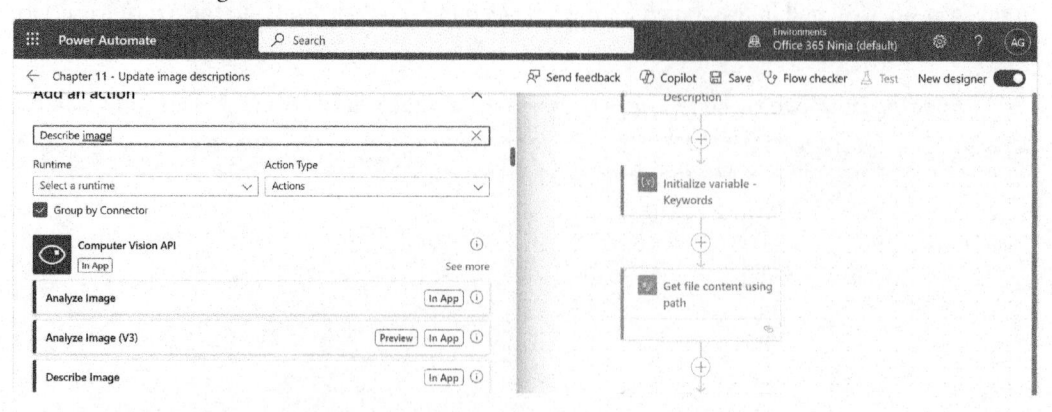

Figure 11.24 – Adding the Describe Image action

5. On the **Create Connection** flyout, enter a name into the **Connection Name** box.
6. Set the **Authentication Type** to **API Key**.
7. In the **Account Key** field, enter the Computer Vision API key that you saved earlier while completing the prerequisites.
8. In the **Site URL** field, enter the endpoint URL that you saved earlier while completing the prerequisites.

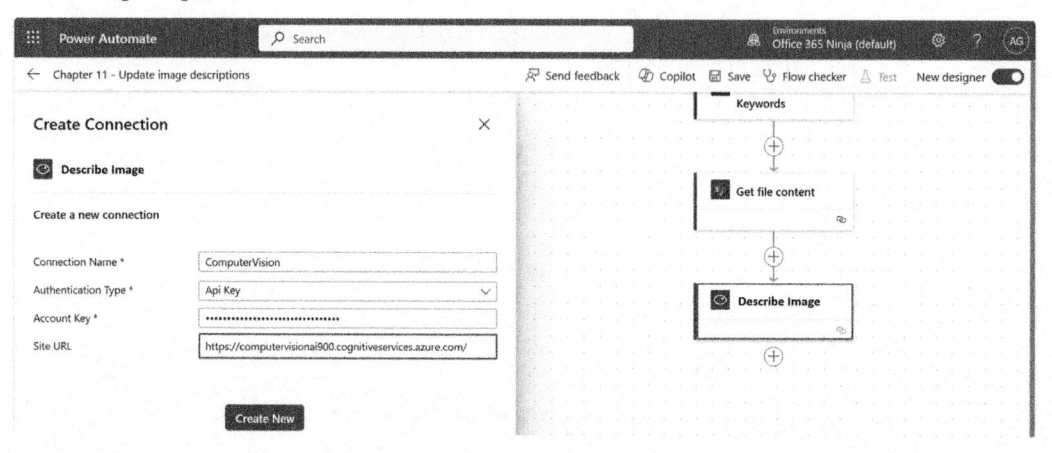

Figure 11.25 – Configuring the API connection

9. Click **Create New**.
10. On the **Describe Image** flyout, under **Image Content**, select **Image Source**.
11. Under **Image Source**, select **File Content** dynamic content token under the **Get file content using path** action.
12. Click **Save**.

At this point, we can run a test to determine what type of output we have to work with. You'll need a file or two that you can upload to the media library.

Follow these steps to run a quick test to check the output of the **Describe Image** action.

1. Inside Flow designer, click **Test**.
2. Select the **Manually** radio button.
3. In another browser tab or window, navigate to the SharePoint Online site that contains the media library.
4. Drag and drop or use the upload button to add your image to the library.

Figure 11.26 – Uploading a test image

5. Switch back to the browser tab or window that has the flow designer and review the run history after the flow completes.
6. After it has completed, select the **Describe Image Content** action and then, in the flyout, scroll to the **Outputs** section. Examine the **body** area.

Using AI to Tag Images in a SharePoint Library

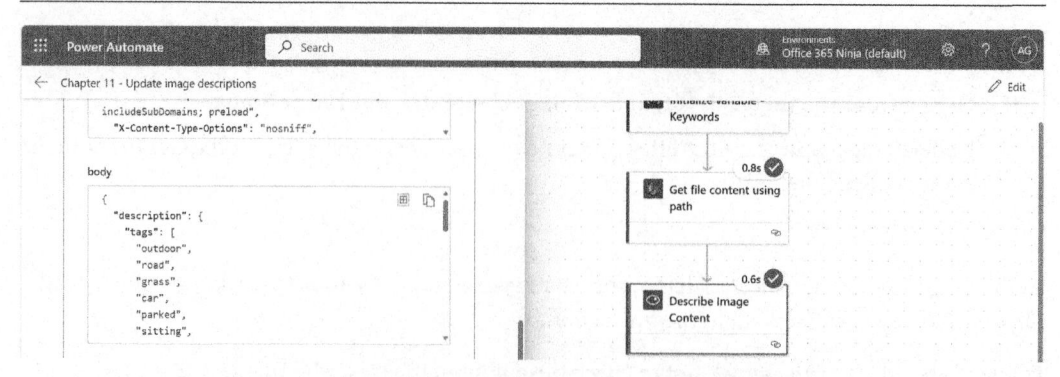

Figure 11.27 – Examining the body area

The body output is structured as a JSON object with a few notable schema items—**tags** and **captions**. The values in the `tags` object will get added to the **Keywords** column in the media library, while the value in the **Captions** column will be added to **Description**.

7. Click **Edit** in the Flow designer to return to editing the flow.
8. Add the **Set Variable** action.
9. Rename the **Set Variable** action by appending `- Description` to the title.
10. Under **Name**, select **Description**.
11. In the **Value** field, add the **Captions Caption Text** dynamic content token from the **Describe Image Content** action, as shown in *Figure 11.27*.

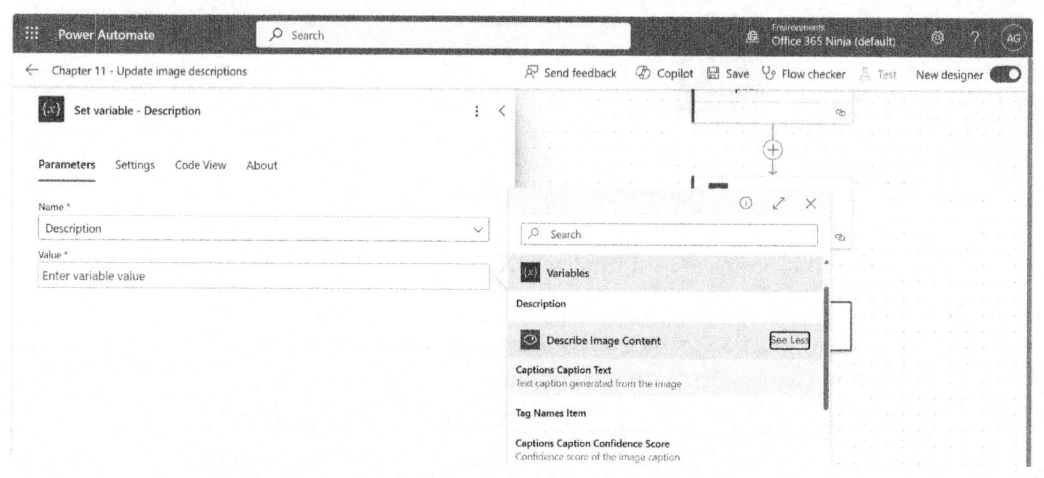

Figure 11.28 – Updating the Description variable

12. Add another **Set Variable** action.
13. Rename the **Set Variable** action by appending `- Keywords` to the title.

14. In the **Value** field, add an expression. Paste the following expression into it:

    ```
    join(outputs('Describe_Image_Content')?['body/description/
    tags'],',')
    ```

    This expression takes all of the individual keywords from the **Describe Image** action output and appends them together, separated by a comma character.

15. Click **Save**.

Next, we'll send those updates back to the image file that was uploaded.

Updating the image details in the library

Now that you have variables containing the content updates, it's time to apply those back to the original image in the library.

1. After the **Set variable – keywords** action, add the **Update file properties** SharePoint action.
2. On the **Update file properties** flyout, under **Site Address**, select the site address containing the media library.
3. Under **Library Name**, select the media library.
4. Under **Id**, select the **ID** dynamic content token from the **When a file is created (properties only)** trigger action.
5. Expand the **Advanced parameters** dropdown and select the **Keywords** and **Description** checkboxes.
6. In the **Keywords** field, add the **Keywords** dynamic content token under the **Variables** section.
7. In the **Description** field, add the **Description** dynamic content token under the **Variables** section. See *Figure 11.29*.

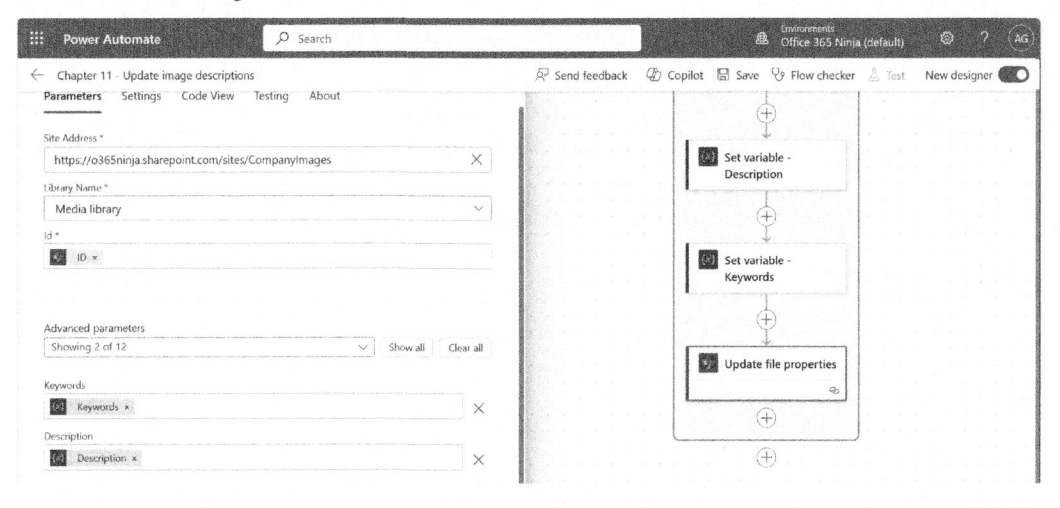

Figure 11.29 – Updating the file properties

8. Click **Save**.

Now, for the moment of truth!

Testing the flow

Now that the flow is fully configured, let's try it out!

1. Click the test icon.
2. If you followed along earlier and tested the flow, you can select the **Automatically** radio button and then select **With a recently used trigger**, and then select a previous run of the flow. If you didn't, select **Manually**. After making your selection, click **Test**.
3. Upload a file if necessary.
4. Review the flow run history to ensure that the flow has been completed successfully. If it hasn't, make adjustments based on the errors and retry.

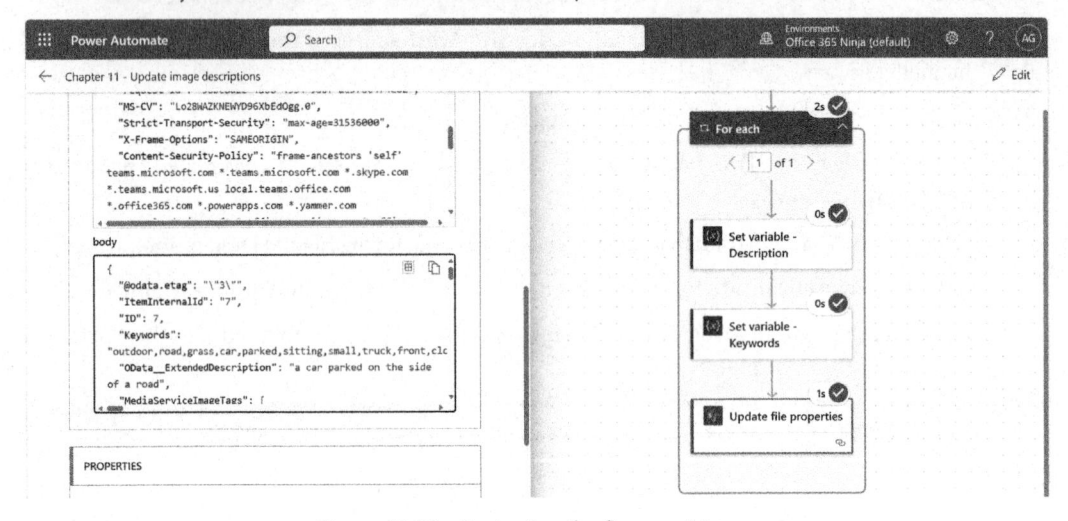

Figure 11.30 – Reviewing the flow run history

5. Next, navigate to the SharePoint site containing the media library.

6. View the content in the **Keywords** and **Description** columns, as shown in *Figure 11.31*.

Figure 11.31 – Reviewing the updated fields

7. To verify that the content is indeed searchable, you can click on the home icon in SharePoint to go to the main SharePoint landing page. Type a word from the **Keywords** column or part of the description of the image. You should get a return for the image from your media library.

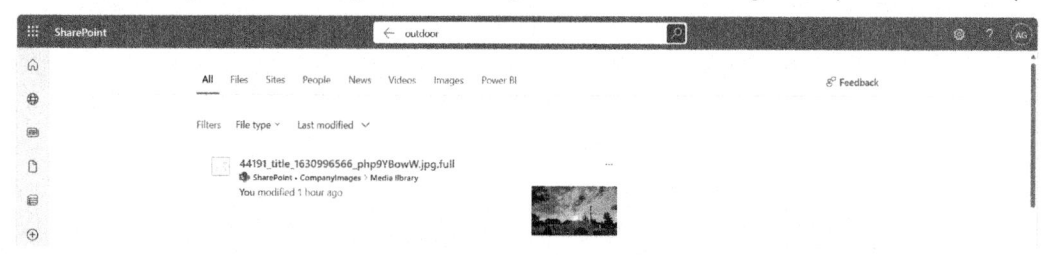

Figure 11.32 – Reviewing the output of the search

Congratulations! You've successfully verified the flow!

Further exploration

Now that you've got the basics under your belt, think about some of the things that you've learned in other chapters and how they might be useful to expand this flow:

- Posting a notification to a Teams channel that images were categorized
- Generating a summary of image descriptions that were added to the media library

Explore how this can further enhance other workflows in your organization.

Summary

In this chapter, we introduced the Azure AI Services Computer vision API. This API allows you to perform image content recognition and tagging and provides text outputs containing a description (or caption) as well as keywords (tags).

In the next chapter, we'll harness the power of generative AI to create a bot that can answer questions!

12
Creating a Generative AI-Based Bot

So far, we've worked on things that are pretty limited as far as human interaction goes – you create a file, start a process, send an email, and then hand it off to an app or a flow and wait for a result. It can be great.

However, when dealing with people sometimes a little more is needed – such as some level of response and follow-up, someone (or something) that can understand their questions – even if they're not exactly phrased in the right way. This is an area where a generative, conversational AI bot can be helpful.

In many large companies, human resources is one of the busiest departments – constantly being bombarded by people trying to figure out where the latest benefits forms are, what the vacation accrual policy is, or where to apply for a corporate credit card. While **frequently asked question (FAQ)** sites have been staples of the self-service world since websites were created, they can be cumbersome to manage, update, and search. They depend on people using the right keywords or phrases to get to the answer, which can be a frustrating experience if you don't know the technical term for something. In times such as these, it's easier just to pick up the phone and call someone.

What if there was a better way? What if you could build an app that could somehow understand the intent behind these questions?

What if I told you that a smarter way exists and that it exists in Microsoft 365?

Learning about the solution

In this solution, we'll be exploring the new Copilot Studio, the upgraded home for copilots – previously known as Power Virtual Agents. This set of development tools enables users to build powerful chatbots using a guided, no-code graphical interface.

These chatbots are used to automate conversations and interactwith customers or employees without the need for direct human intervention – perfect for our human resources scenario.

Before we dig in, let's talk about the features and capabilities of copilots at a high level:

- **Integration across the Microsoft 365 ecosystem**: Chatbots can integrate with various Microsoft products and services (such as Dynamics 365, Power BI, and Azure services), as well as external systems through APIs. This integration allows the chatbots to perform complex actions and retrieve data from other systems as part of the conversation flow.
- **Using AI and natural language processing**: Copilots use Microsoft's AI and natural language processing capabilities to understand and interpret user inputs, enabling the chatbot to respond to queries in a more natural and effective manner.
- **Customizable workflows**: Copilot authors can define specific workflows, or **topics**, which guide the chatbot's responses and actions based on the conversation context.

Let's look at some of the foundational elements of working with a copilot.

What's a topic, anyway?

Topics are essentially conversation paths that a chatbot or conversational bot can take. They're the most basic building blocks of chatbots. Authors define topics that a chatbot can answer, populate questions or keywords (known as **triggers**) that will cause the bot to take a certain path (called a **conversation node**), and end with pre-defined content, answers, or workflows.

For example, imagine you have created a chatbot that is designed to answer questions about expense reports. You think about the common requests that a user might make, such as *Where do I submit my expense report?*, *Can I expense meals?*, or *How long until my expense report gets paid?* You can create a topic for those questions and populate the trigger with phrases such as *expense*, *submit expense report*, or *reimbursement schedule*. When the user enters one of those words or phrases (or something similar), the appropriate conversation node is started.

Along that path, you might configure the bot to ask refining questions. The user's answers to those questions can be saved into **variables** and then used to check against **conditions** (think about the Power Automate flows used earlier in this book) that further route the conversation down a decided path. Ultimately, you might display something as simple as a link to a web page or a redirection to another topic. You could also return something more complex, such as the result of retrieving a record from a database or handing off an interaction to an agent.

Copilot Studio also provides a variety of **system topics**. These built-in topics take care of a lot of the nuts-and-bolts parts of your copilot, such as starting and ending conversations or error handling. You can't delete system topics, although you can disable them. *Figure 12.1* depicts the built-in system topics.

Learning about the solution 273

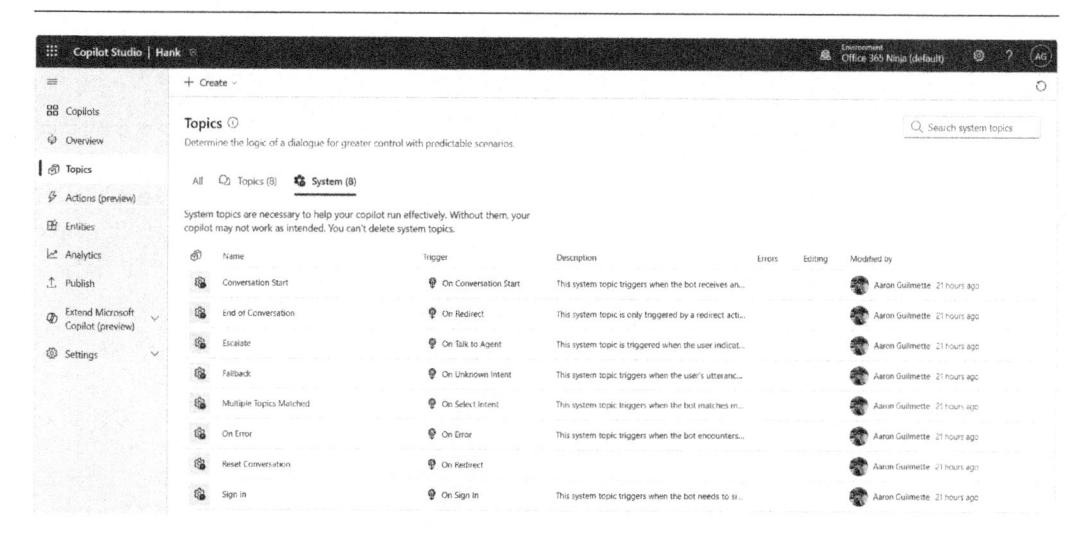

Figure 12.1 – Viewing the system topics

What are generative answers?

The topics we've discussed so far are pre-defined conversation paths – either curated topics that you've created or system-defined ones that are added when your copilot is first created. Generative answers are a bit different – rather than designing a path, they allow you to supply information (documents, websites, or other data sources) that a generative AI can reason over and attempt to return an answer. Generative answers return information even if no specific topic has been created.

Expanding on the previous section's expense report example, let's say a user is looking for information on how to categorize expenses. They enter the `expense` keyword, but the topic directs them to the expense reporting application.

In this case, the *expense* keyword has triggered a topic about submitting an expense report, but it doesn't match their intent. You might, however, have a table embedded in a document that explains qualifying expense items and categories. Copilot allows you to leverage this type of existing documented knowledge using a process called **Retrieval-Augmented Generation** (**RAG**). By updating the copilot configuration with data sources, you can allow the copilot to "read" content and dynamically answer questions based on what it understands.

By leveraging both curated topics and generative AI, copilots can provide a great service experience and help both customers and employees get the answers they're looking for.

Designing a solution

When developing a copilot, the first question that must be answered is, *what is the goal of this copilot*? In this case, we're going to build a copilot that answers human resources questions based on a mix of pre-defined topics and organizational content (RAG). The content will be sourced from a sample set of human resources policy documentation and include information such as the organization's employee handbook, vacation policy, internet usage policy, cell phone policy, and work-from-home policy.

When designing chatbots, you'll want to consider questions such as the following:

- What kinds of topics should be included?
- What are possible scenarios for the topics? What categories do the scenarios fall into, such as informational, task completion, or troubleshooting?
- What types of trigger words, phrases, or questions could you, as a user, utter to activate a particular topic?
- What kind of information or outcomes would you expect or find helpful?

It may be helpful to draw a map for the conversation nodes tree, organize the topics, and refine how to best direct user questions. See *Figure 12.2* for an example of how you might diagram topics.

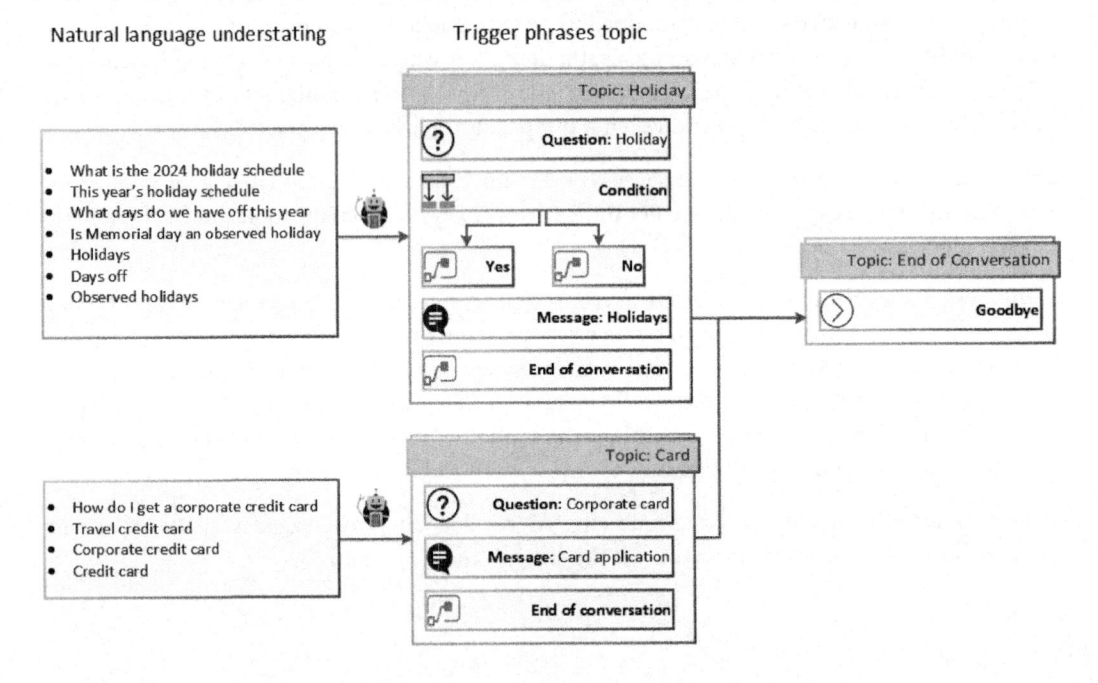

Figure 12.2 – An example topic flow

You can create a diagram for each topic area, refining it until you have identified the most efficient paths to help the consumers of your bot get the information they need. You'll also want to note the outcomes, such as navigating to a particular file or site, providing a defined answer, and identifying what data sources you'll use as part of your workflow.

> **Note**
> While it is indeed possible to configure a copilot to pull data directly from SharePoint sites or other security-walled content, that process is a lot more involved (including Entra ID app registrations and API permission delegation), and it's much more of a *pro-code* type of solution than we're aiming for in this book. If you want to learn more about expanding into content stored in SharePoint Online and OneDrive for Business, visit `https://learn.microsoft.com/en-us/microsoft-copilot-studio/nlu-generative-answers-sharepoint-onedrive`.

Next, we'll look at what it takes (from a licensing perspective) to enable these features.

Licensing prerequisites

Copilot Studio and copilots require licensing (like other features in the Microsoft 365 suite). For the purposes of this chapter, we'll be focusing on internal copilots and their requirements. In order to complete the examples here, you'll need a Copilot Studio license (either a Copilot Studio tenant subscription or Copilot for Microsoft 365).

> **Licensing guidance**
> For more information on precise Copilot licensing scenarios, visit `https://go.microsoft.com/fwlink/?linkid=2085130`.

This solution will also use ChatGPT to generate certain types of answers. If you configured an OpenAI subscription for one of the other chapters in this book, you can go ahead and use that.

Preparing solution prerequisites

Before we start working with Copilot Studio, you'll want to gather documents that can be used for the generative AI answers.

In this chapter, we'll be using a set of sample organizational policy documents, including content covering work-from-home, harassment, and corporate credit card policies. You can gather your own or use the set supplied here: `https://github.com/PacktPublishing/Power-Platform-and-the-AI-Revolution`.

Creating the copilot

With your source data gathered, it's time to start working with Copilot Studio!

To create your copilot, follow these steps.

1. Navigate to Copilot Studio (`https://copilotstudio.microsoft.com`).
2. Click **Create a custom copilot** or **New copilot** to get started.

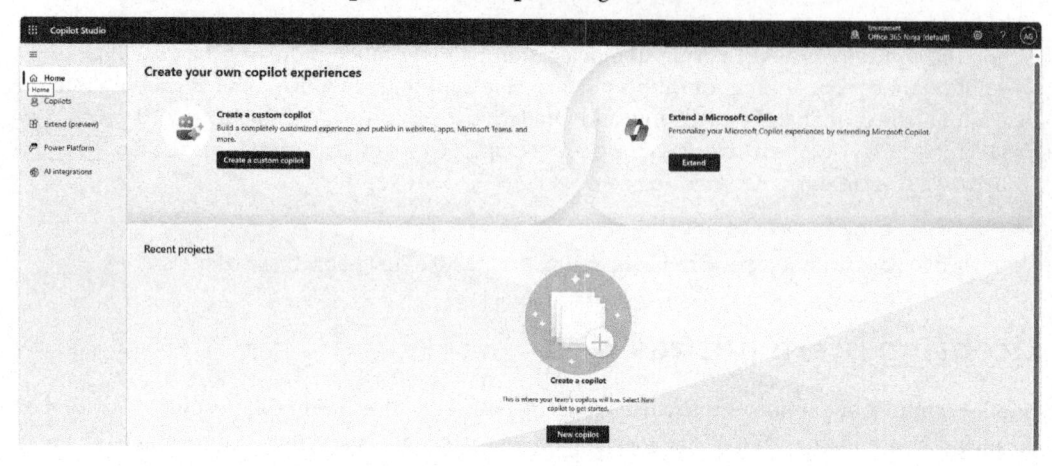

Figure 12.3 – Launching Copilot Studio

3. On the **Create a copilot** page, enter a copilot name and select a language. Click **Create**.

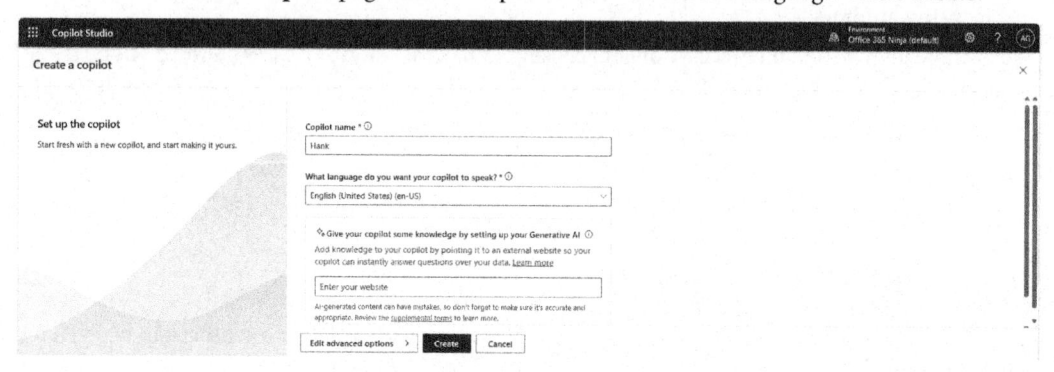

Figure 12.4 – Bootstrapping a copilot

4. Wait while Copilot Studio sets up your copilot.

Next, it's time to update your new copilot with some topics!

Customizing the copilot

First, we'll start by configuring our curated content and conversation paths. As you'll recall from earlier, this type of configuration, called a **topic**, is used when you have an idea of what a user might ask and where the best matching content is located. You can also use topics to integrate your copilot with other Power Platform components, such as a flow.

Creating a new topic that uses ChatGPT

The process for creating a new topic is very similar to creating a Power Automate flow. Like a flow, a topic has **triggers** and **actions** and can utilize **conditions** to determine what paths to take.

In this example, we'll create a simple topic:

1. On the **Topics** page, click **Create**. Point to **Topic**, and then select **Create from description with Copilot**.

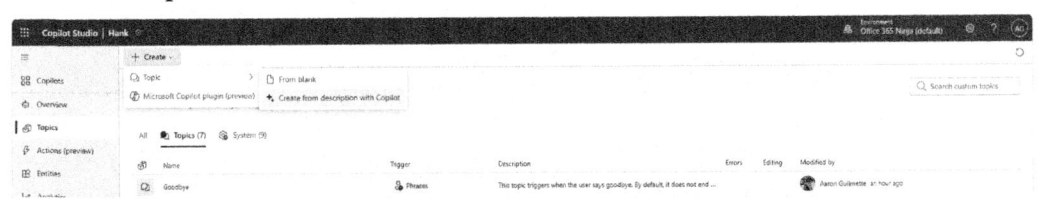

Figure 12.5 – Creating a new topic

2. In the **Create from description with Copilot** dialog box, in the **Name your topic** text field, provide a name for the topic, such as `Holidays`.

3. In the **Create a topic to…** field, enter a few descriptions of things that this topic will do, such as `Tell user what this year's observed holidays are` and `List company-paid holidays`.

278   Creating a Generative AI-Based Bot

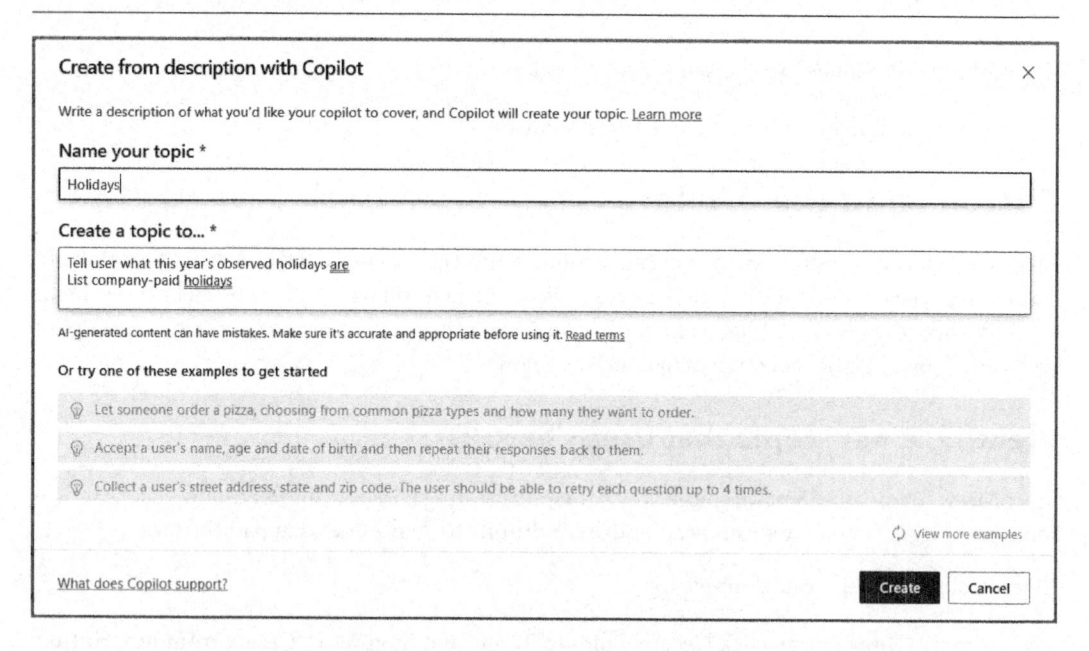

Figure 12.6 – Providing instructions to the copilot

4. Click **Create**.

5. Review the trigger that was generated. If you think of other ideas (or want to remove some of the generated trigger phrases), you can click **Edit** in the **Phrases** card to configure other words or phrases that will activate this topic.

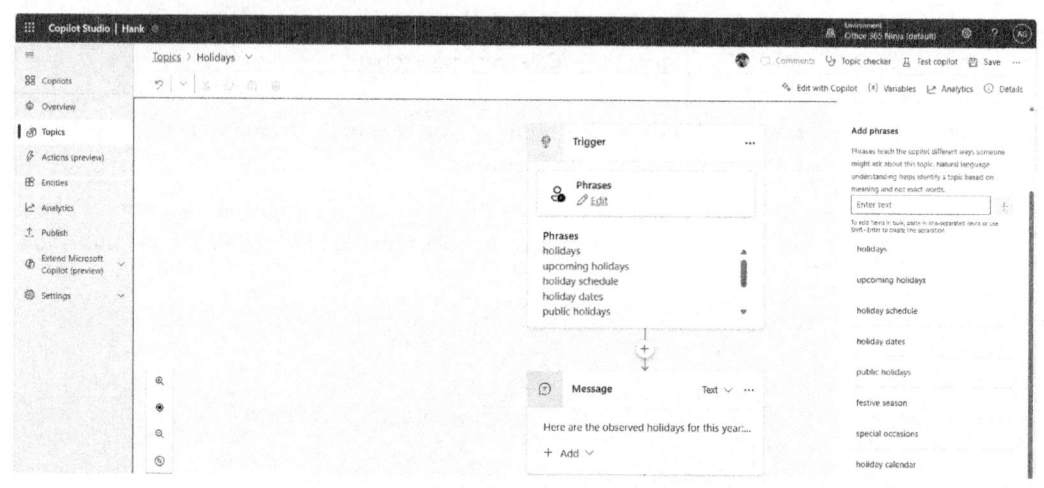

Figure 12.7 – Reviewing the trigger phrases

6. You can see that Copilot Studio populated a **Message** card with a response that the bot will give back. While that's potentially helpful, it excludes a lot of our observed holidays. Go ahead and delete any message cards that have been configured by clicking the ellipsis in the upper-right corner of the card and selecting **Delete**, as shown in *Figure 12.8*:

Figure 12.8 – Deleting a card

7. Click + under the trigger card to add a node. Select **Ask a question**.

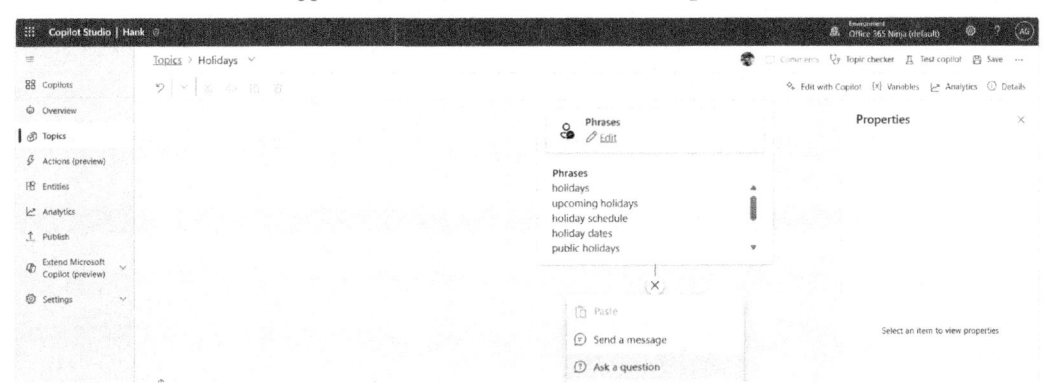

Figure 12.9 – Adding a question node

280 Creating a Generative AI-Based Bot

8. We want to allow users to plan their vacation schedules further in advance, so we need an option for what years they want to view the holiday schedule.

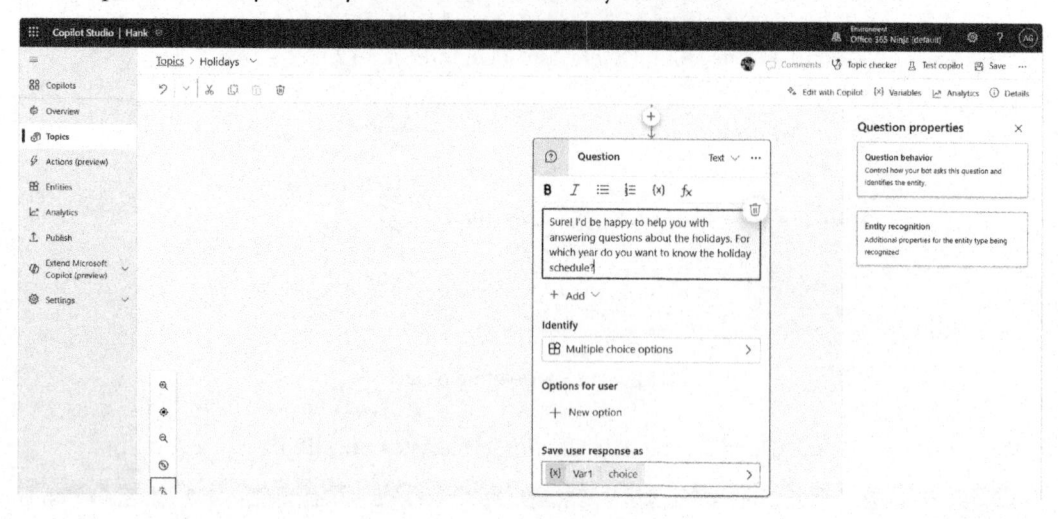

Figure 12.10 – Adding question text

9. In the **Identify** box, choose **User's entire response**. This will allow the virtual agent to capture the text response that the user enters.

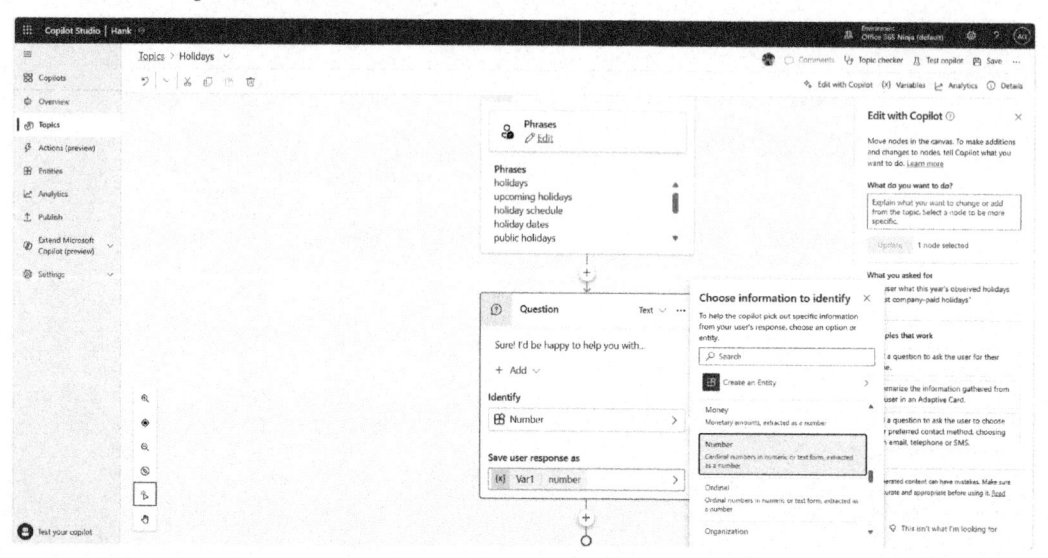

Figure 12.11 – Updating the Identify variable type

Customizing the copilot | 281

10. Under **Save user response as**, click **Var1** and update the name of the variable to something more friendly, such as Year (see *Figure 12.12*).

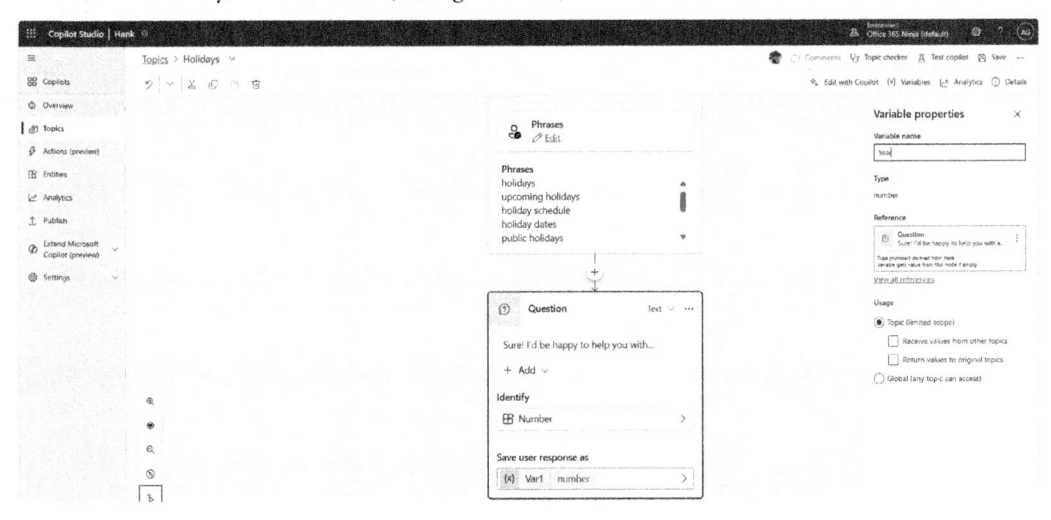

Figure 12.12 – Updating the variable name

11. After the **Question** card, select + and add a node. Then, select **Create a flow**.

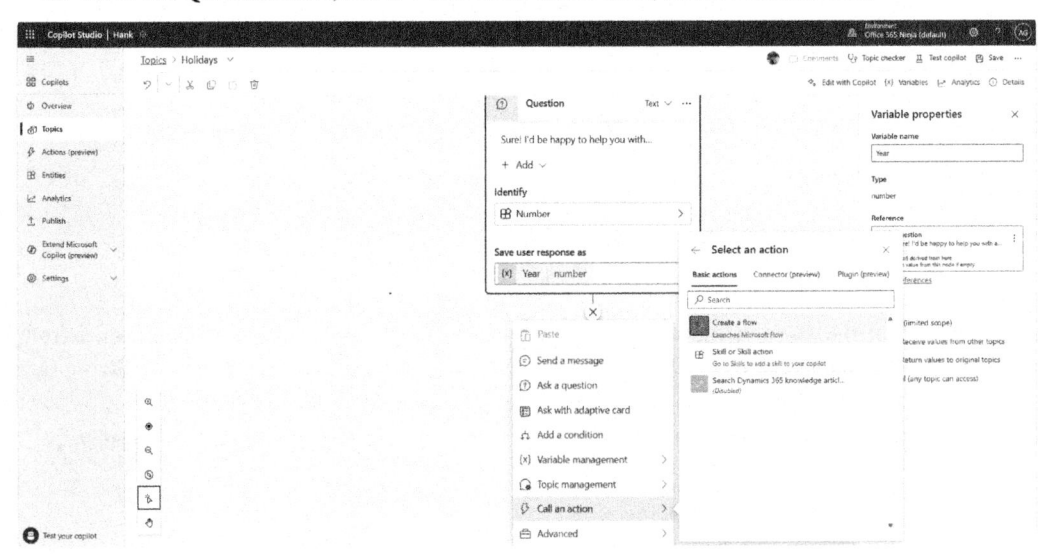

Figure 12.13 – Adding a flow action

282 Creating a Generative AI-Based Bot

12. Wait until a new browser window for Power Automate opens. After a moment, it should appear with two cards added – **When Power Virtual Agents calls a flow** and **Return value(s) to Power Virtual Agents**, as shown in *Figure 12.14*:

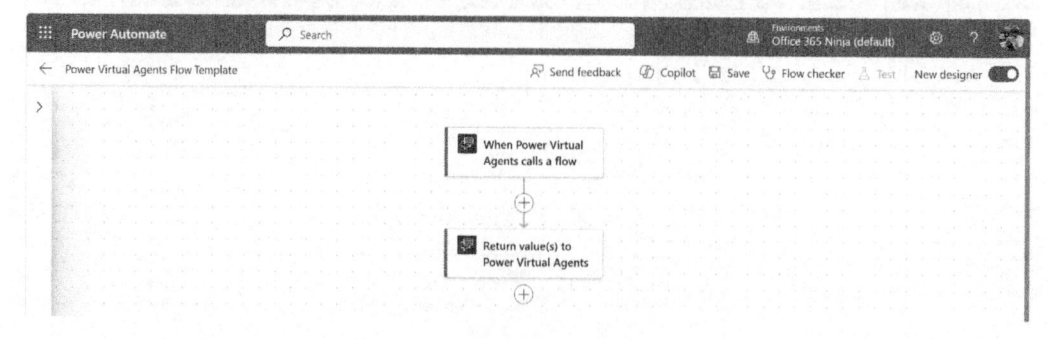

Figure 12.14 – Viewing the Power Automate canvas with PVA actions

13. Select the **When Power Virtual Agents calls a flow** card to customize the input trigger. Click **Add an input**, and then add a **Text** input. Name it something such as `Prompt`, and then place the `Prompt` text in the hint box.

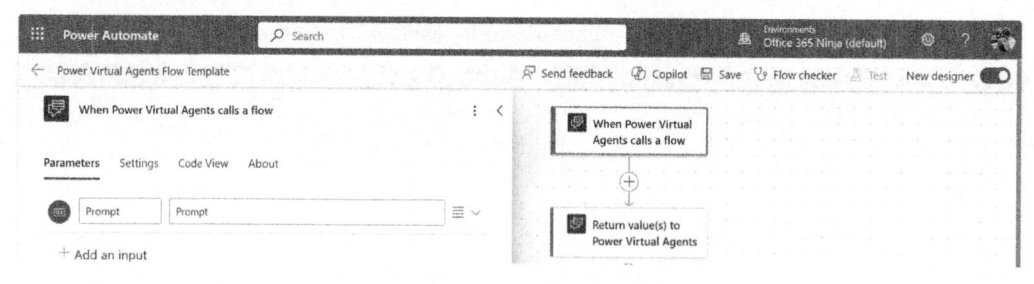

Figure 12.15 – Adding a text input

14. Add an **Initialize variable** action after the trigger. This variable will store the response from ChatGPT. In this example, we'll name it `ChatCompletion` and set its type to **String** (see *Figure 12.16*).

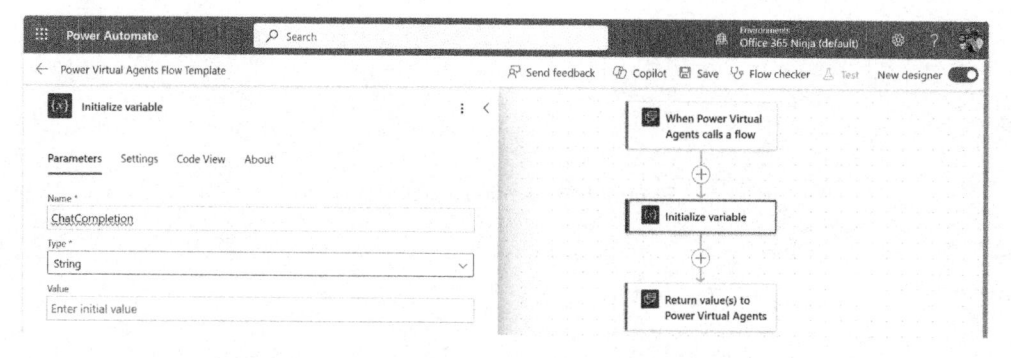

Figure 12.16 – Initializing a variable

15. Add an **HTTP** action.
16. In the **URI** field, enter `https://api.openai.com/v1/chat/completions`.
17. In the **Method** dropdown, select **POST**.
18. Add a header named `Authorization` with the value `Bearer <OpenAI key>` (see *Figure 12.17*).

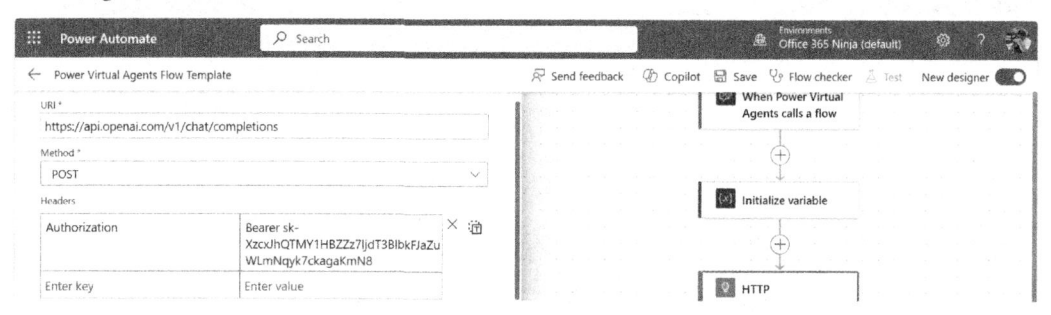

Figure 12.17 – Configuring the HTTP action

19. Enter the following text in the **Body** field. You can replace the holidays as you wish:

```
{
    "model": "gpt-4",
    "messages": [
        {
            "role": "system",
            "content": "You are a helpful HR assistant."
        },
        {
            "role": "user",
            "content": "Generate a list of the following holidays for the year **PROMPT**. The output format should be a bulleted list of the name of the holiday, followed by the day of the week, month, day, and year. For example, \n New Year's Day: Wednesday, January 1, 2024\n. Generate the list using the following holidays: New Year's Day, Martin Luther King Jr Day, Memorial Day, Independence Day, Labor Day, Veterans Day, Thanksgiving Day, Day after Thanksgiving Day, Christmas Eve, Christmas Day, New Year's Eve""
        }
    ],
    "max_tokens": 5000,
    "temperature": 0,
    "n": 1,
    "stream": false,
    "logprobs": null,
```

```
        "stop": null
}
```

20. Replace the **PROMPT** text with the **Prompt** dynamic content token from the **When Power Virtual Agents calls a flow** trigger.

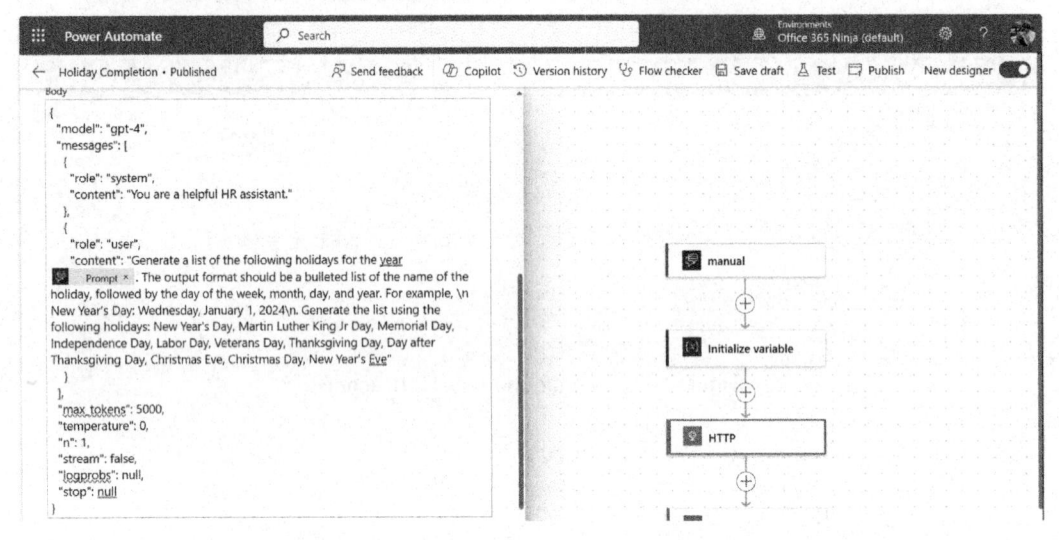

Figure 12.18 – Updating the body with the Prompt dynamic content token

21. After the **HTTP** action, add a **Parse JSON** action.
22. In the **Content** field, select the **Body** dynamic content token from the **HTTP** action.
23. In the **Schema** text area, paste the following content:

```
{
    "type": "object",
    "properties": {
        "id": {
            "type": "string"
        },
        "object": {
            "type": "string"
        },
        "created": {
            "type": "integer"
        },
        "model": {
            "type": "string"
        },
```

```
            "choices": {
                "type": "array",
                "items": {
                    "type": "object",
                    "properties": {
                        "index": {
                            "type": "integer"
                        },
                        "message": {
                            "type": "object",
                            "properties": {
                                "role": {
                                    "type": "string"
                                },
                                "content": {
                                    "type": "string"
                                }
                            }
                        },
                        "logprobs": {},
                        "finish_reason": {
                            "type": "string"
                        }
                    },
                    "required": [
                        "index",
                        "message",
                        "logprobs",
                        "finish_reason"
                    ]
                }
            },
            "usage": {
                "type": "object",
                "properties": {
                    "prompt_tokens": {
                        "type": "integer"
                    },
                    "completion_tokens": {
                        "type": "integer"
                    },
                    "total_tokens": {
                        "type": "integer"
```

```
                    }
                }
            },
            "system_fingerprint": {}
        }
    }
```

If this looks familiar, it should. It's the schema that gets generated when you paste the text from an API call to OpenAI's ChatGPT completions endpoint. You can generate it yourself by creating a manual flow, configuring an HTTP action, and then sending a chat completion request (*steps 15* to *20*). The schema, as you may recall, defines the format of the JSON output object.

Review *Figure 12.19* to see what the configured schema looks like.

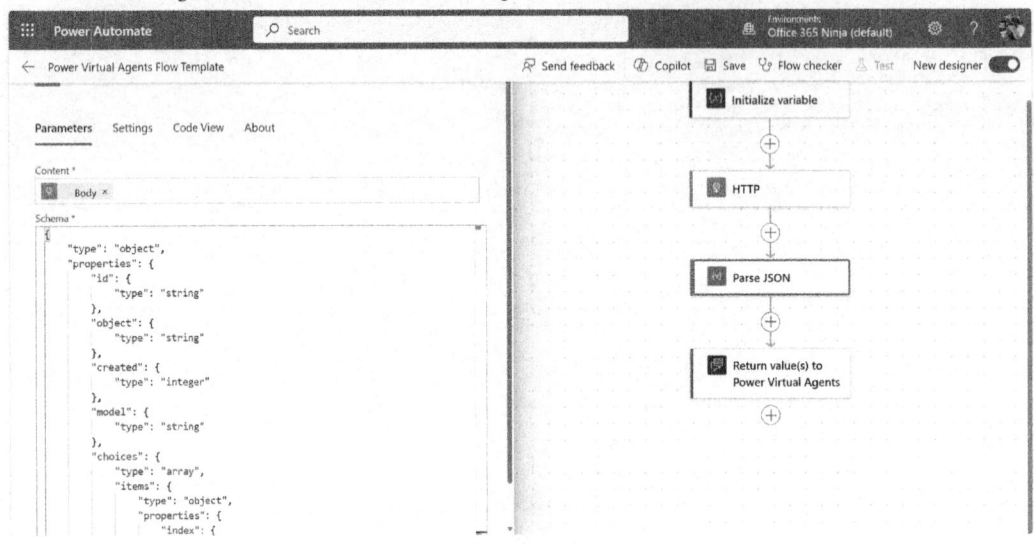

Figure 12.19 – Configuring the Parse JSON action

24. After the **Parse JSON** action, add a **Set Variable** action.

25. In the **Name** dropdown of the **Set Variable** action, choose the variable for **ChatCompletion** that you created earlier.

26. In the **Value** field, select the **Body content** dynamic content token of the **Parse JSON** action, as shown in *Figure 12.20*:

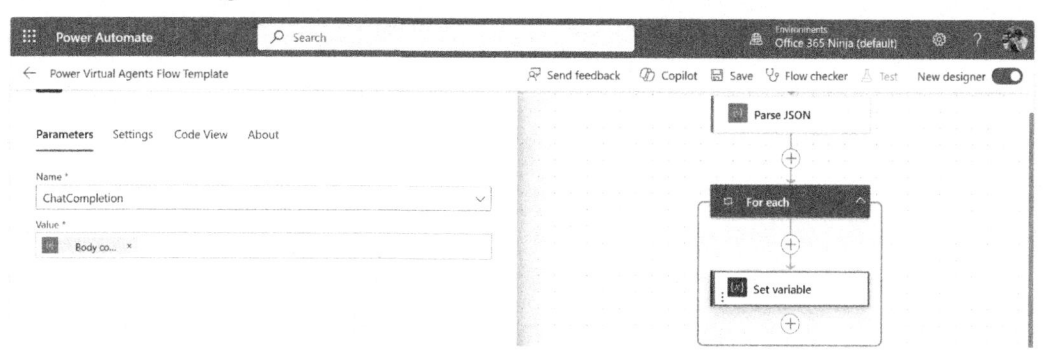

Figure 12.20 – Configuring the Set variable action

27. Select the **Return value(s) to Power Virtual Agents** action.
28. Click **Add an output** and select **Text** as the type.
29. Set the name of the output as Completion.
30. Set the value of the output to be the dynamic content token for the **ChatCompletion** variable.

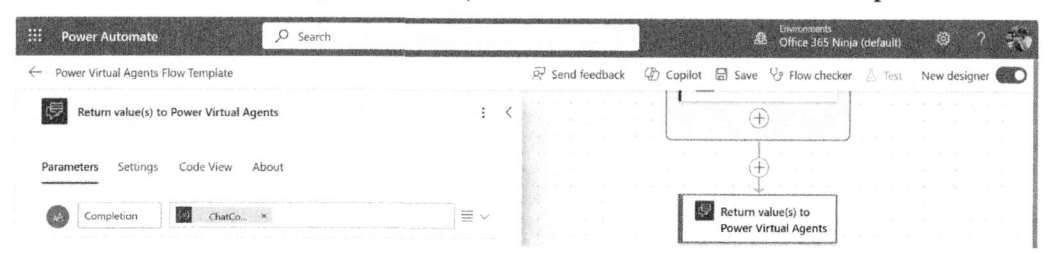

Figure 12.21 – Configuring the return value

31. If desired, rename the flow Holiday Completion (or something similar) so that you can identify it when looking at your flows.
32. Click **Save**.
33. Go back to the browser tab that has Copilot Studio open. You may be asked to refresh it.

288 Creating a Generative AI-Based Bot

34. After the question card, click + to call an action again. This time, the **Holiday Completion** flow should appear for you to select, as shown in *Figure 12.22*:

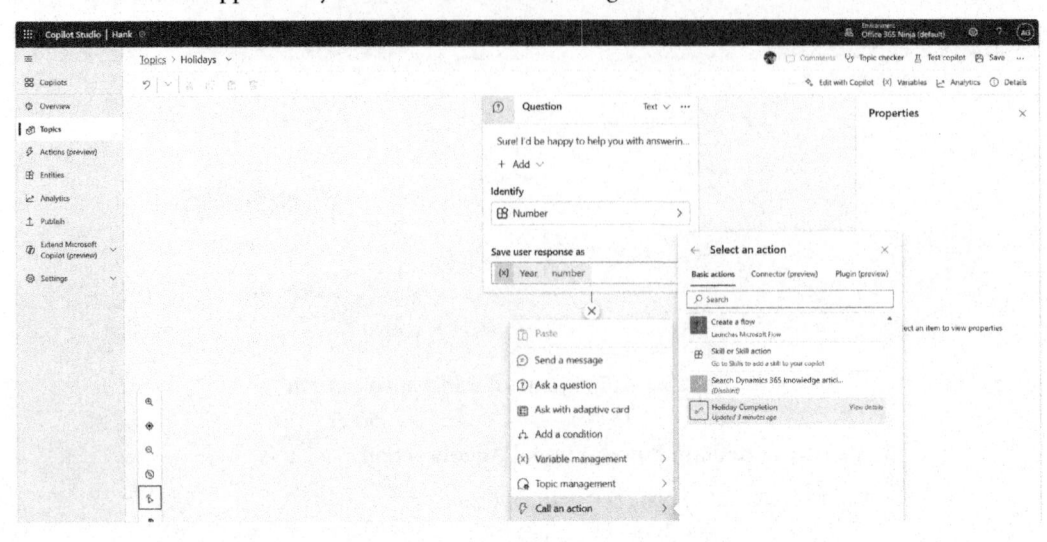

Figure 12.22 – Adding the Holiday Completion action

35. Update the action with the **Prompt** variable (**Year**) that you set up in *step 10*. This will configure the copilot to send the **Year** variable that will be used as the input in the **Holiday Completion** flow.

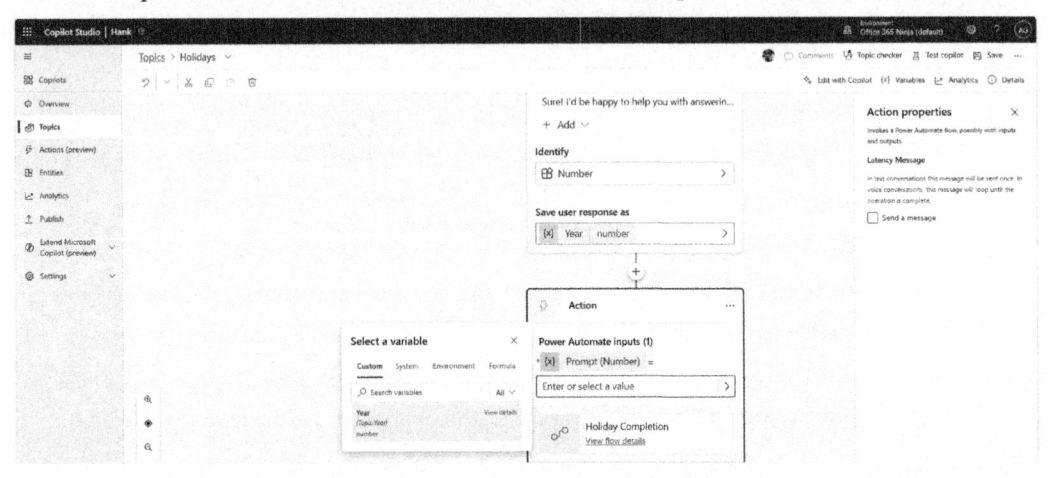

Figure 12.23 – Setting up the variable to send to the flow

Customizing the copilot | 289

36. After the action, click + and add the **Send a message** card.

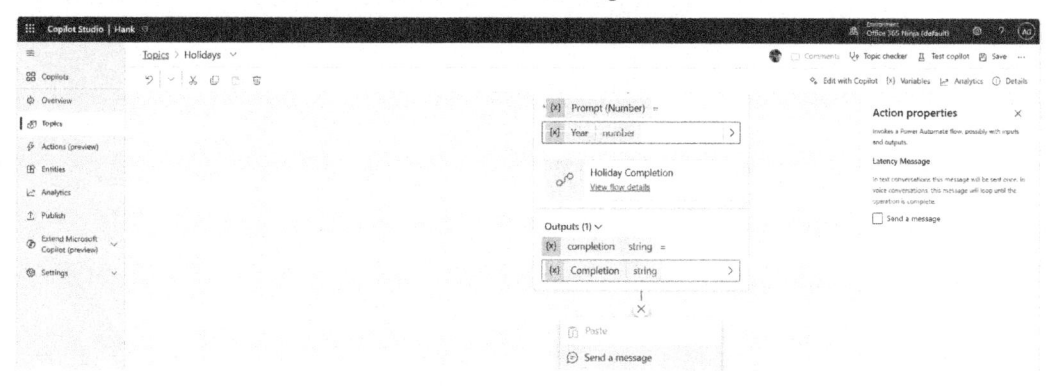

Figure 12.24 – Adding the Send a message card

37. Customize the message card with text. You can select the **{x}** icon to insert the variables that you've used in this node. For example, adding the **Year** variable will display the year that the user entered, while entering the **Completion** variable will insert the value returned from ChatGPT.

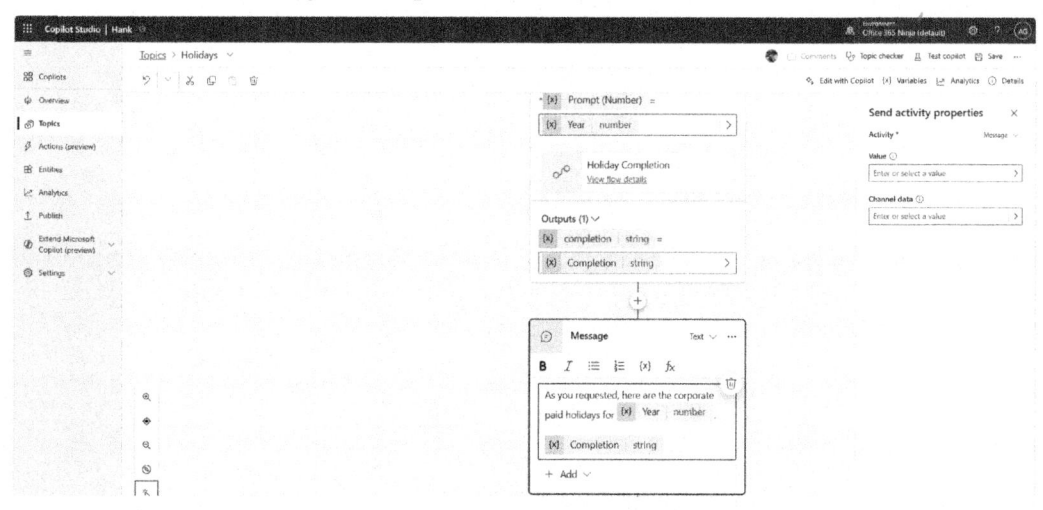

Figure 12.25 – Configuring the message card

290   Creating a Generative AI-Based Bot

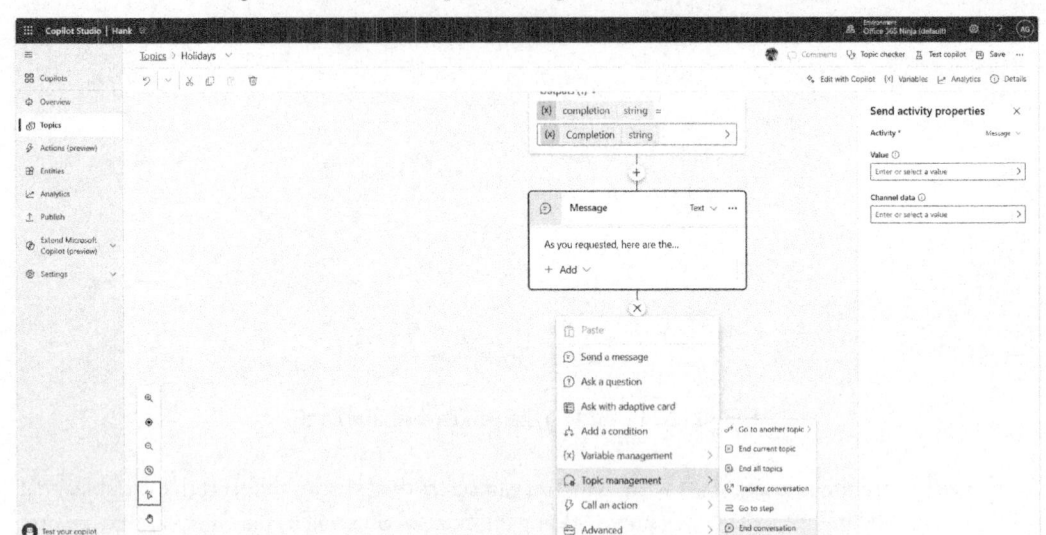

38. After the message card, add a node, point to **Topic management**, and select **End conversation**.

Figure 12.26 – Adding an End conversation node

39. Click **Save**.

Let's move ahead and continue customizing the copilot.

Disabling template topics

Every copilot is created with some base topic templates. Before making your copilot public, you should disable unused or template topics to ensure that your copilot behaves as anticipated and only returns relevant content.

To disable topics, follow these steps:

1. In Copilot Studio, select **Topics**.

Customizing the copilot 291

2. Hover over the **Lesson 1** - a sample topic to expose the **More options** ellipsis.

Figure 12.27 – Exploring topics

3. Click the ellipsis to expand the **More options** panel, and then select either the **Status** toggle to disable the topic or the **Delete** option to delete the topic altogether. If deleting a topic, you will be prompted for confirmation.

Figure 12.28 – Disabling and deleting topics

4. Repeat for the **Lesson 2** and **Lesson 3** topics.

Now, your bot will only respond with appropriate topics.

Adding content for generative AI

At this point, we're going to add our organizational content to bolster our bot's capability to answer questions.

292   Creating a Generative AI-Based Bot

There are three primary content sources for generative AI:

- Public websites
- Files stored in Dataverse
- Files stored in OneDrive for Business and SharePoint Online

Both content from public websites and files stored in Dataverse are very easy to configure and integrate. Files stored in OneDrive for Business and SharePoint Online require substantially more configuration from an authentication perspective, falling more into the *pro-code* category of development.

In this example, we'll add our stock files.

> **Online content**
>
> For the sample online content used to develop this solution, see the *Chapter 12* artifacts located at `https://github.com/PacktPublishing/Power-Platform-and-the-AI-Revolution`.

To start configuring a generative topic, follows these steps:

1. Navigate to Copilot Studio (`https://copilotstudio.microsoft.com`) and open your newly created copilot.
2. On the **Overview** page of the copilot, select **Add files**.

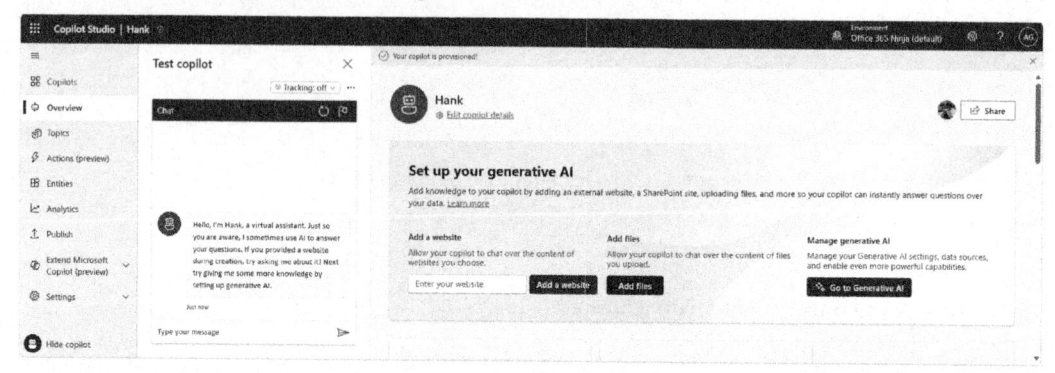

Figure 12.29 – Testing the generative AI response

Customizing the copilot | 293

3. On the **Generative AI** page, either drag your policy document files into the **Upload a document** area or select the **click to browse** link to navigate to your source folder containing the policy document files.

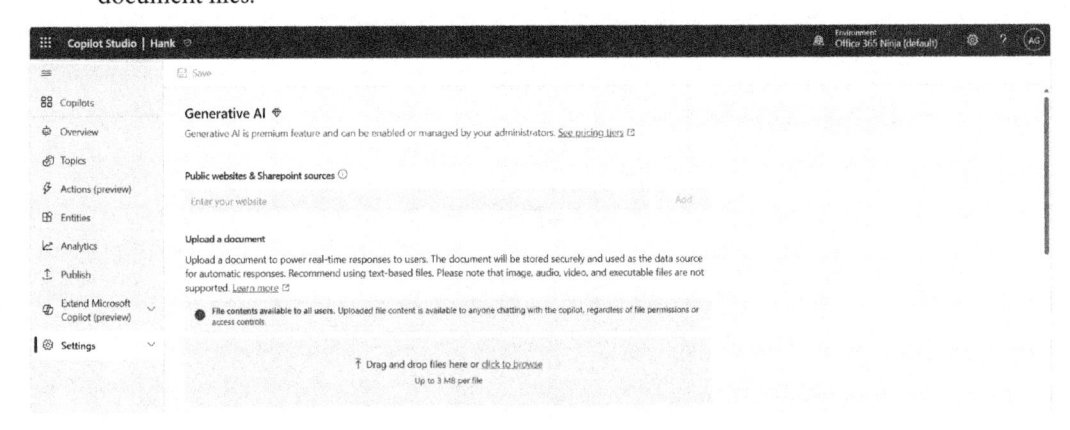

Figure 12.30 – Configuring the generative AI sources

4. After you upload the files to Dataverse, Copilot Studio will initiate an indexing process. After the indexing process has been completed, you'll be able to ask questions about the content in these policy documents!

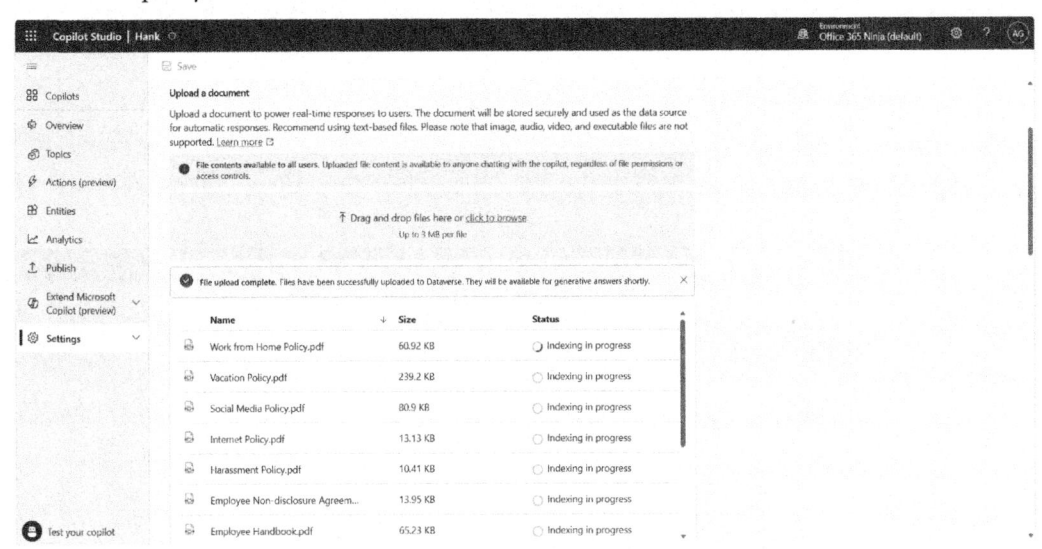

Figure 12.31 – Indexing the policy documents

294   Creating a Generative AI-Based Bot

5. After the content has been indexed, scroll down toward the bottom of the page. Uploading content by itself doesn't enable the generative AI features, so we need to do that as well. Enable the **Boost conversational coverage with generative answers** slide toggle.

Figure 12.32 – Enabling the generative answers feature

6. Click the **Save** icon at the top of the panel. The status bar should update, indicating that Copilot Studio is enabling generative answers, as shown in *Figure 12.33*:

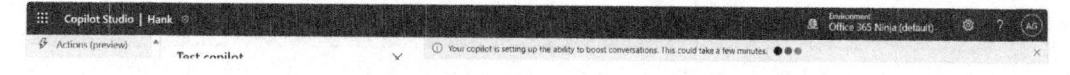

Figure 12.33 – Saving changes

7. To verify that it's ready to go, head back over to **Topics** > **System** and look for the **Conversational boosting** system topic.

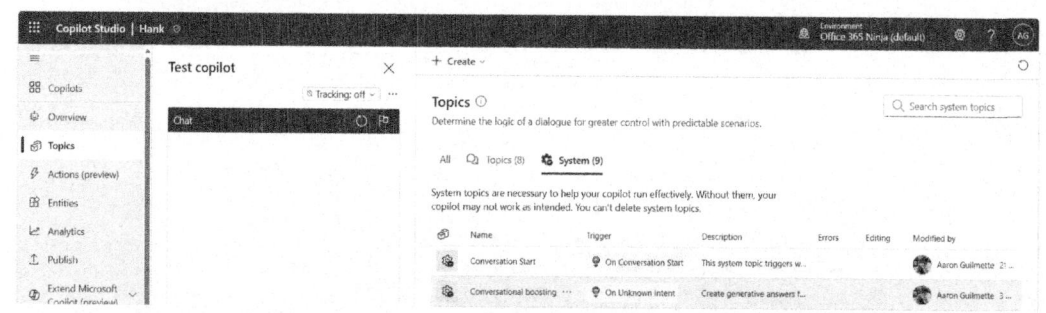

Figure 12.34 – Verifying that the Conversational boosting topic has been created

Next, we'll put our copilot through its paces!

Testing the copilot

In this section, we're going to test both of our copilot configurations – the ChatGPT-based **Holidays** topic and the generative answers.

The Holidays topic

First, we'll test the **Holidays** topic that we created:

1. Click the **Test copilot** button in the navigation bar to open the **Test copilot** chat flyout.
2. Once the flyout has appeared, enter one of the trigger phrases to launch the **Holidays** topic:

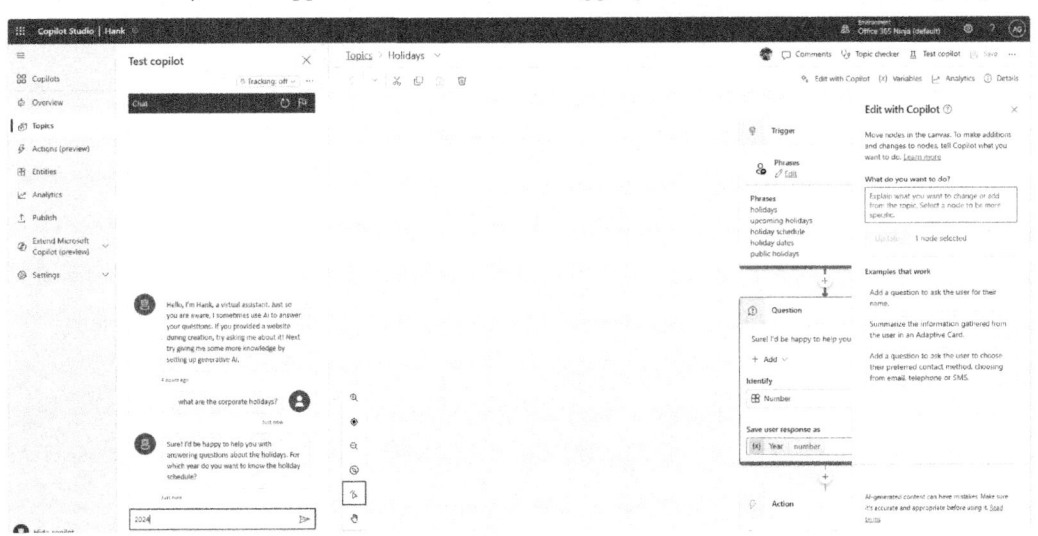

Figure 12.35 – Testing the copilot

3. Review the output. If you've made it all the way through successfully, your bot should respond with the output it retrieved from ChatGPT!

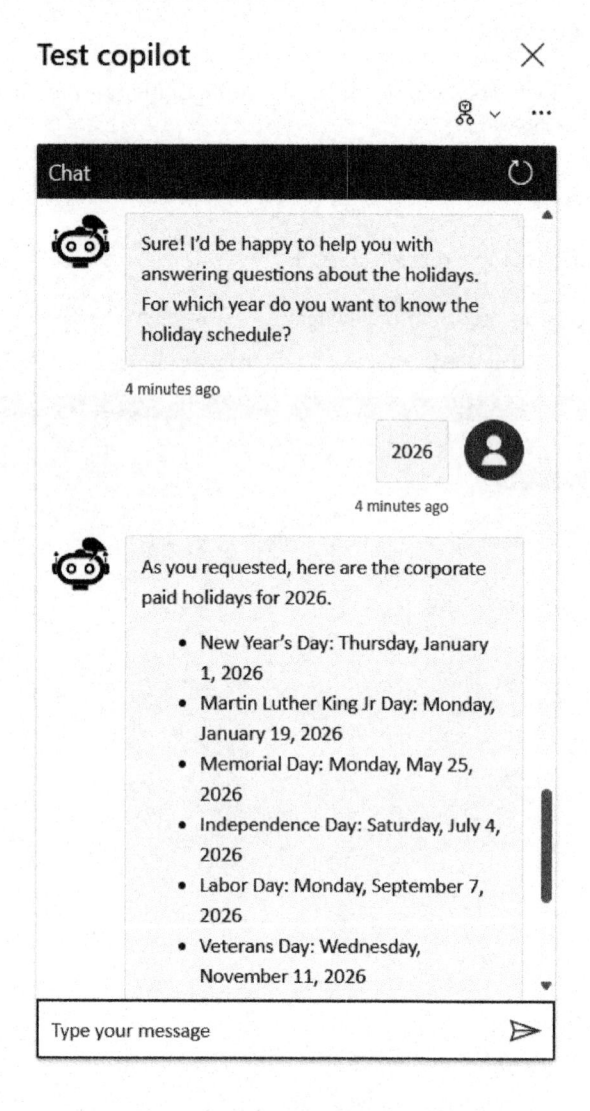

Figure 12.36 – Reviewing the data from ChatGPT

That's pretty great!

Next, let's ask it a question that could only be answered through generative answer boosting.

Generative answers

To see what information generative answers have learned, try asking your new copilot a question that you would be able to obtain from the uploaded documents:

1. In the chat area, ask your copilot a question. In this example, you might ask something such as *What is the discrimination policy?*

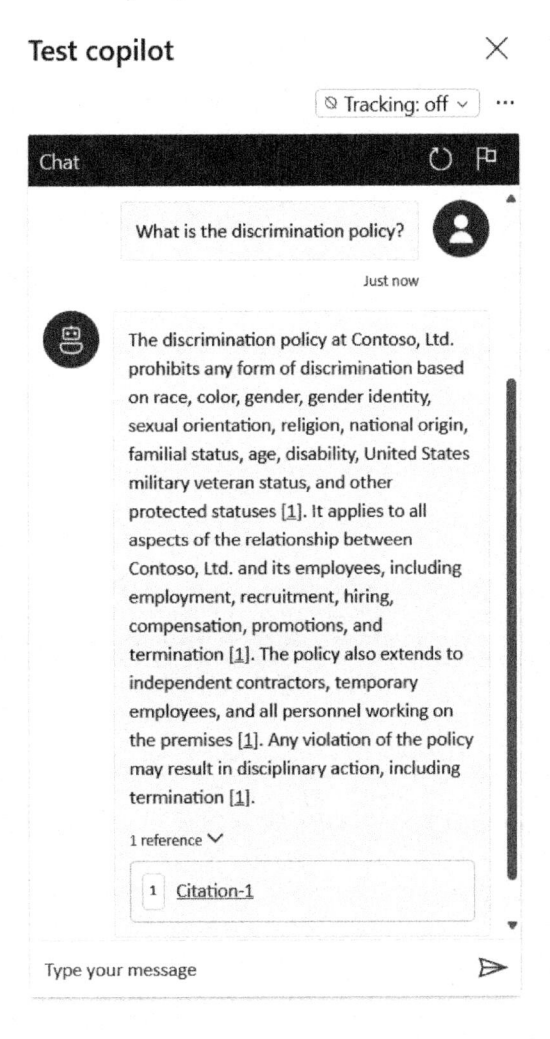

Figure 12.37 – Asking the copilot for a generative answer-based response

2. Click the link for the citation to bring up the uploaded policy document.

Anti-Discrimination Policy.pdf

Equal Employment Opportunity and Anti-Discrimination Policy I. OVERVIEW & SCOPE Contoso, Ltd. of 123 Any Street, Anytown, Michigan 48123, has established an Anti-Discrimination and Equal Employment Opportunity Policy ("Policy"). This Policy applies to all aspects of the relationship between Contoso, Ltd. and its employees, including, but not limited to, employment, recruitment, advertisements for employment, hiring and firing, compensation, assignment, classification of employees, termination, upgrading, promotions, transfer, training, working conditions, wages and salary administration, and employee benefits and application of policies. These policies apply to independent contractors, temporary employees, all personnel working on the premises, and any other persons or firms doing business for or with Contoso, Ltd. Disciplinary action will be taken against any employee or agent in breach of this Policy. II. POLICIES Contoso, Ltd. is an equal opportunity employer committed to complying with all 1. DISCRIMINATION. applicable anti-discrimination laws. Discrimination occurs whenever similarly situated individuals of a different group are accorded different and unequal treatment in the context of a similar situation. Contoso, Ltd. shall not tolerate, under any circumstances, without exception, the exclusion of individuals from an opportunity or participation in any activity because of race, color, gender, gender identity, sexual orientation, religion, national origin, familial status, age, disability, United States military veteran status, and any other status protected by the law. This list is not exhaustive. Nor will Contoso, Ltd. tolerate, without exception, the exclusion of individuals from an opportunity or participation in any activity based on hair texture or protective hairstyles including braids, locs, twists or bantu knots. Our policy of non-discrimination in employment applies, without limitation, to recruitment, hiring, compensation, promotions, transfers, discipline, demotions, terminations, layoffs, access to benefits and training and all other aspects of employment, as well as to selection of volunteers and vendors and provision of services. In addition, our policy of non-discrimination is intended to extend to visitors to our facilities and all of our stakeholders. Contoso, Ltd. is committed to creating and providing a positive work environment that 2. HARASSMENT. is free from harassment. Therefore, the Company will not tolerate workplace harassment of any employee, either by fellow employees or non-employees, of race, color, gender, gender identity, sexual orientation, religion, national origin, familial status, age, disability, United States military veteran status, sexual orientation, gender identity and gender expression, including the exercise of a protected activity (like filing a complaint), or any other reason deemed impermissible under the law. Harassment can include, but is not limited to, offensive verbal conduct such as foul or obscene language, epithets, suggestive statements or innuendo, derogatory comments, or 'jokes." Harassment may further include touching, gestures, or other offensive physical conduct, or creating, displaying, or reading offensive graphic or written materials in the workplace that relate to the sex, race, religion, color, national origin, age, or disability of an employee. Any of these behaviors is considered harassment if it would make a reasonable person experiencing the conduct uncomfortable in the workplace, or if it could hinder the person's job performance. All employees, including supervisors, other management personnel, and independent contractors, are required to abide by this Policy. Violation of the Policy will result in disciplinary action, up to and including discharge. No person will be adversely affected in employment with Contoso, Ltd. as a result of bringing complaints of harassment. Contoso, Ltd. is strongly opposed to sexual harassment, and that such 3. SEXUAL HARASSMENT. behavior is prohibited both by law and by company policy. Sexual harassment is unwelcome sexual advances, requests for sexual favors, and other verbal or physical conduct of a sexual nature constitute harassment when (1) submission to such conduct is made either explicitly or implicitly a term or condition of employment; (2) submission to or rejection of such conduct by an individual is used as a basis for employment decisions, promotion, transfer, selection for training, performance evaluations, benefits, or other terms and conditions of employment; or (3) such conduct has the purpose or effect of creating an intimidating, hostile, or offensive work environment or substantially interferes with an employee's work performance. Contoso, Ltd. prohibits inappropriate conduct that is sexual in nature at work, on Company business, or at Company-sponsored events including the following: comments,

Figure 12.38 – Reviewing the source material for the copilot's answer

Congratulations! You've built a copilot with two different types of AI-enhanced content!

Further exploration

This just scratches the surface of what a copilot can be for your organization. You can build a giant copilot to reason over tomes of data, or several smaller, more targeted copilots that can be used to help provide users with answers based on organizational knowledge.

What are some ideas that you might have to expand on this copilot? Consider using conditions to navigate to new conversation nodes and topics, such as the following:

- Create a topic about corporate credit cards and provide a multiple-choice option to navigate to the card request application or the expense reporting site.
- Integrate a question at the end of a curated topic to find out whether the answer was useful. If not, link to the **Conversational booster** topic and let the user ask generative answers for more details.

Summary

In this chapter, we explored different ways to integrate generative AI into copilots (formerly known as Power Virtual Agents). You were able to send requests to ChatGPT to obtain answers for corporate holidays using a specifically crafted prompt, while RAG allowed you to provide answers to questions based on organizational content that you uploaded to Dataverse.

Each of these ideas can be expanded to create even more functional copilots.

In the next chapter, we'll take this copilot and make it available for people to use!

13
Publishing a Generative AI-based Bot

In the previous chapter, you were able to build a chatbot (or **copilot**, in the new vernacular) that leveraged two different generative AI features—sending data to ChatGPT to evaluate and loading documents in Dataverse for Generative Answers to reason over.

In this final chapter, we'll walk through the necessary steps to publish the chatbot and make it available so people can start asking questions.

With any further ado, let's get going!

Publishing a bot to Teams

Publishing a bot is going through the steps to make it available to users. Microsoft uses the term **channels** to describe the services, apps, or destinations where your bot will be published.

Depending on the type of bot you've created, you may want to publish it to Microsoft Teams, a public website, Facebook, or other services. The ability to publish bots to different locations will depend on its authentication settings.

In this example, we're going to make the bot available to Microsoft Teams users. By default, your bot is configured for Teams and Power Apps authentication, so it makes sense to start here.

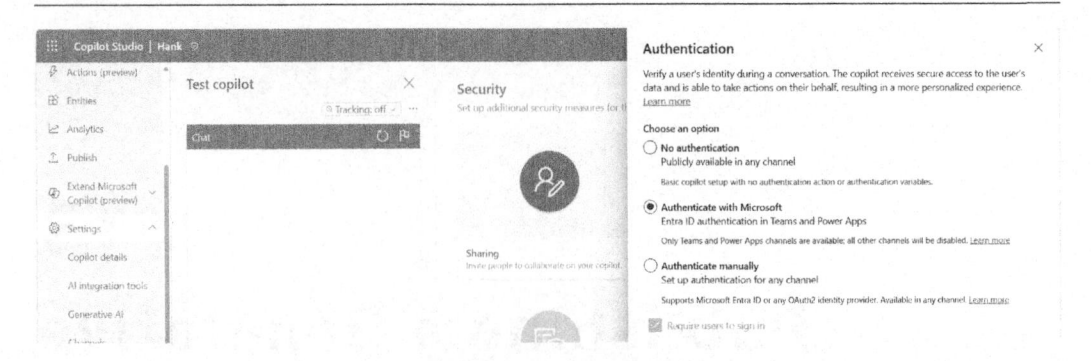

Figure 13.1 – Viewing the bot's authentication configuration

Publishing the bot

To publish the bot to Teams, you can simply follow these steps:

1. Navigate to Copilot Studio (https://copilotstudio.microsoft.com) and select your bot.
2. In the navigation menu, expand **Settings** and select **Channels**.

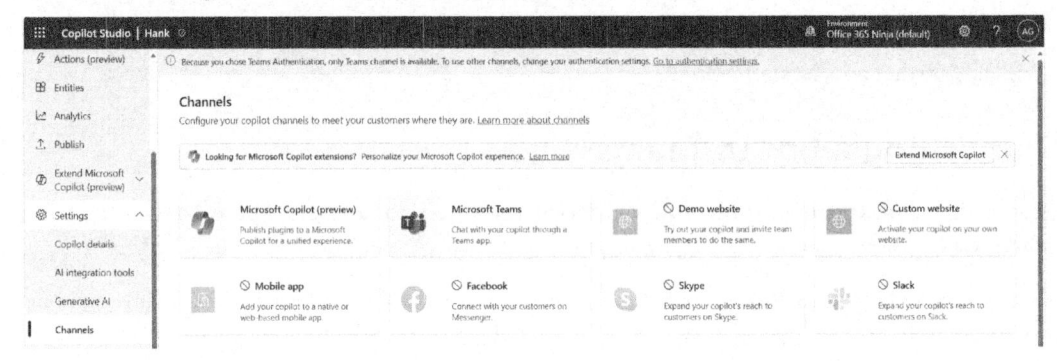

Figure 13.2 – Viewing the Channels page

3. Select **Microsoft Teams**.

4. On the **Microsoft Teams** flyout, at the bottom of the page, click **Turn on Teams**.

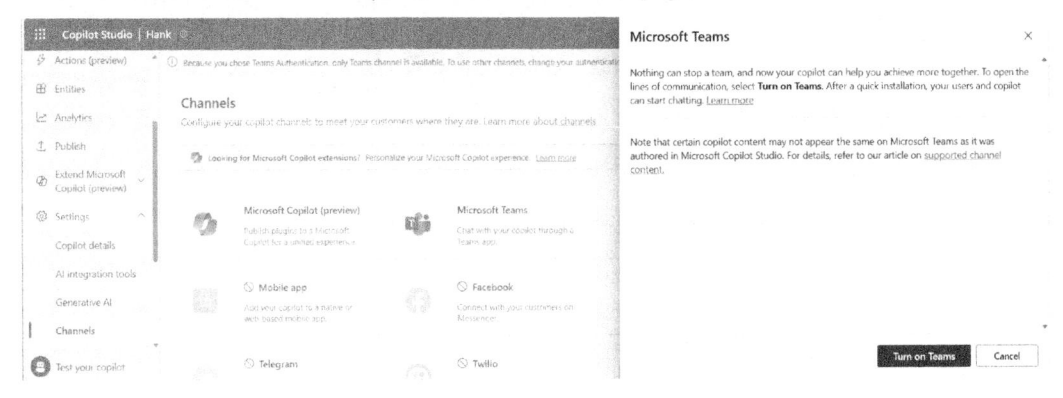

Figure 13.3 – Enabling the copilot for Teams

5. Confirm that it has been enabled.

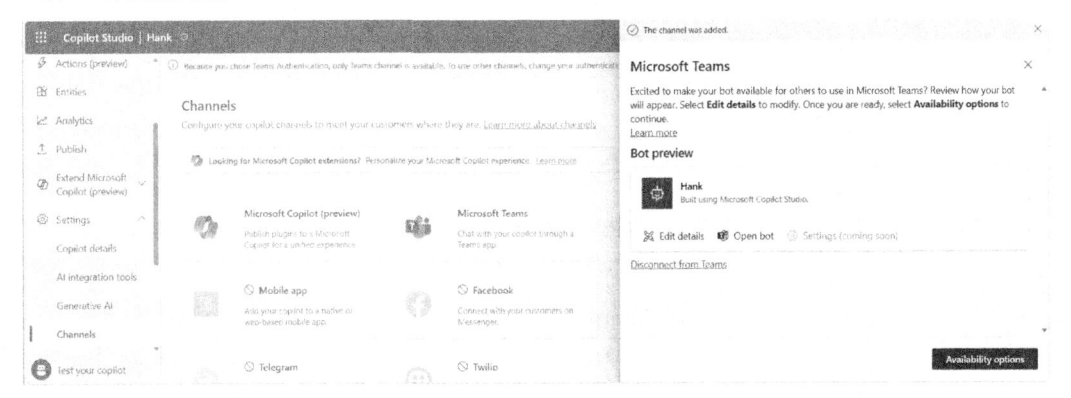

Figure 13.4 – Confirming that Teams integration has been enabled

If desired, you can click **Edit details** to change the display characteristics of your bot, including the icon, icon color, descriptions, and whether this bot can be added to a team (or whether it's just a bot along the left rail). When you're done updating the settings, click **Save**.

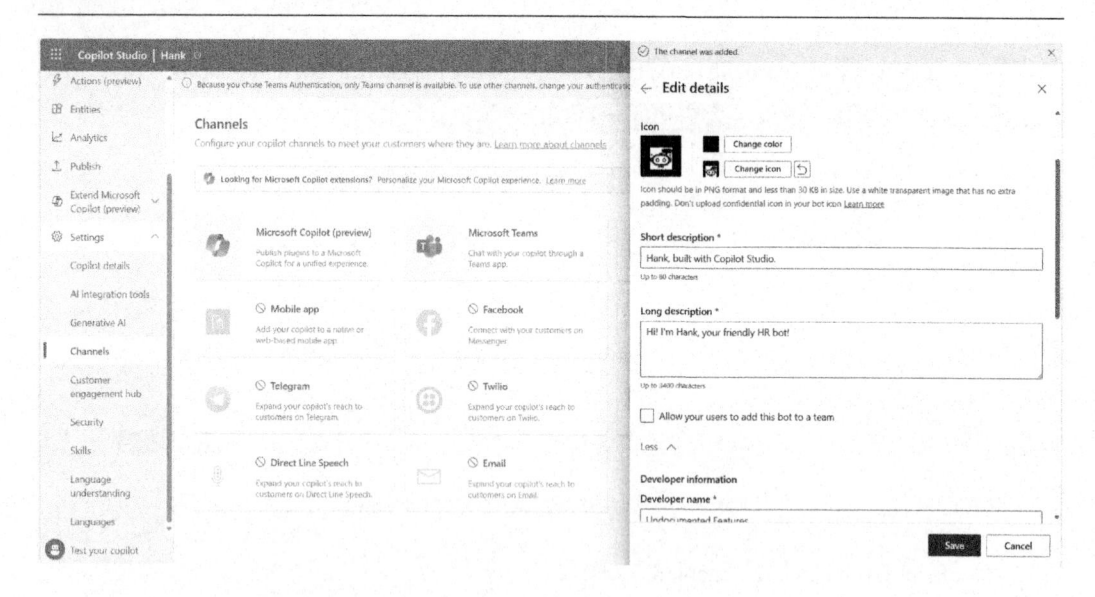

Figure 13.5 – Configuring additional bot settings

6. Select **Availability options**.

7. Under **Show in Teams app store**, you can select **Show to my teammates and shared users** to make it available to your peers, or you can click **Show to everyone in my org**. The **Show to everyone in my org** option will generate a custom app request in the Teams admin center (which will need to be approved by an administrator).

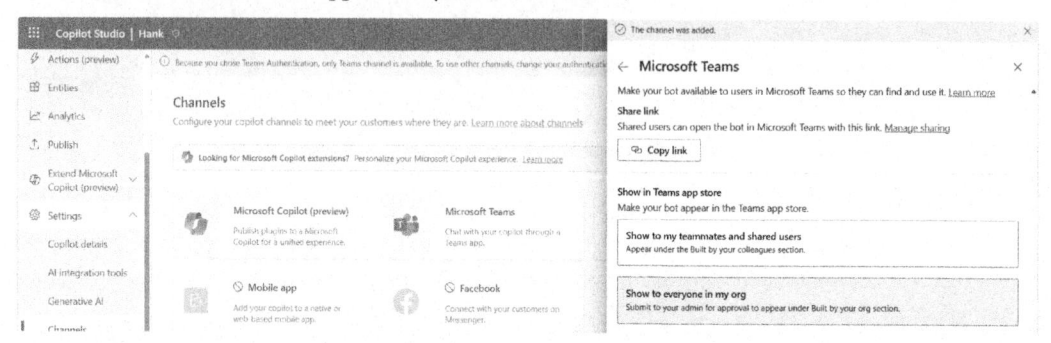

Figure 13.6 – Sharing the bot

8. Click **Show to everyone in my org**. Then, on the next page, click the **Submit for admin approval** button.

9. Select **Publish** in the navigation menu.

10. If your bot wasn't automatically published, click **Publish**.

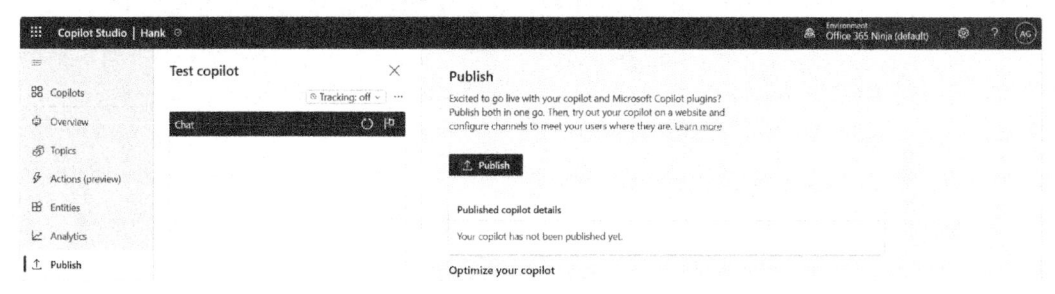

Figure 13.7 – Starting the publishing process

11. When prompted to confirm, click **Publish**.

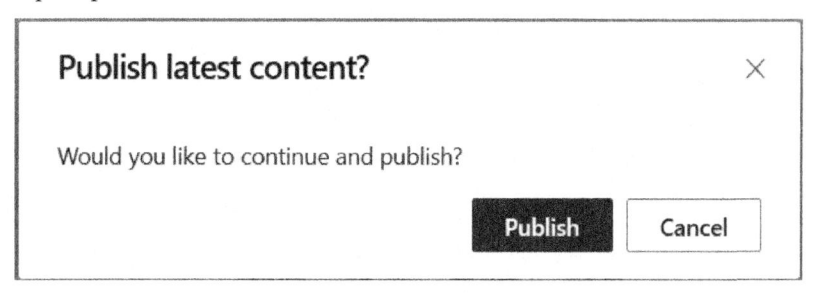

Figure 13.8 – Confirming the publishing action

Next, we'll take a look to see how our bot looks in Teams.

Testing the bot

In this section, you'll get to see how your bot works inside Teams. Follow these steps:

1. From the **Channels** > **Microsoft Teams** flyout, select **Open bot**.

Figure 13.9 – Opening the bot in Teams

2. You can launch either the desktop or web version of Microsoft Teams.
3. Once Teams has launched, you should be presented with your chatbot. Click **Add**. This will install your app into the left rail in Teams.

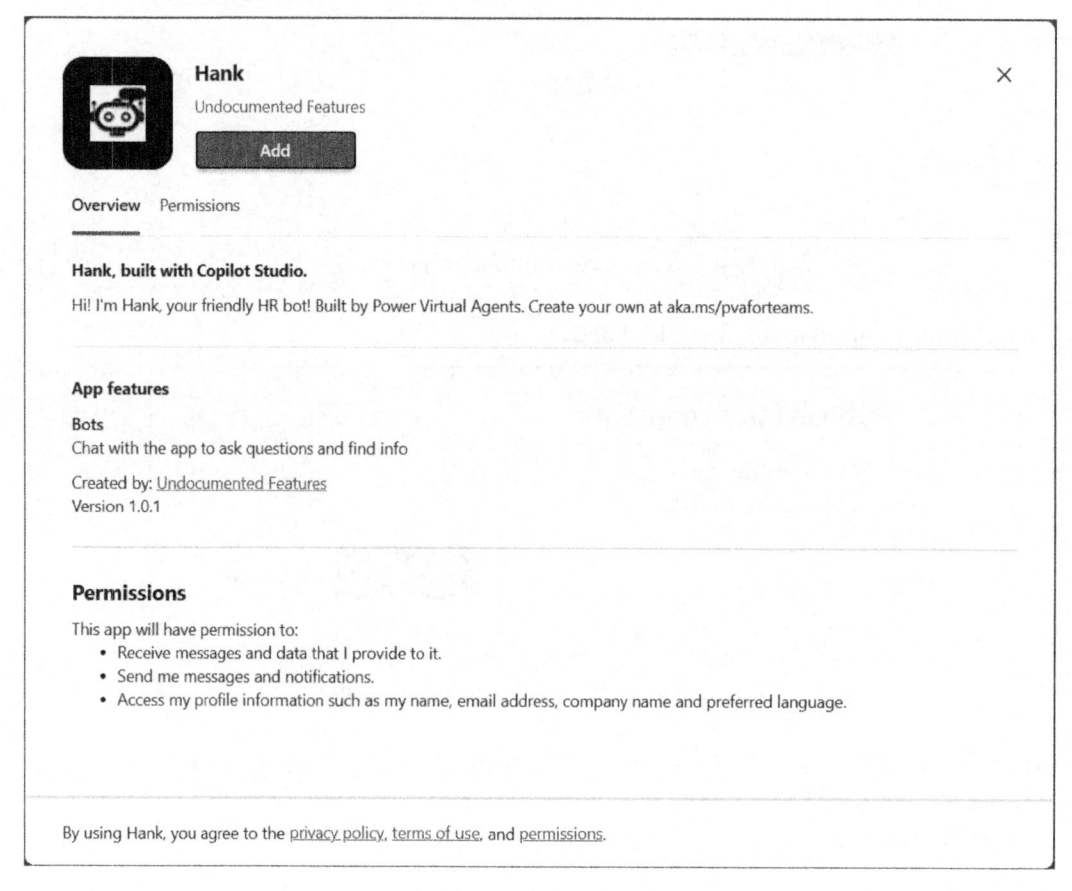

Figure 13.10 – Adding your chatbot

4. You can then ask it questions, just like when you were testing it previously.

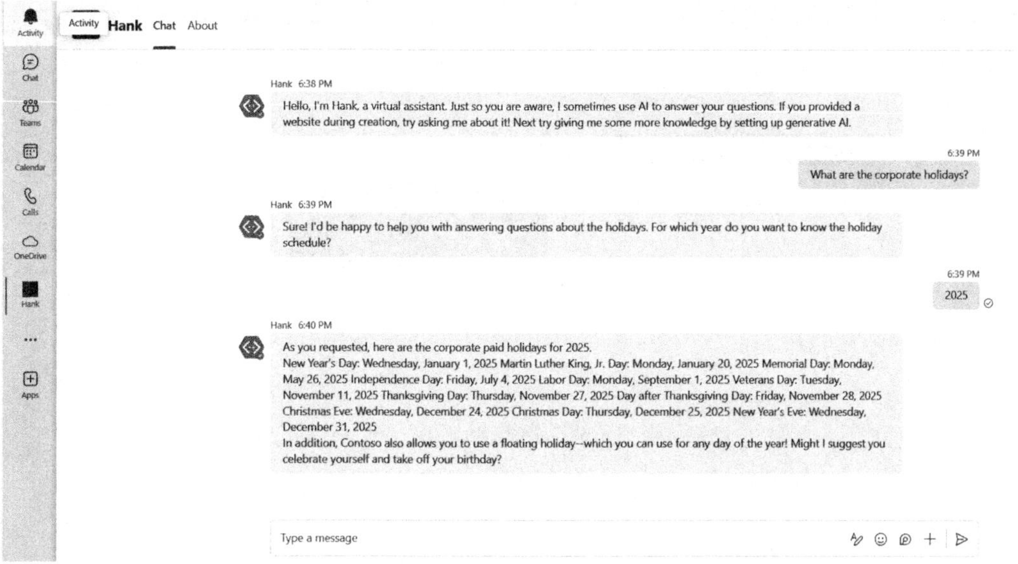

Figure 13.11 – Asking the Teams bot questions

Now that you've tested it out, it's time to approve it and make it available organization-wide!

Approving the bot

Approving the bot is a relatively simple exercise, though you will need administrative rights for Microsoft Teams. You can approve the bot following this quick process:

1. Navigate to the Microsoft Teams admin center (`https://admin.teams.microsoft.com`).

2. In the navigation menu, expand **Teams apps** and select **Manage apps**.

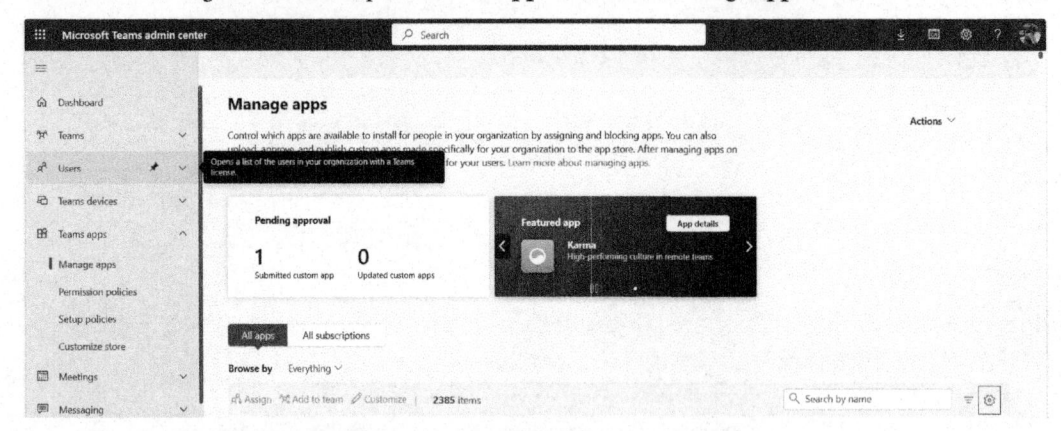

Figure 13.12 – Managing the Teams App store

Notice there is one custom app pending approval.

3. In the **Search by name** box, start typing the name of your bot. Notice that your bot app has a status of **Blocked**, as shown in *Figure 13.13*.

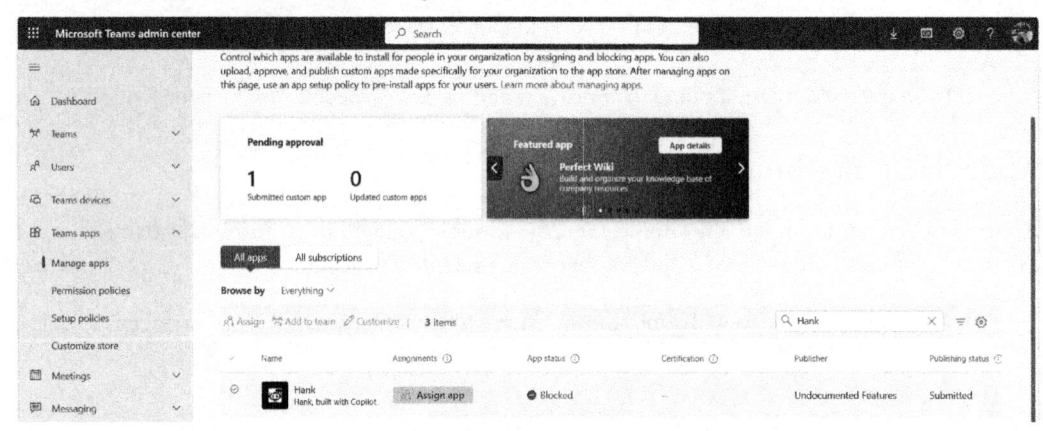

Figure 13.13 – Viewing the bot app's status

4. Click the **Name** of the app.
5. Click **Publish** to make the app available in the Teams app store.

Figure 13.14 – Publishing the bot app

6. When prompted to confirm, click **Publish**.

Other users in your Microsoft 365 organization can now go and look for the bot in the Teams app store!

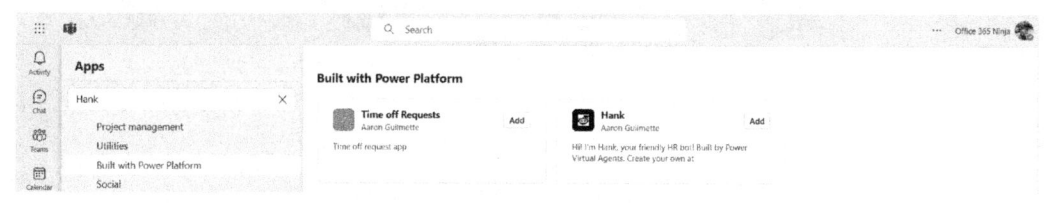

Figure 13.15 – Locating the bot in the Teams app store

Next, we'll look at publishing the bot to some other channels, such as a public website.

Publishing a bot to a website

Most of the time, you'll create bots that target either internal or external users—since those categories of users have different needs.

In this section, we're going to switch the authentication method for the bot we just built so that it can be used on a public channel (such as a website or Facebook). In the real world, you'll likely be building different bots for different scenarios.

310 Publishing a Generative AI-based Bot

> **No website? No problem**
>
> If you don't have a developmental website to work with—that's okay! You can go to https://www.wordpress.com and sign up for a free hosted website. We'll be using a WordPress site in this example.

To publish the bot to a website, follow these steps:

1. Navigate to Copilot Studio (https://copilotstudio.microsoft.com) and select your bot.
2. Expand **Settings** and choose **Security**.
3. On the **Security** page, select **Authentication**.

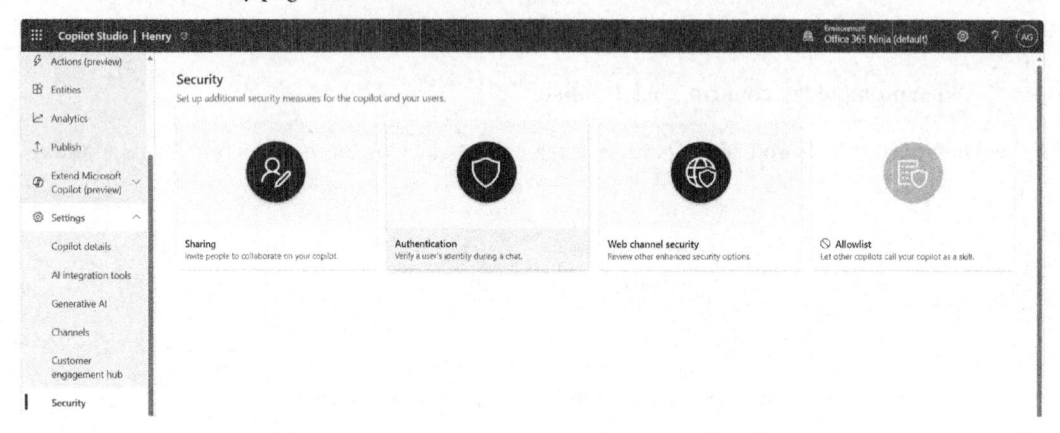

Figure 13.16 – Updating the security settings for the bot

4. On the **Authentication** flyout, select **No authentication** and click **Save**.

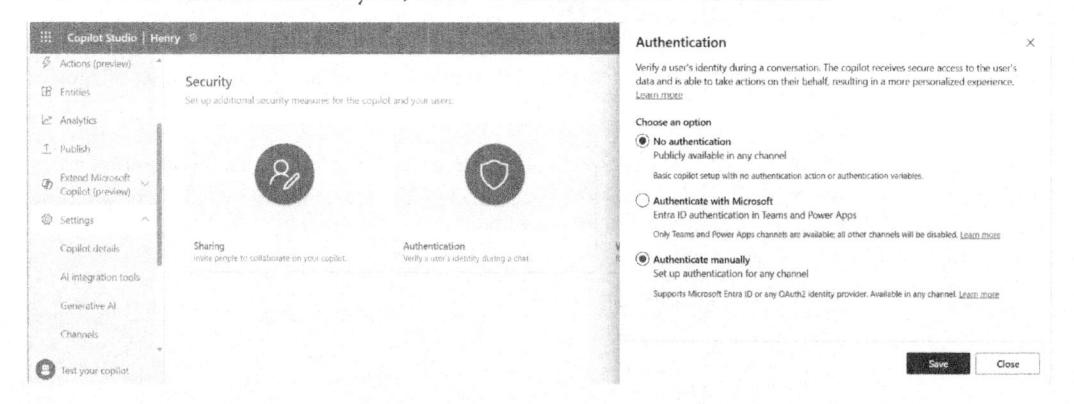

Figure 13.17 – Selecting No authentication

5. Review the **Save this configuration?** dialog box and click **Save**.

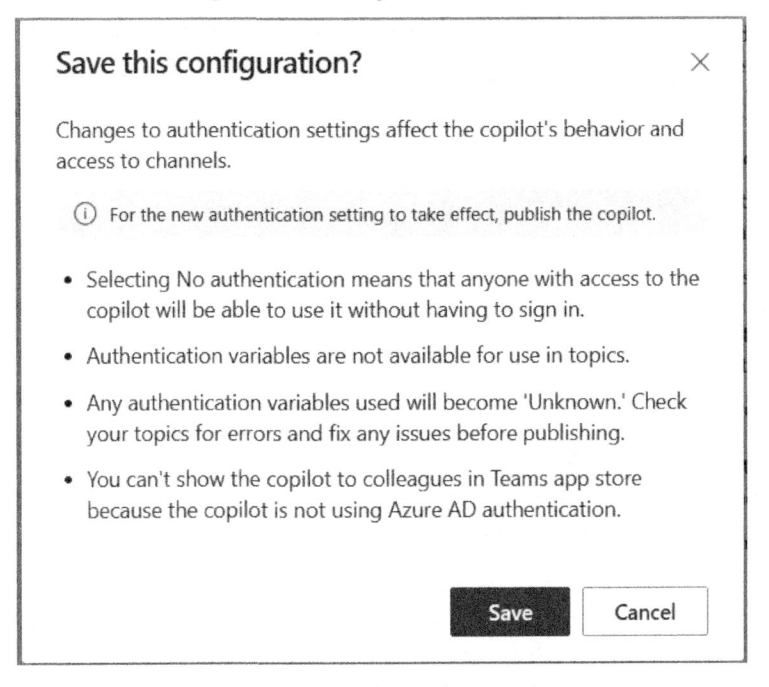

Figure 13.18 – Reviewing the Save dialog box

6. Under **Settings**, click **Channels**. Note that the other channels are now unlocked.

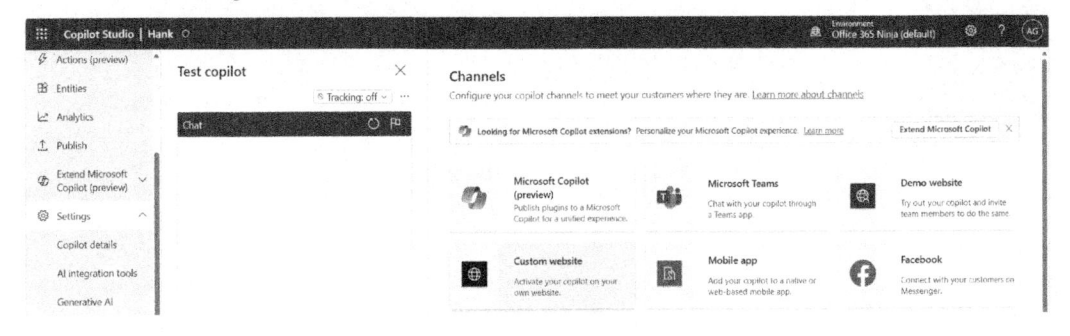

Figure 13.19 – Viewing available channels

312   Publishing a Generative AI-based Bot

7. Select the **Custom website** channel.
8. On the **Custom website** flyout, you should see a section labeled **Default embed code**. We'll use this code on our site.

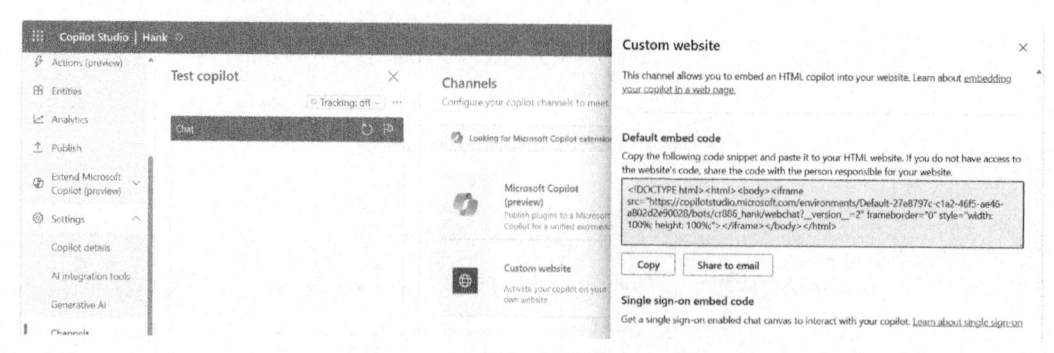

Figure 13.20 – Viewing the custom website code

9. In a new browser window, navigate to your website's administration interface.
10. Create or edit a page.
11. Next, you'll need to get to the HTML or Text view of your site. If you're using WordPress, you can do that by clicking the **Text** tab of the composition window, as shown in *Figure 13.21*.

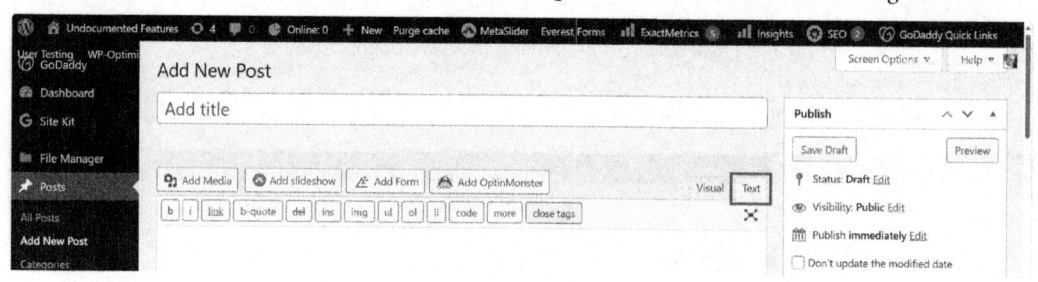

Figure 13.21 – Switching to the text/HTML view

12. Switch back to the browser tab that had the Copilot Studio custom website code. Copy the code and paste it into the HTML editor. Depending on your theme, you may need to edit the size parameters. For example, it may be useful to remove the `"style=width:100%; height:100%"` tag so that you can see what the native display size is. See *Figure*.

Figure 13.22 – Updating the website code

13. Click **Publish** to publish the post or page on your site.

That's it!

Publishing a bot to Facebook

Bots can also be an extension of your business on social media sites such as Facebook. In this example, we'll publish a bot to respond to questions through Facebook Messenger.

> **Get Facebooking!**
> In order to integrate with Facebook, you'll need an existing Facebook business app. You'll also need to register with Facebook Developer (`https://developers.facebook.com`).

To get started, follow these steps:

1. Navigate to Copilot Studio (`https://copilotstudio.microsoft.com`) and select your bot.
2. From the navigation pane, expand **Settings** and select **Channels**.
3. Select **Facebook**.

314　Publishing a Generative AI-based Bot

4. Notice the fields that appear on the **Facebook** flyout, including **Facebook app ID**, **Facebook app secret**, **Page ID**, and **Page access token**.

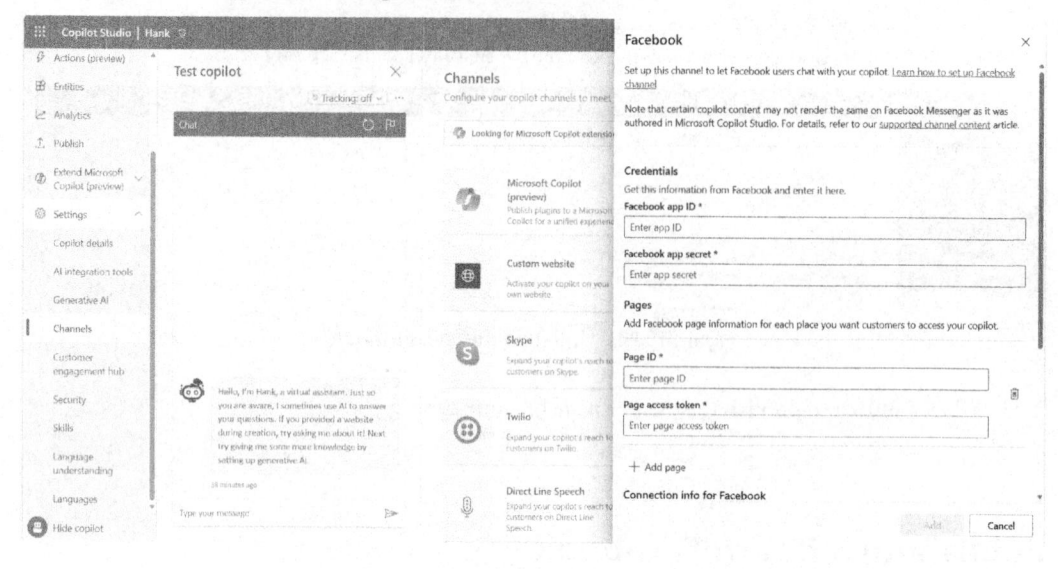

Figure 13.23 – Viewing the Facebook settings flyout

5. Open a new browser tab. Navigate to `https://developers.facebook.com` and sign in with the ID that manages your organization's Facebook page or app.

6. From the navigation menu, select **My Apps**.

Figure 13.24 – Logging in to the Facebook Developers site

7. Select your existing app or page.

Figure 13.25 – Selecting your Facebook page or app

8. Expand **App settings** and select **Basic**.

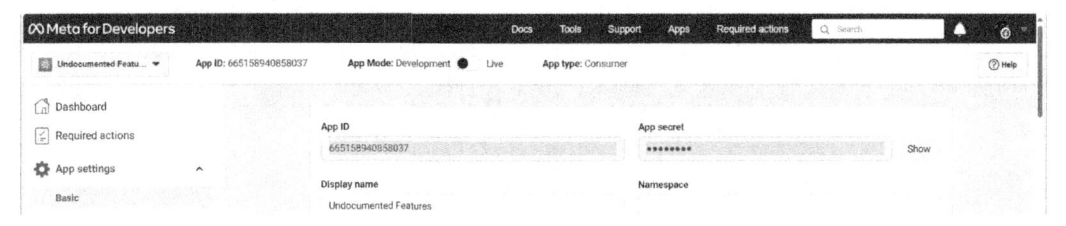

Figure 13.26 – Getting the Facebook security data

9. Copy the **App ID** and **App secret** values to the corresponding locations in the Copilot Studio Facebook channel setup.
10. On the Facebook Developer settings page, select **Advanced**.
11. Enable the **Allow API access to app settings** toggle and click **Save changes**.

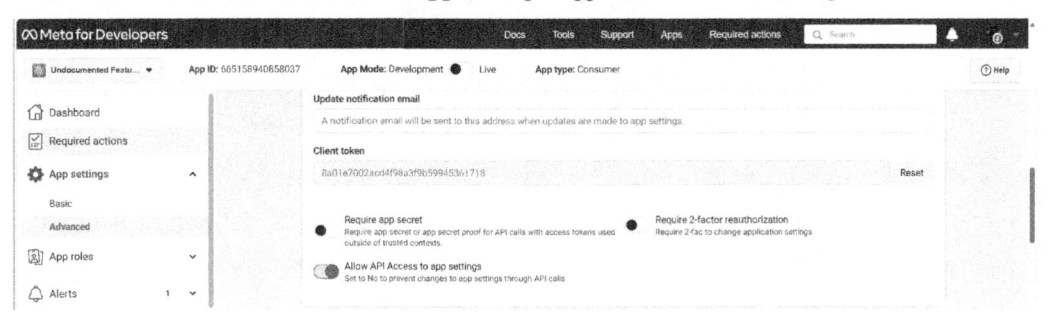

Figure 13.27 – Enabling API access

316   Publishing a Generative AI-based Bot

12. Click **Dashboard**, and then select **Set up** for the **Messenger** app.

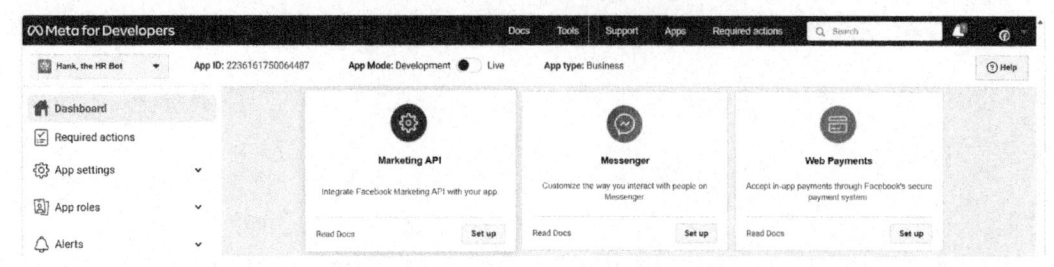

Figure 13.28 – Setting up the Messenger app

13. Depending on the current state of your Facebook property, you may need to set up a new page or connect an existing page. You'll need this to generate an access token. In this case, we have an app and a page but need to connect them for Messenger, so we'll click **Connect**.

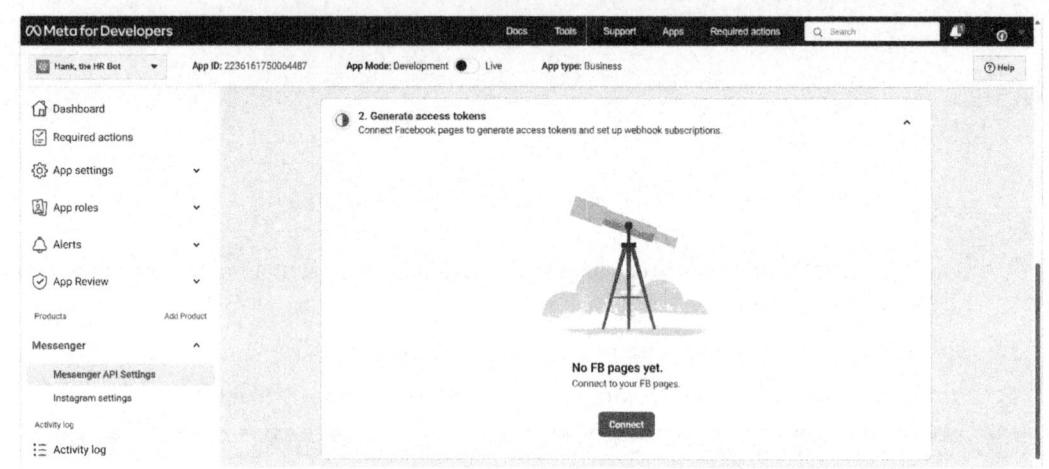

Figure 13.29 – Connecting the bot app to a Facebook page

14. Upon connecting, acknowledge the data access. Click **Continue**.

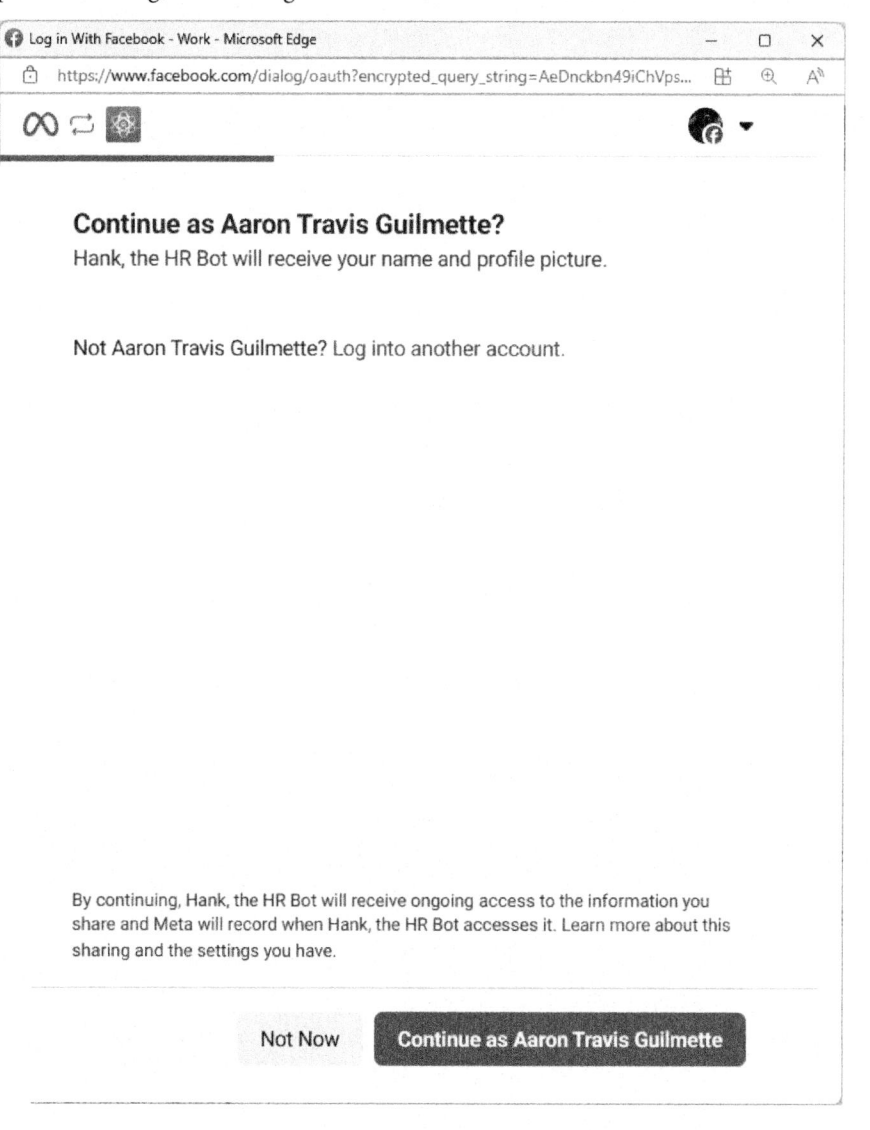

Figure 13.30 – Acknowledging the data access confirmation

318　Publishing a Generative AI-based Bot

15. Confirm which assets your bot will access. In this case, we're just going to allow it to access the HR bot Facebook app.

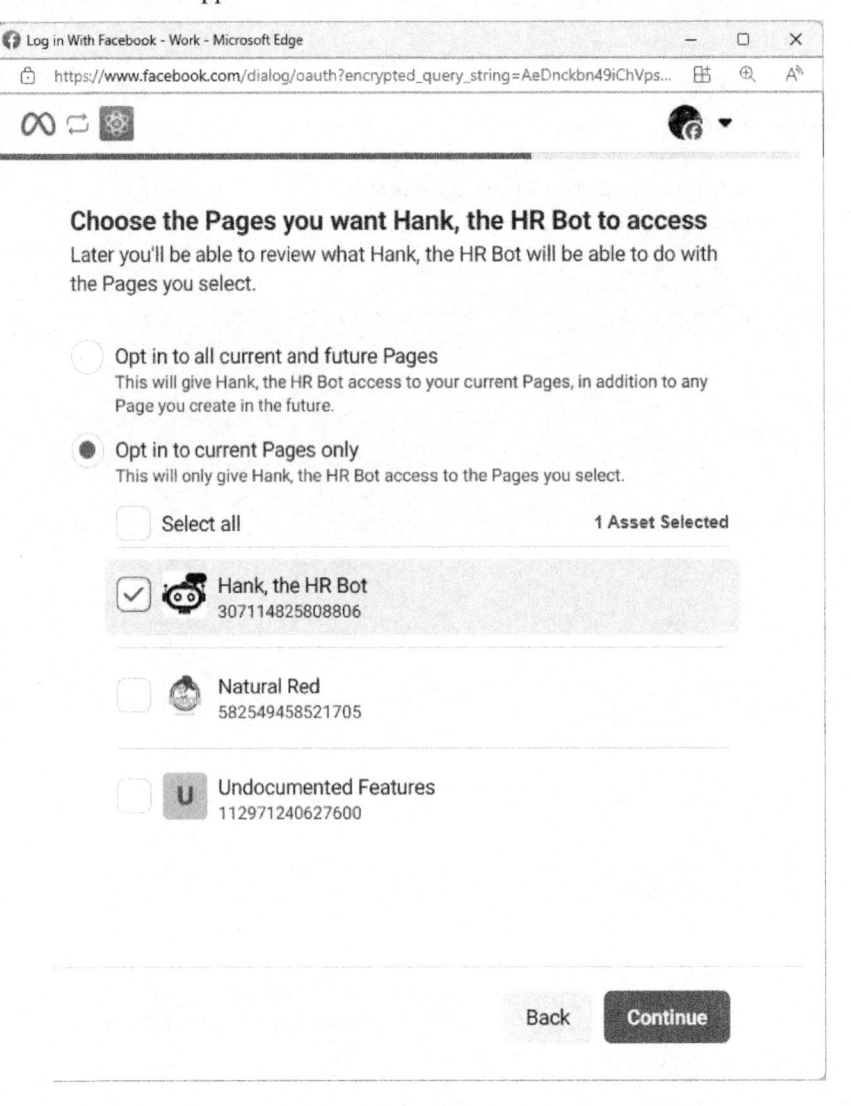

Figure 13.31 – Granting access

16. After the page is connected, you can generate an access token, as shown in *Figure 13.32*:

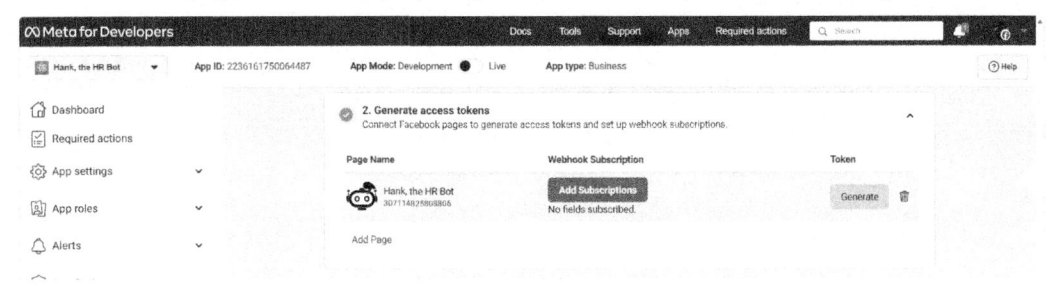

Figure 13.32 – Generating an access token

17. Click **I Understand** and then copy the token to the clipboard.

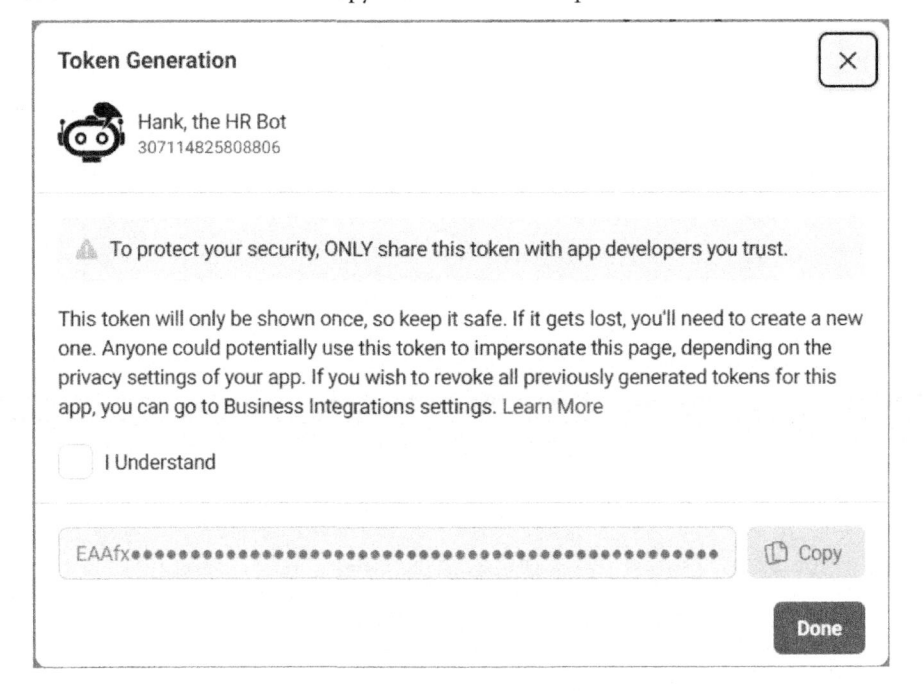

Figure 13.33 – Acquiring the page access token

18. Paste the access token into the **Page access token** field in Copilot Studio.

19. On the Facebook Developer page, click the **Page ID** value and paste it into the **Page ID** field in Copilot Studio.
20. Click **Add** on the **Facebook** flyout in Copilot Studio to save the configuration and generate **Callback URL** and **Verify token** values.

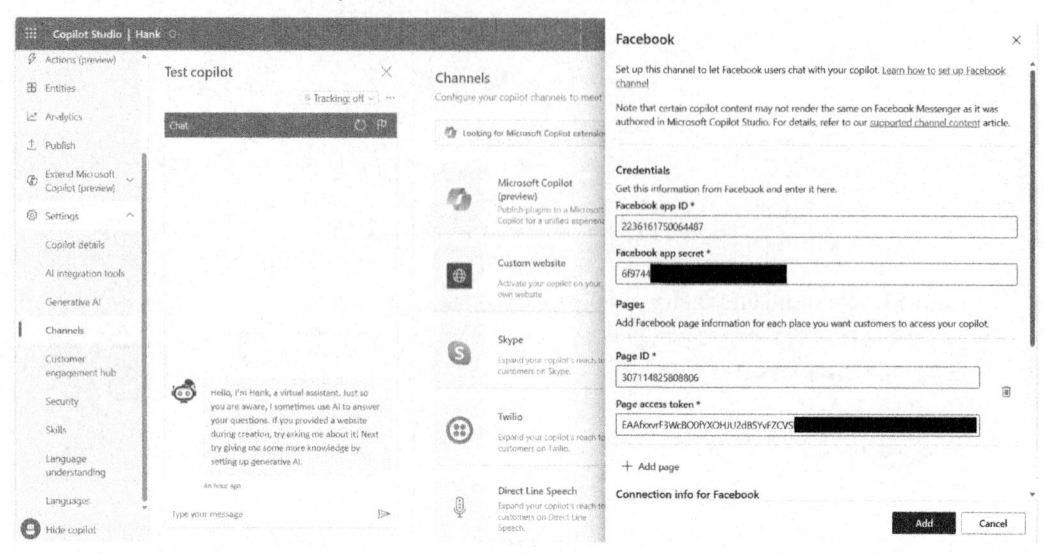

Figure 13.34 – Configuring the Facebook flyout

21. Under **Configure webhooks**, click **Configure**.

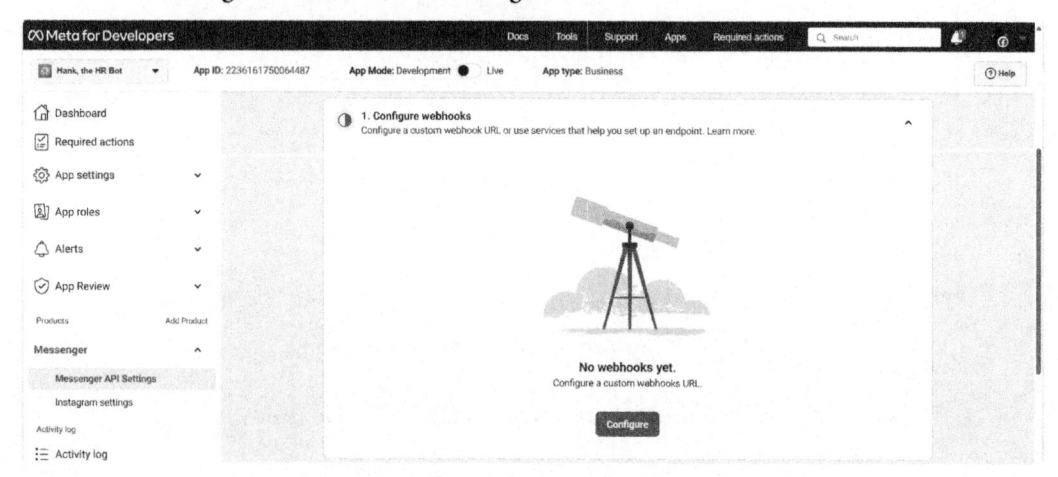

Figure 13.35 – Configuring a webhook

22. Copy the **Callback URL** and **Verify Token** parameters from the Copilot Studio **Facebook** flyout page to the appropriate fields, and click **Verify and save**.

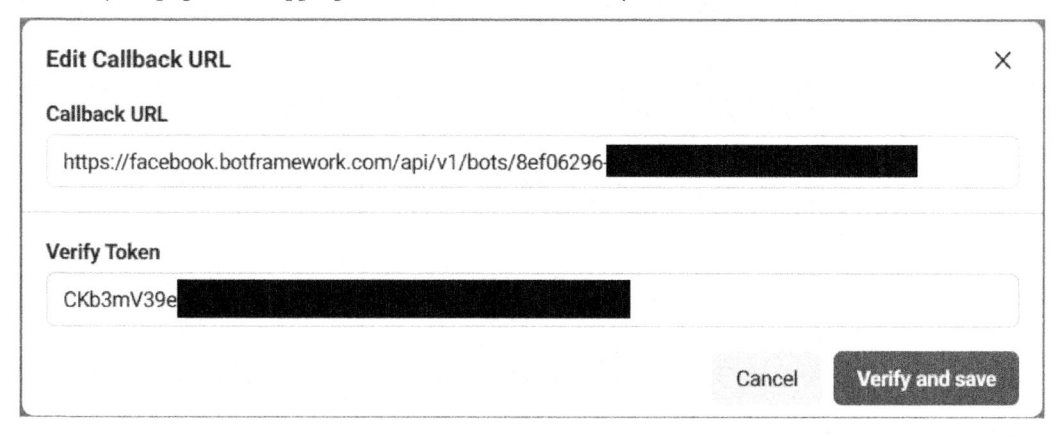

Figure 13.36 – Updating the webhook settings

23. Click **Manage** next to the **Webhook Fields** field.

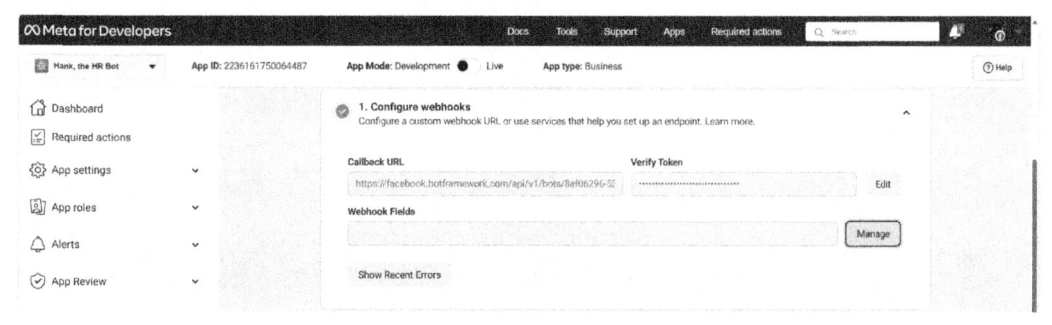

Figure 13.37 – Managing webhooks

24. In the **Webhook fields** dialog box, click **Subscribe** for each of the following fields:

    - `messages`
    - `messaging_postbacks`
    - `messaging_optins`
    - `message_deliveries`

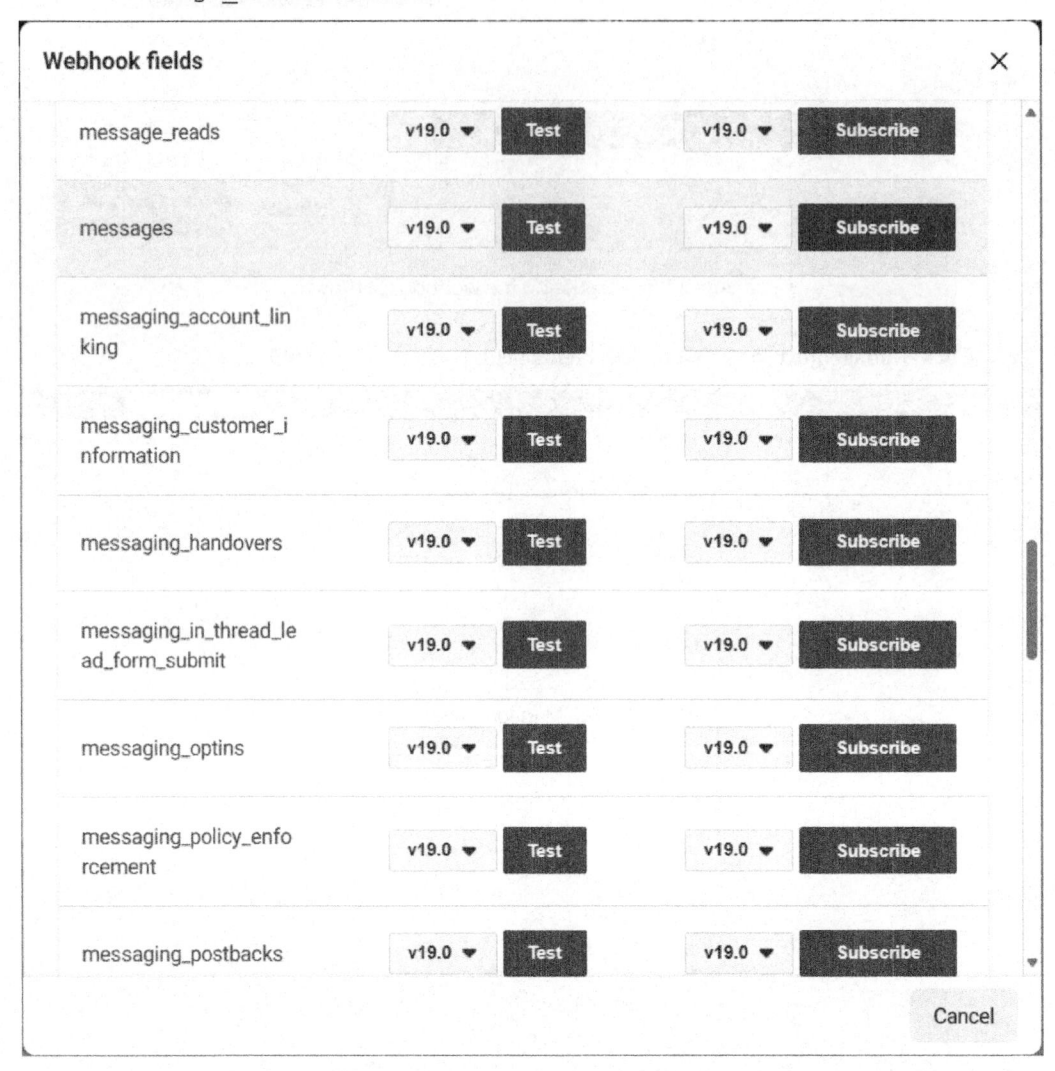

Figure 13.38 – Subscribing to webhooks

25. Click **X** to close the dialog box.
26. Ensure the **Webhooks Fields** field has been updated.

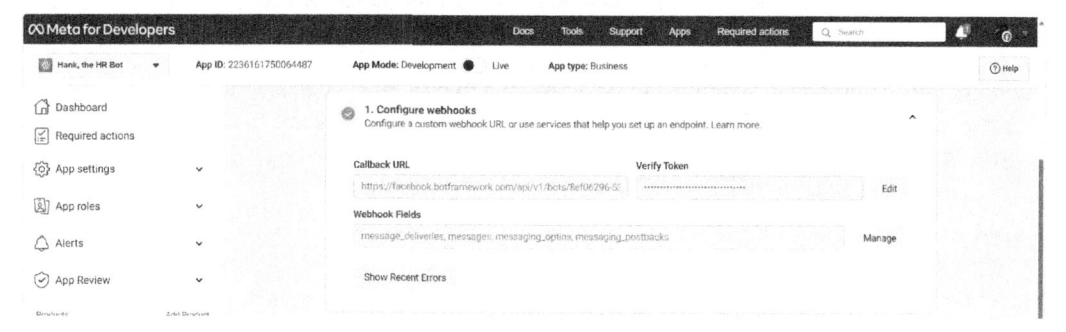

Figure 13.39 – Confirming the webhook fields have been updated

27. After configuring these items, you'll need to submit your bot app for review with Facebook by expanding **App Review** and clicking **Submit for Review**. If your business is not currently verified with Facebook, you'll need to complete that by supplying supporting documentation. Facebook does this to ensure that APIs are not abused and adhere to responsible data protection practices.

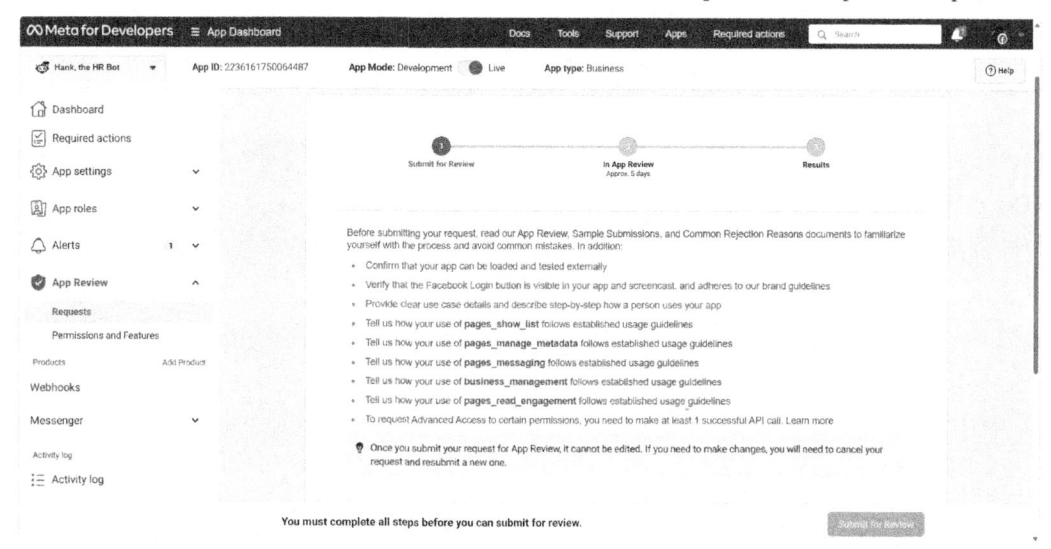

Figure 13.40 – Submitting the bot for review with Facebook

Once that is complete, your bot can begin answering questions through Facebook Messenger!

Publishing a bot to other endpoints

In addition to integrating with popular social media and communications apps, you can also extend your conversation bot to other applications.

For more information on developing bot integrations and other pro-code solutions, see `https://learn.microsoft.com/en-us/microsoft-copilot-studio/publication-connect-bot-to-custom-application`.

Summary

This chapter guided you through extending your bot to places such as Teams, a public website, and Facebook. In each of these scenarios, you learned how to integrate the conversation bot you developed, extending its reach and usefulness.

That's it for this book. I hope you had as much fun exploring the powerful capabilities of generative AI, OpenAI, and AI Builder solutions in Azure and Microsoft Power Platform as I did writing about them!

Index

A

actions 5, 6, 277
AI Builder 8
   custom models 8
   prebuilt models 8
AI Copilot 6
AI-Enabled Resume Screener
   attachment and candidate record,
      processing 215-218
   candidate record,
      updating 218-220, 225-227
   confirmation messages, sending 228, 229
   flow, creating 213
   flow, testing 230, 231
   information, extracting from
      resume 218-220
   resume, evaluating with prompt 220-224
   solution, designing 197, 198
   solution prerequisites configuration 199
   trigger and variables, configuring 213-215
AI model 2
AI, to tag images
   computer vision 263-267
   flow, creating 260
   flow, testing 269, 270
   image details, updating in library 268, 269
   solution, designing 255
   solution prerequisites configuration 255
   trigger, configuring 260-262
algorithm 1
Anomaly Detector service 11
API access
   configuring, for ChatGPT 21-24
application life cycle management (ALM) 74
**application programming
     interfaces (APIs)** 10
arrays 117
artificial intelligence (AI) 1
automation
   enabling 90-94
Azure
   configuring 16
   OpenAI service resources, setting up 19-21
Azure AI Services
   working with 10, 11
Azure Cognitive Services
   reference link 12
Azure Computer Vision 251
   face detection 254
   image analysis 253
   image classification 251
   object detection 252

Index

optical character recognition (OCR) 254
semantic segmentation 253
Azure Developer CLI
  download link 25
Azure OpenAI services
  API access, requesting for 16-19

B

Bard 13
  URL 13
bot
  approving 307-309
  publishing, to Facebook 313-323
  publishing, to other endpoints 324
  publishing, to Teams 301-305
  publishing, to website 309-313
  testing 305, 306
bounding box 252

C

canvas apps 74
  reference link 74
canvas frontend app
  creating 86-90
channels 301
chatbots 271
  designing, considerations 274
ChatGPT
  API access, configuring for 21-24
  data, retrieving from 41
  limitations, to create flows 49
  URL 27
  used, for building app 60-64
  used, for creating flows 47-50
  working with, as user 27-29

ChatGPT Plus
  used, for creating flows 52-56
ChatGPT's JSON output
  working with 43-45
Claude 13
  URL 13
code-first authoring 5
collections 117
columns 77
Common Data Service 73
computer vision service 10
  creating 255, 256
  working with 263-268
conditions 272, 277
connectors 5
Content Moderator service 11
context 28
controls 7
conversation node 272
Copilot for Security 6
Copilots 5, 6
  actions 6
  creating 276
  customizing 277
  entities 6
  features and capabilities 272
  licensing prerequisites 275
  responses 7
  testing 295
  topics 6
  triggers 6
  used, for building app 64-70
  used, for building Power App 73
  used, for creating flows 56-60
Copilot Studio 6, 271
Copliot in Viva Sales 6
custom models 97
Custom Vision service 11

D

dall-e-3 39
data
   retrieving, from ChatGPT 41
data cards 7
data elements
   configuring 74-80
data sources 7
Dataverse environment
   creating 72, 73
deepfakes 3
Describe it to design it feature 56

E

Encodian 115, 116
Encodian Flowr connector 117
   input formatting 117, 118
   Merge Presentations action 119
   Populate PowerPoint action 119
   tokens 118
entities 6, 76
Entra ID
   used, for creating user identities 71
Entra ID user creation
   reference link 71
environment 72
event registration and identity validation
   solution, designing 153, 154
   solution prerequisites configuration 155
   workflow 154
event registration and identity validation workflow
   confirmation messages, sending 185-189
   file request link, generating 173-178
   flow, configuring to handle form submission 167

   flows, creating 167
   flows, testing 189-194
   identity document, processing 178-185
   Microsoft Form data, processing 167-172
Executive Summary, with GPT
   content, sending to GPT 238-245
   document, converting 237, 238
   document, populating 245, 246
   file, saving 245, 246
   flow, creating 235
   flow, testing 247, 248
   solution, designing 233
   solution prerequisites configuration 234
   trigger, configuring 235-237

F

Facebook
   bot, publishing to 313-323
face detection 254
Face service 10
few-shot learning 50
fields 77
flow, creating 124
   data, sending to Encodian connector 142-148
   Generate Content Summaries scope, creating 124-129
   Generate Slides scope, creating 139-141
   GPT prompt, customizing 132-138
   JSON parameters, configuring 129-132
flows 5
   creating, with ChatGPT 47-50
   creating, with ChatGPT Plus 52-56
   creating, with Copilot 56-60
   testing 148-151
formulas 7
frequently asked question (FAQ) sites 271

G

galleries 7
generative adversarial networks (GANs) 1, 2
Generative AI 1, 3, 16
  content, adding for 291-294
generative answers 273, 297, 298
Generative Pre-trained Transformer (GPT) 12
Git
  download link 25
gpt-3.5-turbo 39
gpt-4 39
gpt-4-turbo 39

H

Holidays topic
  testing 295, 296

I

image analysis 253
image classification 251
Images API 12, 39

J

JavaScript Object Notation (JSON) 41-43, 117, 118
  reference link 118
JSON formatter
  URL 118

L

Language Model for Dialogue Applications (LaMDA) 13
Language service 11
Language Understanding (LUIS) service 11
large language model 2
leave request app
  prerequisites configuration 71
licensing prerequisites 98, 99, 115, 116
low-code software 5

M

Maker Portal
  URL 74
Merge Presentations action 119
Microsoft 365 Copilot 6
Microsoft Partner
  reference link 10
Microsoft Teams team
  creating 102, 103
Midjourney 13
  URL 13
model-driven apps 74
  reference link 74
model-driven backend app
  creating 80-86

N

natural language understanding (NLU) 6
neural networks 1
no-code software 5
Node.js 14+
  download link 25

O

object detection 252
one-shot learning 50
OpenAI API 12

OpenAI GPT-3 completions 37-41
OpenAI Gym 12
OpenAI models
  working with 12
OpenAI Platform 12
  reference link 13
OpenAI Scholars Program 12
OpenAI service resources
  setting up, in Azure 19-21
optical character recognition (OCR) 254

P

Personalizer service 11
personally identifiable information (PII) 11, 16
Populate PowerPoint action 119
Postman
  URL 244
Power Apps 4, 7
  automation, enabling 90-94
  building, with Copilot 73
  canvas frontend app, creating 86-90
  ChatGPT, used for building app 60-64
  controls 7
  Copilot, used for building app 64-70
  data cards 7
  data elements, configuring 74-80
  data sources 7
  formulas 7
  galleries 7
  model-driven backend app, creating 80-86
  screens 7
  working with 60
Power Automate 4, 5
  actions 5
  ChatGPT's JSON output 43-45
  connectors 5

flows 5
flows, creating with ChatGPT 47-50
flows, creating with ChatGPT Plus 52-56
flows, creating with Copilot 56-60
triggers 5
working with 47
Power BI 5
Power Fx 5
Power Platform 4
  configuring 25, 26
Power Platform licensing 9, 10
  reference link 10
PowerPoint template
  creating 122, 123
PowerShell 7+
  download link 25
pre-built models 97
prompt frameworks
  reference link 132
prompts 28
prompts, sending to ChatGPT 30
  HTTP method 30-36
  OpenAI GPT-3 completions 37-41
Python 3.9+
  download link 25

Q

QnA Maker service 11

R

recurrent neural networks (RNNs) 1, 2
responses 7
response tokens 30
responsible AI 3
  reference link 3

Retrieval-Augmented Generation (RAG) 273
robotic process automation (RPA) 4

S

scope 124
screens 7
semantic segmentation 253
sentiment analysis 98
sentiment analysis flow
   configuring 103-112
   testing 112-114
shared mailbox
   creating 100, 101
shot learning 50
solution 74
   designing 274
solution prerequisites
   configuring 100
   Microsoft Teams team, creating 102, 103
   shared mailbox, creating 100, 101
solution prerequisites configuration, AI-Enabled Resume Screener
   AI model, configuring 204
   AI model, publishing 211
   AI model, testing 211
   AI model, training 204-211
   Cloudmersive connector, enabling 212, 213
   job descriptions, configuring 203
   shared mailbox, creating 199
   SharePoint document library, provisioning 201
   SharePoint lists, provisioning 202
   SharePoint Online, configuring 201
   team, creating 200

solution prerequisites configuration, AI to tag images
   computer vision service, creating 255, 256
   SharePoint library 257-260
solution prerequisites configuration, Executive Summary with GPT
   cloud storage provider, setting up 234
   document template, preparing 234
   subscriptions, enabling 234
solution prerequisites, event registration and identity validation workflow
   Anyone links, enabling 157-159
   input form, building 165, 166
   SharePoint library, provisioning 159
   SharePoint list, provisioning 160
   SharePoint Online, configuring 156
   SharePoint Online settings, updating 161, 162
   SharePoint site, configuring 156, 157
   Teams meeting, establishing 163, 164
Speech service 11
system topics 272

T

tables 76
tags 118
Teams
   bot, publishing to 301-305
token 29, 30, 118, 234
Tokenizer 29
   URL 239
topics 6, 272, 277
   creating, that uses ChatGPT 277-290
   disabling 290, 291
Translator service 11
triggers 5, 6, 272, 277

U

user identities
  creating, in Entra ID 71

V

variables 272
variational autoencoders (VAEs) 1, 2
Visual Studio Code
  download link 25

W

website
  bot, publishing to 309-313
what-you-see-is-what-you-get (WYSIWYG) 5
Wikipedia articles
  interacting with 120-122
Workflow Definition Language
  reference link 261
workstation
  configuring 25

Z

zero-shot learning 50

‹packt›

packtpub.com

Subscribe to our online digital library for full access to over 7,000 books and videos, as well as industry leading tools to help you plan your personal development and advance your career. For more information, please visit our website.

Why subscribe?

- Spend less time learning and more time coding with practical eBooks and Videos from over 4,000 industry professionals
- Improve your learning with Skill Plans built especially for you
- Get a free eBook or video every month
- Fully searchable for easy access to vital information
- Copy and paste, print, and bookmark content

Did you know that Packt offers eBook versions of every book published, with PDF and ePub files available? You can upgrade to the eBook version at packtpub.com and as a print book customer, you are entitled to a discount on the eBook copy. Get in touch with us at customercare@packtpub.com for more details.

At www.packtpub.com, you can also read a collection of free technical articles, sign up for a range of free newsletters, and receive exclusive discounts and offers on Packt books and eBooks.

Other Books You May Enjoy

If you enjoyed this book, you may be interested in these other books by Packt:

Microsoft Power Platform Enterprise Architecture

Robert Rybaric

ISBN: 978-1-80461-263-7

- Understand various Microsoft Dynamics 365 CRM, ERP, and AI modules for creating Power Platform solutions
- Combine Power Platform capabilities with Microsoft 365 and Azure
- Find out which regions, staging environments, and user licensing groups need to be employed when creating enterprise solutions
- Implement sophisticated security by using various authentication and authorization techniques
- Extend Microsoft Power BI, Power Apps, and Power Automate to create custom applications
- Integrate your solution with various in-house Microsoft components or third-party systems using integration patterns
- Migrate data using a variety of approaches and best practices

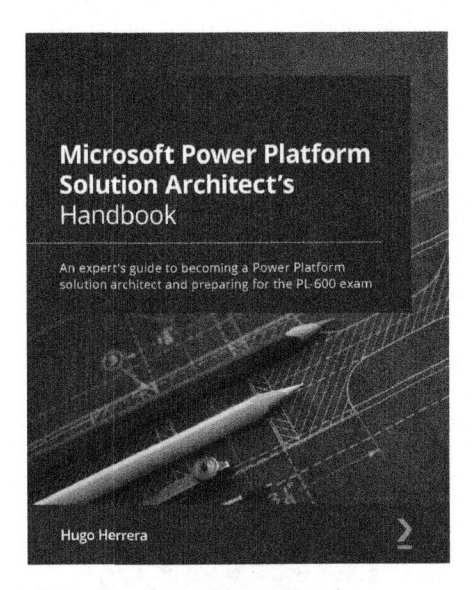

Microsoft Power Platform Solution Architect's Handbook

Hugo Herrera

ISBN: 978-1-80181-933-6

- Cement the foundations of your applications using best practices
- Use proven design, build, and go-live strategies to ensure success
- Lead requirements gathering and analysis with confidence
- Secure even the most complex solutions and integrations
- Ensure compliance between the Microsoft ecosystem and your business
- Build resilient test and deployment strategies to optimize solutions

Packt is searching for authors like you

If you're interested in becoming an author for Packt, please visit `authors.packtpub.com` and apply today. We have worked with thousands of developers and tech professionals, just like you, to help them share their insight with the global tech community. You can make a general application, apply for a specific hot topic that we are recruiting an author for, or submit your own idea.

Share Your Thoughts

Now you've finished *Power Platform and the AI Revolution*, we'd love to hear your thoughts! Scan the QR code below to go straight to the Amazon review page for this book and share your feedback or leave a review on the site that you purchased it from.

`https://packt.link/r/1835086365`

Your review is important to us and the tech community and will help us make sure we're delivering excellent quality content.

Download a free PDF copy of this book

Thanks for purchasing this book!

Do you like to read on the go but are unable to carry your print books everywhere?

Is your eBook purchase not compatible with the device of your choice?

Don't worry, now with every Packt book you get a DRM-free PDF version of that book at no cost.

Read anywhere, any place, on any device. Search, copy, and paste code from your favorite technical books directly into your application.

The perks don't stop there, you can get exclusive access to discounts, newsletters, and great free content in your inbox daily

Follow these simple steps to get the benefits:

1. Scan the QR code or visit the link below

    `https://packt.link/free-ebook/978-1-83508-636-0`

2. Submit your proof of purchase
3. That's it! We'll send your free PDF and other benefits to your email directly

Printed in Great Britain
by Amazon